THE WEDDING DRESS

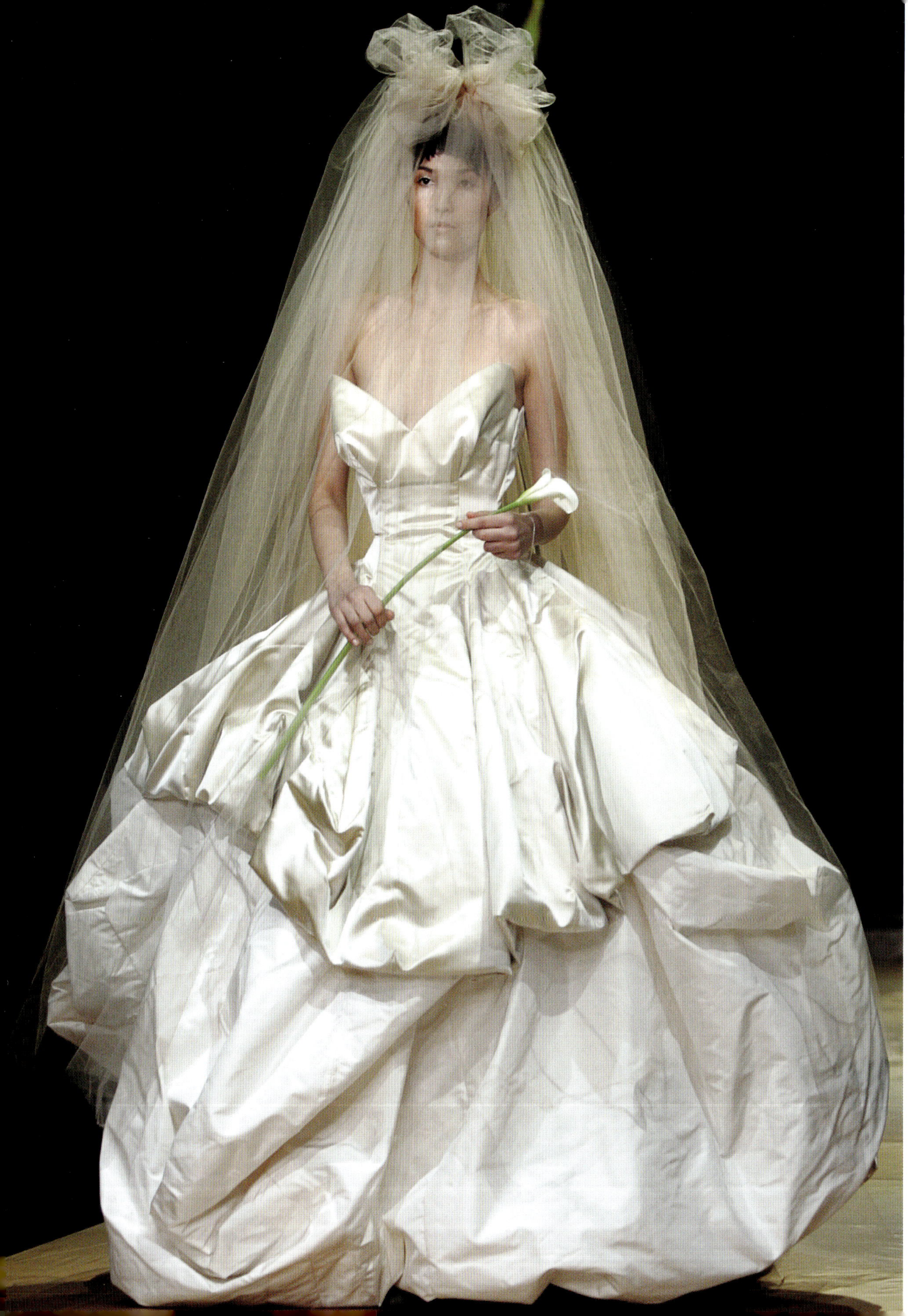

THE WEDDING DRESS

THE 50 DESIGNS THAT CHANGED THE COURSE OF BRIDAL FASHION

Eleanor Thompson

PRESTEL
Munich · London · New York

Published by Prestel
A member of Verlagsgruppe Random House GmbH

Prestel Verlag
Neumarkter Strasse 28
81673 Munich
Tel.: +49 89 41 36 0
Fax: +49 89 41 36 23 35

Prestel Publishing Ltd.
14-17 Wells Street
London W1T 3PD
Tel.: +44 (0)20 7323 5004
Fax: +44 (0)20 7323 0271

Prestel Publishing
900 Broadway, Suite 603
New York, NY 10003
Tel.: +1 212 995 2720
Fax: +1 212 995 2733
E-mail: sales@prestel-usa.com

www.prestel.com

Originated in Hong Kong by Cypress Colours (HK) Ltd.
Printed and bound in China by Hung Hing

Library of Congress Cataloging-in-Publication Data
Thompson, Eleanor.
The wedding dress : the 50 designs that changed the course of bridal fashion / Eleanor Thompson.
pages cm
"Conceived, edited, and designed by Marshall Editions"–Title page verso.
Includes bibliographical references and index.
ISBN 978-3-7913-4873-5
1. Wedding costume–History. 2. Brides–Clothing–History. 3. Fashion design–History. 4. Fashion designers–Biography. I. Marshall Editions Ltd. II. Title.
GT1752.T47 2014
391.4'8–dc23
2013030459

ON THE COVER
Catherine Middleton wore an Alexander McQueen wedding dress designed by Sarah Burton for her 2011 wedding to Prince William, Duke of Cambridge.

OPPOSITE THE TITLE PAGE
Vivienne Westwood's Wake Up, Cave Girl! collection gown of 2007.

Contents

Introduction

Twenty-first century brides have a dizzying array of wedding dresses to choose from. Magazines, blogs, and books abound with inspirational images to suit every style of wedding, running the gamut from traditional to avant-garde, bohemian and vintage to classic. Yet, so often, the press returns to the same dresses that have stood the test of time: the regal glamour of Grace Kelly's dress, Princess Diana's fairy-tale-princess confection, and the classic elegance of Wallis Warfield Simpson's two-piece suit, to name but a few. These traditional archetypes have been recently joined by the striking creations of contemporary designers, worn by celebrities like Gwen Stefani, who wed in a white and hot-pink dress created by British designer John Galliano. But why is it that certain wedding dresses stand above the crowd and, decade after decade, captivate brides-to-be? This book uncovers what it takes for a wedding dress to become an icon, revealing the stories behind its conception and the details that make it magical.

The romantic tradition

One of the most important dresses a woman will ever wear, the wedding gown is invested with emotions and dreams. Many designers understand that their role in creating an iconic wedding dress is wish-fulfillment, materializing the hopes and fantasies of a bride. As a ceremonial garment associated with an important rite of passage, the wedding dress is ingrained with symbolism and traditions dating back over the centuries. All the dresses in this book have been chosen because, in some way, they reflect the most valued traits, ideals, and aspirations of bridalwear. The white wedding dress is the ubiquitous standard-bearer. Without a doubt, the first iconic wedding dress was the one that instigated the mass trend for white. In 1840, Queen Victoria unwittingly set an international custom for romantic white wedding dresses. To this day, white wedding gowns like Olivier Theyskens's magnificent 2008 design for Lauren Davis are created as symbols of romantic love.

A sign of the times

Some white wedding dresses have achieved their iconic status by rebelling against tradition and playing with the associations and qualities of this symbolic color. Until the latter part of the twentieth century, the white wedding dress drew upon Christianity's association of white with purity and innocence—values many contemporary designers recognize are incongruous with twenty-first century life. Produced in 1965, Yves Saint Laurent's curious take on the white wedding dress—a knitted cocoon-like garment—is an emblem of the changing attitudes toward marriage in the twentieth century. With one dress, Saint Laurent began a new tradition in bridal design: to question the meaning of the white wedding dress to contemporary society. As time passed, Saint Laurent's statement was picked up by Christian Lacroix, Joe Casely-Hayford, Yohji Yamamoto, Jean Paul Gaultier, Rei Kawakubo, Viktor & Rolf, and Karl Lagerfeld, all of whom have made poignant political and cultural comments about the spectacle of white weddings. Designers have also chosen to comment on the associations of a traditional white wedding dress by departing from it altogether. Gowns of deep purple, rich red, and bright pink embody the dynamism of twenty-first century wedding culture, embracing multi-faith, same-sex, and countercultural marriage ceremonies.

The future of fashion

Stripped of religious and out-dated cultural meanings, white—pure and dramatic—is the perfect canvas to showcase the intense craftsmanship of couture. In Cristóbal Balenciaga's skillful hands the white wedding dress was distilled to its most essential form. His breathtaking sculptural dresses of the late 1960s, with no surface embellishment and few joining seams, are testament to the technical agility of the couturier.

The perfect wedding dress is not only a dream for a bride but often for designers, too—a chance to realize their conceptual objectives and express the highest levels of their craft. Gianni Versace's provocative silver micro-mini that closed his Fall/Winter Atelier collection in 1997; Catherine Walker's impeccably tailored gown made for Lady Helen Windsor in 1992; and Alexander McQueen's sensuous body-skimming dress, created for Plum Sykes in 2005, are all prime exemplars of their designers' unique technical and creative achievements. These three dresses, like their historical counterparts, have come to stand as monuments to craftsmanship, skill, and artistic vision following their designers' premature deaths.

Gowns such as Versace's, designed for the runway rather than the church aisle, frequently serve as a marker of new artistic tendencies. Often created to form the dramatic centerpiece of a couture collection, a wedding dress is usually the final design to be revealed by a designer during a catwalk show. Drawing the themes of the collection together in one extraordinary ensemble, these showstopping dresses demonstrate the highest fulfillment of the designer's vision in a uniquely compelling way. These one-off ensembles can be hugely important in the history of fashion.

The craft of couture

The skill, labor, and time required to produce a couture gown sets it above the average wedding dress design. Custom-made creations for individual clients can take up to six months and many fittings to design and create, involving specialist seamstresses, dyers, beadworkers, and embroiderers.

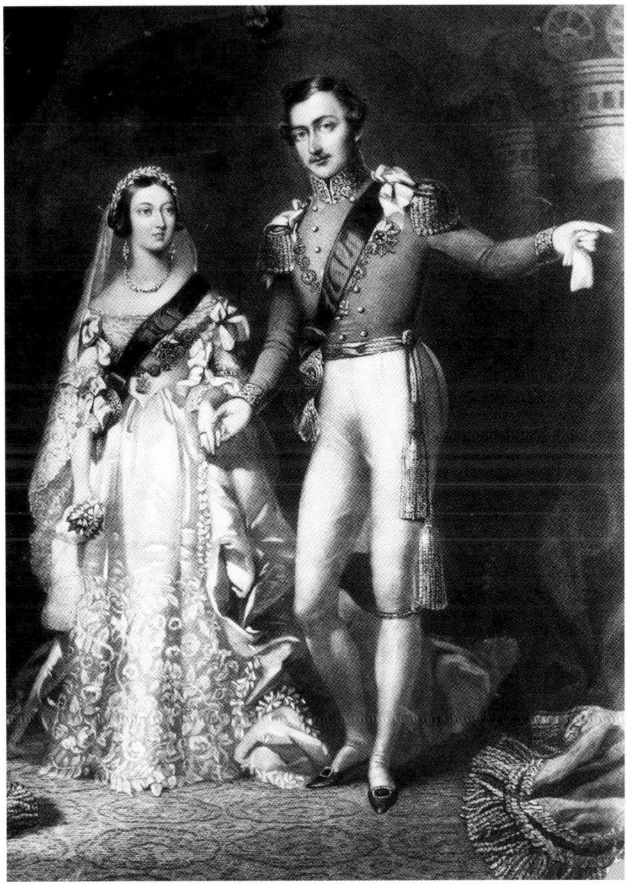

PICTURING THE DETAILS
Illustrations can be a rich source of design inspiration, offering a clear guide to details that may be missed by archive photography. Queen Victoria's dress (page 12) wasn't clearly photographed before the lace flounce on the skirt was removed. This illustration indicates it was attached to the lower half of the skirt.

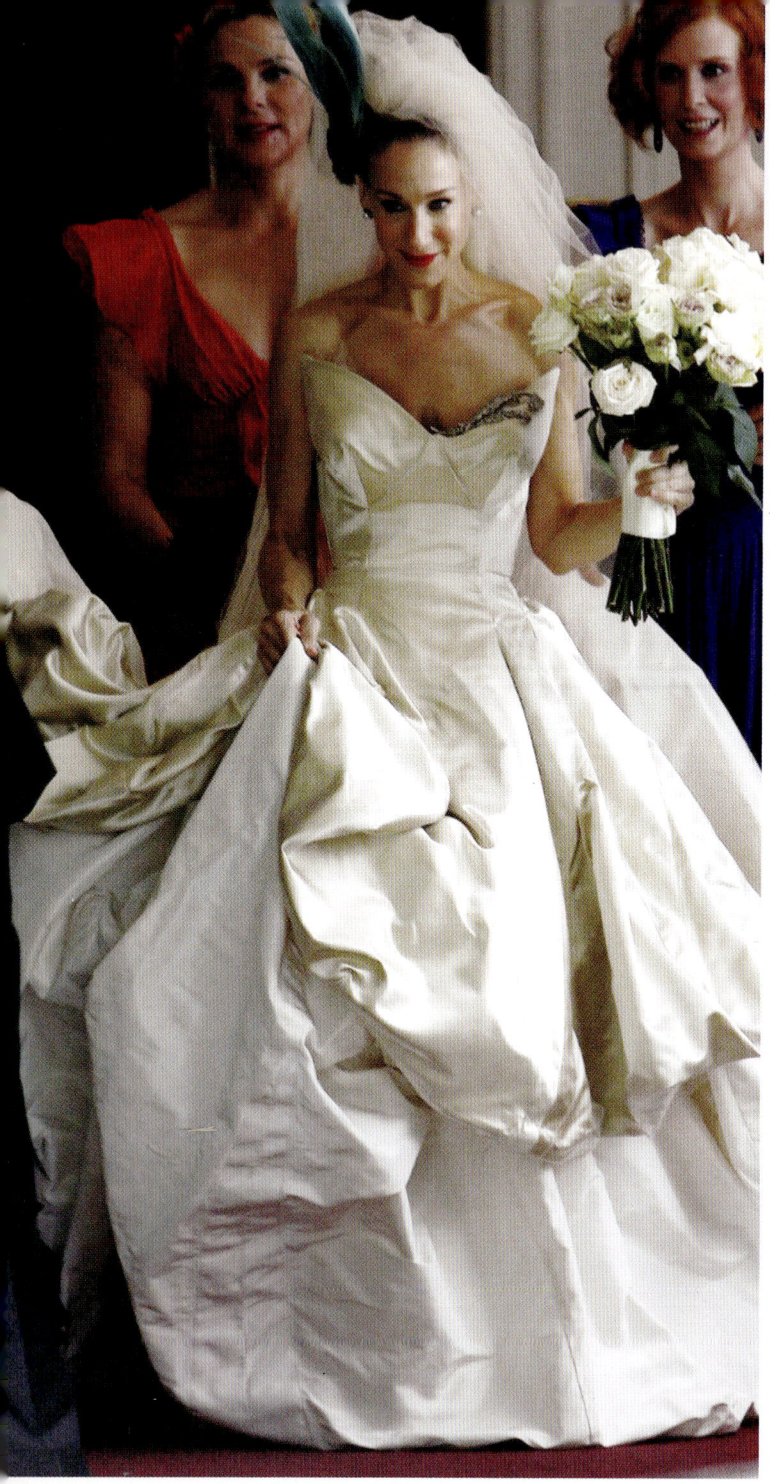

THE BRIDE AND THE DRESS
The adaptation and accessorizing of Vivienne Westwood's 2007 Wake Up, Cave Girl! couture collection gown (see page 144) emphasizes how a bride's individual style can make a dress iconic.

Every last detail of a couture wedding gown, from intricate surface embellishments to hidden internal seams, are refined to perfection before they can be debuted—usually just for a few hours of wear at a one-off event.

Yamamoto intentionally revealed the process of creating an iconic gown in the deconstructed wedding dress he showcased in 2000. The design literally turned the wedding dress inside out, exposing the normally hidden marks of couture construction. Unsurprisingly, the cost of luxurious wedding gowns can run into hundreds of thousands of dollars. That said, the value of an iconic wedding dress need not necessarily be reflected in its price tag, nor must it be handcrafted. Viktor & Rolf's sell-out, limited-edition wedding dress, created for retail chain H&M in 2006, was priced at just $349. For a fraction of the price of a couture dress, brides were able to buy the exclusivity and status of limited, avant-garde design.

Iconic gowns for iconic women

Many of the gowns in this book were designed for celebrity brides. Ever since Consuelo Vanderbilt's spectacular marriage ceremony to the ninth Duke of Marlborough in 1895, the press have slavishly reported on high-profile weddings. The continued profuse coverage of royal and celebrity brides has embedded certain wedding dresses in the public's imagination and evoked millions of bridal fantasies.

From gowns designed for Queen Victoria to Victoria Adams, the future Mrs. Beckham, the dresses that most often capture the popular imagination are those that manage both to meet the public's expectations and make a personal statement at the same time. On Catherine Middleton's wedding day, over two billion people watched as the future queen unveiled her much-anticipated wedding gown, taking her place alongside Princess Diana and Grace Kelly as a model princess bride. Sometimes, the expectation is that a bride will break from tradition rather than follow it. In these cases, more eclectic and unusual dresses can capture the limelight. Like their traditional counterparts, these emblems of counterculture remain a combination of public expectation and private statement, brilliantly captured by the designer of the dress. The dark, gothic romance of Dita Von Teese's purple Vivienne

Westwood wedding dress is just as compelling and relevant to many brides-to-be as the more traditional wedding dresses of her mainstream counterparts.

Von Teese and Westwood were a perfect match; the British designer's signature corsetry and draped fabric accentuated the star's sensuous pin-up glamour. Likewise, in the pairing of Sarah Burton and Catherine Middleton, John Bates and Marit Allen, and John Galliano and Kate Moss, the designer was able to channel the bride's personality into a unique ensemble that would be celebrated by both the popular and fashion press as a result.

What does it mean to be iconic?

Sometimes just small changes to a designer's standard catwalk model can elevate a dress from beautiful to iconic. Von Teese's purple wedding dress originally featured on Westwood's runway show in a muted gold color; the same designer's 2007 Wake Up, Cave Girl! wedding dress was adapted with a sparkling trim and an ever-so-slightly more fitted bodice to suit the fictional but still highly influential desires of *Sex and the City*'s Carrie Bradshaw; Giambattista Valli's tulle ruffled skirts were given a surprising, hidden feature just for one special bride, the shoe designer Charlotte Dellal.

While it is true to say that celebrity wedding dresses become iconic after being taken to the public's heart, not all iconic dresses have met with universal admiration. Editor of *Vogue* magazine Edna Woolman Chase wrote of Wallis Warfield Simpson's hugely popular wedding ensemble that "[Simpson] and Mainbocher might have done better than they did." While others thought it enduringly elegant, the *Vogue* editor dismissed it as "dull … to look at."

Selecting just fifty iconic wedding dresses out of the many hundreds of beautiful and famous examples is no easy task, nor is pinning down the slippery definition of iconic. In this book, it signifies designs that have broken new ground, set trends, inspired multiple imitations, or represented the wedding dress in its most sublime form. This selectivity has ruled out many wonderful and well-known gowns. In the 1920s Chanel, Patou, and Lelong all championed revolutionary knee-length designs, but Poiret's dress has been selected for the book since it is one of the earliest known surviving wedding dresses of this style. In the 1930s Alix, Callot Soeurs, Vionnet, and Charles James produced bias-cut wedding gowns of breathtaking beauty. However, of these designers it is widely recognized that Vionnet was the pioneer of the bias-cutting technique, while James, also featured, harnessed it in 1934 to make a surprising and unconventional gown for Barbara Beaton. In a similar way, although the house of Alexander McQueen has undertaken many commissions for one-off bridal gowns for celebrities, actresses, fashionistas, and socialites—all designs unsurpassed in their originality—none of these gowns have had as great an impact as the one McQueen personally designed for his friend Victoria "Plum" Sykes.

Inspiration for brides-to-be

For most brides, their wedding is a chance to wear a dress that has been designed and custom-fitted using couture techniques. Even if the dress is bought ready-to-wear, it can be embellished or accessorized in a unique way. From the range of dresses in this book, spanning the romantic to the revolutionary, there is inspiration for every bride-to-be. These gowns can't be found in a bridal store, but each and every one has something unique to offer. Some, like Christian Lacroix's black bejeweled gown, shout their statements loudly. Others, such as Jean Muir's discreetly top-stitched dress, whisper of their quality and individuality. Elements of all these gowns can be translated into styles to suit all personalities and budgets. Even the most avant-garde creations offer up surprising sparks of inspiration. For undiluted femininity, look no further than Lagerfeld's distressed Miss Havisham-inspired gown. Pared down, its allover frou-frou feathers could become a pretty, soft-focus embellishment. With some obvious modification, the outré sexuality of Gaultier's transparent lingerie dress could transform into a sensual corseted dress perfect for an empowered bride. The avant-garde dresses in this book offer silhouettes, garment shapes, and fabrics and textures to inspire new directions. The best advice for choosing bridalwear, the most important dress of any bride's life, is to take your time and reflect on your options—so be drawn deeper into the secrets of these iconic wedding dresses and let them reveal your own dream style.

01

William Dyce

1840 For Queen Victoria

Queen Victoria's white gown broke with centuries of royal bridal customs, sparking the most enduring bridal tradition of all time.

When Britain's Queen Victoria wed her cousin, Albert of Saxe-Coburg-Gotha, in 1840, the bride wore a crinoline-style court dress of heavy ivory silk satin. Trimmed with white lace, this simple yet elegant gown was a powerful personal statement that instigated the paradigm of the white wedding dress.

Contrary to popular belief, white had been used for bridal gowns prior to Queen Victoria's wedding, in particular for the dresses of wealthy nobility. White was a difficult color to create and maintain and sent a clear message of affluence (women of lesser means wore their "best dress" of any color). However, before Queen Victoria's marriage, centuries of English princesses married in shimmering gowns woven with threads of silver and gold. These were topped with velvet and ermine robes paired with formal, jeweled tiaras and crowns. A most unusual royal bride, Queen Victoria deliberately broke with these traditions.

Personal and romantic

Politics usually prevailed over romance in royal marriages of the nineteenth century. Acts of foreign policy, marriages forged alliances between nations. In these circumstances, opulent wedding dresses were used to show off the wealth and power of the bride's nation. Surprisingly, in an era of arranged marriages, Queen Victoria's was a true love match. In addition, unlike other royal brides, she held a huge amount of power and influence. She entered the marriage as queen in her own right—her future would be actively leading the nation, not acting as a decorative royal consort. Queen Victoria was aware of the political message of royal weddings and it seems she was determined to make hers a personal moment for herself and her husband. So she eschewed a grand display of wealth in favor of a prettily romantic dress made by her personal dressmaker, Mary Bettans.

Following the fashionable 1840s silhouette, Queen Victoria's gown was distinguished by a décolleté bodice with a Bertha collar that drew attention to the sweeping lines of her bare neck and shoulders. Although low across her chest, this neckline would have been considered appropriate for formal attire. The sharply pointed, dropped V-waist, surrounded by deep pleats sewn into the waistband of the dome-shaped skirt, emphasized the queen's slender waist. Queen Victoria's choice of accessories touchingly acknowledged the romance of her nuptials: her veil was fastened to her head with a wreath of orange blossom, a symbol of fertility and purity, and myrtle, representing love and domestic happiness.

TRENDSETTER IN WHITE
Though not the first white wedding ensemble in history, Queen Victoria's white dress and veil have influenced the choices of Western brides for nearly two centuries.

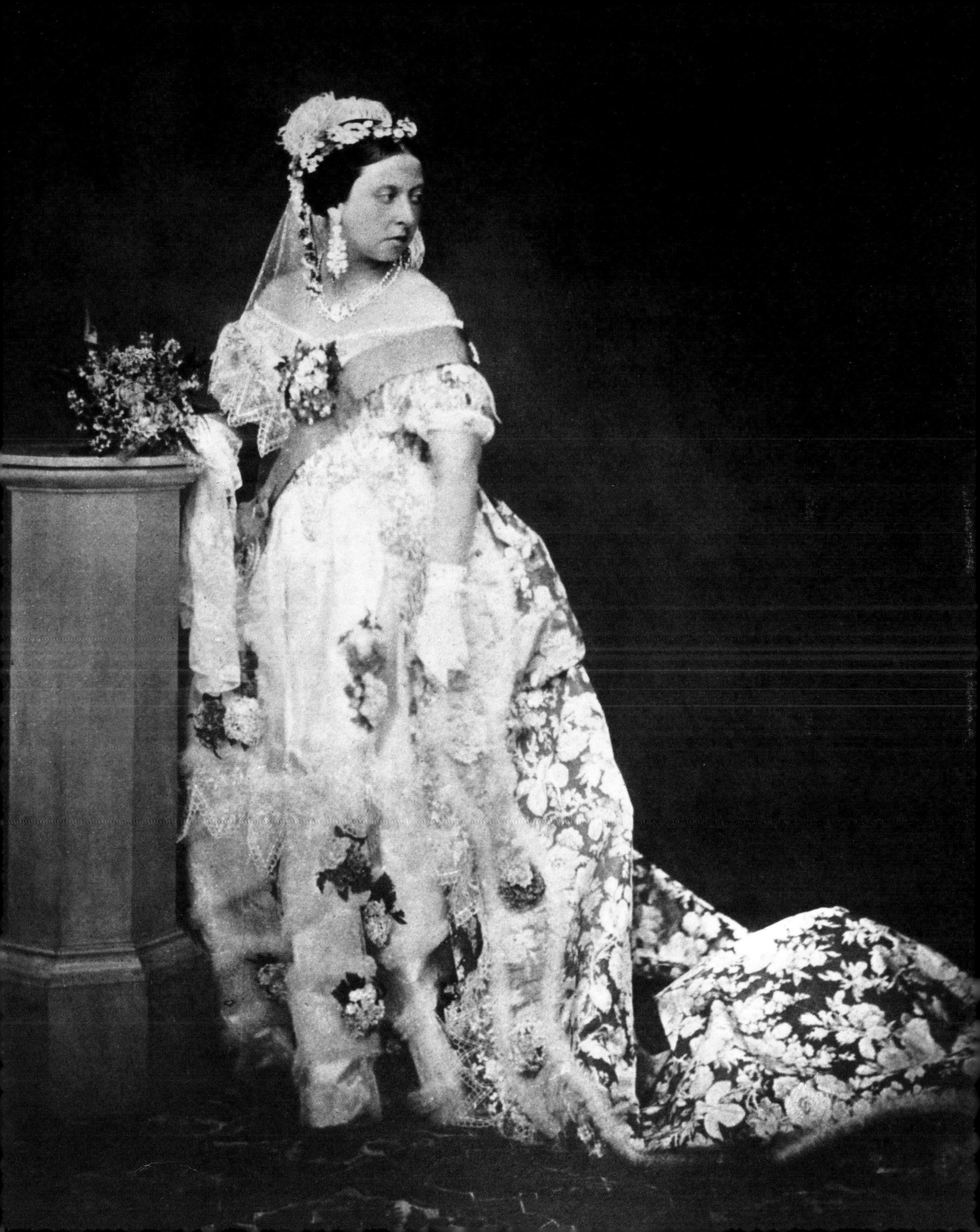

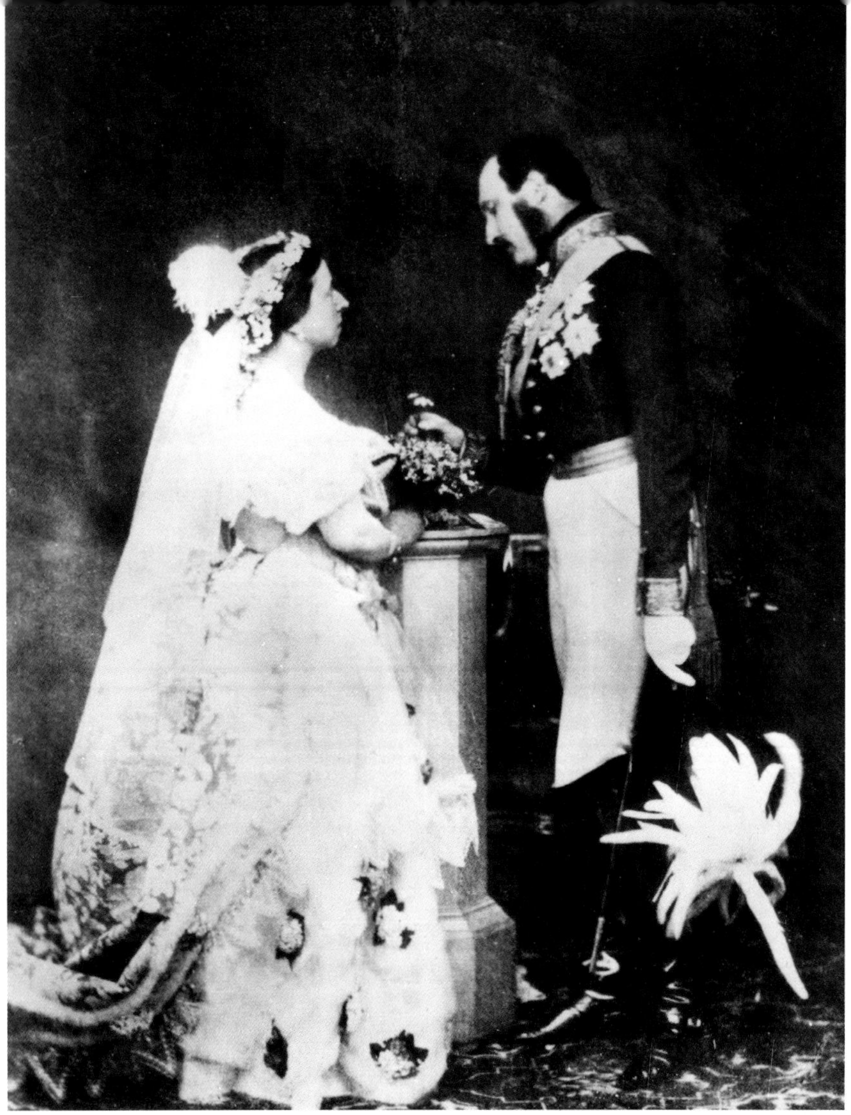

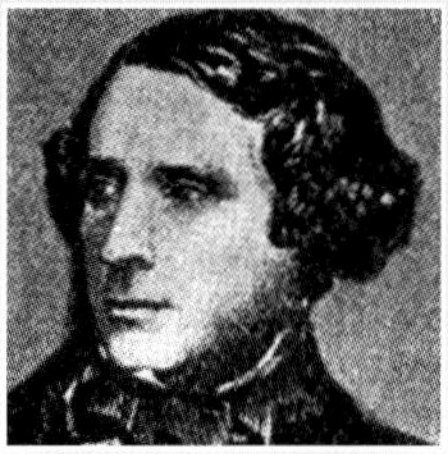

William Dyce
1806–1864

A distinguished Scottish artist involved in the formation of the British public art education system, Dyce's ideas on education fed into the influential South Kensington Schools system. Dyce started his career at the Royal Academy Schools before studying the works of Titian and Poussin in Rome. He took charge of the School of Design in Edinburgh, Scotland, before heading the newly established Government School of Design, in London (renamed London's Royal College of Art in 1896). He left the school in 1843 to concentrate on his painting. Victoria's dress was Dyce's sole fashion project.

English craftsmanship

As head of state, Queen Victoria recognized her duty to the nation and displayed her patriotism by selecting English fabrics for her gown. The queen's patronage of Spitalfields silk and Honiton lace gave these cottage industries, badly affected by the industrial revolution, welcome stimulus. The lace commission gave employment to 200 local women for nine months. In a much-publicized commission, the distinguished painter William Dyce designed the dress, including the motif for the lace. Dyce showcased the fine craftsmanship of the lace, choosing white as the color that best highlighted the qualities of the fabric. It is said that the designs were later destroyed so that the queen's dress might remain perfectly unique. The lace flounce on the skirt became the queen's favored memento, which she had recycled onto other garments many times. Following Prince Albert's death in 1861, this reminder of her wedding day became an even more treasured possession.

Images of the wedding were extensively reproduced, sparking a fashion for white wedding dresses among those that could afford them, most famously Queen Victoria's daughter, Princess Victoria, and daughter-in-law, the future Queen Alexandra. Over the course of Victoria's reign, the white wedding dress, veil, and orange-blossom wreath became the key traditional elements that we know today.

A SYMBOL OF LOVE
Pinned to the front of her bodice Victoria wore a sapphire and diamond brooch, a wedding gift from Albert—a small spot of color upon the white expanse of her dress.

THE DRESS

STYLE Romantic

SHAPE Crinoline

FABRIC Spitalfields silk satin and Honiton lace

COLOR Ivory

HIDDEN DETAILS

- The train, attached at the waist, extends 18 ft (5.5 m).
- Victoria's jewels included a sapphire and diamond brooch, a Turkish diamond necklace and earrings, and the insignia for the Order of the Garter.
- The veil measures 1½ yd (1.4 m) square.
- The lace flounce on the skirt measures 4 yd (3.7 m) in length, and ¾ yd (0.7 m) in depth.

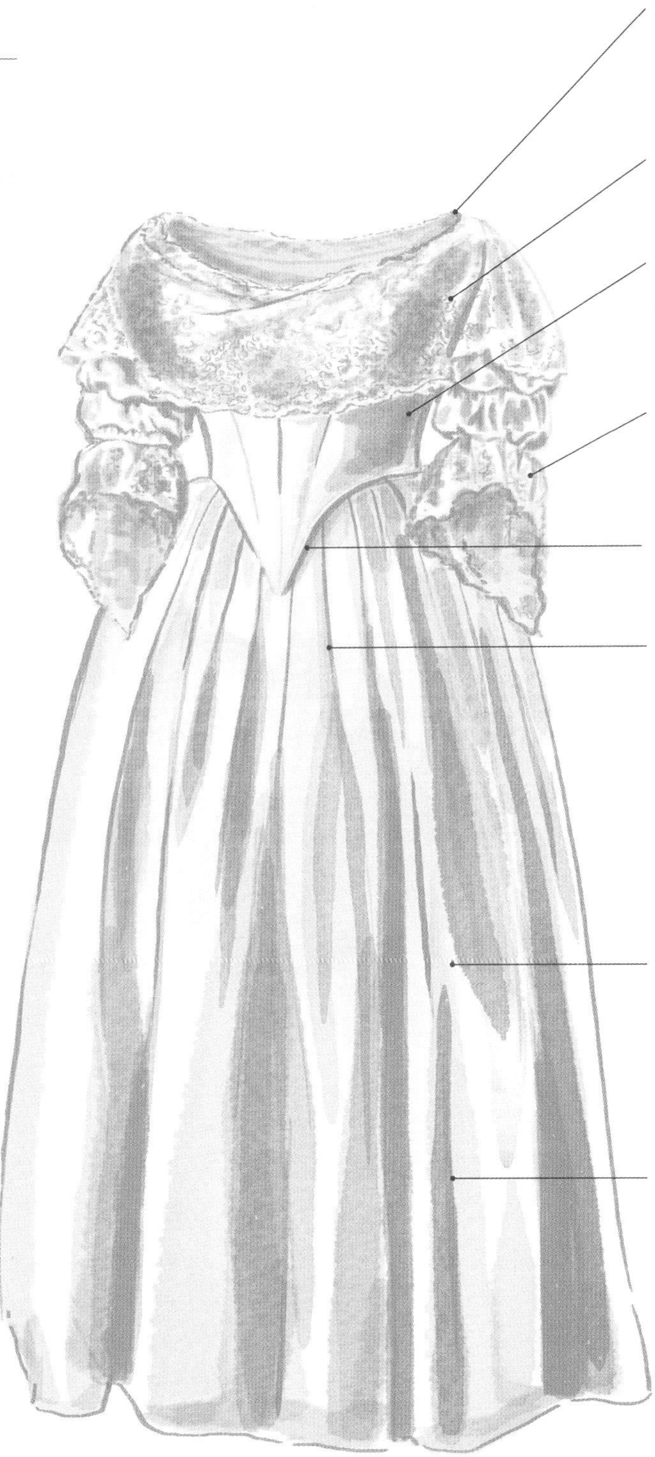

02

Charles Frederick Worth

1895 For Consuelo Vanderbilt

One of the most lavish wedding gowns of its era, Charles Frederick Worth's creation for American heiress Consuelo Vanderbilt provided a public feast and stimulated the press's obsession with celebrity wedding dresses.

So-called dollar duchesses—rich American brides whose inheritances reinvigorated the fortunes of financially ailing British aristocratic families—were the celebrities of their day. The marriage of Consuelo Vanderbilt, the granddaughter of a pioneering rail magnate, to the ninth Duke of Marlborough reputedly involved the transfer of vast sums of money to the groom and was unsurprisingly the subject of considerable gossip. The press reported on every detail of the event, paying particular attention to what the bride wore. *Vogue* magazine published an illustrated article on her trousseau and the *New York Times* devoted nearly two pages to describing her bridal lingerie. Society magazine *Town Topics* told its readers, "It is delightful to know that the clasps of Miss Vanderbilt's stocking supporters are of gold, and that her corset-covers and chemises are embroidered with rosebuds in relief."

Lavish and public

Naturally, Vanderbilt's luxurious wedding dress befitted her standing as "American royalty." Commissioned from the most famous couturier of the day, Worth, the dress was said to have cost $6,720.35 (over $180,000 in today's money). It followed the fashionable 1895 silhouette: enormous puffed sleeves and a bell-shaped skirt emphasizing a slender waist, cinched with a wide sash. The *New York World* newspaper reported that the bride had a 20-inch (50.8-cm) waist, a measurement achieved through corsets worn underneath as well as integral boning sewn into the bodice. The dress was cut from rich creamy white satin covered with flounces of point d'Angleterre lace and tendrils of orange blossom. The train was 15 feet (4.6 m) long, falling in a straight line from box pleats at the shoulders. It was edged in its entirety with a border of rose leaves tied by true-lovers' knots, that was wrought in silver-thread embroidery and pearls. This symbolism presented a public statement of a love match, masking the reality that this was a union of duty and familial obligation. Although the marriage did not last, the event set the standard for lavish wedding dresses to be consumed as very public spectacles.

DAILY DELIGHTS
Wealthy brides' dresses provided exciting news for the new dailies and mass-produced women's magazines of the late nineteenth century.

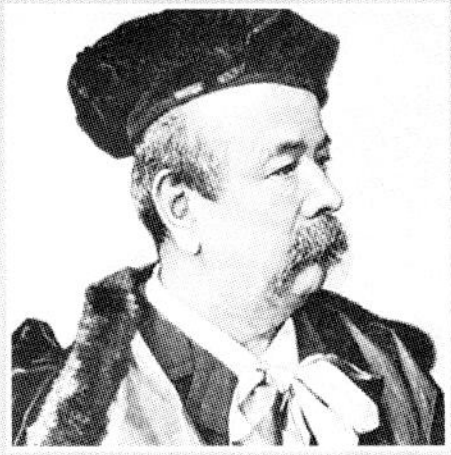

Charles Frederick Worth

1825–1895

Often referred to as the father of haute couture, Worth is credited with transforming dressmaking from a craft into a business. He promoted a new way of working, with the designer leading the creative process. His clients chose from a series of preprepared designs that could be tailor-made to their measurements. Born in Britain, Worth established his first salon in Paris in 1858. His designs were noted for their use of lavish fabrics and trimmings, their attention to fit, and the inclusion of details from historic dress. Worth's popularity as a designer was secured in the 1860s when he won the patronage of France's Empress Eugénie. The House continued under the direction of his sons Jean-Philippe and Gaston-Lucien. The Worth family's involvement with the house ended in 1952. It shut down couture operations four years later.

THE DRESS

STYLE Extravagant

SHAPE Hourglass

FABRIC Satin and point d'Angleterre lace

COLOR Cream

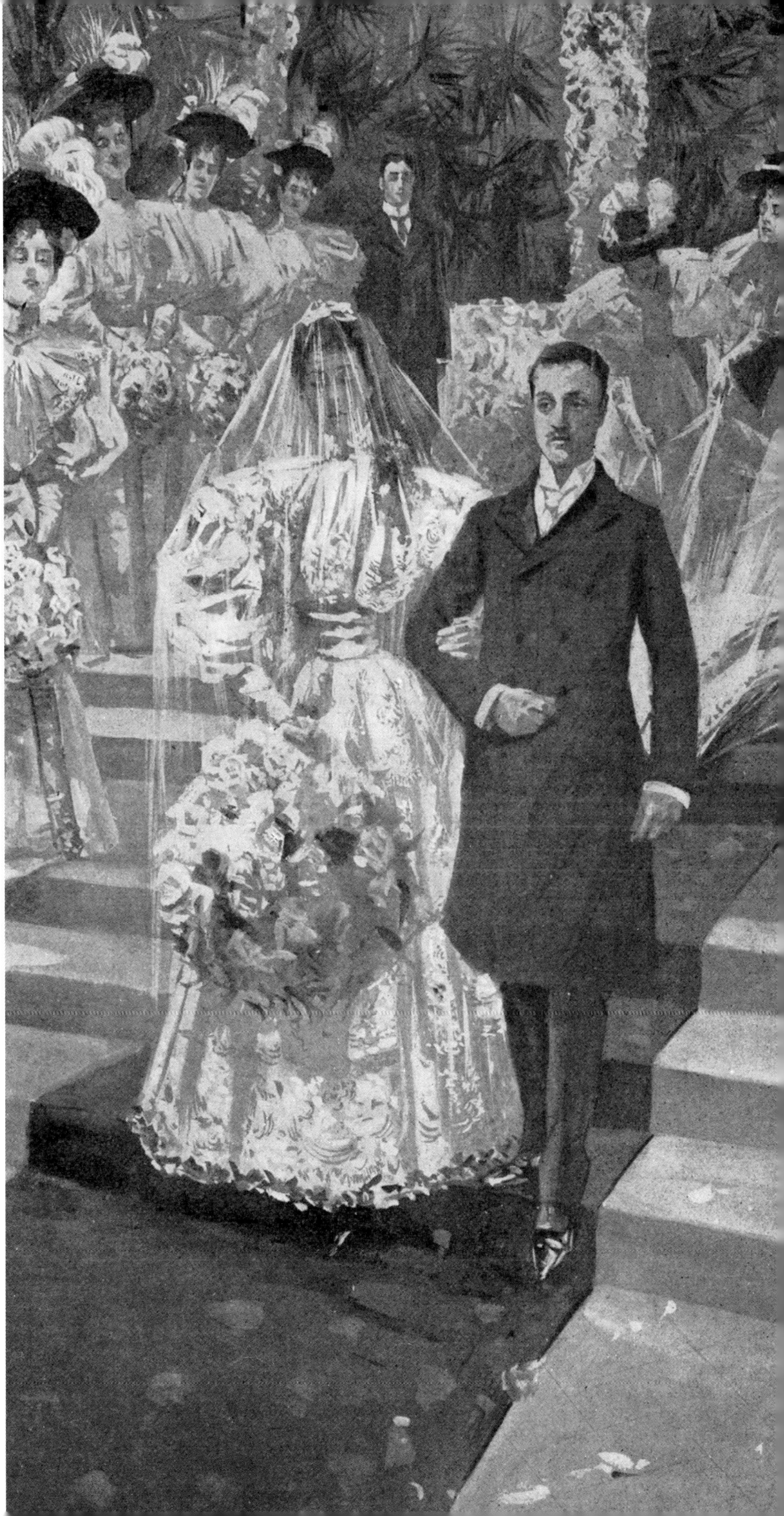

03

House of Worth

1898

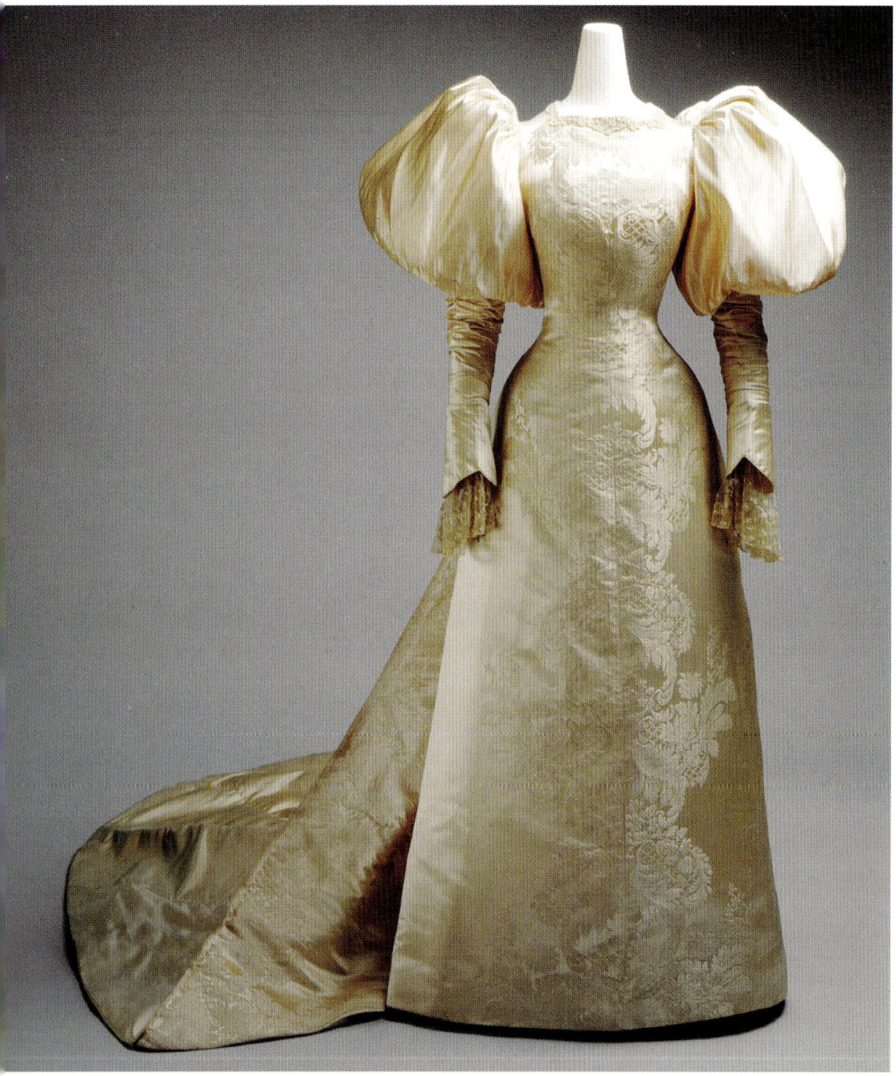

STATUESQUE SYMMETRY
The fabric is mirrored from selvedge to selvedge, perfectly pieced together to maintain the motif.

This perfectly balanced masterpiece is typical of the impeccable tailoring and finishing that made the House of Worth the most prestigious label for late nineteenth-century brides.

The simple, clean lines of this dress are utterly reliant on the skill of the dressmaker, engaging fabric and tailoring in complete harmony to realize a unified vision of a statuesque bride. The gown was perfectly molded into its hourglass form using panels cut from a stiff silk brocade. The fabric's design was pieced together to create a flawlessly matched image along the central front seam of the dress, drawing the eye up and down from neck to hem. The swirling, foliate motif of the fabric further emphasized the curvaceous silhouette of the dress. The House of Worth's exceptional dressmaking techniques were demonstrated in even the smallest details of the garment: tiny hand-stitched cartridge pleats at the shoulders created the structure that gave the gigot sleeves their voluminous form. With the artistic prowess of a sculptor, the dressmaker balanced the proportions of the gown; the enormous sleeves counteracted by the dimensions of the skirt and a train cascading out from the waist. The attention to

THE DRESS

STYLE Restrained elegance

SHAPE Hourglass

FABRIC Silk brocade

COLOR Cream

HIDDEN DETAILS

- Tiny, hand-stitched cartridge pleats at the shoulders create the structure that gives the gigot sleeves their voluminous form.
- The edges of the cuffs are trimmed with bands of piping.

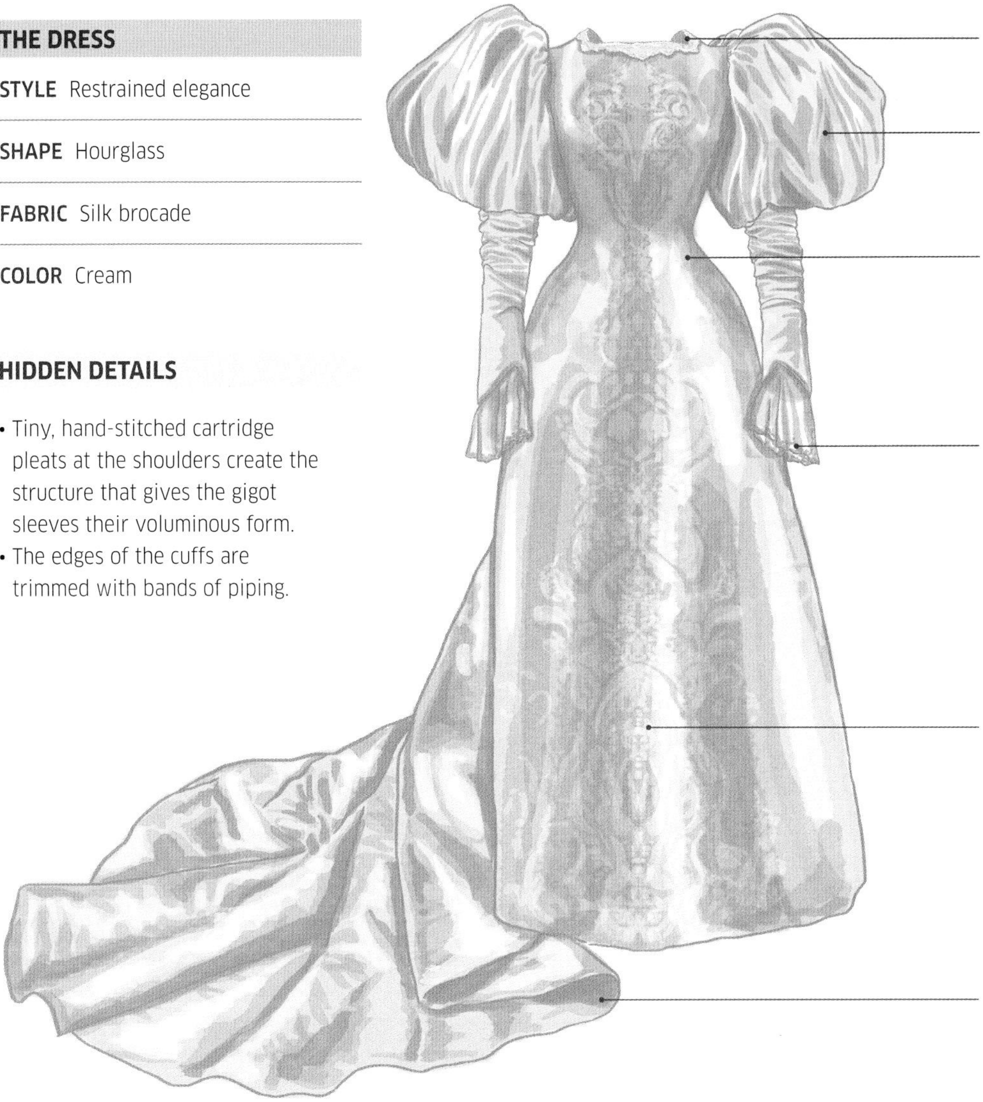

detail displayed in this iconic couture dress sets it apart from the mass-produced designs that were coming onto the market during this time as a result of the industrial revolution.

Attention to detail

Following Charles Frederick Worth's death in 1895, the business passed to his two sons, Jean-Philippe and Gaston-Lucien. Under their direction, the house continued Worth's aesthetic, drawing inspiration from historic sources—in this dress the design of the sleeves, with puffed upper arms and a fitted lower sleeve extending over the hand, has its precedent in sixteenth-century styles.

Inspiration for mass-market dreams

Under the helm of the Worth brothers, the House of Worth expanded its influence across the Atlantic, attracting wealthy American brides prepared to travel to Paris for the intensive process of commissioning a bespoke wedding dress like this one. New mass-market women's magazines avidly reported upon society weddings, and the couture creations worn by wealthy brides provided the inspiration for the mass-produced designs flooding the market from the late nineteenth century onward. The dream, if not the reality, of a luxury couture wedding gown was now within reach of many women.

04

William Wallace Terry

1922 For Princess Mary

Vogue magazine described the first royal wedding dress to be featured in its pages as a combination of "youthful simplicity and royal splendor."

Princess Mary, daughter of King George V, chose a fashionably loose, low-waisted medieval-style bridal gown girdled with silver cord that resonated with romantic connotations of courtly love.

As *British Vogue* reported, the dress design deftly fused contemporary styling with the regalia and pomp expected of a royal princess, a template adopted by countless future royals. Princess Mary's dress was crafted by London's leading court dressmaker, William Wallace Terry, from ivory-colored silk gauze embroidered with pearls and crystal beads in a trelliswork of roses mounted upon a foundation of glistening silver lamé.

Captured on camera

The wedding was filmed by no less than four rival cinematographic companies, who distributed the film nationally on the day and internationally within a month of the wedding. The films presented a previously unrealized understanding of what the public wanted to see. In place of the fleeting, snatched glimpses of the bride's dress offered by earlier cinematic reportage, Princess Mary was filmed on her way to and from Westminster Abbey and also waving from the balcony of Buckingham Palace. Another first was the release of sketches and descriptions of the gown, allowing the dress to be reproduced with accuracy. A near-identical version, imported by Franklin Simon & Co., New York, was soon modeled by Hollywood actress Marion Davies.

The broadcast of Princess Mary's wedding dress spread the dream that any bride could become a princess for the day.

ROYAL TRENDSETTING
Princess Mary's medieval-style gown set the style for royal brides: a blend of contemporary influence and regal pomp.

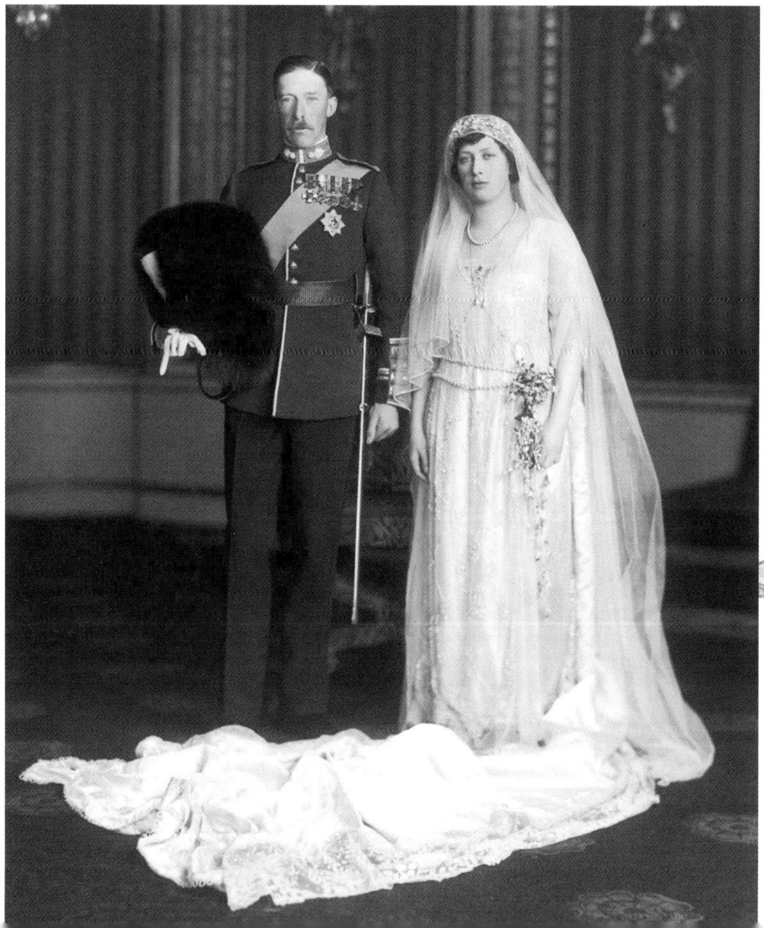

William Wallace Terry

CIRCA 1880S–1950S

Later taking the professional name of Reville, William Wallace Terry established the London court dressmaker, Reville & Rossiter, in 1905 with Sarah Rossiter. The house was appointed court dressmakers to Queen Mary in 1910, designing the queen's coronation gown in 1911. In 1912, Terry bought out Sarah Rossiter and in 1919 the name changed to Reville Ltd.

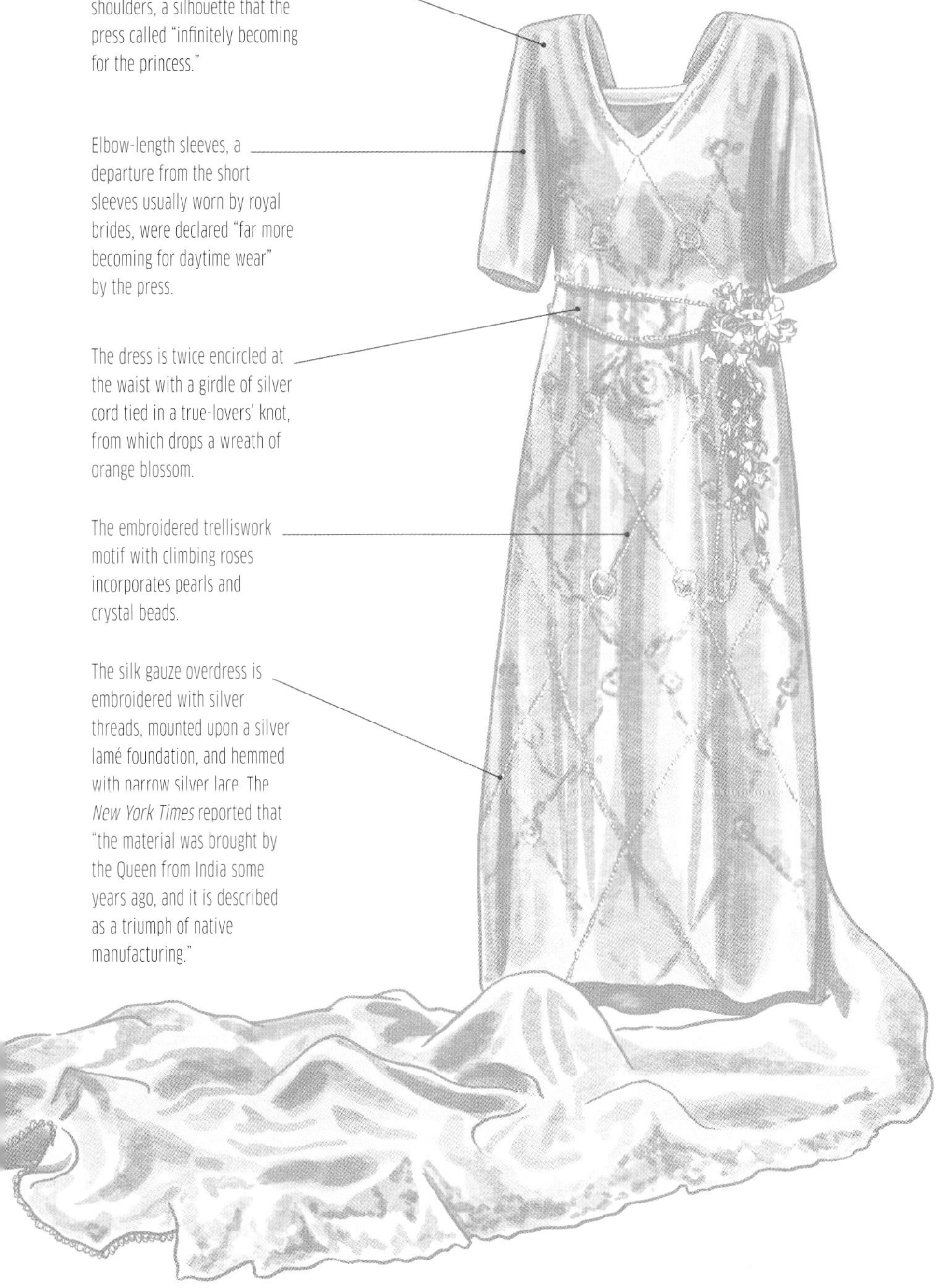

THE DRESS

STYLE Medieval

SHAPE Straight

FABRIC Silk gauze, lamé, duchesse silk satin, and Honiton lace

COLOR Ivory and silver

HIDDEN DETAILS

- Emblems of the British Empire—the British rose, Irish shamrock, Scottish thistle, Australian wattle, Indian lotus, Canadian maple leaf, and New Zealand fern—are embroidered on the train in silver thread.
- A deep border of Honiton lace, a gift from the bride's mother, Queen Mary, trims the train.

05

Paul Poiret

1925

Paul Poiret's knee-length dress, one of the earliest surviving short wedding dresses, ushered in the era of the flapper bride.

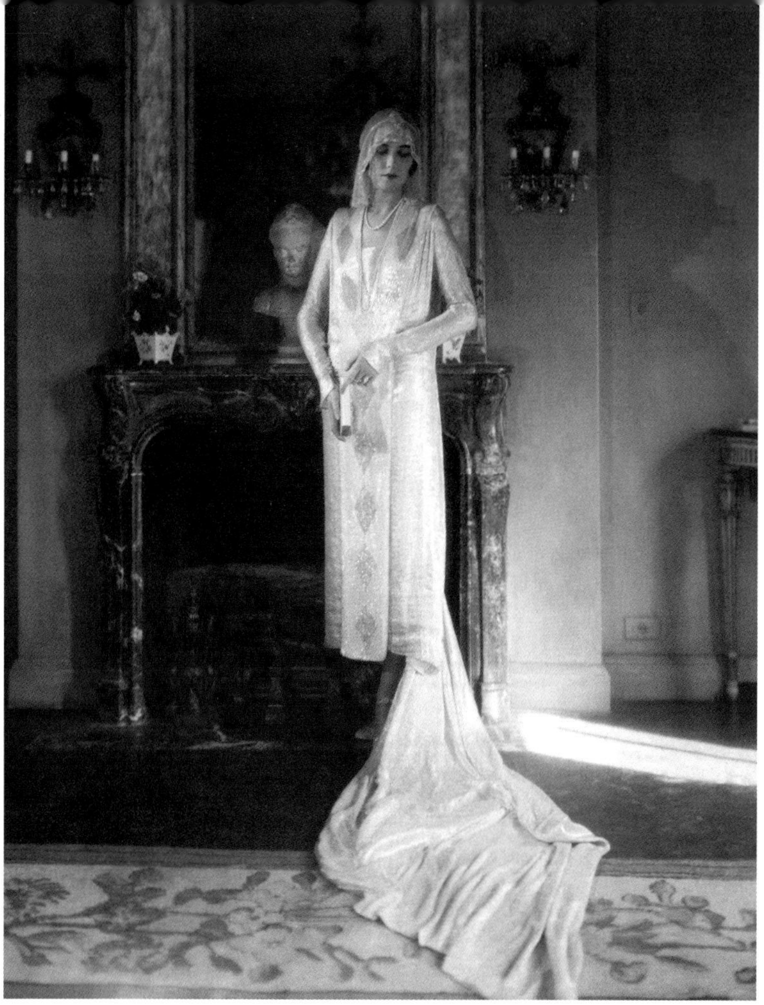

NEW HEIGHTS
Poiret's modernist wedding dress survives in the collection of the Metropolitan Museum of Art, New York. Although no photos of Poiret's dress remain in print, this contemporary Lanvin dress shows the knee-length silhouette.

The 1920s swept away the stultifying conventions of postwar society. To a soundtrack of jazz music, newly emancipated women danced fast and furiously toward modernity. Couturiers Coco Chanel, Jean Patou, and Lucien Lelong responded to this brave new world by developing the decade's iconic streamlined silhouette. This radical new fashion aesthetic had its origins in the structural simplicity of Poiret's designs.

Poiret advocated garments cut along straight lines and constructed of simple rectangular shapes. As early as 1910 he introduced the chemise gown, a pared-down garment without shaping, bust darts, or inserts, simply sewn together at each side. Understandably, Poiret's loose gowns are credited with freeing women from the constraints of corsetry and paved the way for the ideal of "la garçonne," whose boyish physique was the feminine archetype of modernism. This wedding gown drew upon Poiret's loose chemise dress, but its complex construction cleverly incorporated an aristocratic court train attached to the shoulders—a tradition that survived the decade. The gown was cut from silk charmeuse mounted upon a long-sleeved silk chiffon underdress. The back of the dress, an elongated rectangle pleated to the shoulders, fell into a long, straight-edged train trimmed with a band of silver lamé. The same decorative trimming, applied across the back of the shoulders and down the sides of the dress, mirrored the edging on the train. The trimming extended around to the front of the dress where it looped up and down, providing a visual counterpoint to the simple, straight lines of the silhouette.

Poiret's wedding dress created the prototypal 1920s bride; unrecognizable from her forebears, she was svelte, slim-hipped, and flat-chested, yet irrefutably feminine. In the decades since 1925, hemlines have fallen and risen, and corsetry has come and gone, but the loose, short wedding dress continues to evoke the idea of a free-spirited "modern" bride.

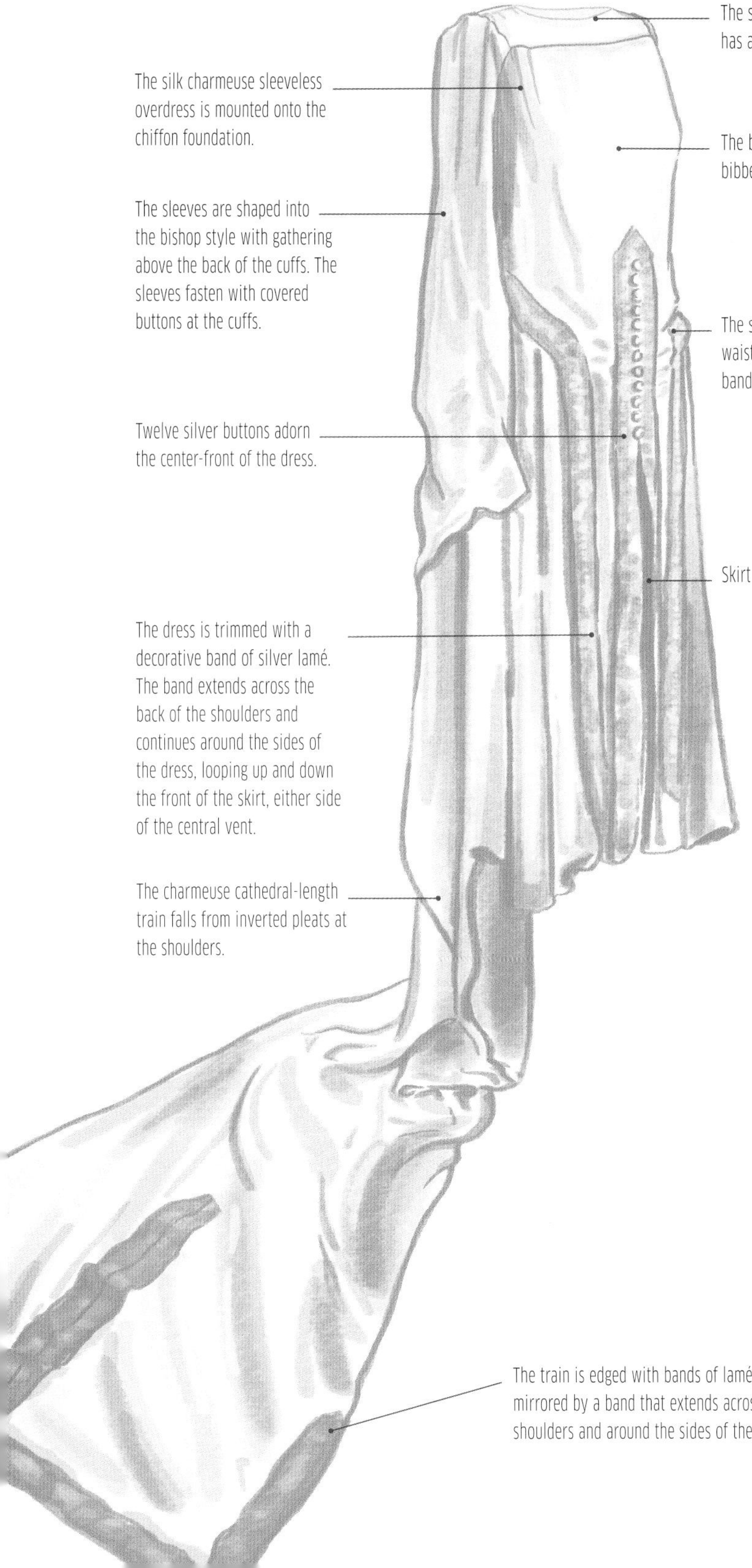

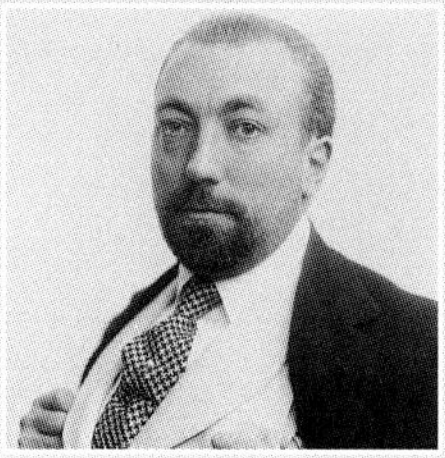

Paul Poiret
1879–1944

Paul Poiret was a technical and aesthetic innovator, dubbed the "king of fashion" during the 1910s. Poiret opened his first salon in 1903, following positions at the established couture salons of Jacques Doucet in 1898 and Worth in 1901. He is famous for breaking with the conventions of dressmaking–draping rather than tailoring and liberating women from corsets and petticoats. Poiret's aesthetic, influenced by his collaboration with artists, was characterized by acidic colors and exotic and Asian influences.

THE DRESS

STYLE Modern

SHAPE Narrow, straight cut

FABRIC Silk charmeuse, silk chiffon, and lamé

COLOR Cream and silver

HIDDEN DETAILS

- Silk satin skirt under the silk chiffon skirt.
- Concealed lamé shoulder straps.

06

Jeanne Lanvin

1926

Jeanne Lanvin's designs channeled the new aesthetic of the 1920s while retaining a wistful spirit of nostalgia that chimed perfectly with the aspirations of romantic young brides.

In 1925, a new style called art deco was premiered at the International Exposition of Modern Industrial and Decorative Arts in Paris. Inspired by modern art movements including cubism, it provoked a fashion for geometric and angular patterns. Lanvin responded by declaring: "Modern clothes need a certain romantic feel."

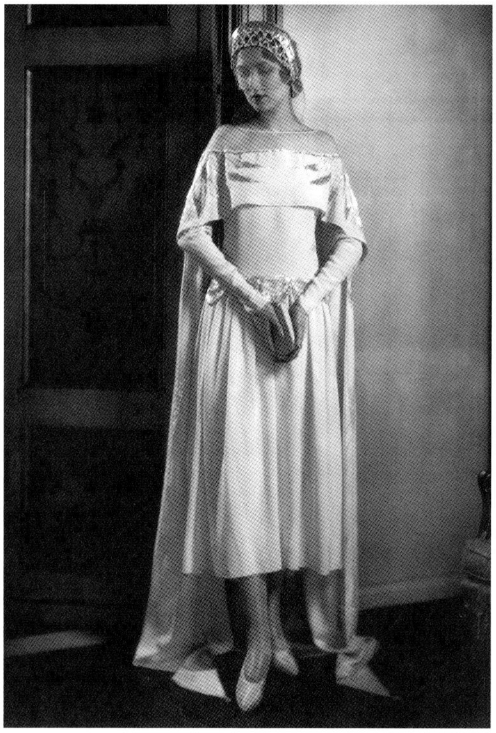

A CERTAIN ROMANCE
This Lanvin dress, of similar style to the cream 1926 dress, is decorated with striking bands of metallic embroidery. The photograph captures Lanvin's easy balance of romanticism and modernity.

The robe de style

Lanvin's signature silhouette was known as the "robe de style." It featured a full skirt gathered into the waist of a slim-fitting bodice, an adaptation of panniered eighteenth-century dresses. By 1926, the garçonne look had reached its peak: boyish and streamlined, its tubular, drop-waisted silhouette was the antithesis of the picturesque robe de style. The elongated lines of this wedding dress, with close-fitting sleeves ending in trumpet-shaped cuffs, was an elegant compromise between the frothily romantic robe de style and the severity of the garçonne shift dress.

Characteristically, Lanvin treated the simple shape of the dress as a canvas for bold, finely worked decoration. Striped bands embroidered in contrasting cream and bronze metallic threads wound around neck and waist and up and down the front of the dress in mirrored V configurations. From neck to waist and bottom hem to waist, the embroidery converged in the center-front of the dress in a swirling rosette motif. The rope-like bands harked back to the revival of medieval-style girdles that graced fashionable wedding dresses earlier in the decade but were worked in a stylized, trompe l'oeil effect that reflected the geometric dynamism of art deco style.

HIDDEN DETAILS

- Cream threads are embroidered in chain stitches.
- Metallic threads are embroidered in split stitches.
- The contrasting bands of cream and bronze embroidery dovetail at the center-back of the neck and waist.

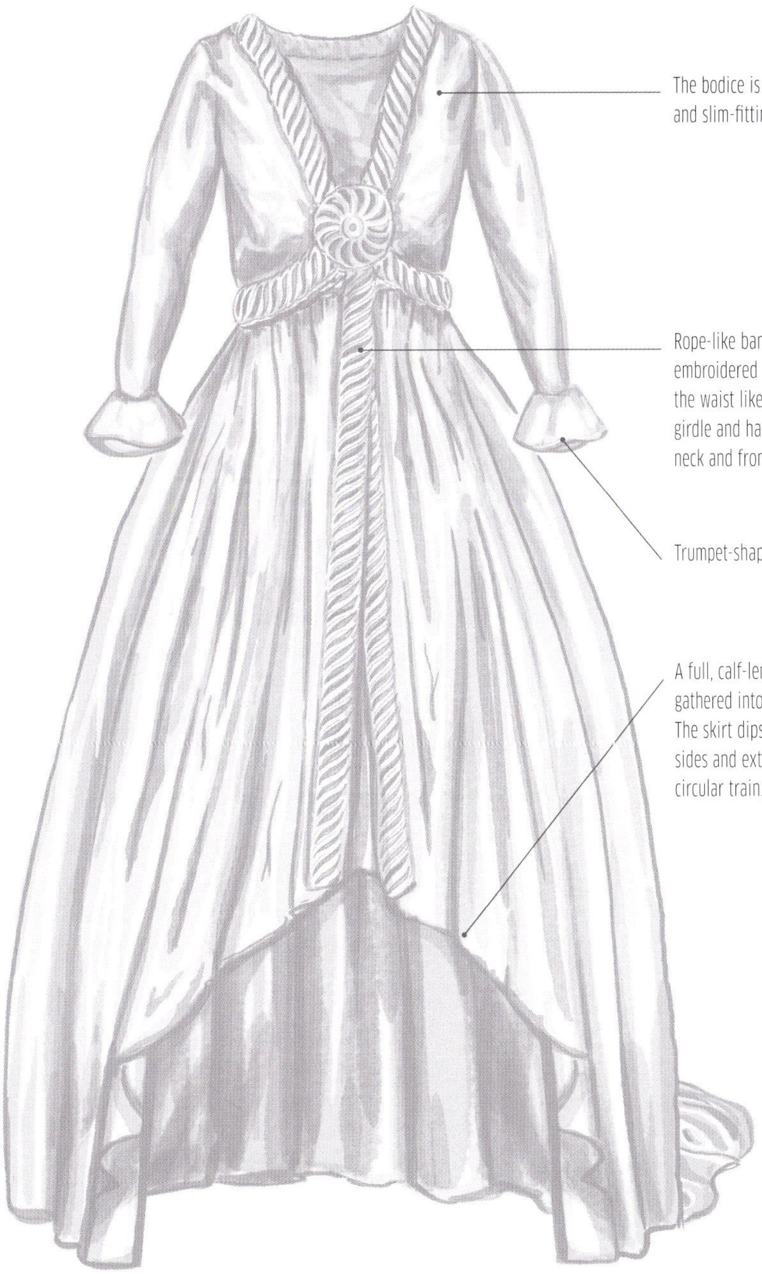

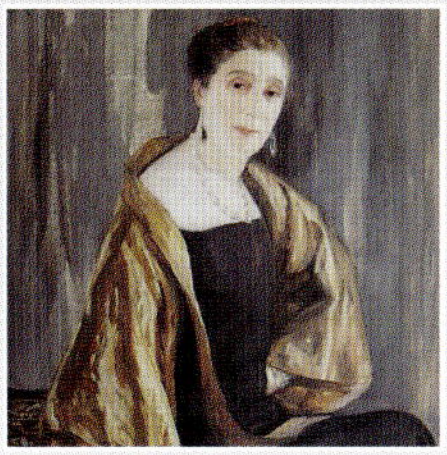

Jeanne Lanvin
1867–1946

Lanvin is the oldest fashion house in Paris, established in 1909 by Jeanne Lanvin. Lanvin trained as a milliner, beginning her career at age thirteen. A decade later, in 1889, she opened a hat boutique on the rue du Faubourg Saint-Honoré. When Lanvin began creating dresses for her daughter, the youthful simplicity of her designs won over an adult clientele, and in 1909 she branched out into womenswear. In the same year, Lanvin was inducted in the Chambre Syndicale de la Haute Couture. Lanvin's signatures were the robe-de-style silhouette, her use of pretty, feminine color, and finely worked embellishments.

THE DRESS

STYLE Romantic modernism

SHAPE Robe de style

FABRIC Silk satin

COLOR Cream

07

Madeleine Vionnet

1929

Madeleine Vionnet's bias-cut wedding dress, intersected with curved lines, epitomizes the sleek, sinuous aesthetic of the 1930s.

In 1926, *Vogue* magazine reported that Vionnet had "a mind that was logical, a thought process that was architectural, and a cutting technique that was mathematical." All of these skills are artfully demonstrated in the creation of this wedding dress, composed of intricately pieced-together geometric panels trimmed with silver cord. To make this smooth, silk panne velvet gown, Vionnet deconstructed the body into a series of planes and angles. These imagined lines were translated into an array of flat, triangular shapes that the designer then reconstructed around the body's solid three dimensions. All of the designer's gowns started with basic geometric shapes such as rectangles, squares, and circles. It was Vionnet's ethos that the couturier should be a "geometrician," as the human body "makes the geometrical figures to which the materials should correspond."

Queen of the bias cut

Vionnet understood the potential of different types of fabric—how they would move and form around the body. This in-depth knowledge of the qualities of different fibers and weave structures led her to refine a method of cutting and draping fabric that respected the rounded or elliptical planes of the body. She maximized the elasticity of fabric by cutting pattern pieces diagonally across the fabric's grain (known as fabric cut on the bias). Vionnet understood that the bias-cut technique would allow fibers to expand and contract around the curvilinear form of the body, so moving in tandem with it. Freedom of the body was Vionnet's priority: "It is a pity to go against nature," the designer declared. Embracing bias-cutting allowed the designer to celebrate, rather than constrain, the curves of the female body.

The construction of this weblike wedding dress is evidence of Vionnet's mastery of the complexities of the bias-cutting technique. Each pattern piece was cut on the bias and stitched together so that the pieces draped continuously around the body, maintaining the grain line. Fabrics were preconditioned to behave according to the designer's will—weighted and hung before being cut and sewn. "I never came across any fabric that disobeyed me," she once remarked. In Vionnet's hands, lightweight silk panne velvet expressed its innately sensuous qualities. Its soft pile pressed in one direction, the fabric spiraled seductively around the contours of the body.

Vionnet always worked in the round. Never sketching, she prepared new gowns by placing half-sized dressmaking models on a rotating piano stool, slashing into the fabric to fit the geometric shapes to the curving lines of the body. In this instance, Vionnet's method was dramatically exposed by highlighting lines

SLEEK AND SEDUCTIVE
Vionnet rejected corsets. The bias-cut dress brought the body into close contact with the dress—the bride would have worn specially designed underwear or a slip under the dress.

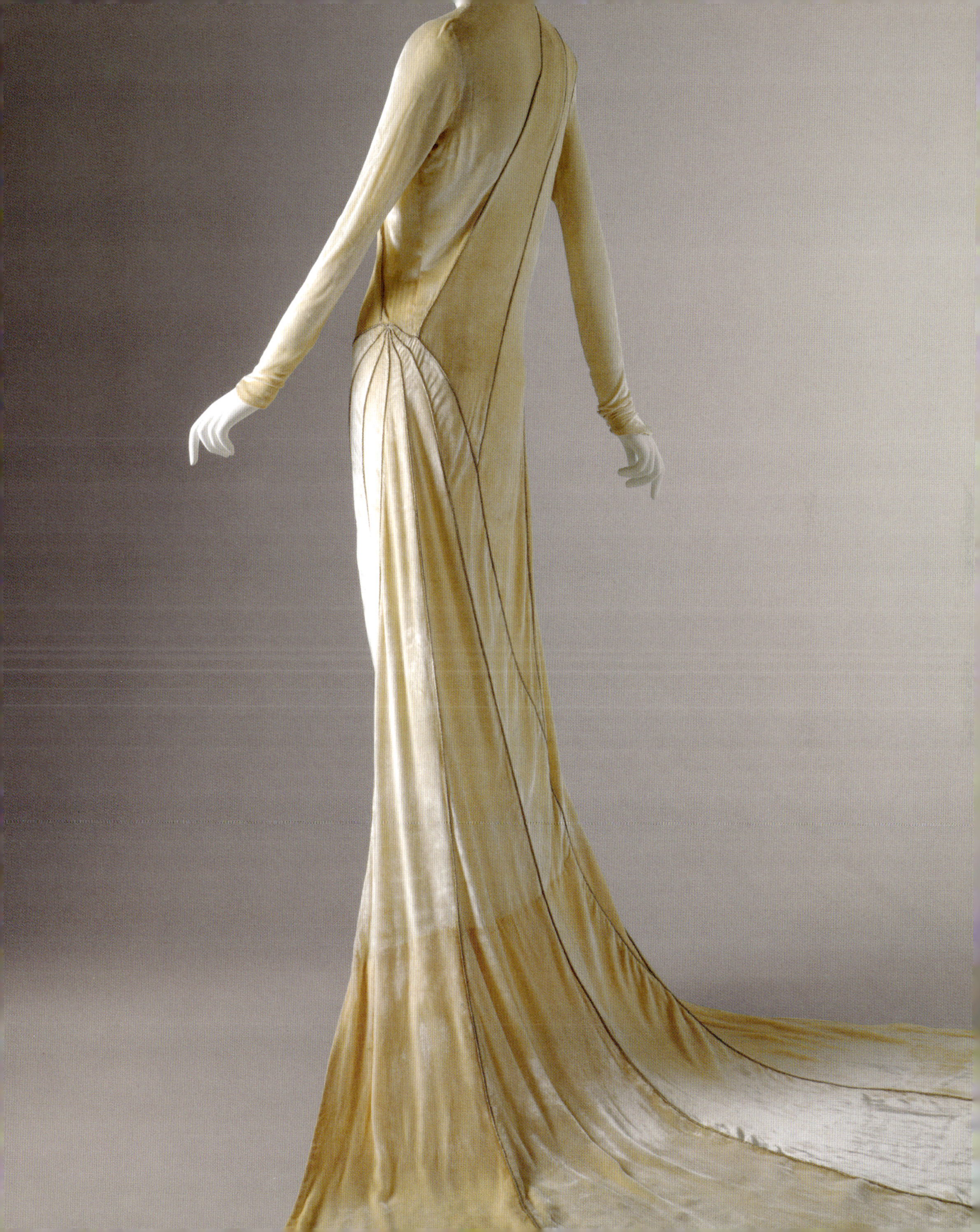

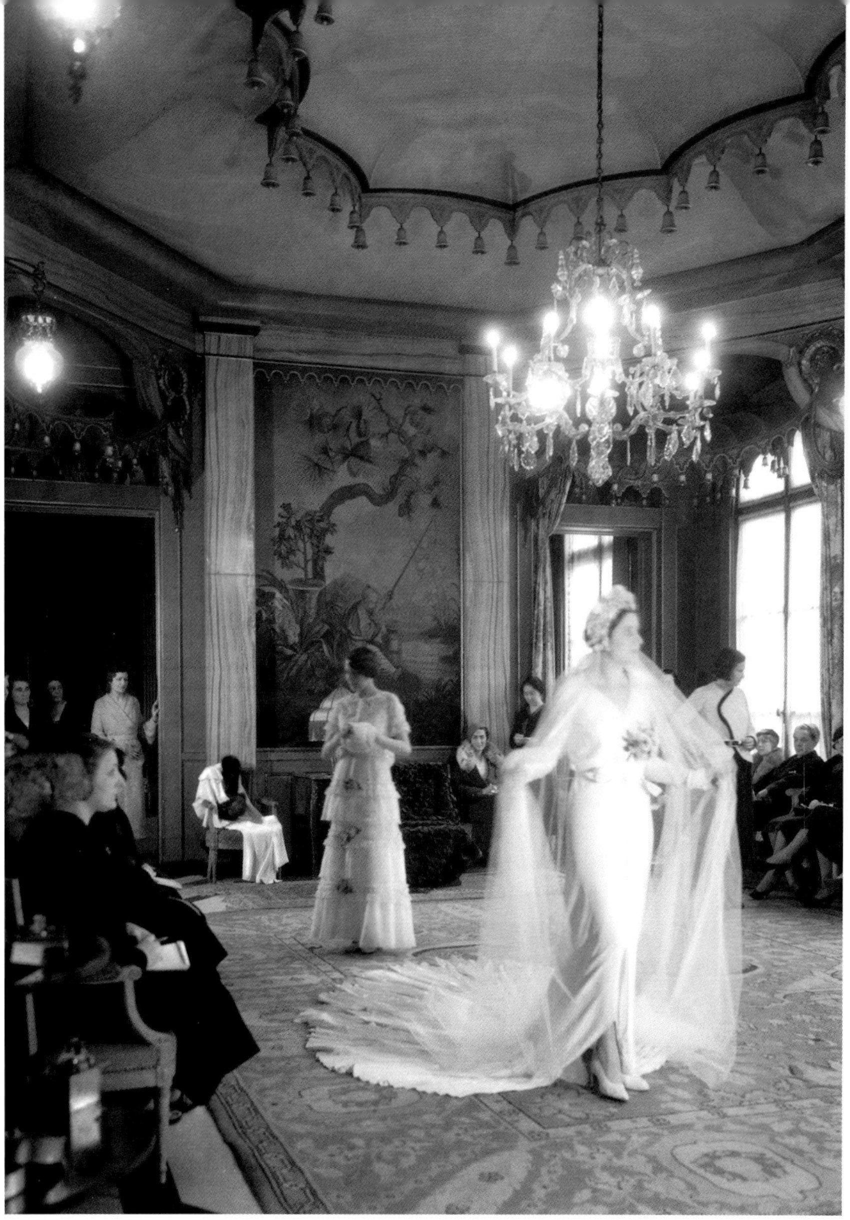

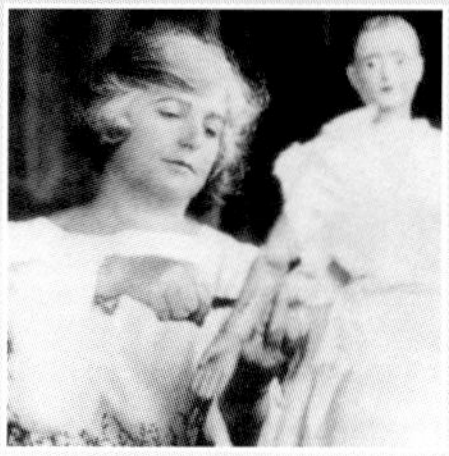

Madeleine Vionnet
1876–1975

French couturier Madeleine Vionnet entered the dressmaking profession as an apprentice at the age of eleven. After working for a lingerie maker, she honed her skills at several Parisian couture houses, becoming première d'atelier at the House of Callot Soeurs in 1901 and modéliste (designer) at the House of Doucet in 1907. In 1912, she established her own couture house in Paris. Breaking free of established practices, she advanced and popularized the technique of bias-cutting. Vionnet was celebrated for her expertise in draping and her preoccupation with the minute details of dressmaking.

THE NEW SILHOUETTE
The work of Vionnet was echoed in the designs of her contemporaries, including this dress by Callot Soeurs (1931).

of silver cord arcing around the body. Radiating from the left hip, the cord curved backward in sinuous lines down the length of the circular cathedral train and forward to the calf-length asymmetric hem, which was softened with scalloped shaping. Applied over the seams, this decorative trimming gave an aesthetic validity to the telltale signs of the craft of dressmaking. Vionnet was adamant that the "functional hardware" of dressmaking should be incorporated into the design of a garment.

The revolution

Vionnet's revolutionary construction techniques coincided with developments in contemporary art that sought to reject previous artistic traditions: futurism's exploration of movement and cubism's transformation of perspective. Vionnet's new silhouettes and radical reappraisal of the body mirrored aspects such as cubism's recomposition of the body in abstract form. Vionnet was at the forefront of the early twentieth century's avant-garde cultural practice, ushering in a new, streamlined aesthetic and a modern, liberated femininity.

THE DRESS

STYLE Early art deco

SHAPE Streamlined and sinuous

FABRIC Silk panne velvet

COLOR Ivory

HIDDEN DETAILS

- The dress was worn with a veil of off-white cotton-thread rose point lace.

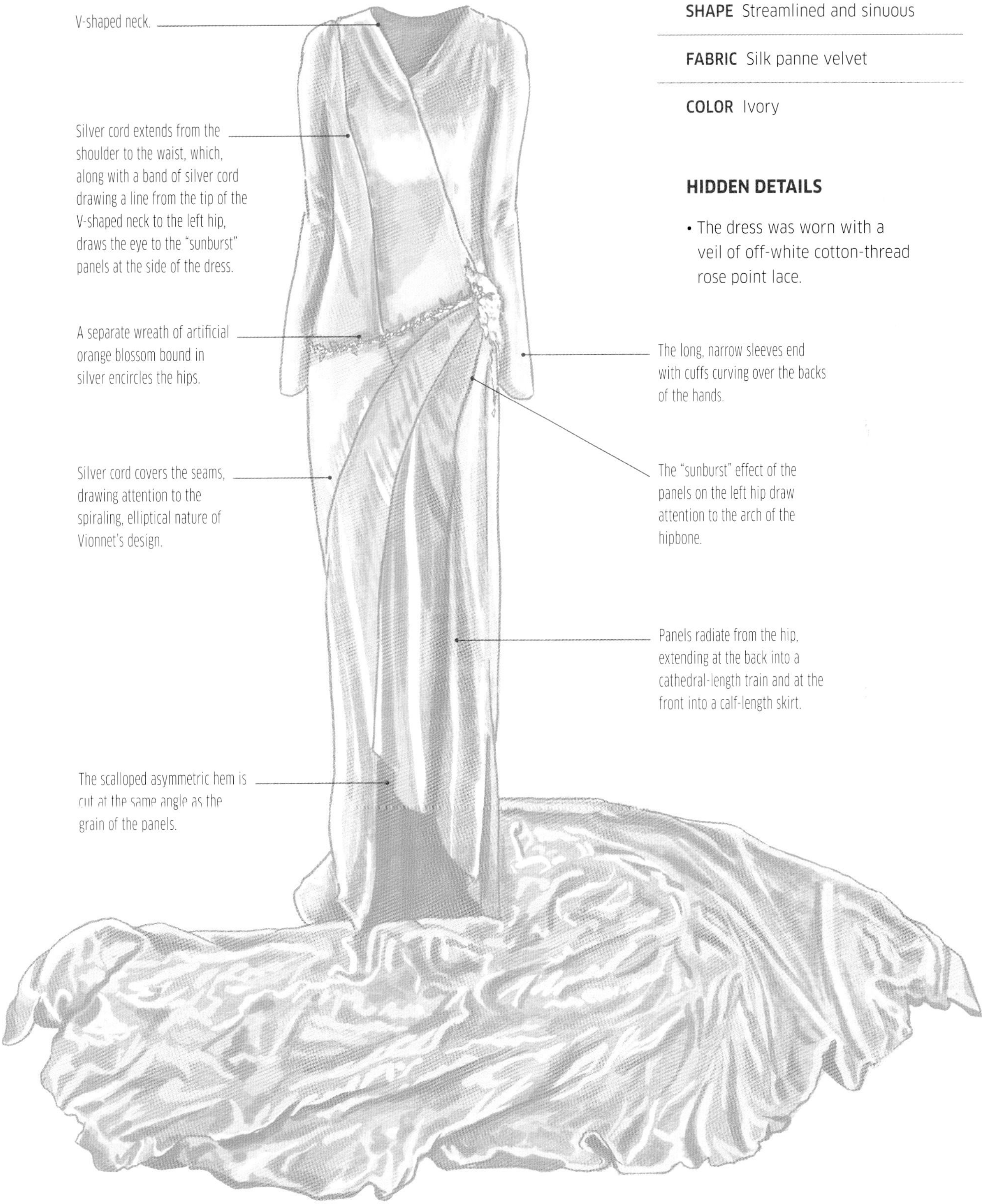

08

Charles James

1934 For Barbara "Baba" Beaton

The inventive construction of Charles James's carefully molded design pushed the boundaries of the bias-cut wedding gown.

James was a restless maverick who constantly challenged the conventions of fashion design. His modus operandi was to imagine and master the infinite variations of fashion's limited number of silhouettes and shapes. In 1934, James put his unique spin on the decade's ubiquitous bias-cut column silhouette. His creamy ivory silk satin gown was composed of five separate panels: the main section of the dress stretched around the torso; narrow raglan sleeves cut in one piece with the yoke; and a deep skirt flounce extending into a train attached to two final pieces—pointed streamers that trailed behind the bride. Seams sweeping around the body connected the sleeves and skirt flounce to the central panel. The dress was devoid of fastenings of any particular significance, just a hook and loop at the neck. James relied on the elasticity of the bias-cut fabric to enable the garment to be pulled over the bride's head.

Building on bias-cut techniques

James was a perfectionist in the extreme, working and reworking the intricacies of a design, often for months on end, until he was convinced they couldn't be improved. The simple lines of this design are deceptive because every seam and dart maximized the fit and the aesthetic of the gown. James once said, "All my seams have meaning—they emphasize something about the body." His attention to detail is evident in the dress's pleasing symmetry and rhythm, which were achieved by the mirroring and echoing of seams, darts, and folds in elongating V shapes.

Like all gowns cut on the bias, the satin stretched around the torso, but, rather than allow the fabric to fall organically and skim the body, James manipulated its drape with carefully placed darts that cleaved the satin to the bride's curves. At the front of the dress, all the lines drew the gaze sharply upward, while at the back they moved downward. Caressing the line of the hips and bust, extended darts emphasized the feminine shape—a testament to James's intention to celebrate the female figure through design. At the back of the dress, seams with a practical function to fit the main dress to the yoke were arranged into a more formal pattern.

The most dramatic element of the dress was the train. With its complex, almost architectural construction, it anticipated James's later experiments with rigid forms, such as his sculptural gown of 1948 (see page 42). Contemporary bias-cut wedding dresses fell like waterfalls into soft puddles of fabric. James inverted this mode by training the fabric at the back of the skirt into sculptural drapery divided into two clear linear streamers.

MOLDED TO THE CURVES
James's column design expanded on bias-cut dress designs, using darts and seams to further shape the gown.

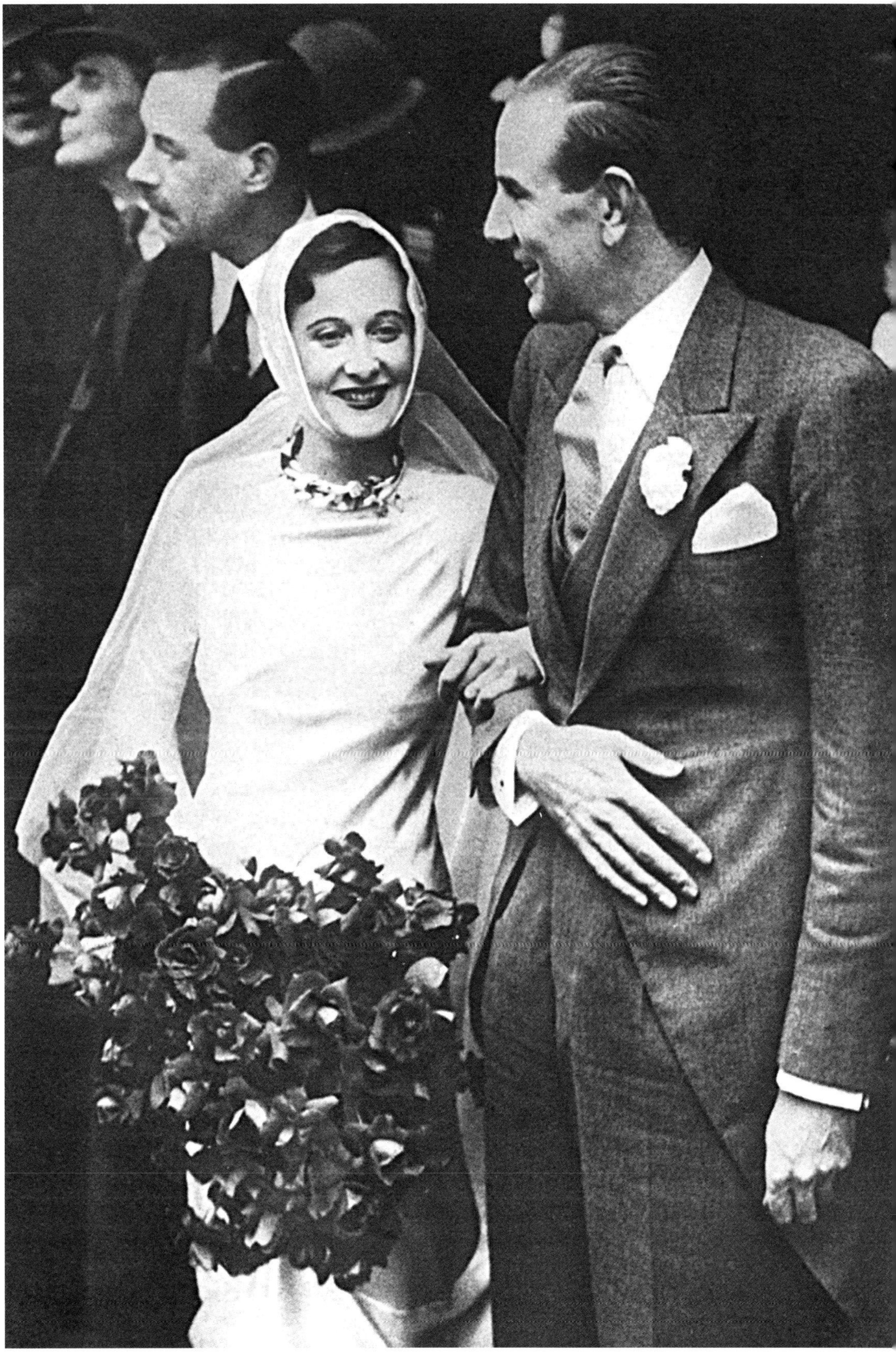

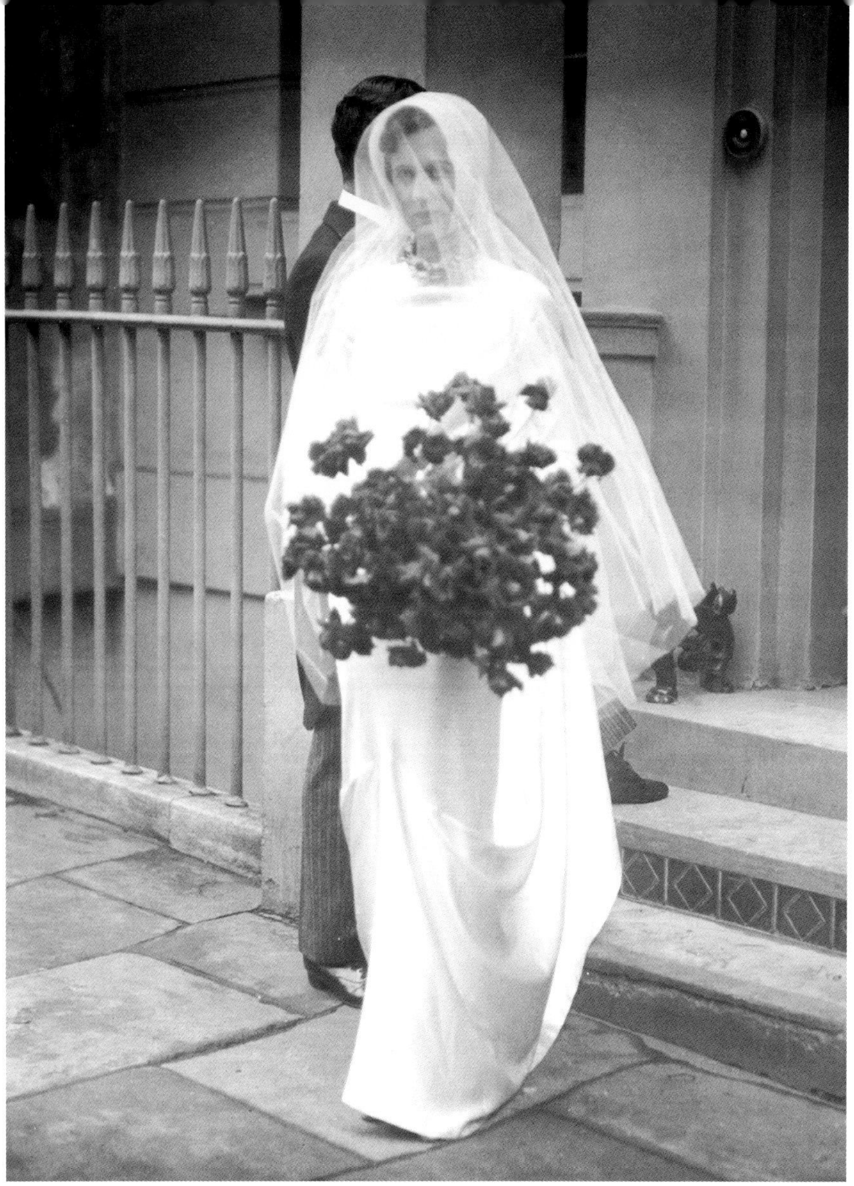

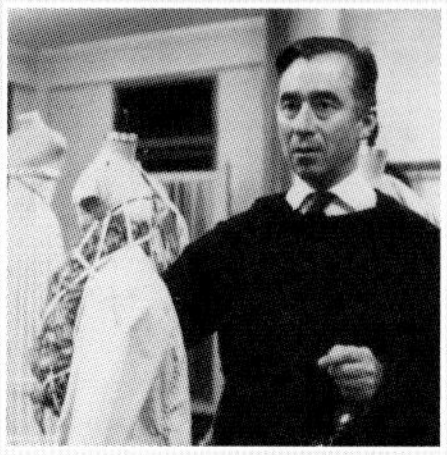

Charles James
1906–1978

James opened a hat shop under the name Charles Boucheron In 1926. Three years later, he established his first dressmaking salon in London. Over the following decade James split his time between London, Paris, and New York, initially creating prototypes for mass-produced copies and later individual couture creations. Tragically, the designer died alone and penniless. The late 1940s and 1950s were the peak of his career, but his creative successes were matched by business failures, exacerbated by his mercurial character.

INSTANT CLASSIC
James's take on the prescribed column dress of the 1930s was as dramatic as the bride's crimson bouquet.

Definitive and dramatic

James created the "trailing dress" for the British socialite Barbara "Baba" Beaton. Being dressed by James on her wedding day was a mark of the bride's adventurous taste and spirit. A James creation was guaranteed to be incomparably original, but there was no guarantee that there would actually be a dress ready on the day. The designer's notoriously obsessive fastidiousness on occasion prevented garments from leaving his studio in time for the event for which they had been commissioned.

The unique modernity of James's design was further enhanced by the spectacular crimson design scheme at the church ceremony. This was created by the bride's brother, the famous photographer and designer Cecil Beaton, who stage-managed the wedding. Baba Beaton carried a huge bouquet of red roses. She accessorized her dress with an unusual head covering inspired by the headdresses worn by nuns under their hoods. Over the dress's high cowl neck she wore a wax orange-blossom choker.

James's gown transcended the vagaries of 1930s fashion. It was the epitome of the designer's originality, as covetable today as the day on which it was worn.

THE DRESS

STYLE Innovative

SHAPE Bias-cut column with train

FABRIC Silk satin

COLOR Creamy ivory

HIDDEN DETAILS

- Two sharply sloping diagonal bust darts on either side curve around the body, fanning out over the hips and across the back of the dress, almost meeting at the center-back seam.
- The fitted cuffs have faced points and press-stud fastenings.
- There is a small opening at the back of the dress, fastened at the neck with a hook and loop.

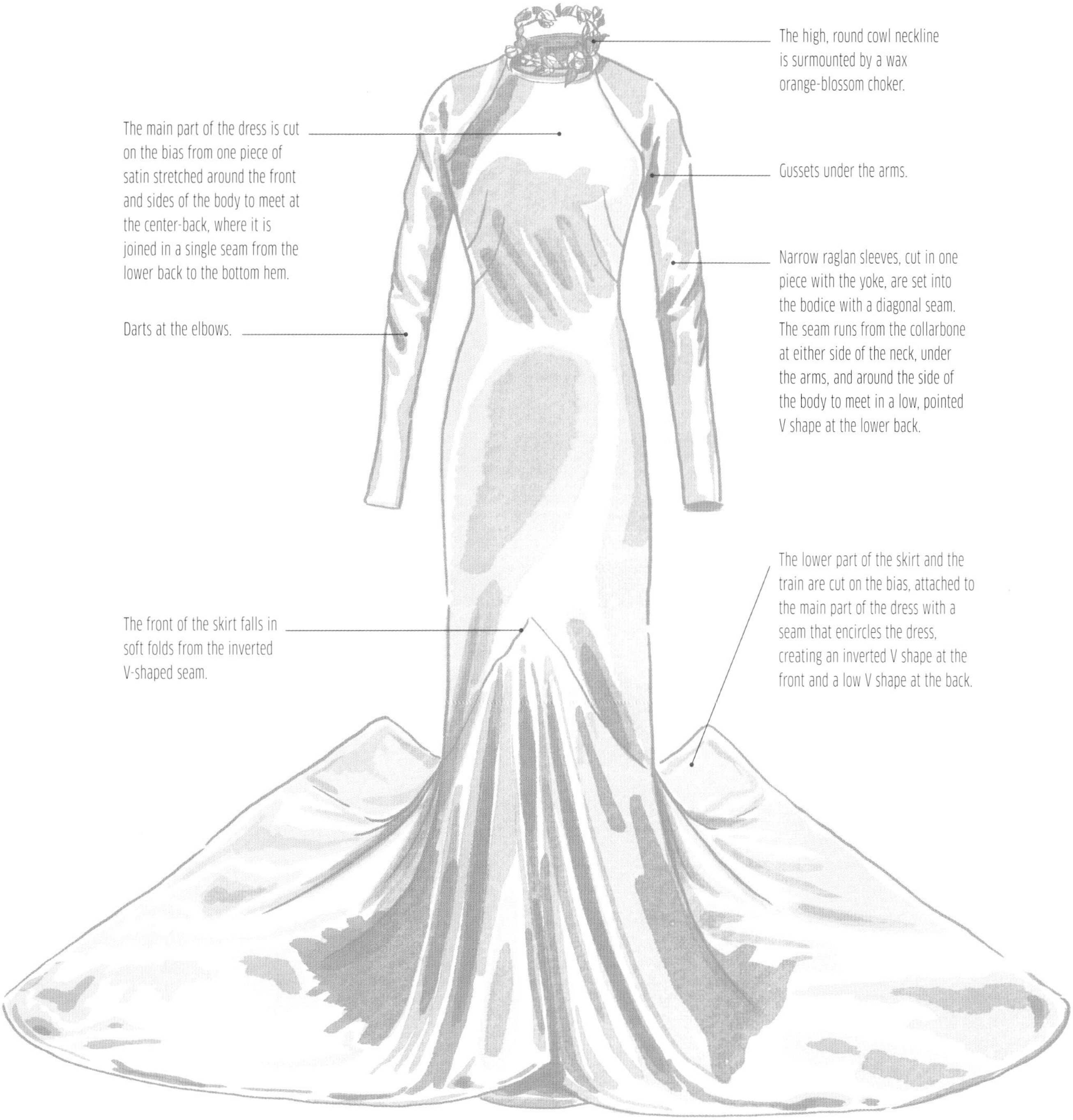

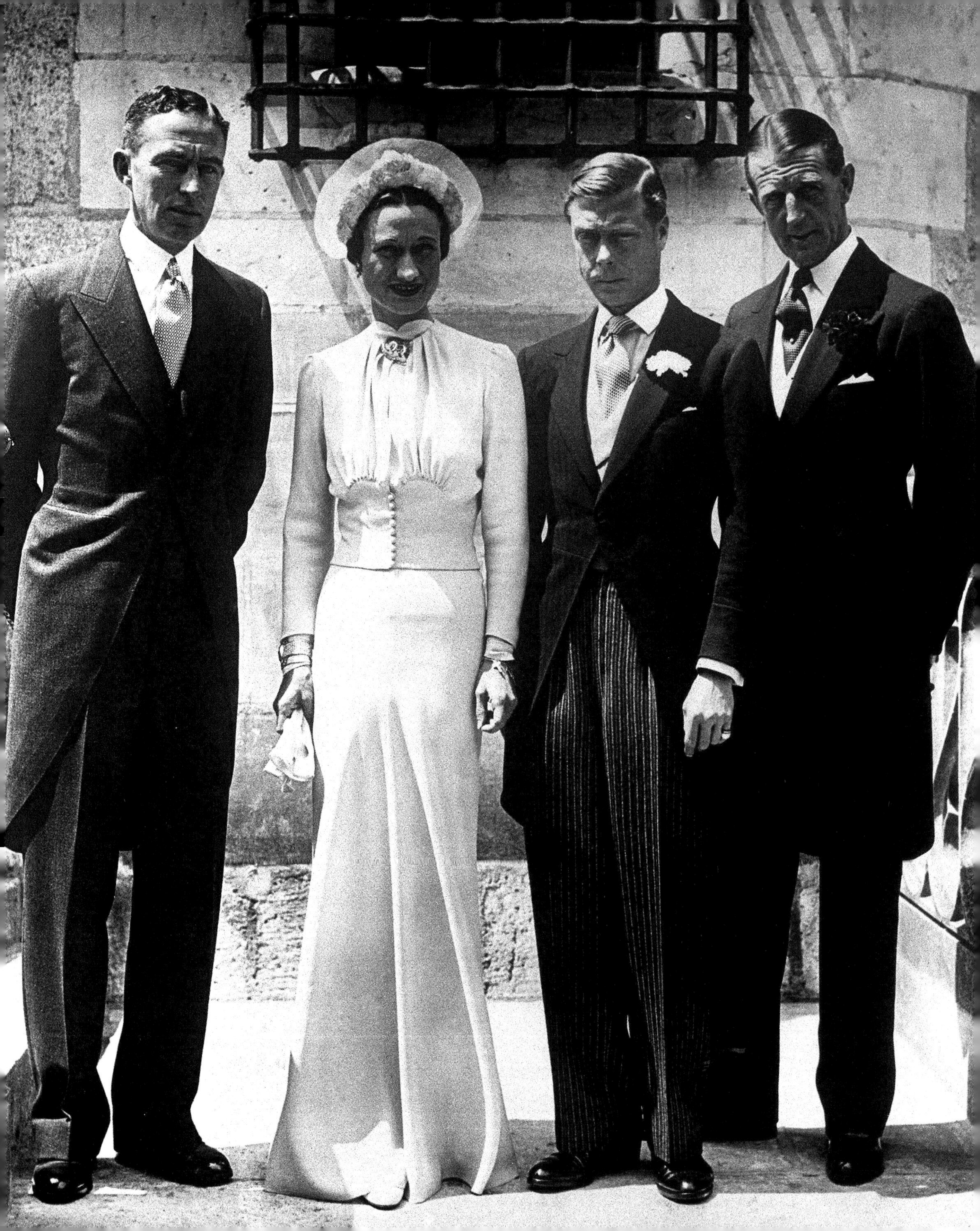

09

Mainbocher

1937 For Wallis Warfield Simpson

Modest and restrained yet flattering and elegant, Wallis Warfield Simpson's pale blue ensemble was an unusual royal wedding outfit. But her marriage to the Duke of Windsor was no conventional fairy tale.

In order to marry his twice-divorced American bride, King Edward VIII was forced to abdicate the throne. In such delicate circumstances, the couple opted in favor of a quiet service in the Château de Candé in Monts, France. As always, the future Duchess of Windsor was dressed entirely appropriately for the occasion. Her sublimely simple outfit was designed by the Paris-based American couturier Mainbocher.

Mainbocher's artistic vision of understated elegance and opulent simplicity accorded perfectly with Wallis Simpson's sharp, streamlined aesthetic. Simpson said of her style, "I've never again felt correct in anything but the severe look I developed." The dress bears hallmarks of Mainbocher's masterful cutting and meticulous attention to detail. Cut on the bias, the sleek column dress and internally corseted jacket emphasized Simpson's slender form, while the gently puffed sleeves flattered and softened her muscular shoulders. Mainbocher said of his client, "She has a fabulous figure, because she is not scrawny."

The simplicity of the outfit relied on balance and symmetry, observed in every element of its cut and construction, most notably in details like the V-shaped seams. Rows of small covered buttons that fastened with correspondingly small rouleau loops were typical of Mainbocher's labor-intensive detailing. A most unusual decorative feature on the dress was secreted beneath the jacket: a puckered zigzag seam at the center-back of the neck suggested a healing wound, unlike the smoothness that characterized the rest of this design. The significance of this private detail remains a secret shared between the designer and the bride.

Overnight sensation

The outfit was accessorized with plain court shoes, gloves specially created to accommodate her wedding ring, and a crescent-shaped hat made of straw, mounted with blue coq feathers backed by a layer of tulle. A brooch was fastened on her collar and on her wrist she wore a diamond charm bracelet with nine crosses, each inscribed with a significant event in the duke and future duchess's lives. The dress, jacket, shoes, and gloves were all made from fine silk crepe dyed "Wallis Blue," a signature shade of pale grayish-blue created by Mainbocher to match the bride's eyes.

Simpson knew what impact her choice of wedding dress would make. Two weeks before the nuptials, *Life* magazine reported, "Women of the world were little absorbed in the conventional satin gowns of England's

CLEAR BIAS
The elegant dress is a simple structure of silk cut on the bias, with boning at the jacket waist to draw it in.

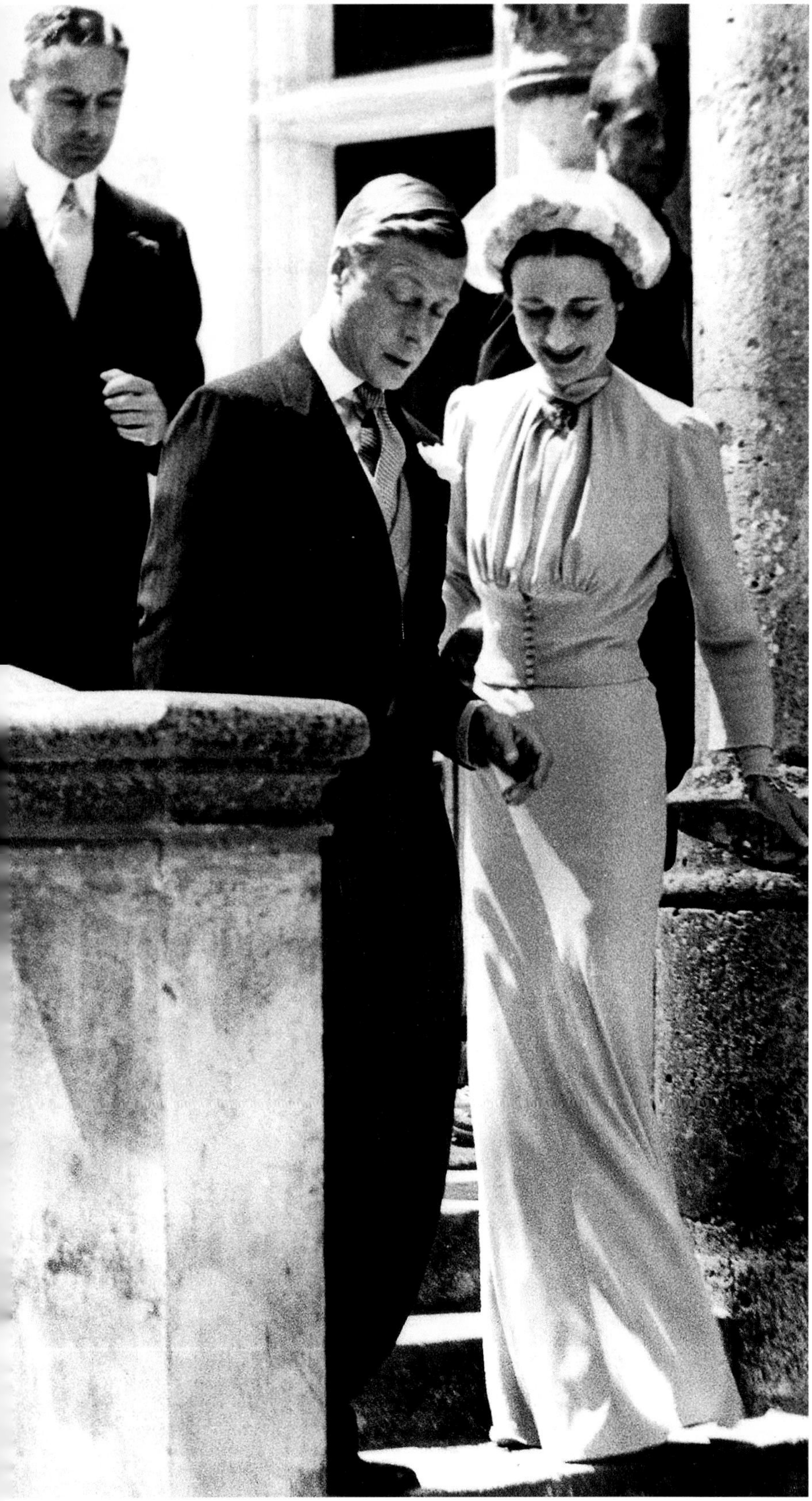

new queen. What Mrs. Wallis Warfield Simpson would wear, however, roused their avid curiosity." As the article implies, interest in Simpson's wedding dress overshadowed that of the coronation outfit of her rival, Elizabeth, the future Queen consort. It has also been suggested that Simpson was aware of the communicative potential of her wedding ensemble and gave some thought as to how her sartorial choices might impress upon the British public what they were missing by rejecting her. Was it coincidence that she chose to wear a halo-shaped hat and the bracelet given by Edward to mark milestones in their relationship? Like royal brides such as Queen Victoria, Simpson used her wedding outfit to convey personal messages about her nuptials.

The wedding dress was an overnight sensation, particularly with royalty-smitten Americans. Despite its design being a closely guarded secret, copies were being put into production practically at the moment the couple's vows were exchanged. Less than a week after the wedding, variations of the $250 original were being snapped up in American department stores. They ranged in price from $25 in Bonwit Teller to $8.90 in Klein's cash-and-carry store. Elements such as the covered buttons and corseted insert in the jacket were widely copied by other designers.

The timeless elegance of Mainbocher's wedding ensemble endures as an icon for the controversial royal bride. Chic and proper, it continues to inspire second-time brides. When the divorced Nancy Shevell married twice-wed Paul McCartney in 2011, she wore an understated suit that had a gathered bodice and vertical row of covered buttons, echoing Mainbocher's design.

THE MOST COPIED DRESS IN HISTORY
Following the news coverage, "Wally" dresses could be found in department stores throughout America.

Mainbocher
1890–1976

Born Main Rousseau Bocher in Chicago, Mainbocher began his career in fashion as an editor for *Vogue Paris* before realizing his own creative ambitions as a designer and opening a salon at 12 avenue George V, Paris, in 1929 (at which time he changed his name).

His success designing the future Duchess of Windsor's wedding dress secured him a devoted clientele of society ladies, who followed him to America upon the outbreak of World War II. Mainbocher remained in his New York salon until 1971, after which he returned to Europe for the rest of his life.

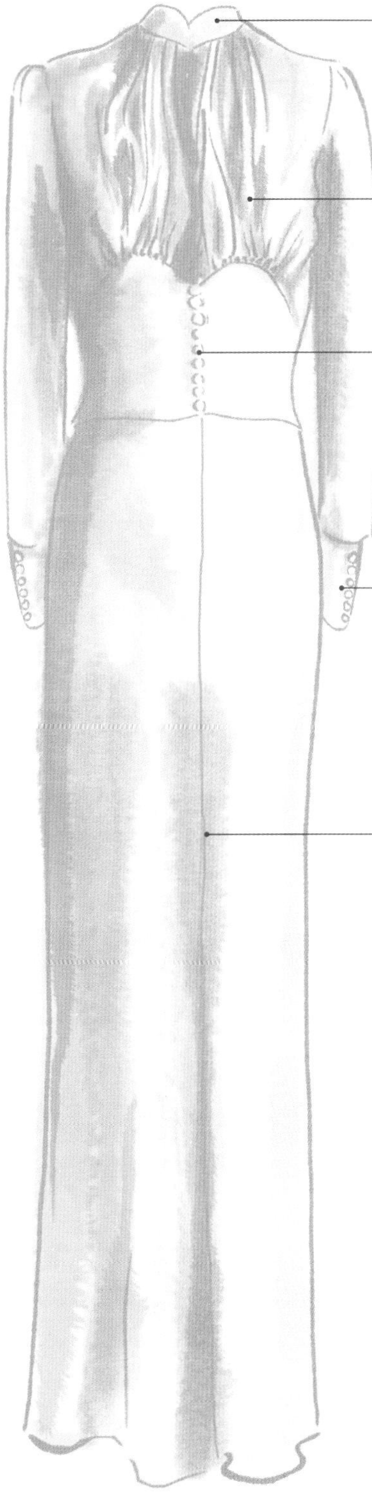

THE DRESS

STYLE Elegant minimalism

SHAPE Column

FABRIC Silk crepe

COLOR "Wallis Blue"

HIDDEN DETAILS

- A puckered zigzag seam at the center-back of the dress's neck suggests a healing wound.
- The shoulder seams are recessed at the top of the sleeves to create a smooth line underneath the jacket.

10

Elsa Schiaparelli

1938

Drawing on unlikely associations with a mythical monster, Elsa Schiaparelli's surrealist design displaced bridal traditions and reinvented the veil as canvas for experimentation and expression.

Schiaparelli had a reputation as a true nonconformist. *Time* magazine described the designer as "madder" and "more original" than any of her contemporaries. The designs she produced between 1936 and 1939 incorporated the theories and imagery of surrealism. In 1938, at the time the International Surrealist Exhibition had just opened in Paris, Schiaparelli presented her now infamous Circus collection, which she recollected as her "most riotous and swaggering" collection. The show closed with a discreetly long-sleeved, full-skirted white wedding dress—the image of virginal purity and modesty. However, in place of the usual plain white veil, the designer paired her gown with a veil embroidered with sapphire blue bugle beads. Arrayed in a trompe l'oeil effect, the embroidery suggests wild, wavy strands of hair or slithering snakes. These glittering tresses bring to mind the mythical Greek Gorgon, Medusa—a beautiful woman turned into a hideous monster who literally petrified those who looked upon her. The tale of Medusa has continued to fascinate designers, her face later becoming the logo of the house of Versace.

Subverting myths and traditions

The origins and symbolism of the bridal veil are steeped in their own mythology. Some sources say they were worn in the medieval period to ward off evil spirits, but from a practical perspective, when marriages were arranged, the veil was employed to prevent a groom from looking at the bride's face until after he had taken his vows. The act of lifting the veil symbolized the shift of responsibility for the bride from father to groom, and represents the bride's submission to and willingness to obey her husband. By the twentieth century the veil had value as a symbol of purity, chastity, and innocence.

Schiaparelli designed for the modern, active woman—her clothes enabled women to articulate themselves in public in ways they had never done before. In this respect, her embroidered veil could be read as a bold statement about the status quo of marriage. With her characteristic imagination and daring, Schiaparelli's design reframed the meek, dutiful bride as a serpent-haired demon with the power to turn her groom to stone.

MEDUSA BRIDE
The cotton net veil is embroidered with blue bugle beads in a trompe l'oeil motif suggesting slithering snakes or wild, wavy hair.

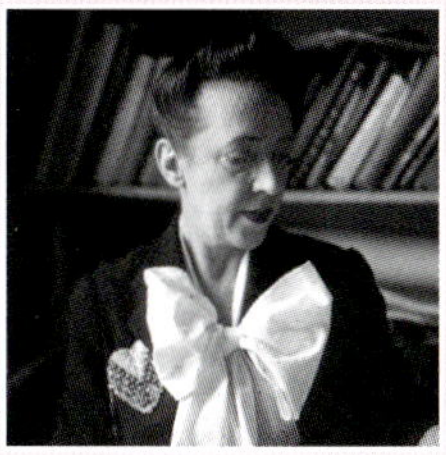

Elsa Schiaparelli
1890–1973

Dare to be different, Schiaparelli urged women. Influenced by her collaboration with artists, most famously Salvador Dalí, Schiaparelli used clothing as an expressive medium. Born in Rome, she moved to New York in 1916 and relocated to Paris in 1922. Schiaparelli began designing in 1924 after meeting Paul Poiret (see page 20). Her first independent collection, presented in 1927, included the now famous trompe l'oeil bow sweater. The 1930s proved to be her peak creative period, during which time she pioneered the concept of themed collections and the fashion show as performance.

THE DRESS

STYLE Surrealist

SHAPE Full skirt; bouquet-length drop veil

FABRIC Silk; cotton net and bugle-beaded veil

COLOR White and blue

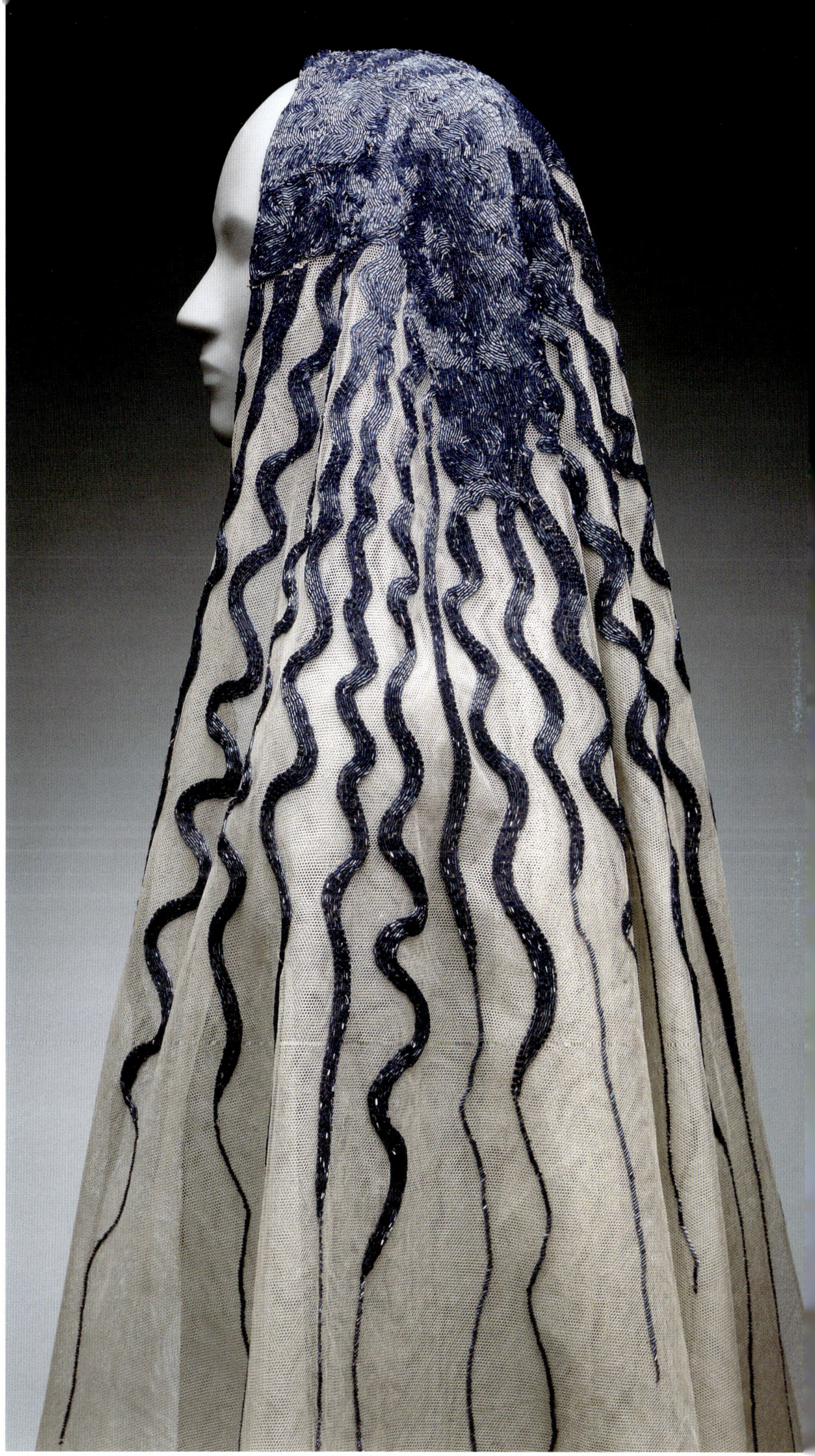

11

Norman Hartnell

1947 For Princess Elizabeth

Princess Elizabeth's ravishingly embroidered wedding dress shone as a luminous symbol of renewal for postwar Britain.

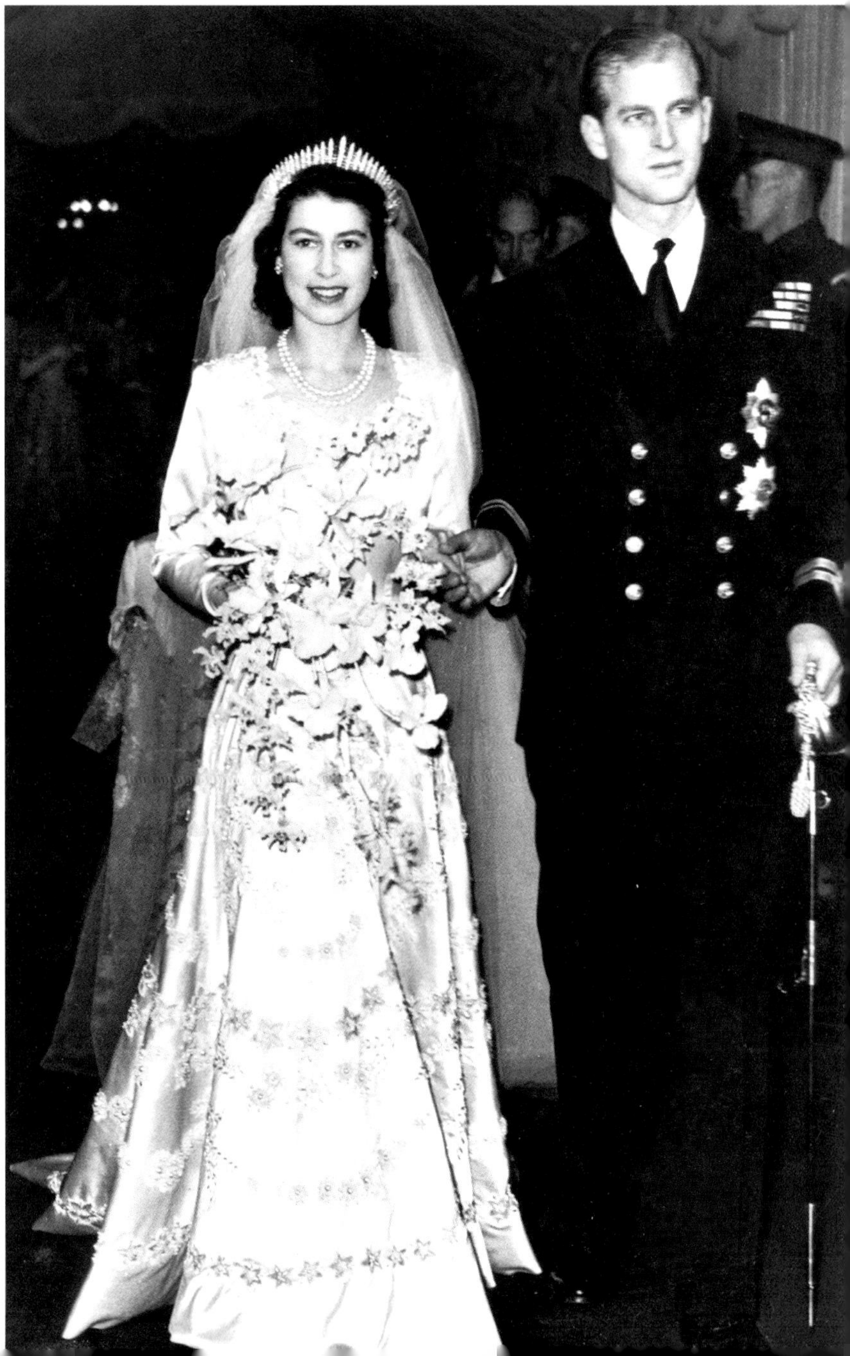

In July 1947, when Princess Elizabeth became engaged to Philip Mountbatten, Britain was still in the grip of austerity, nearly two years after the end of World War II. The marriage of England's fresh-faced future monarch to the dashing lieutenant presented a beacon of hope and relief to a nation fatigued by the deprivation and heartache of war. The bride's dress was commissioned from London's leading court couturier, Norman Hartnell, whose theatrical training perfectly equipped him to realize the spectacle and pageantry expected of the royal gown. Hartnell drew inspiration from Sandro Botticelli's painting *La Primavera* (circa 1482), recognizing in this allegory of renewal the promise of recovery pinned to the royal wedding. The design of the dress was based loosely on the flower-strewn dress worn in the painting by the goddess Flora—symbolizing love and the advent of spring. Hartnell's ivory satin dress and train were bedecked with shimmering floral garlands and flowing sprays of corn. These emblems of love and fertility were embroidered with white seed pearls, sparkling crystals, and glistening silver threads. Hartnell described the process of creating the embroideries in his autobiography, *Silver and Gold*. He laid

LA PRIMAVERA
The princess accessorized her dress with a pearl necklace to match the pearl embroidery on the dress.

out yards of tracing paper on the floor of his workroom. First marking a central line from the shoulder, he filled in a line of syringa and orange blossoms. Then, sitting cross-legged on the floor, he marked in the rest of the floral motifs "assembled in a design proportioned like a florist's bouquet." Hartnell then returned to the design and filled in any gaps with more leaves and blossoms.

A bright future

Fashion historian James Laver described the visual effect produced by the embroidery as "A color scheme surprising in its range, for a whole gamut of shades and contrasts can be held within the span of color which has itself no color." The freshness and delicacy of Hartnell's embroidery was mirrored by the gentle structure of the gown, which emphasized, without constraining, the curves of the bride's youthful physique. The dress was cut from supple satin ordered from the Scottish firm of Winterthur. It had a tailored bodice gently molded to the bride's body, square shoulders, a cutout sweetheart neckline mounted on transparent tulle, narrow long sleeves, and a low pointed V-waist. Below the waist, a full-length skirt cut on the cross fell in soft folds, extending into a deep circular train. The bride also wore a magnificent 13-foot (4-m) court train attached to the shoulders of her dress. Made of ivory-colored silk tulle, the train was decorated with appliqué satin flowers. The satin was made at Lullingstone Castle. Reputedly, the Queen Mother specifically requested that this stiff, lustrous satin be used. A silk tulle veil and ivory satin peep-toe, sling-back, high-heeled sandals, trimmed with silver and seed pearl buckles, made by Edward Rayne, completed the bride's ensemble.

Cheering a downtrodden nation

With wartime restrictions and rationing still in place, Hartnell's vision was not easily realized. The pearls for the embroidery, 10,000 in total, had to be sourced from America. The provenance of the satin had to be ascertained after rumors spread that it was made from "enemy" Italian and Japanese silkworms. The Palace confirmed that the threads came from Chinese worms. In a touching gesture of national solidarity, hundreds of women across the country sent the Princess their clothing coupons in the post so that she could realize, with her dress, the nation's collective desire for luxury and ceremony. Princess Elizabeth's beautifully worked wedding dress validated the dreams of a nation of brides still suffering the after-effects of war.

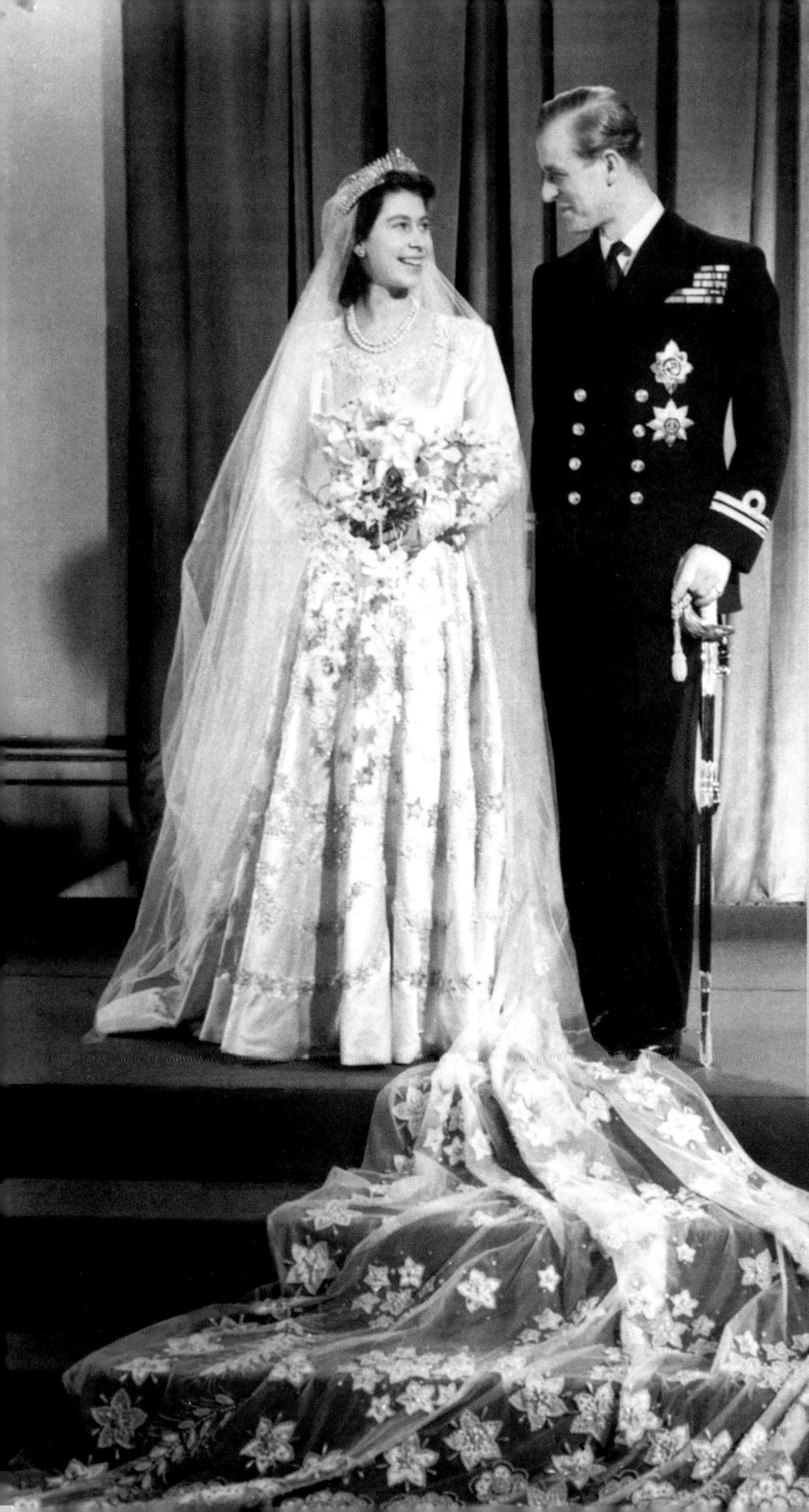

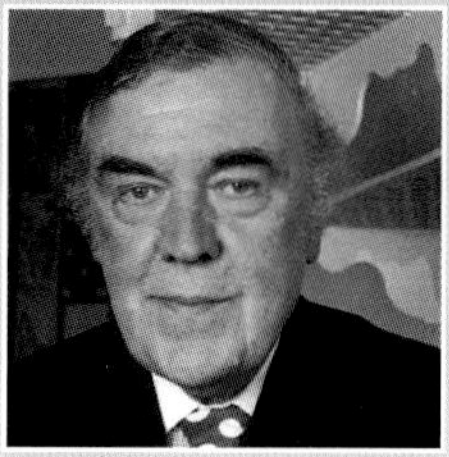

Norman Hartnell

1901–1979

Norman Hartnell was Britain's most celebrated mid-twentieth-century designer. As a student, he designed for Cambridge University's amateur dramatics society. Establishing his own salon in 1923, Hartnell made his name designing for London's court society, securing the official appointment of dressmaker to the royal family in 1938. Hartnell designed the wedding dress of Princess Elizabeth and that of her sister, Princess Margaret, in 1960, as well as Elizabeth's coronation robes in 1953. Hartnell is best remembered for his signature show-stopping embroidered ball gowns and quintessentially English style.

A SYMBOL OF LOVE AND SPRING
Sparkling with embroidered pearls and crystals, the spectacular 13-foot tulle train was regal and magnificent yet light and fresh.

THE DRESS

STYLE Youthful and romantic

SHAPE Soft hourglass

FABRIC Silk satin

COLOR Ivory

HIDDEN DETAILS

- Attached at the shoulders was a 13-foot (4-m) tulle train embroidered with floral motifs and ears of corn worked in pearl, crystal, and appliqué duchesse satin.
- Fastens at the center-back with buttons.

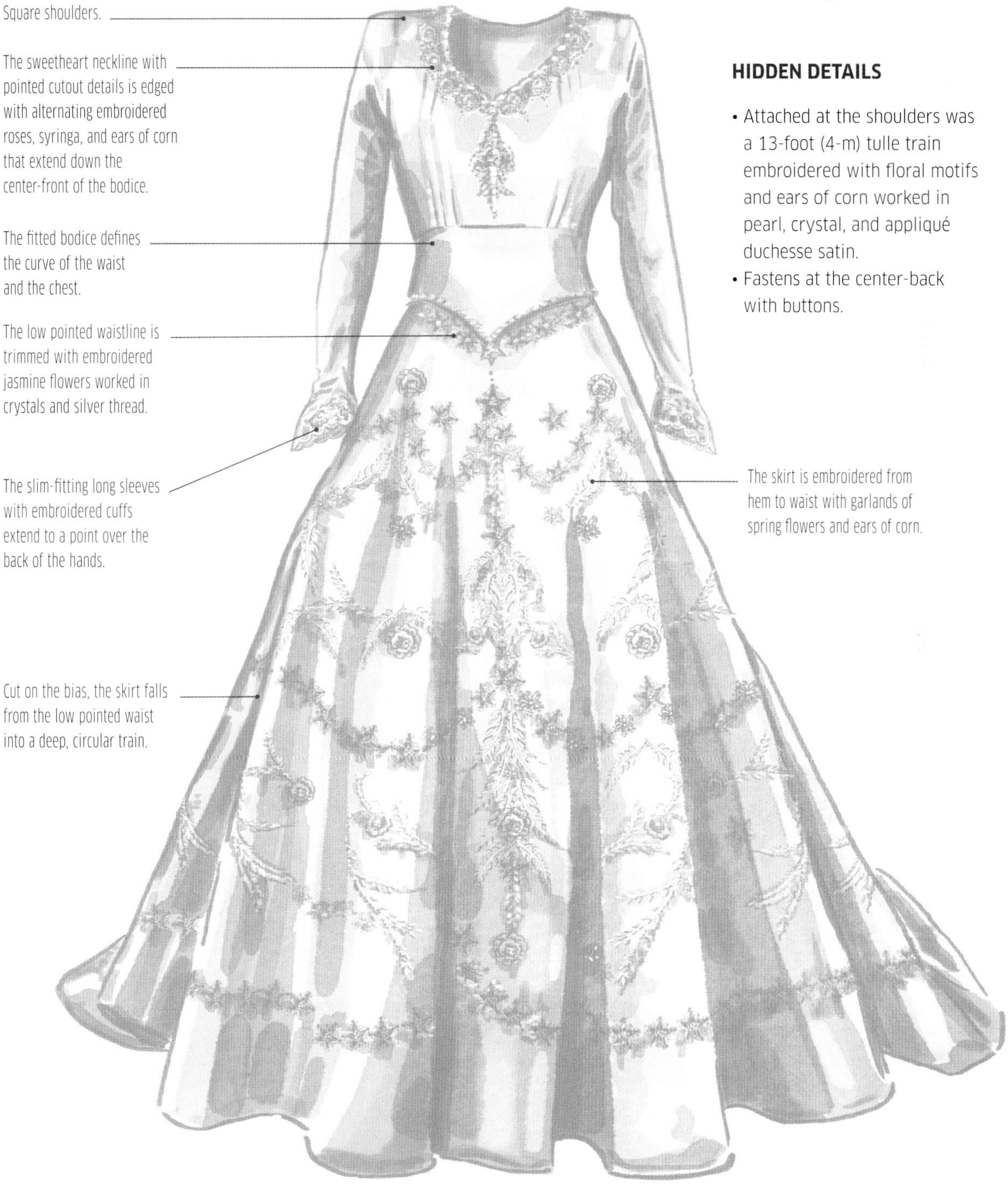

12

Charles James

1948

This seashell-pink satin wedding dress, which Charles James produced at the pinnacle of his career, is the epitome of the designer's creative genius.

James's reputation as fashion's greatest architect was sealed by the artistry with which he sculpted fabric into original compositions. Lacking any formal dressmaking training, James developed his own methodology built upon concepts that he drew from architecture, sculpture, and mathematics. James enhanced and reshaped the female form with his complex dressmaking techniques. The designer, who had begun his career as a milliner, treated the female body as a block upon which he built his creations. He trained fabric around the curves of the body with his signature precision-cutting and geometric seaming. Exploiting the structural potential of heavyweight fabrics, James was able to extend garments beyond the body's boundaries, supporting them with underpinnings based on Victorian prototypes. (For more about James, see page 30.)

Designed for a Madame X

This wedding dress, fusing the prevalent New Look silhouette with a reinterpretation of an 1880s-style bustle and corsetry, was an excellent example of the designer's unorthodox technical processes and unique personal aesthetic. Created from stiff silk satin disciplined into a structure exaggerating the female form, the dress resonated with a powerful eroticism suggestive of John Singer Sargent's oil painting *Madame X (Madame Pierre Gautreau)* (1883–1884), by which James was very likely inspired.

James's design demanded a strength of presence to take control of its sensuous styling. A pleated sweetheart neckline exposed an expanse of décolletage, with twisted straps slipping suggestively over the shoulders. A tightly corseted bodice—dissected with razor-sharp seams meeting in the pointed waist—smoothed the torso into a sleek bullet. The polonaise-inspired skirt, sculpted over the hips with deftly draped fabric, formed a gravity-defying bustle falling to an asymmetric hem. An ivory satin underskirt toned perfectly with the pearlescent-pink overskirt, a combination of colors that confirmed *Vogue* magazine's 1948 accolade of James as the "master of color comparatives."

James transformed historical references and contemporary fashion into a wedding dress of universal modernity. By the late 1940s, the designer's rare wedding dresses were highly valued as works of sculptural art, and today they have achieved cult status.

ARTISTRY AND FORM
James didn't make dresses—he built them in layers, using the female body as a blank form.

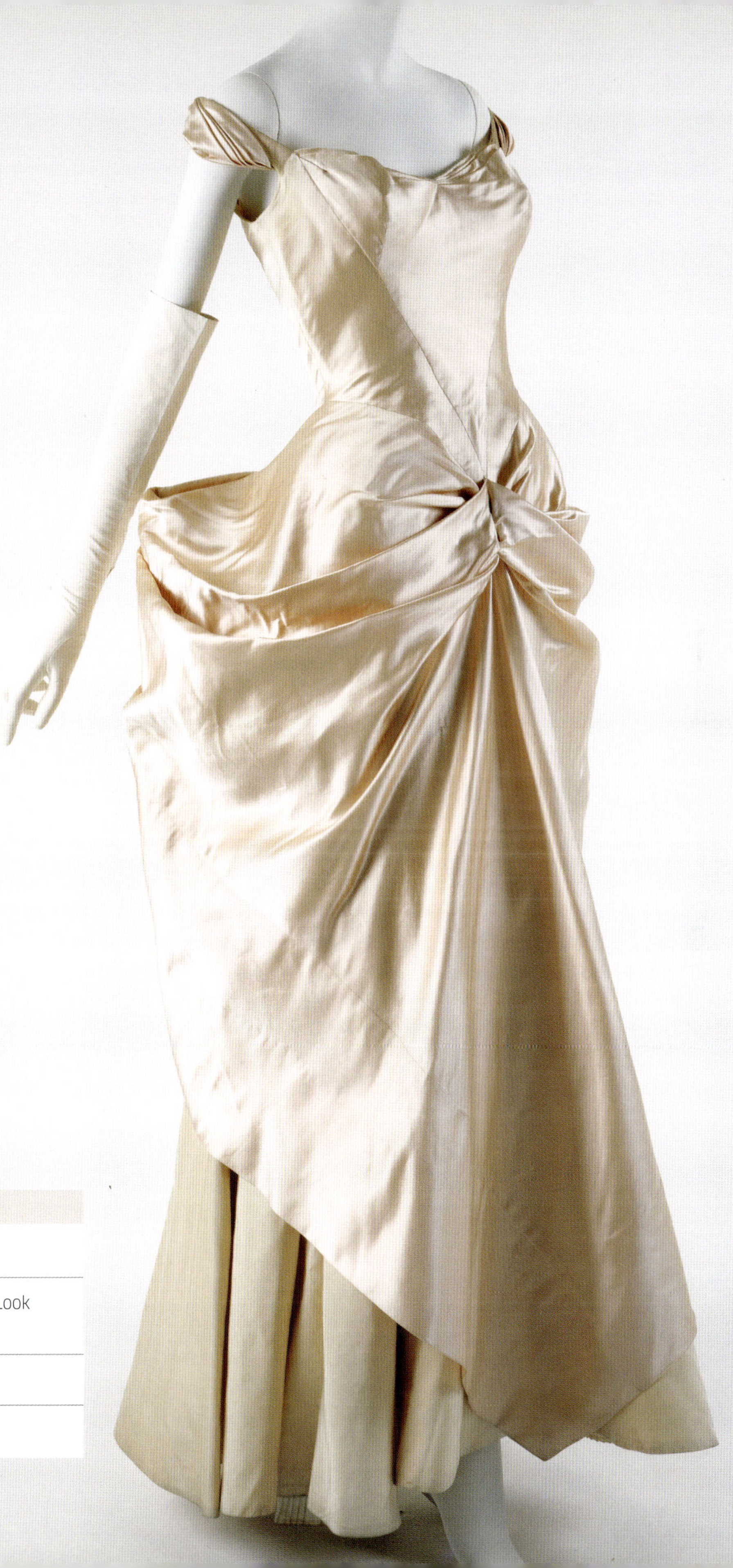

THE DRESS

STYLE Sculptural

SHAPE Reinterpreted New Look and neo-Victorian

FABRIC Silk satin

COLOR Pale pink and ivory

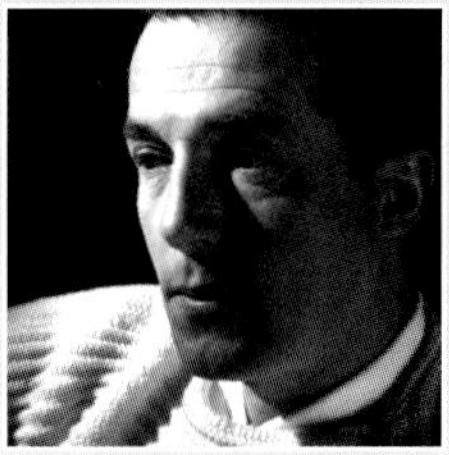

Hardy Amies
1909–2003

British couturier Hardy Amies was Queen Elizabeth II's longest-serving dressmaker. During the 1950s, he set up a boutique aimed at the general public that eventually supported his couture business. He received the royal warrant in 1955 from Queen Elizabeth II, and held it until his death.

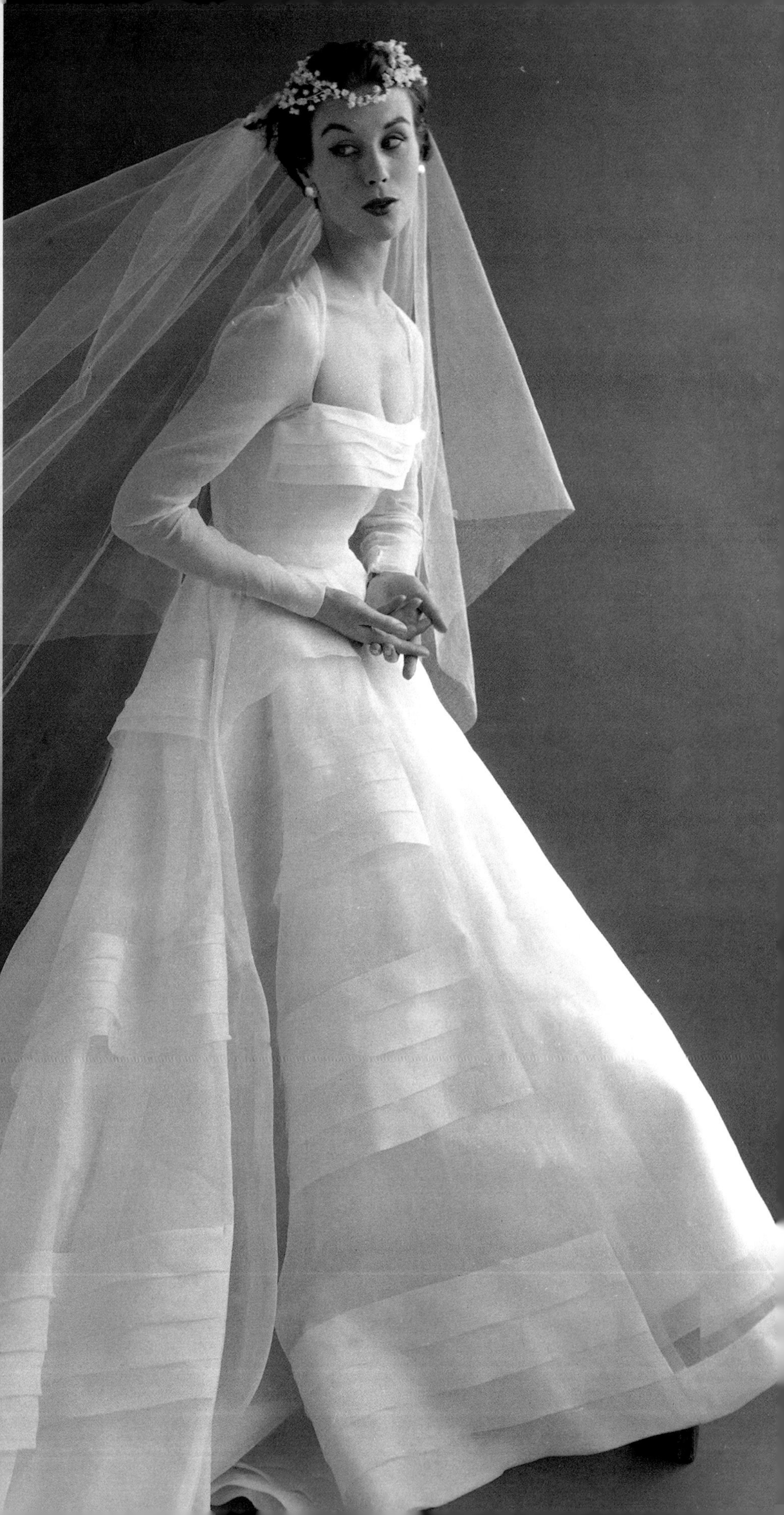

13

Hardy Amies

1953

Hardy Amies's sculptural dress, executed in fine cotton organdy, challenged the supremacy of the ubiquitous silk wedding dress.

In the 1950s, the silk wedding dress was the ultimate symbol of luxury, the ideal for brides who had been forced to "make do and mend" their clothes during World War II. For those who couldn't afford silk, synthetic fibers such as nylon and rayon, emulating silk's lustrous qualities, were affordable alternatives, exploited by the emerging mass-produced ready-to-wear bridal market.

Simple and striking

In the north of England, a Manchester-based lobbying group known as the Cotton Board was set up to address cotton's perceived inferiority to silk. At one of the Board's fashion shows in 1953, Amies unveiled a wedding gown of striking simplicity that rivaled the most sumptuous of silk dresses. Amies translated the style of Christian Dior's immensely popular New Look into a gown that utilized the qualities of sheer, crisp cotton organdy and heavy cotton poplin. The dress had a boned, tight-fitting bodice with a square neckline, edged with four horizontal tucks and sloping shoulders echoing the silhouette of Dior's famous Corolle line. Beneath the tiny cinched waist, the dress flowed gracefully into a full trained skirt that maximized the airy lightness of diaphanous organdy. Amies cleverly created fullness free from heaviness by supporting the skirt with two crease-resistant cotton poplin petticoats. At either side of the dress, panels with horizontal bands of tucking, growing incrementally in size from waist to hem, gave an added illusion of fullness. Unlike the padded waists required to hold skirts made of heavier fabrics, the cotton skirt delivered the desired fullness weightlessly. The pared-down elegance of Amies's design is captured in the promotional photograph shown at left.

Despite the best efforts of Amies and other designers—including Michael Sherard, who designed a fitted, tucked organza couture wedding dress in 1951, and Horrockses, who produced a white cotton piqué dress for the bride on a budget—the Cotton Board's challenge failed to topple silk from the bridal pedestal. Amies's design nonetheless remains an outstanding example of the possibilities of cotton, inspiring brides and designers to look beyond the realm of silk.

COTTON COUTURE
A promotional photograph taken by John French, of model Myrtle Crawford, shows the weightless translucence of the cotton fabric.

THE DRESS

STYLE New Look

SHAPE Sculptural

FABRIC Cotton organdy

COLOR White

14

Ann Lowe

1953 For Jacqueline Bouvier

Far from being a personal choice, Jacqueline Bouvier's first wedding dress was selected on her behalf as a symbol of social standing.

Joseph "Joe" Kennedy, patriarch of the powerful Kennedy clan, was alert to the popularity of his son John, a handsome, charismatic senator, and viewed his nuptials to Jacqueline Bouvier as an important public relations opportunity. Overriding the wish of the Bouvier family for a quiet, private affair, he masterminded a grand public celebration with 1,200 invited guests and huge media coverage. Joe Kennedy involved himself in every detail of the wedding, including Bouvier's dress.

Bouvier had developed a strong sartorial identity—she knew that slim-fitting dresses with firm lines suited her tall, slender figure best. It is said that she had hoped to commission a contemporary couture gown, but, at her fiancé's behest, she acquiesced to her future father-in-law's request that she wear an ultra-traditional dress. Bouvier was to be presented as the new princess of American royalty.

Ann Lowe, an African American dressmaker, was selected to create the gown. Lowe designed for the matrons of many Social Register families, including the Du Ponts and Auchinclosses. Her design used 50 yards (45 m) of ivory silk taffeta fashioned into a huge circular skirt decorated with bands of tucking

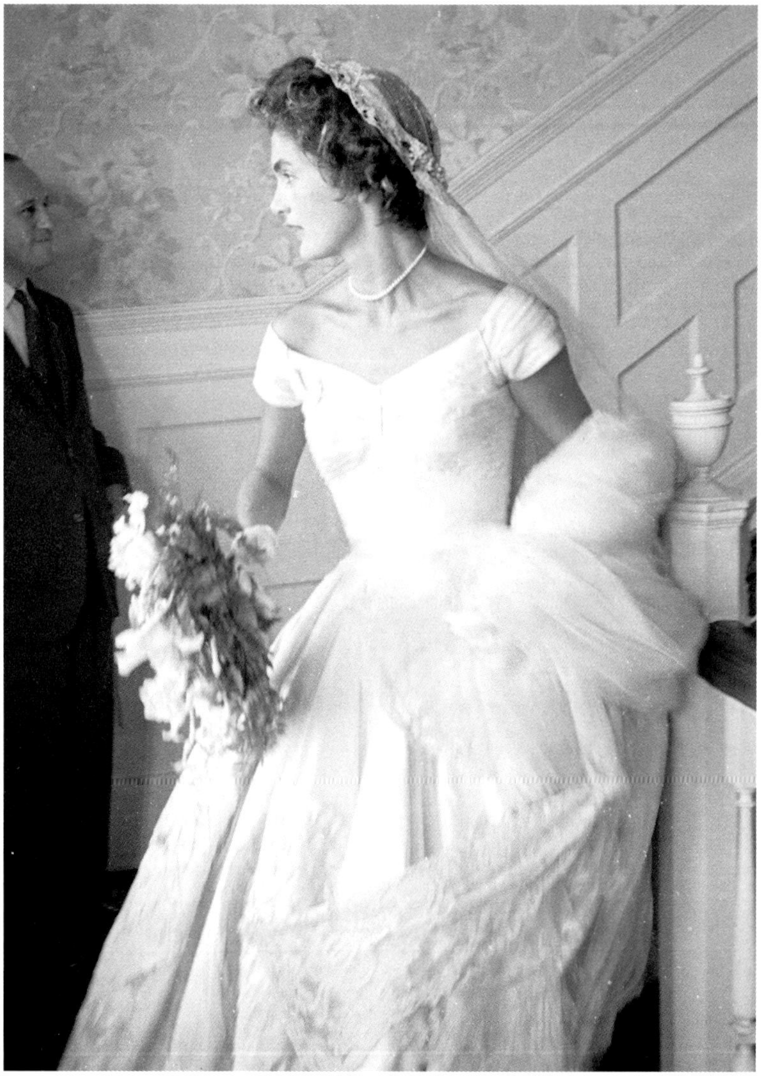

FRAMING THE FACE
The bands of fabric and the neckline of the dress were designed to draw the eye up toward the face.

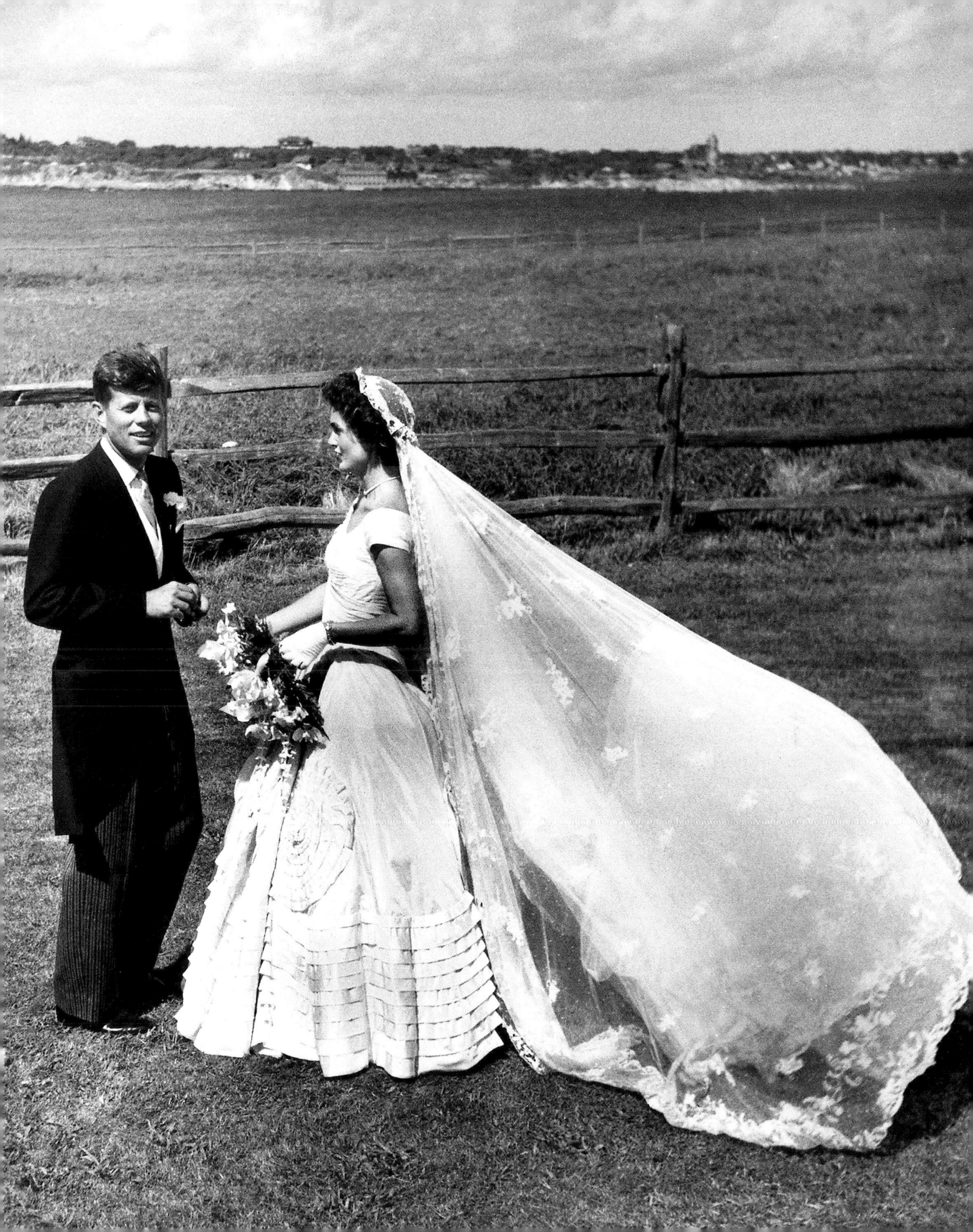

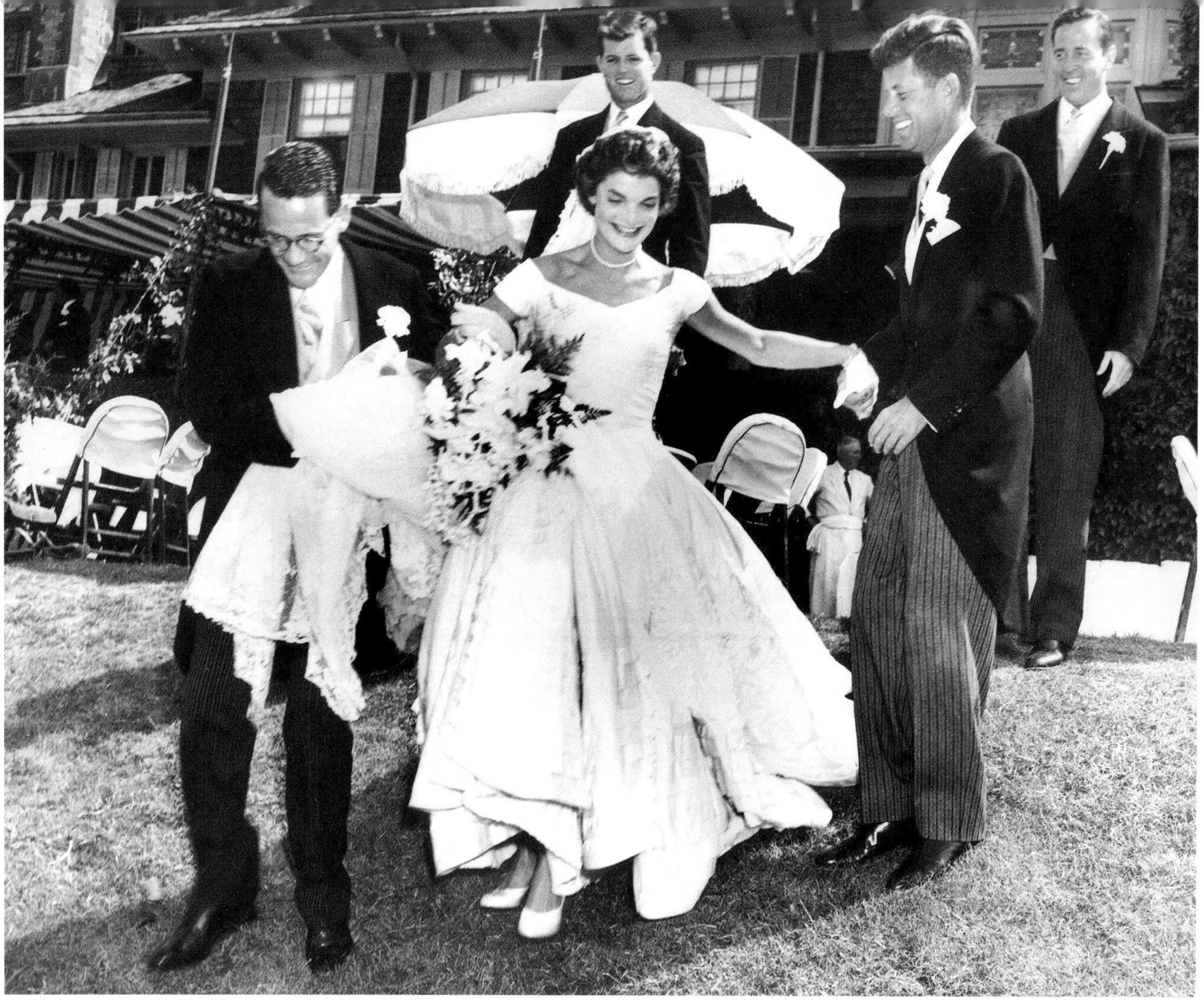

and tiny wax flowers. Its shape and decoration drew on the 1860s crinoline skirt, though Bouvier likened it to a lampshade. Perched atop this bouffant foundation was a tight-fitting bodice and portrait neckline that revealed elegant swathes of bare shoulder. Bouvier noted that the tight bands across the bodice emphasized her flat chest. With its complex detailing, the dress took two months to complete.

While the dress bore the influence of the Kennedy family, Bouvier's rose point lace veil was inherited from her grandmother. It was attached to her hair with a small tiara of lace and traditional orange blossoms. She wore a single strand of Bouvier family pearls at her neck, a diamond leaf pin, and a diamond bracelet—gifts from her future parents-in-law and husband, respectively. The family heirloom accessories and the historical styling of the dress may have been allusions to the lineage of the Kennedy and Bouvier families.

Leaving a legacy

Although Bouvier confessed to "hating" her "clumsy gown," it achieved her father-in-law's ambitions by living on as one of the most memorable bridal dresses in recent history. On the occasion of her second marriage in 1968 (see page 72), Bouvier fulfilled her original wish for a contemporary dress. She chose a straight lace-covered design by Italian couturier Valentino. The dress became an instant icon of Jackie's popular style and transformed the fortunes of the fashion house.

MAKING HISTORY
Although Bouvier's first marriage earned an instant place in the history books, it was her second, self-chosen dress that most influenced fashion history (see page 72).

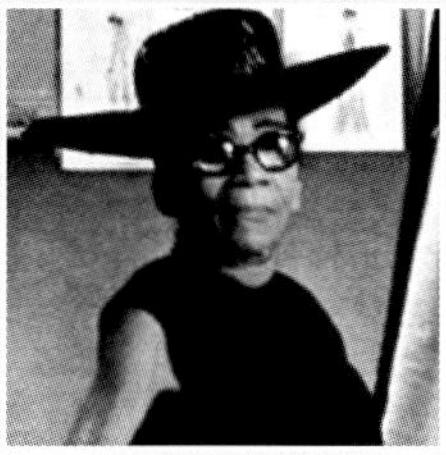

Ann Lowe
1898–1981

Born in Clayton, Alabama, the great-granddaughter of a slave and a plantation owner, Ann Cole Lowe graduated fashion school in New York City in 1917. The designer went on to open a dress salon in Tampa, Florida, before returning to New York in 1928. Lowe worked on commission for stores like Saks Fifth Avenue and Madeline Couture, and briefly operated Ann Lowe Originals on Madison Avenue in New York.

Lowe designed the dress Olivia de Havilland wore in 1947 to accept her Academy Award for Best Actress in *To Each His Own.*

THE DRESS

STYLE Neo-Victorian

SHAPE Full bouffant skirt, tight bodice

FABRIC Silk taffeta

COLOR Ivory

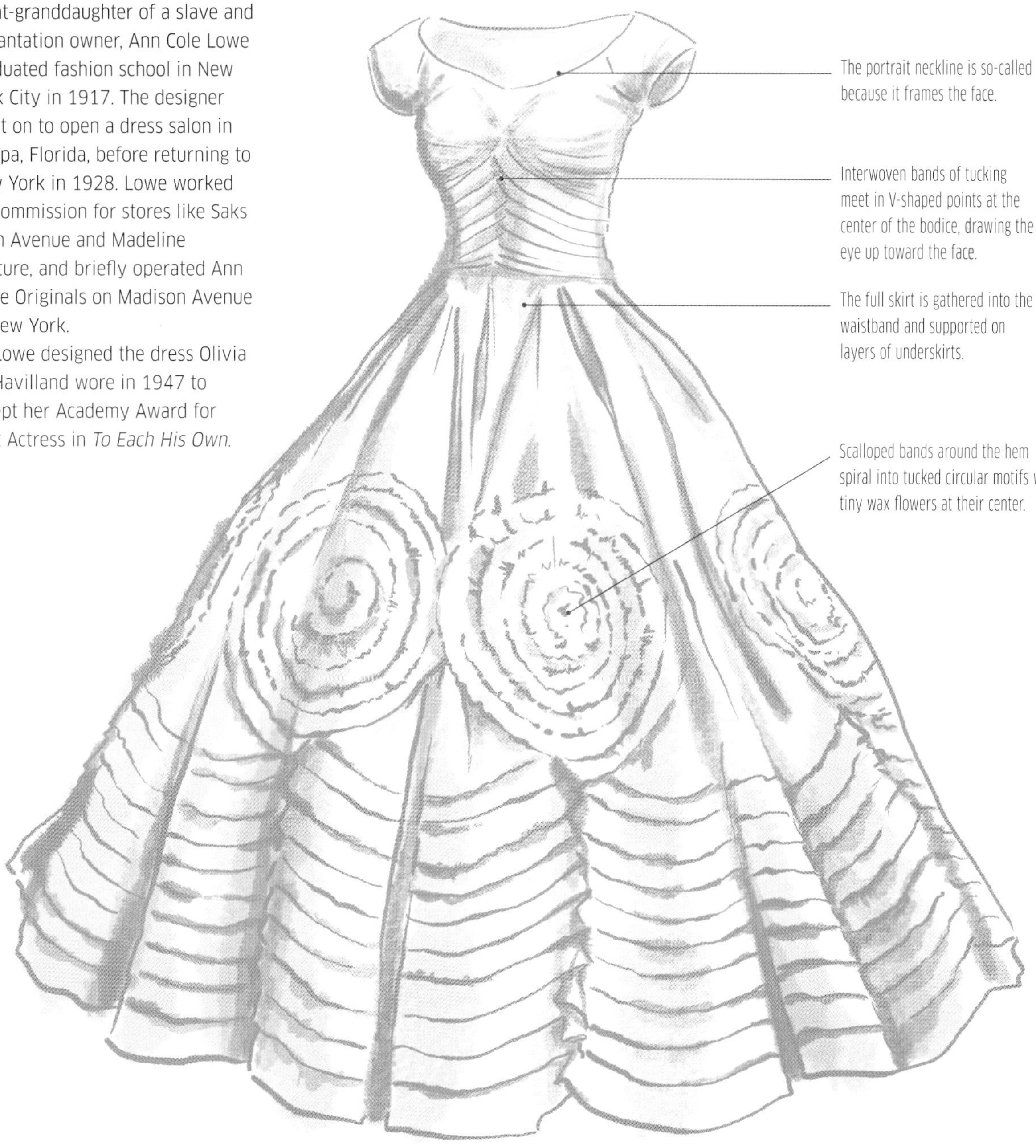

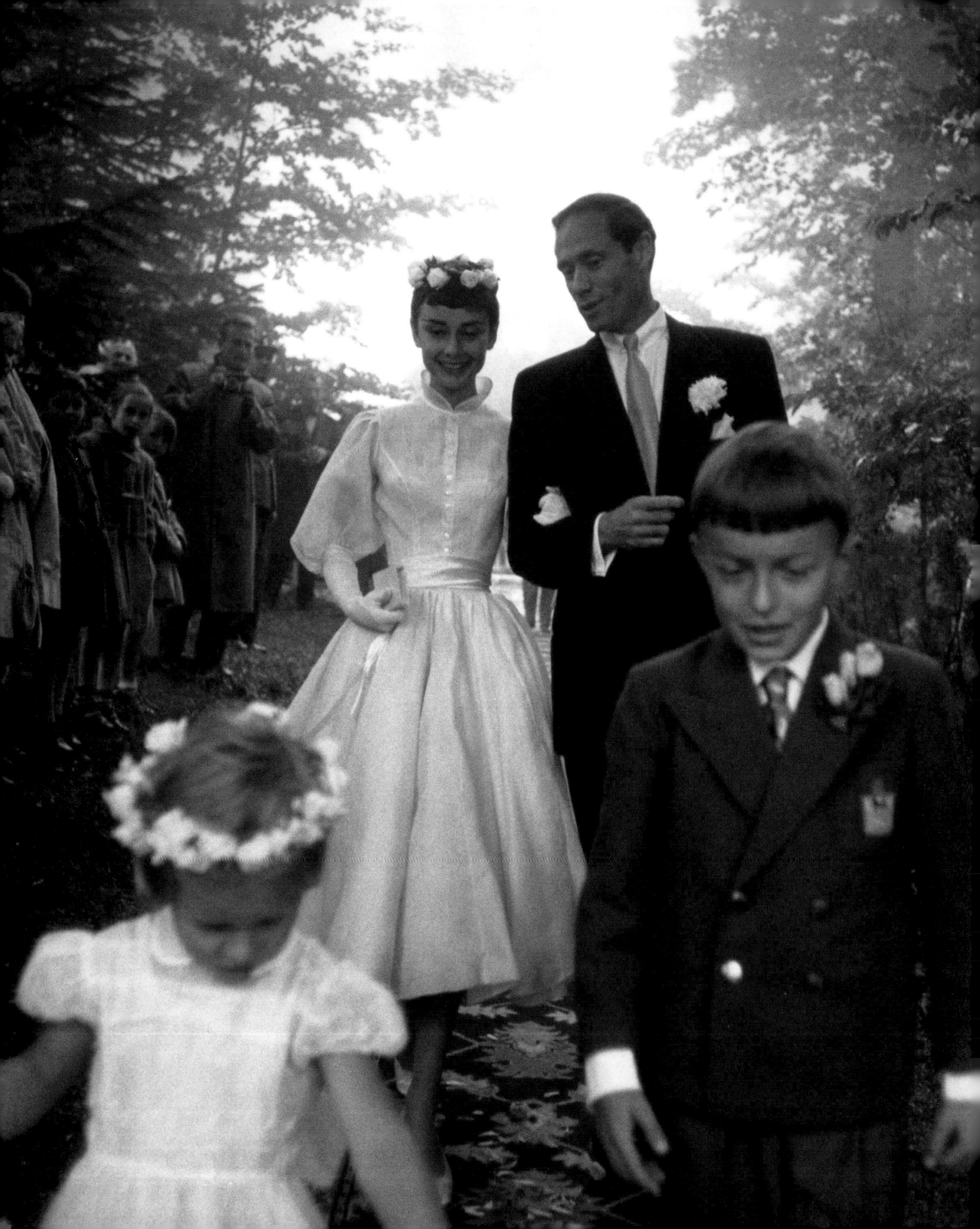

15

Pierre Balmain

1954 For Audrey Hepburn

Prettily romantic, Audrey Hepburn's tea-length, ballerina-style silk organdy dress captured the zeitgeist of the 1950s.

On the occasion of her marriage to *Ondine* co-star Mel Ferrer, Audrey Hepburn wore a pretty ballerina-style dress designed by Pierre Balmain. The French couturier's design perfectly complemented the star's petite frame. Its soft full skirt, large billowing sleeves caught at the elbow, and wide sash emphasized the actress's tiny waist. A high stand-up collar framing her elfin face drew attention to her straight and slender neck. The ensemble was completed with a coronet of real roses perched upon her "child-like head," characterized by photographer Cecil Beaton in *Vogue* magazine as "compact as a coconut with its cropped hair and wispy monkey-fur fringe."

The trendsetting ballet bride

Hepburn's gamine, waif-like figure and doe-eyed, urchin looks redefined glamour in the early 1950s. The star, discovered in 1951, had trained as a ballerina in the Nazi-occupied Netherlands. Partly as a consequence of the malnutrition she suffered during this period, Hepburn was forced to abandon her dream, but she retained her ballerina's grace. Cecil Beaton observed of her posture: "A rod-like back continues the vertical line of the nape... Audrey Hepburn's stance is a combination of an ultra fashion plate and a ballet dancer. Indeed, she owes a large debt to the ballet for her bearing and abandon in movement, which yet suggest a personal quality, an angular kinship with cranes and storks."

Hepburn was ideally suited to the new soft and youthful styles of wedding dress that were developing in the 1950s in response to mainstream fashion. Rigid silhouettes fashioned from stiff ribbed silks and duchesse satin gave way to shorter full skirts made of light tulle, chiffon, and organdy. Skirts that hit above the ankle were termed "tea-length" or "ballerina-style." In 1954, Dior introduced the H-line that lowered waists and raised busts with the idea of suggesting the "tapering figure of a young girl." The look was achieved with "Degas bodices," cut like a ballerina's costume. With her ballerina's figure, Hepburn became the standard-bearer of the new chic style.

Hepburn's supremely fashionable wedding dress cemented her status as a trendsetter and style icon for modern young women. Two months after her September wedding, which took place in Bürgenstock, Switzerland, *Vogue* magazine featured a photograph of the event alongside Beaton's profile of the star. Beaton eulogized the actress's unconventional beauty, stating, "Audrey Hepburn's appearance

BALLERINA STYLE
Though her career as a ballerina was tragically short, Hepburn blossomed into an icon for the new ballet-inspired style of the 1950s.

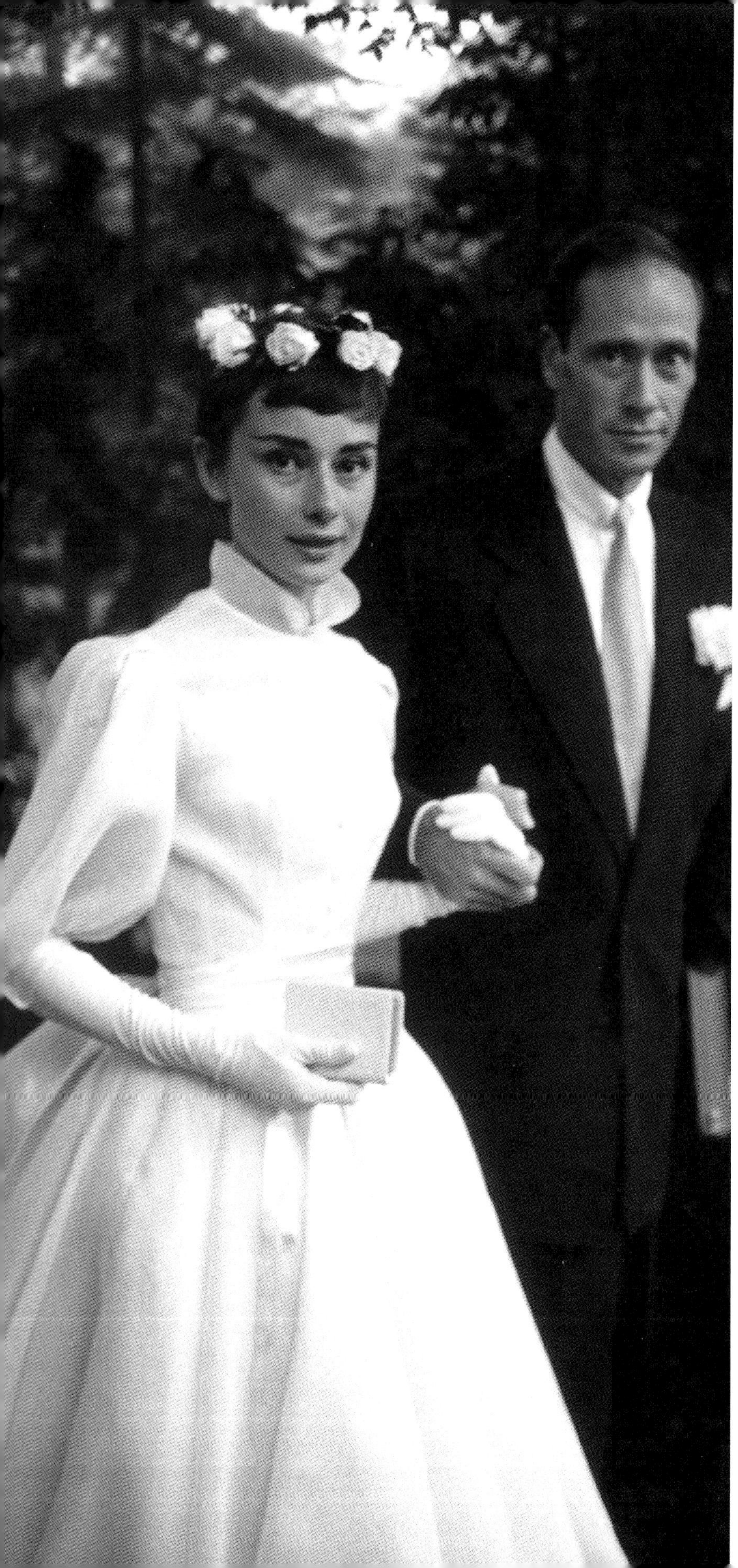

succeeds because it embodies the spirit of today." The article concluded that the actress was likely to be the "embodiment of our new feminine ideal."

Art imitating life

Following Hepburn's lead, brides who considered themselves young, modern, and up-to-the-minute began to wear the new shorter-length wedding dress. The style had the added benefit that it could easily be reworn after the wedding for semiformal occasions. Two years after Hepburn married in her calf-length dress, *Harper's Bazaar* declared that the ballet-length was the choice of the career girl. In a case of art imitating life, the star wore another ballerina-style dress in the 1957 musical-comedy film *Funny Face*. Designed by Hubert de Givenchy, the tulle-skirted confection, featuring a bateau neck and dropped waist, is as iconic as Hepburn's Balmain dress, reflecting and contributing to the continued popularity of ballerina-style wedding gowns.

One of the most influential fashionistas of all time, Hepburn created yet another iconic bridal look at her second marriage, to Andrea Dotti, in 1969—a pink wool funnel-necked minidress with matching kerchief from her favorite designer, Givenchy. But it is, perhaps, Balmain's simple white wedding dress that is the most enduring icon of the star.

THE STYLIST'S CHOICE
A style icon of her time and of all times, Hepburn's exquisite taste was made famous by her movie career and is typified in her choice of wedding gowns.

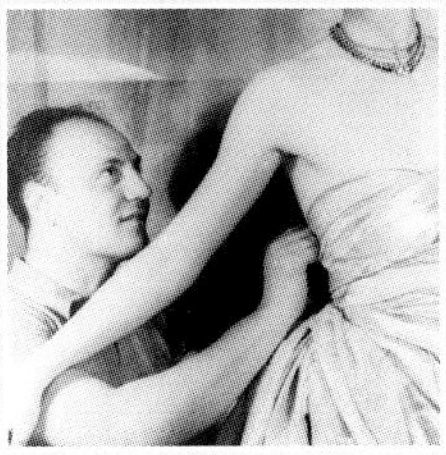

Pierre Balmain
1914–1982

French couturier Pierre Balmain was described by fashion historian Farid Chenoune as "one of the supreme practitioners of the New Look Generation." Balmain worked for the houses of Molyneux and Lucien Lelong before establishing his own couture salon in 1945. His signature simple elegance, focused on impeccable construction, won him a clientele of women famed for their style. The house of Balmain continued after his death. Oscar de la Renta, chief designer from 1992 until 2002, was credited with restoring the company's fortunes and stylistic reputation.

THE DRESS

STYLE Softly feminine

SHAPE Ballerina

FABRIC Silk organdy

COLOR White

HIDDEN DETAILS

- Fastens at the center-front with tiny buttons.
- Strapless sweetheart bodice underneath.

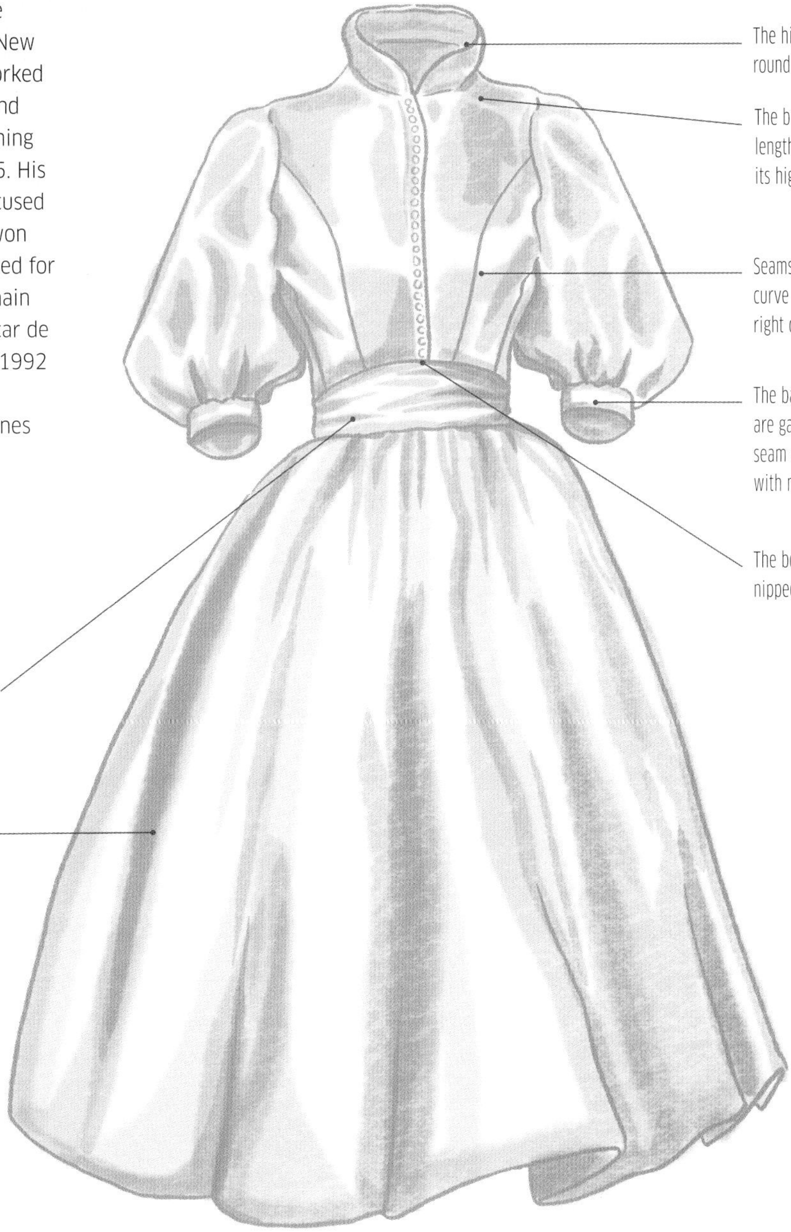

16

Helen Rose

1955 For Grace Kelly

Grace Kelly's dress played the starring role in her fairy-tale wedding to Prince Rainier of Monaco, transforming the actress from movie-star princess into real-life European royalty.

The dress gave a faultless performance. Composed of a fitted lace bodice and bell-shaped satin skirt fused together with a pleated cummerbund, the design was modest—erring on severe—yet luxurious. Helen Rose's design struck the perfect balance between regal dignity and Hollywood glamour.

Rose, chief costume designer at Metro-Goldwyn-Mayer (MGM), the film studio where Kelly was under contract, was tasked with designing the most hotly anticipated costume of the actress's career. Rose artfully translated the drama of the occasion into a design that complemented the star's natural beauty. Her design played out the sculptural and textural possibilities of the dress to maximum effect, contrasting diaphanous silk tulle with rich, pearl-encrusted rose point lace, delicate Valenciennes lace, and the dull luster of peau de soie satin. The subtle interplay of textures was more than a match for the "princely plumage" of the groom's military uniform. The dress's subtle detailing and uncomplicated hourglass silhouette shone on the grandiose stage of Monaco's Saint Nicholas Cathedral, and through the camera lens—Rose was mindful from the outset that images of the dress would be instantly broadcast all around the world.

A study in grace and modesty

The simple lines of the dress belied its complex construction, involving four separate parts. The bodice was seamlessly molded to the star's figure like a second skin. Each elaborate lace motif was individually detached from its original ground and pieced together onto the silk tulle of the bodice, a painstaking task that occupied two seamstresses for a month. To ensure the bride's appropriately demure demeanor, the sheer lace was backed with a strapless boned bodice of silk crepe, its sweetheart neckline faintly discernible beneath the lace. A mini-crinoline attached to the waistline of the underbodice supported the second piece of the ensemble—a skirt whose distinctive bell shape was created by pleats all around the waist, its rigid lines held in place by three layers of integrated petticoats.

At the back of the dress, the skirt fanned out into a gentle train, split down the middle. Here, Rose entertained Kelly's audience with interesting detailing: a triangular lace insert peeking out between curtains of silk, held together with three delicate bows. One press

TO CAP IT ALL
The bride wore a cap topped with a wreath of tiny wax orange blossoms, openwork leaves of seed pearls, and small wired lace motifs.

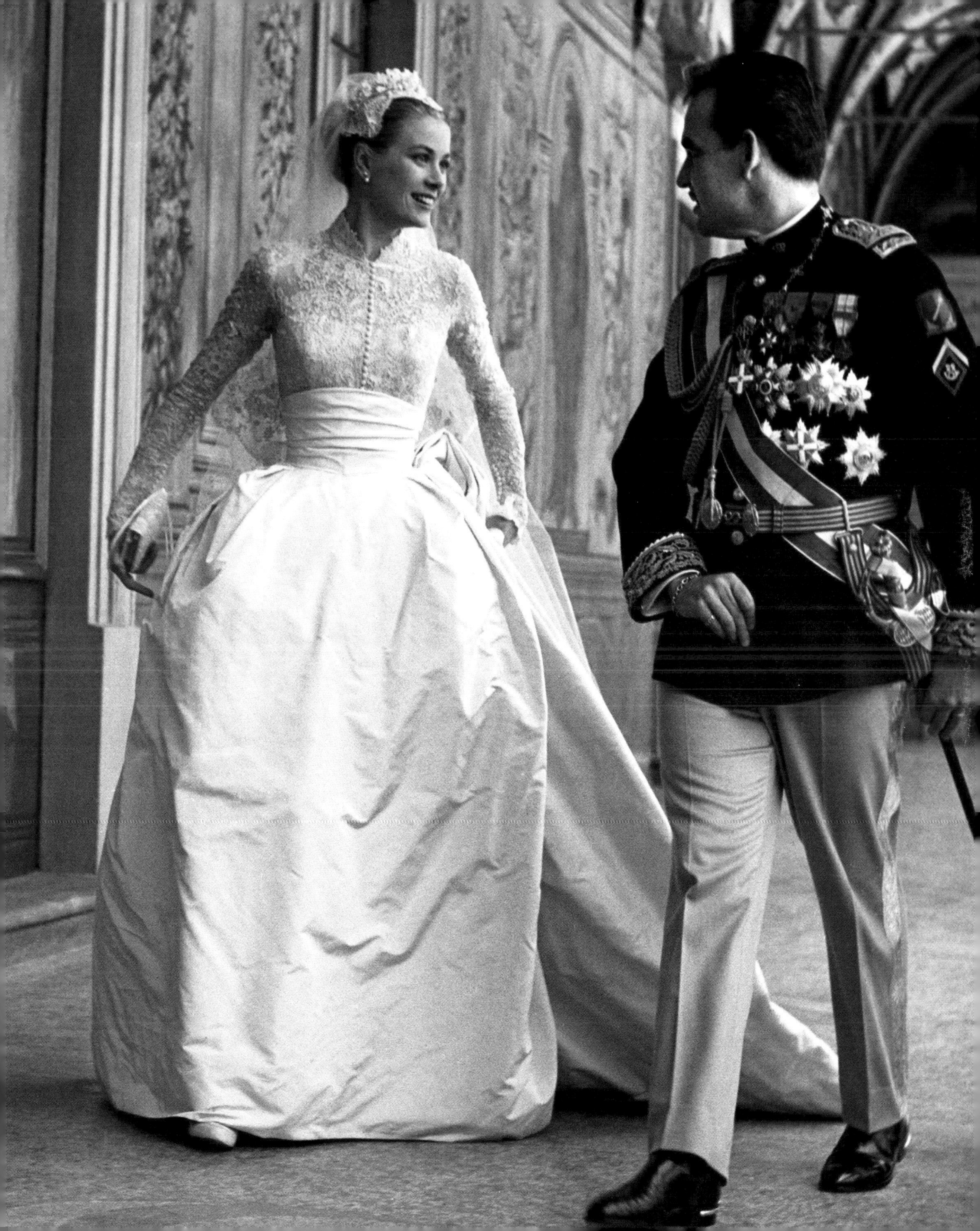

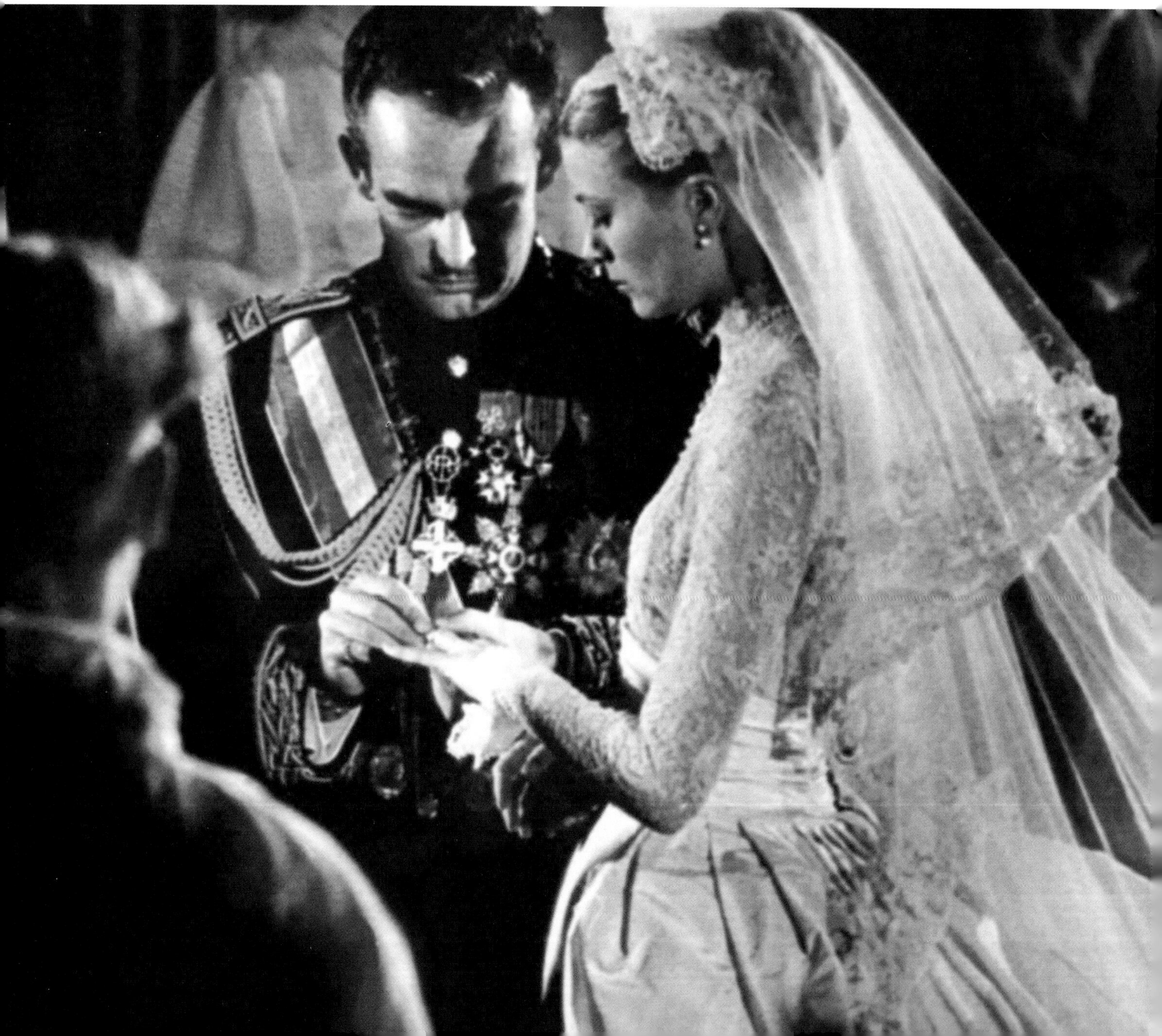

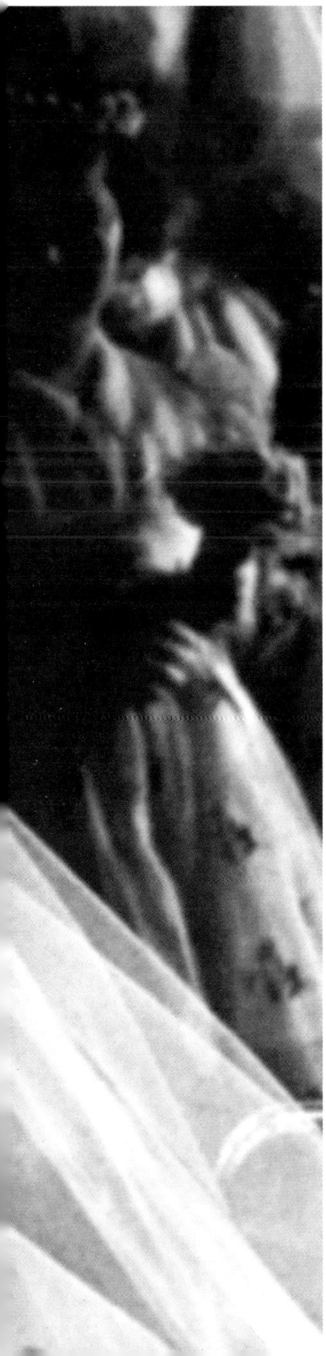

report described the train as "like a river of whipped cream along the plush red floor." A steel-boned, pleated cummerbund unified the separate components of the dress while drawing attention to Kelly's 21-inch (53-cm) waist. The outfit was completed by an intricately adorned Juliet cap perched on the back of the bride's head. The circular silk tulle veil, attached to the cap, was designed especially so that the bride's features were still clearly visible while it was covering her face.

The cost of Hollywood royalty

It took thirty-five milliners, seamstresses, embroiderers, beaders, and dyers—all employees of MGM's costume department—nearly two months to complete the ensemble. The lavish fabrics and manufacturing costs, excluding the designer's salary, were estimated in the region of $7,200 (over $60,000 today). MGM maximized the opportunity to capitalize on the intense interest in the nuptials of their biggest star by gifting the bride her gown. The company's publicity greatly exaggerated its opulence, stating that its design used 25 yards (23 m) of peau de soie taffeta, 25 yards (23 m) of silk taffeta, 100 yards (91 m) of silk tulle, and 300 yards (274 m) of Valenciennes lace. In fact, the finished dress used only about a quarter of these amounts.

From the full-length sleeves covering the backs of her hands to the high neckline, the dress radiated an air of restrained elegance that Kelly worked to perfection. Clutching her matching lace-covered prayer book as she walked down the aisle, Kelly was every inch the serene princess bride. The iconic images of her wedding dress are so embedded in popular culture that the cummerbund, sweetheart bodice, Juliet cap, and bell skirt are viewed as trademark Grace Kelly, cited as the inspiration for wedding gowns from ready-to-wear boutiques to couture examples worn by future princesses such as Catherine Middleton.

ROMANTIC TOUCHES
Kelly's veil was edged with appliquéd lace motifs including two tiny lovebirds.

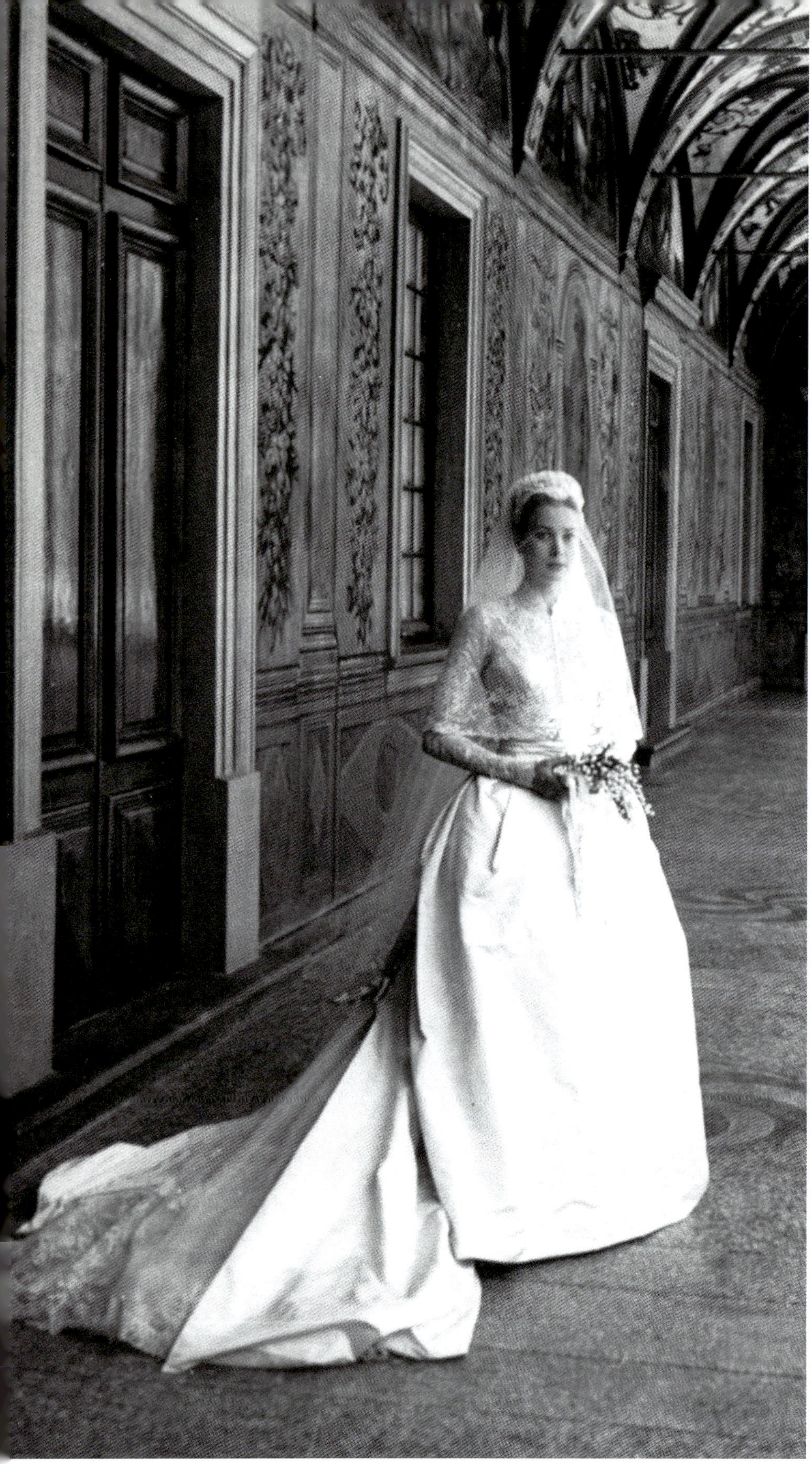

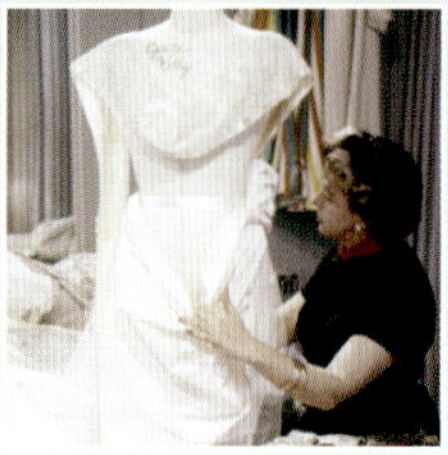

Helen Rose
1904–1985

American costume and clothing designer Helen Rose created the most celebrated wedding dresses of the 1950s for brides on- and off-screen. Between 1943 and 1966 she worked for film studio Metro-Goldwyn-Mayer (MGM), dressing the stars of more than 200 films, winning two Oscars for her work, and famously designing the wedding dresses of MGM actresses Grace Kelly and Elizabeth Taylor (1950). Her restrained and elegant signature style often paired the nipped-in waist and billowing skirts of Dior's New Look with a sweetheart-shaped bodice.

SEAMLESS LACE APPLIQUÉ
The bodice achieved a seamless look with lace motifs that were detached from their original ground and re-embroidered onto the shaped tulle.

THE DRESS

STYLE Regal and romantic

SHAPE Hourglass

FABRIC Lace and satin

COLOR Ivory

HIDDEN DETAILS

- Attached to the waist of the bodice is a slim slip edged in lace and weighted at the center-back seam. Over the slip is a mini-crinoline, 14 in (35 cm) long, held out by a hoop and with four stiff lace-edged ruffles.
- Peeking through the split in the train is a triangular insert made from two layers of silk tulle, edged in lace and appliquéd with lace motifs. A silk taffeta underskirt with four ruffles of synthetic net lies underneath the insert, holding out the lace.

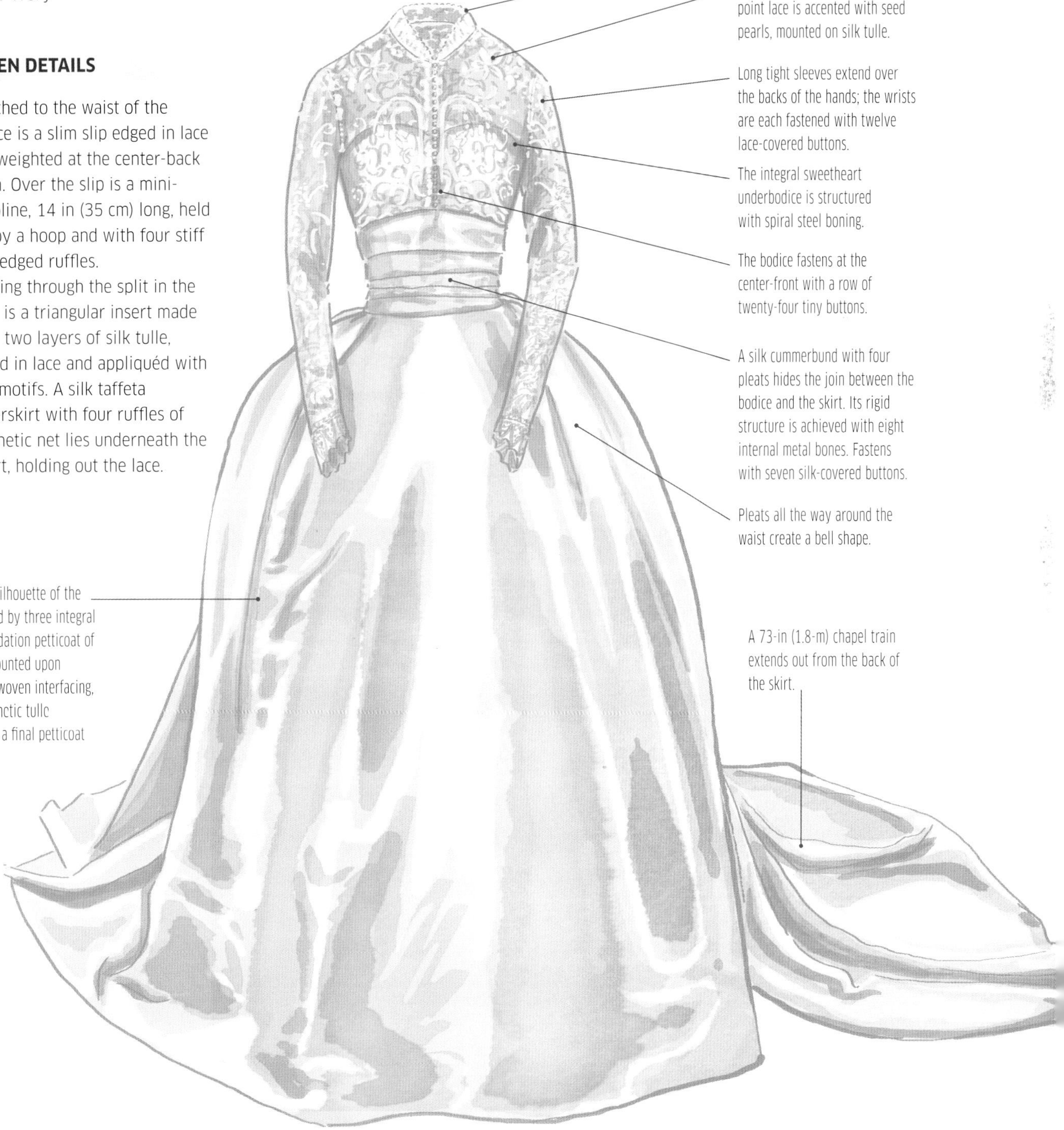

17

Yves Saint Laurent

1965 Fall/Winter

Yves Saint Laurent's knitted cocoon gown began a vogue for questioning the very form of the white wedding dress.

In 1965, Saint Laurent presented his latest Fall/Winter line, featuring his now famous color block Mondrian-inspired shift dresses. The show concluded with a most unusual wedding dress fashioned from bulky cream-colored wool. Knitted in bands of textured stitches that formed a cylindrical shape, rounded over the top of the head and tapering at the ankles, it entirely encased the bride's body, leaving only her face, hands, and feet visible. Strange and shocking, the effect was somewhere between a woollen mummy, a limbless white matryoshka doll, and an oversized insect cocoon.

An object explained within its form

This baffling, somewhat phallic form defied all expectations of wedding couture. Was it supposed to be a sculpture or a wearable garment? Did it feel cozy and comforting or heavy and itchy? Did the garment mean to protect or trap the bride? Was she emerging from its depths, metamorphosed into a newly married woman—like a butterfly breaking free from its silk cocoon—or was she being led to her death in a knitted sarcophagus, bound and buried by her new status? Like the Russian nesting dolls its form appeared to reference, the dress was itself a *mise en abyme* of distorted, opaque associations. In other words, while no clear meaning is presented by the dress, tantalizing clues suggesting the intentions of the designer were bound into its construction.

Saint Laurent's design practice probed the spatial possibilities of dress. He famously stated, "A dress is not architecture, it's a house: it is not made to be contemplated but to be lived in." The geometric jersey dresses he produced for his Fall/Winter 1965 collection were nonetheless architectural—with technical precision, their interior construction yielded to the curves of the wearer while presenting an illusion of graphic flatness and extreme simplicity. The confident modernity of this line testified to the designer's claim that "Chanel freed women, and I empowered them."

By contrast, the structure of his cocoon wedding dress was more like a prison than a house. Unlike the rest of the collection, it severely limited movement, trussing up the bride with its thick satin ribbons. The bride's hands emerged from slits at either side of the waist. The placement of the slits deliberately enforced an attitude of submissiveness and servility, with the hands either taking up a prayer pose or placing one meekly on top of the other. Bound up and bow-tied like a paper-wrapped gift, the bride could do nothing other than passively await her release.

It is hard not to read the dress—created on the cusp of the sexual revolution by a designer

THE ADVANCE OF AVANT-GARDE
Yves Saint Laurent's knitted cocoon dress, shown here at a 2002 retrospective, reconceptualized and interrogated the tradition of the white wedding dress.

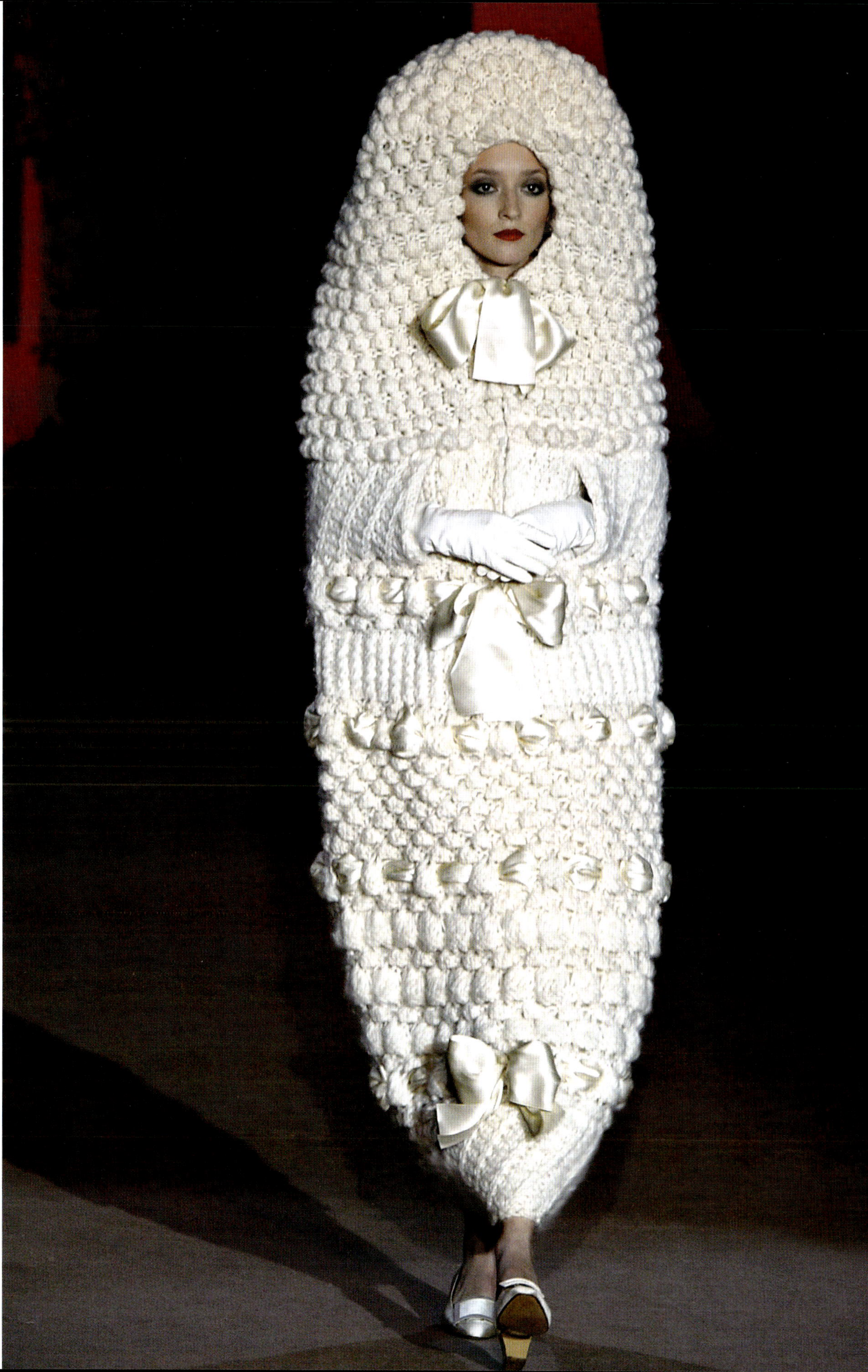

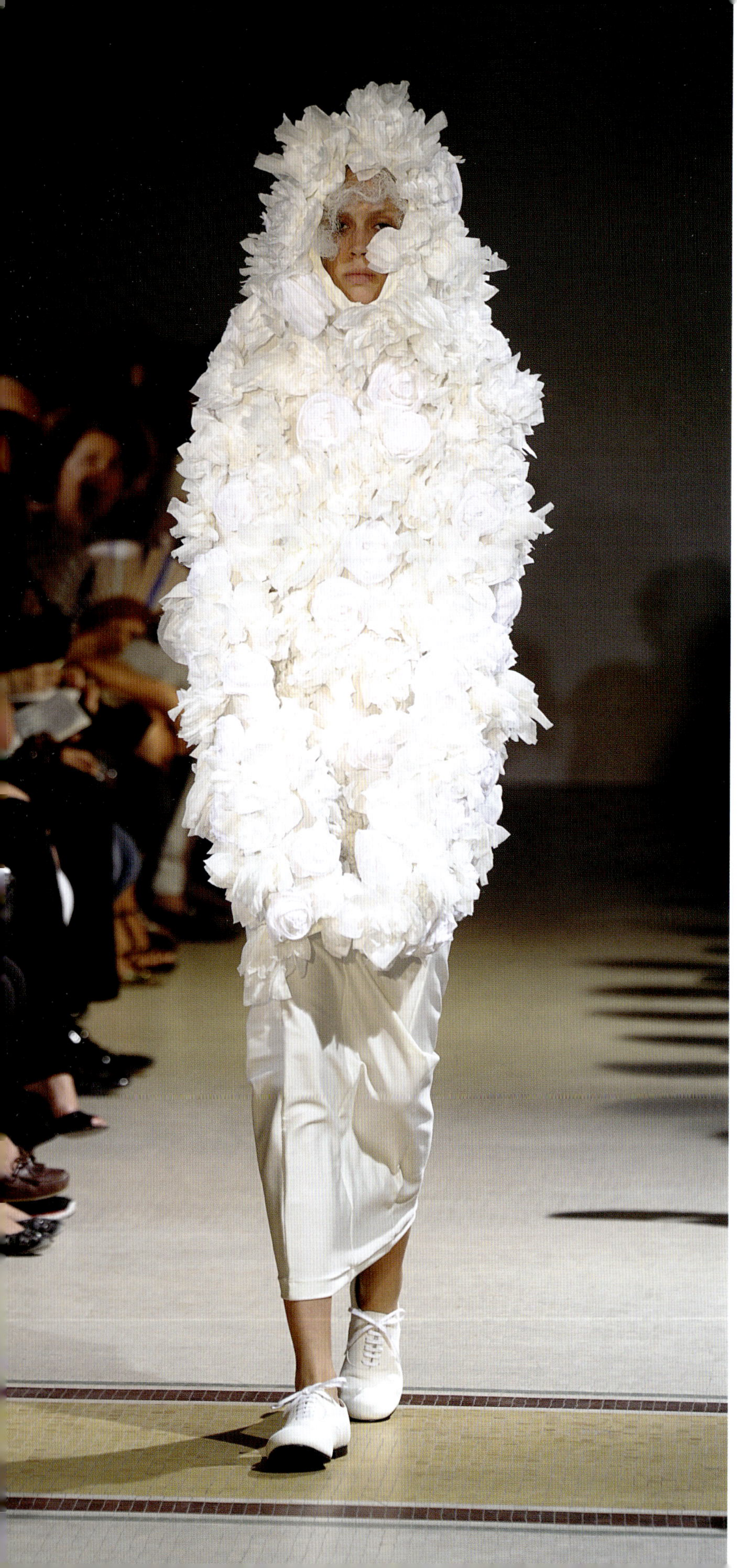

who celebrated worldly, liberated women—as anything other than a comment on the oppressive nature of the marriage institution. However, the materiality of the dress suggests a more nuanced interpretation of its symbolism.

Knit with meaning

The dress is knit in a variation of the stitches found in Aran-style fisherman's sweaters. The centuries-old tradition of textured knitting, developed throughout the British Isles, houses a lexicon of stitches that endow a unique identity to the wearer. Knit by fishermen's wives, they provide a heartfelt way of identifying loved ones lost at sea.

In Aran knits, a honeycomb pattern is a symbol of the hard-working bee. Used on this dress, it most likely makes a reference to the bride's sexuality—she is a flower awaiting pollination—and yet her apparel does not easily facilitate that act. The intricacy with which the ribbons are woven into the dress would necessitate slow, steady patience to undo. Fishermen's protective Aran sweaters are traditionally made of untreated wool that retains natural lanolin to give the garment a degree of water resistance. This association also reinforces the idea of the cocoon dress as a defensive barrier against the world.

The legacy of Saint Laurent's strange knitted wedding dress is found in the conceptual practice of avant-garde designers including Jean Paul Gaultier, who closed his Fall/Winter 1998 collection with a bridal couple in his-and-hers Aran-knit outfits. Comme des Garçons and Yohji Yamamoto have also echoed Saint Laurent's treatment of materials, his investigation of the spatial properties of dress, and his deliberately obtuse conceptualization of the symbolism and meaning of bridalwear.

HOMAGE TO THE COCOON

Comme des Garçons presented a revised cocoon dress as part of the Spring 2012 collection (see page 168).

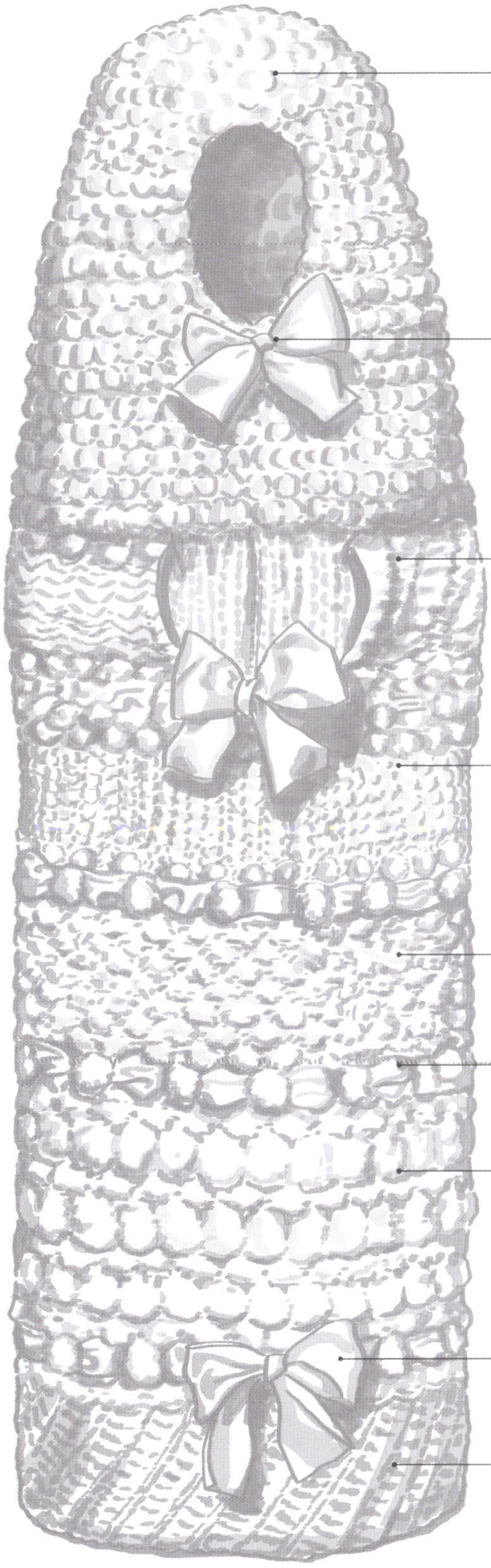

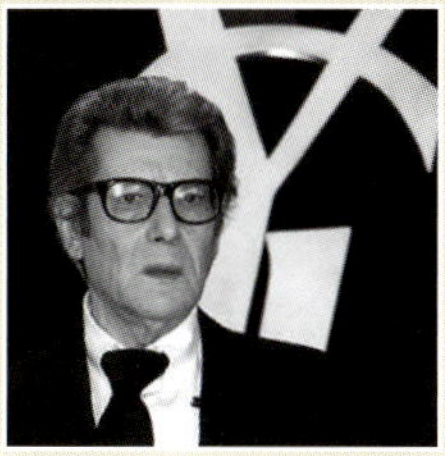

Yves Saint Laurent

1936–2008

Yves Saint Laurent anticipated the changes that would occur in the fashion industry during his forty-five-year career: the rise of ready-to-wear, branding and licensing, and the influence of global conglomerates. Born in 1936, Saint Laurent moved to Paris at age eighteen to study couture and found a job assisting Christian Dior. Succeeding the designer in 1957, the twenty-one-year-old shook up Dior's traditional style. Upon being replaced at Dior, Saint Laurent opened his own business in 1962. Predicting the decline of couture in the face of ready-to-wear, he opened the Rive Gauche prêt-à-porter boutique in 1966. The designer credited himself with creating "the contemporary woman's wardrobe." His ground-breaking aesthetic combined masculine and feminine, classic and avant-garde.

THE DRESS

STYLE Avant-garde architectural

SHAPE Cocoon

FABRIC Wool, satin

COLOR Cream

18

John Bates

1966 For Marit Allen

Marit Allen's futuristic wedding ensemble defined cutting-edge style for forward-thinking young brides of the 1960s.

Fashion journalist Marit Allen, later remembered for her work as a costume designer, commissioned John Bates—one of the most adventurous designers of her acquaintance—to make her wedding outfit. Bates created a streamlined white gabardine minidress and coat with "space-age" inspired metallic detailing. The sleeveless A-line shift dress featured a deep silvered yoke and a stand-up collar. Its matching double-breasted coat was trimmed with dome-shaped buttons, silver bands around the cuffs, and a dramatic silver collar with wide, pointed lapels. Bates produced the unique ensemble especially for Allen, but under his ready-to-wear line Jean Varon. Each piece bears the Jean Varon label.

Allen was editor of the Young Ideas pages at *British Vogue*—a trendsetting journalist who was the voice of her generation. The designers and styles she showcased on her pages had a huge impact on the youth-dominated cultural landscape of the 1960s. She endorsed the innovative new talent of the growing youthquake. Many leading lights of 1960s fashion received their first significant exposure through Allen, who also modeled their designs for *British Vogue* and happily wore them on the swinging London scene.

Space-age brides

In the early 1960s, space exploration fired the imaginations of young designers like Bates and André Courrèges, who formally launched the "space-age" look in 1964 with a collection of white and silver garments fashioned from novel fabrics such as shiny PVC. For Allen's ensemble, Bates manipulated the smooth, pliable qualities of cotton gabardine—a tough twilled fabric famously invented by Thomas Burberry for his raincoats—shaping it into angular garments with rigid, hard-edged lines that held their shape away from the curves of the body. The space-age look presaged a future free of constraints for sexually, socially, and sartorially liberated women.

In the progressive circles in which Allen moved, certain traditions of bridalwear were rendered obsolete; veils and trains looked anachronistic with the popular, short sleek hairstyles launched by Vidal Sassoon. Bates responded to his modern bride with a contemporary, minimalist reinterpretation of a veil—an oversized collar designed to be worn upright to frame her face. Although the 1960s did enact great positive changes for women, especially political and sexual freedoms, even the most avant-garde bride still clung to some degree of formality and convention in her wedding dress. Although fashionably short, Bates's combination of a dress and matching coat, covering the bride's bare arms, made the outfit appropriate for Allen's church wedding.

FUTURISTIC BRIDE
The space-age look is achieved with shiny PVC trimmings on the coat. The bride insisted that it was Bates, not Mary Quant, who was the originator of the miniskirt.

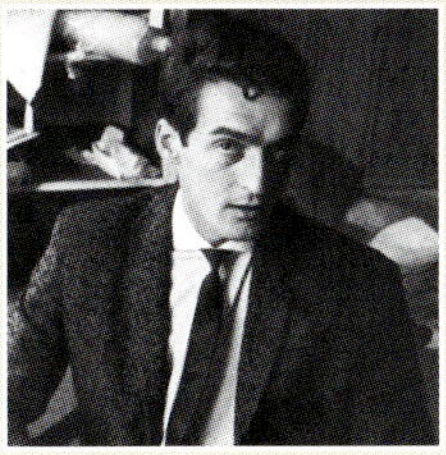

John Bates
1938–

British-born John Bates designed under the name Jean Varon from 1959 until the 1980s. He aimed to produce innovative fashion that could be afforded on a secretary's wage. In 1965, his midriff-baring mesh dress was chosen as the Dress of the Year and donated to the Fashion Museum, Bath. The same year, he designed memorable op art and futuristic costumes for the character Emma Peel in the renowned British TV series *The Avengers.* Bates is acknowledged as one of the big four names of British fashion in the 1970s, with Jean Muir (see page 74), Bill Gibb, and Zandra Rhodes (see page 82).

THE DRESS

STYLE Futuristic

SHAPE A-line shift

FABRIC Cotton gabardine and metallic polyester film on a PVC ground

COLOR White and silver

HIDDEN DETAILS

- The shiny, metallic effect was achieved by applying metallic polyester film onto a blue PVC resin mixed with gums.

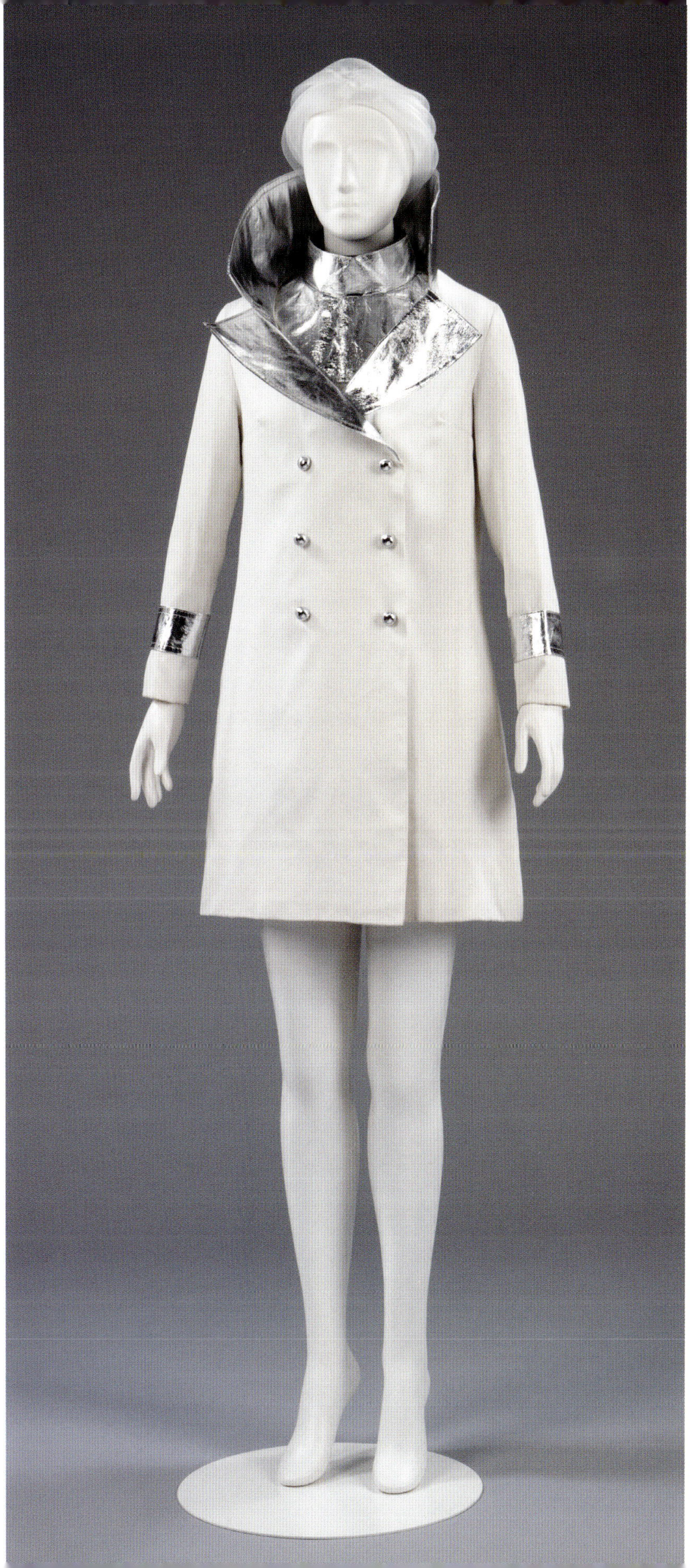

19

Jean Patou

1967

Jean Patou's sweeping fur-trimmed coatdress captures the romanticism of the late 1960s love affair with Hollywood-inspired, whimsical, winter-wonderland weddings.

Patou's sculptural maxicoat, executed in silk zibeline—a thick, lustrous fabric—softened the mid-1960s modernistic, streamlined silhouette with delicate mink trim applied to the hem, cuffs, and collar.

As the 1960s progressed, fashionable brides began to look backward as well as forward to the space-age future, inspired by Hollywood's vision of pre-revolutionary Russia or medieval England in films such as *Doctor Zhivago* (1965) and *Camelot* (1967). These epic historical love stories, played out against snowy landscapes, popularized maxicoats, fur trimmings, hoods, muffs, and frog fastenings. The costumes worn by Julie Christie and Vanessa Redgrave in these films were also directly referenced in the hooded, mink-trimmed ensemble worn by British pop star Lulu when she married Bee Gees musician Maurice Gibb in 1969. In contrast to later versions of the style, Patou's coatdress is a master class in understated elegance, its slim-fitting front extending into a train falling in folds from the shoulder. Refined details like the narrow set-in sleeves, neat flapped pockets, and concealed fastenings are a testament to the craft of haute couture.

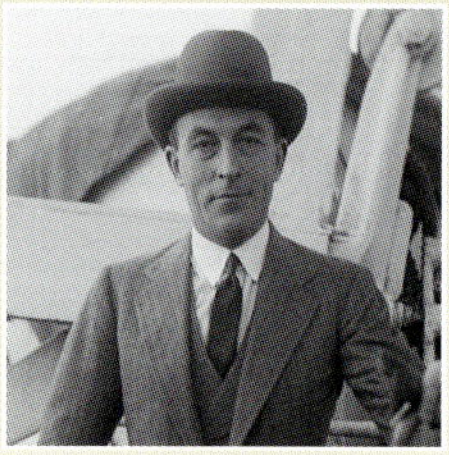

Jean Patou

1880–1936

Jean Patou operated a fur and dressmaking business before opening a couture salon in Paris and establishing the Jean Patou brand. In his heyday, the 1920s, Patou was credited with developing the garçonne look along with Chanel, introducing sportswear styles into fashion, and was celebrated for his geometric knitwear. Patou died in 1936, but the company continued after his death. From 1963 to 1974, Michel Goma was the house's chief designer, assisted by Jean Paul Gaultier. Patou stopped producing fashion in 1987 to focus on perfumes.

THE DRESS

STYLE Winter wonderland

SHAPE Slim-fitting coatdress

FABRIC Silk zibeline and mink

COLOR White

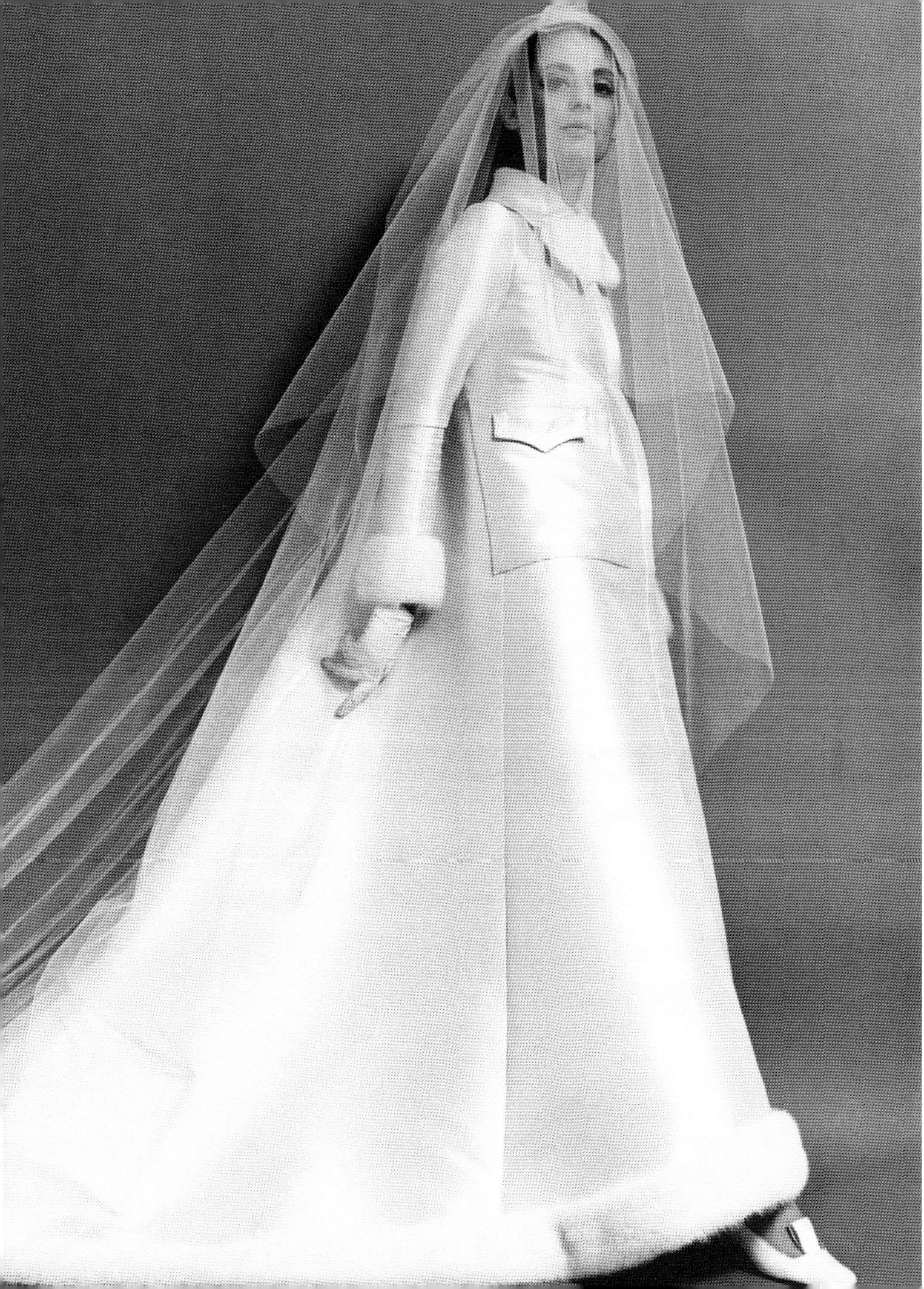

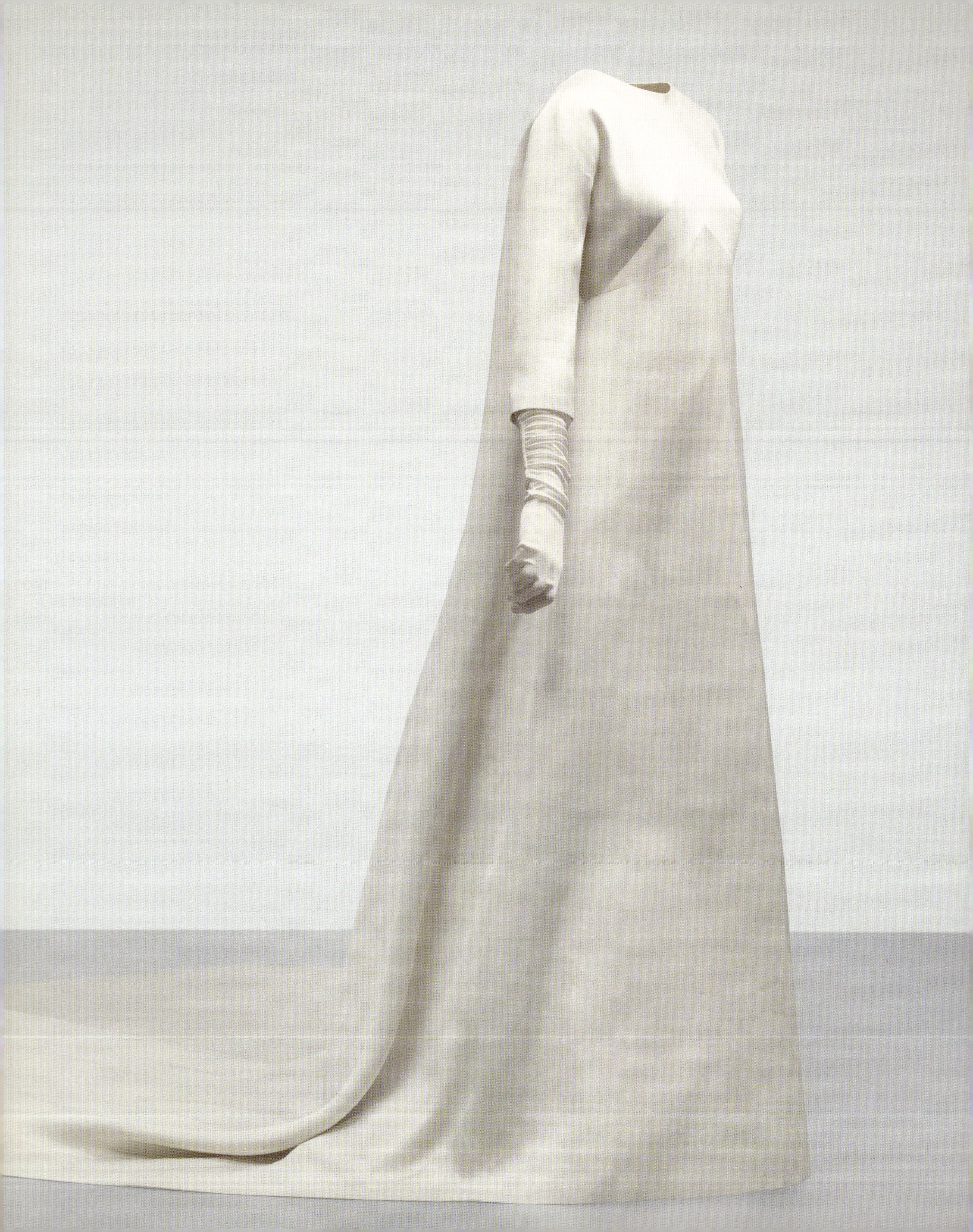

20

Cristóbal Balenciaga

1968

Cristóbal Balenciaga's trapezoid wedding dress, created on the eve of the closure of his haute couture house, distilled the designer's credo into a work of sublime architectural austerity.

Balenciaga was a legend in his own lifetime, a true innovator and virtuoso who dedicated the latter part of his career to simplifying and abstracting fashion's forms. Between 1967 and 1968, shortly before he abruptly terminated his business, he designed a group of pure white silk gazar wedding gowns representing the apotheosis of his achievements. The first of these dresses, produced in 1967, was sculpted into a cone shape with a trapezoid silhouette using just one seam. Falling without interruption from the shoulders to the floor, the dress's pure lines were achieved by a razor-sharp cut. Its simplicity was a tribute to the designer's meticulous tailoring skills and intuitive ability to sculpt fabric. "Balenciaga created not only a style but a technique. He was the architect of haute couture," said his pupil Givenchy.

The single-seam wedding dress was a prototype from which Balenciaga produced at least two further wedding dresses in 1968, through which he adapted and refined his cut and placement of seams. One dress, photographed by David Bailey, featured a dramatic seam across the front. Placed on the bias, it laterally dissected the dress with absolute precision from one hem to the other, creating angles that projected and suspended the fabric away from the body in a highly original multifaceted shape. The seams in the version pictured here created an inverted V shape framing the bust, shaped with surgically sharp darts that together worked to taper the fabric into a dynamic A-line silhouette.

Wedding dress as living sculpture

Balenciaga envisioned his wedding gowns as three-dimensional entities encircling the body and spiraling away from it. They were the product of the designer's quest, begun in the 1950s, to tailor sculptural forms. His success in this endeavor can be attributed to his deep knowledge of the possibilities of rigid textiles and in letting the material determine the cut of the garment. Balenciaga developed silk gazar, a stiff yet easily manipulated fabric, with Swiss manufacturer Abraham in 1958. By using this distinctive fabric, the designer was able to conceive a voluminous shape contained by crisp lines.

Though geometric and architectural in form, the dress retained a fluidity, thanks to the designer's deft manipulation of the fabric, subtly changing its shape with movement like a living sculpture. Its fluid lines, characteristic of Balenciaga's work of this period, altered the way clothing related to the female body. This original, unrestrictive silhouette, releasing

CLEAN WHITE LINES
The crisp lines of Balenciaga's design are accentuated by the use of pure white fabric.

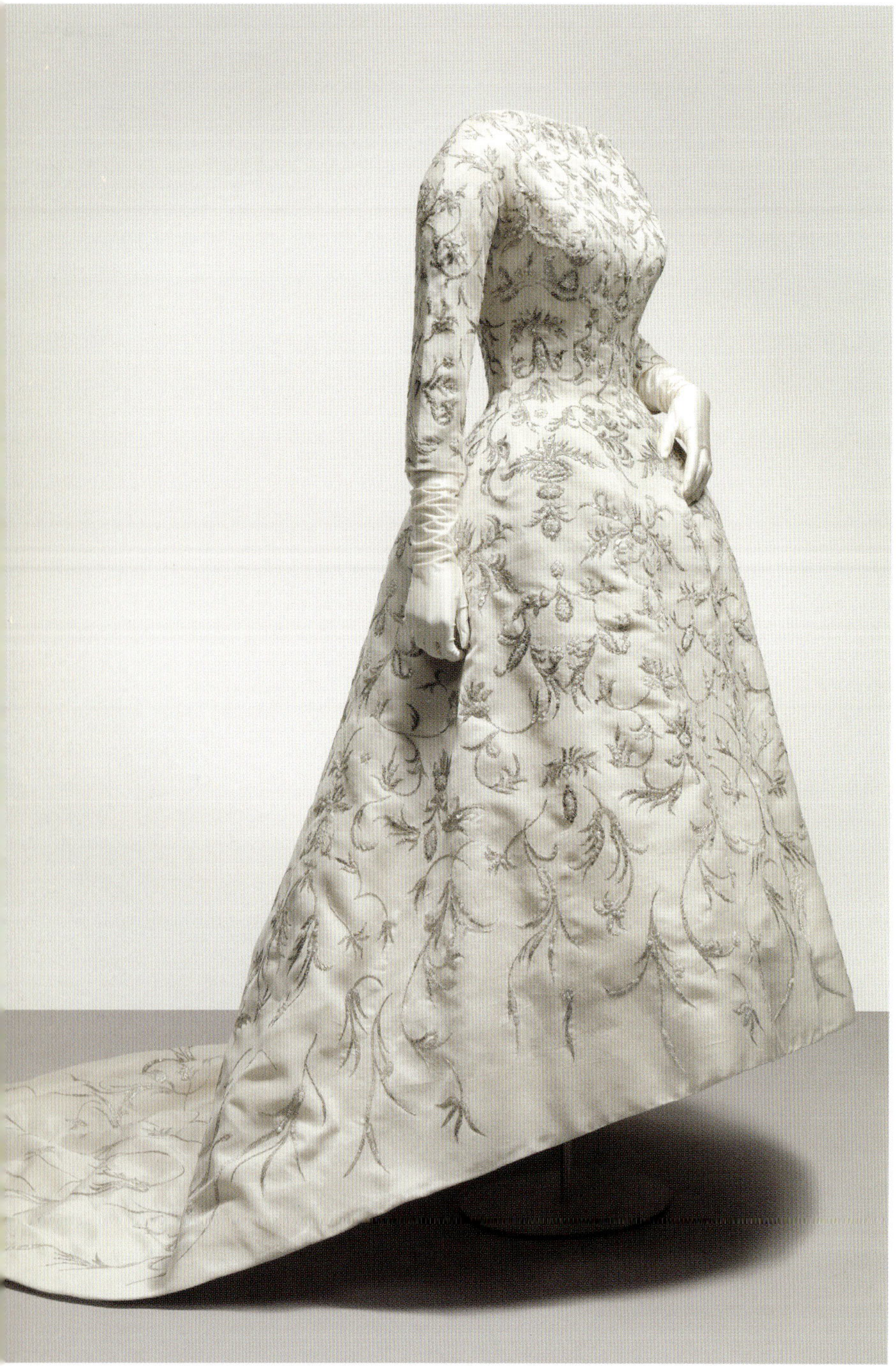

the waist, was particularly radical in terms of bridalwear, traditionally designed to contain and emphasize that area of the body.

A strength and inspiration

A devout Catholic all his life, Balenciaga's religious beliefs imbued his severe aesthetic and creative process—he worked with focused discipline and obsessive exactitude. Inspired by the austerity of monastic clothing, Balenciaga stripped his garments back to their purest, most essential state. Nowhere was the ever-present influence of the church more evident than in these wedding dresses, which are completely free of surface decoration. With no embellishment to obscure the cut, the clean lines—accentuated by the purity of color—brought the designer's technical mastery to the fore.

Balenciaga dressed many high-profile brides, including Sonsoles Díez de Rivera (dress shown at left), Doña Fabiola de Mora y Aragón (later Queen of Belgium), and María del Carmen Martínez-Bordiú y Franco, granddaughter of the Spanish dictator. However, Balenciaga himself recognized that to wear his designs required a strength of character. This was particularly true of his wedding dresses. Thus the impact of his archetypal designs of 1967–68 were felt less in the mainstream bridal market and more in haute couture, where Balenciaga inspired legions of designers. "Haute couture is like an orchestra, whose conductor is Balenciaga," Christian Dior said of his Spanish counterpart. "We other couturiers are the musicians and we follow the directions he gives."

TOWARD THE TRAPEZOID
This asymmetric ivory silk wedding dress was designed in 1957 for Sonsoles Díez de Rivera. The silver metallic embroidery was inspired by the dresses of Madonna statues in Seville, Spain. The simple, dramatic lines of the dress and its ecclesiastic references were refined over a period of ten years to produce the unadorned sculptural white wedding dresses.

HIDDEN DETAILS

- The back of the dress, with a seam down the center, is cut from two triangular panels.
- Fastens down the center-back with press studs.
- Lined with ivory silk taffeta.

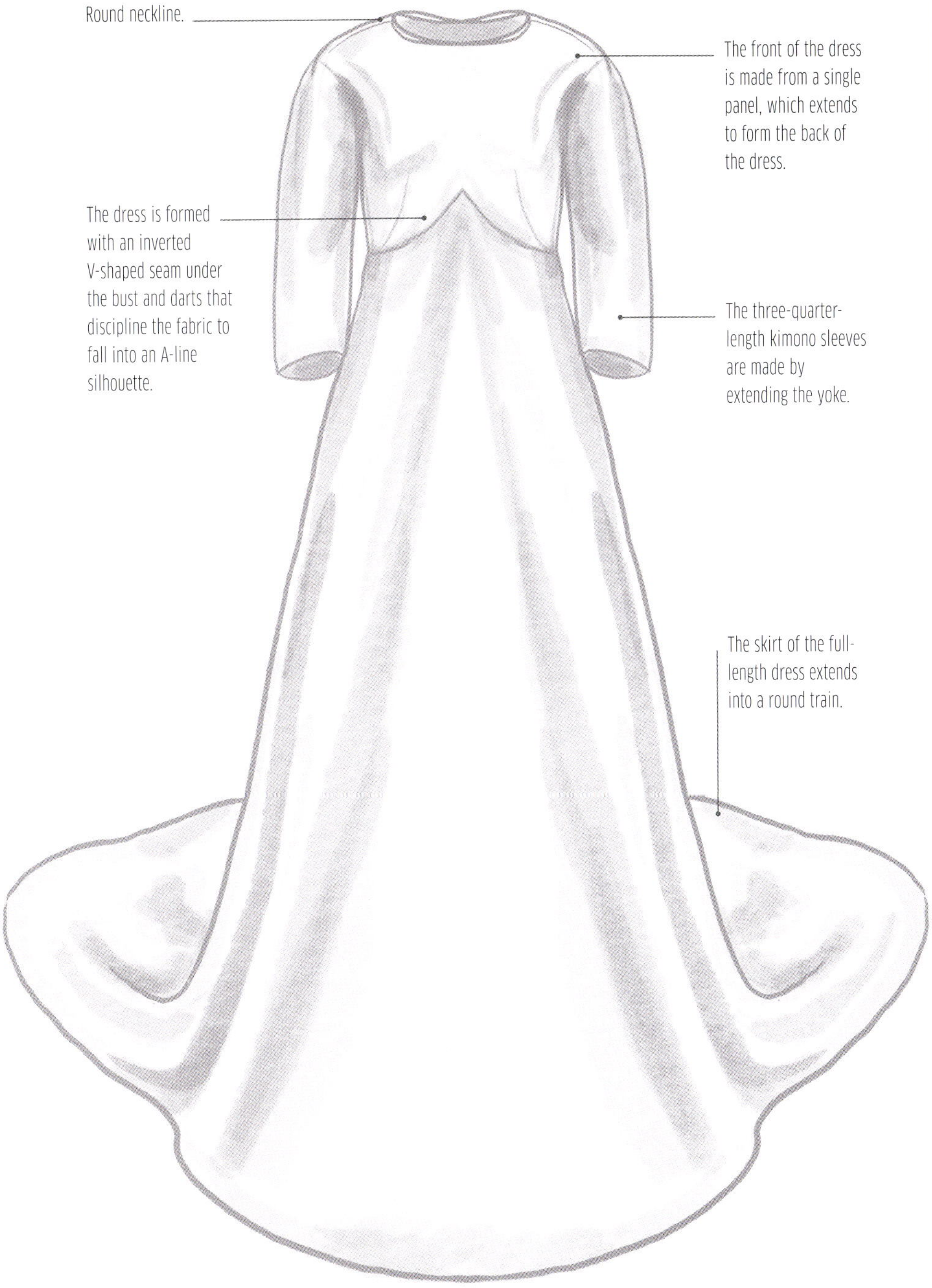

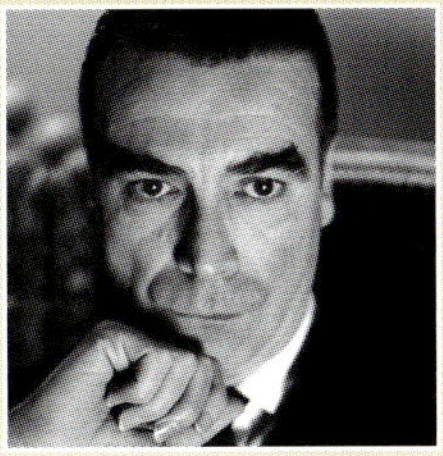

Cristóbal Balenciaga
1895–1972

As a child in Spain, working alongside his seamstress mother, Balenciaga learned how to sew, drape, and cut dresses. Balenciaga founded his company in 1918, but in 1936 the Spanish Civil War forced the designer to relocate to France, where the fashion press were soon praising his immense influence upon French fashion. When Balenciaga died, *Women's Wear Daily* exclaimed, "The King is dead."

Today the label continues to pay homage to its founder under notable creative directors Nicolas Ghesquière (1997–2012) and Alexander Wang (2012–present).

THE DRESS

STYLE Minimalist

SHAPE Trapezoid

FABRIC Silk gazar

COLOR White

21

Valentino Garavani

1968 For Jacqueline Kennedy

Jacqueline Kennedy's selection of a minidress from Valentino Garavani's landmark White Collection irrevocably altered the image of second-time brides and gave a temporary boost to the ailing haute couture industry.

In 1968, Garavani showcased his White Collection, a Spring/Summer line composed entirely of garments in shades of white, cream, and beige rendered in sensuous fabrics. The collection received exuberant praise from the fashion press, with *Vogue* magazine hailing it as "the talk of Europe" and calling the designer "the idol of the young, a new symbol of modern luxury." From this collection, Jacqueline Kennedy, the widow of American President John F. Kennedy, chose an ecru silk georgette and lace dress to wear at her nuptials to Greek shipping magnate Aristotle Onassis.

The straight, unfitted design featured a short, knife-pleated skirt under a floating "pullover"-style bodice with a funnel neck. Decorated with scallops of appliquéd lace, its long, balloon-shaped lace sleeves were caught with deep cuffs. Sartorially, the dress couldn't have been more different from the formal gown the bride had worn, little over a decade previously, at her heavily orchestrated wedding to John F. Kennedy (see page 46).

When the press published photographs of the Onassis's private wedding on the Greek island of Skorpios, the startling image of the

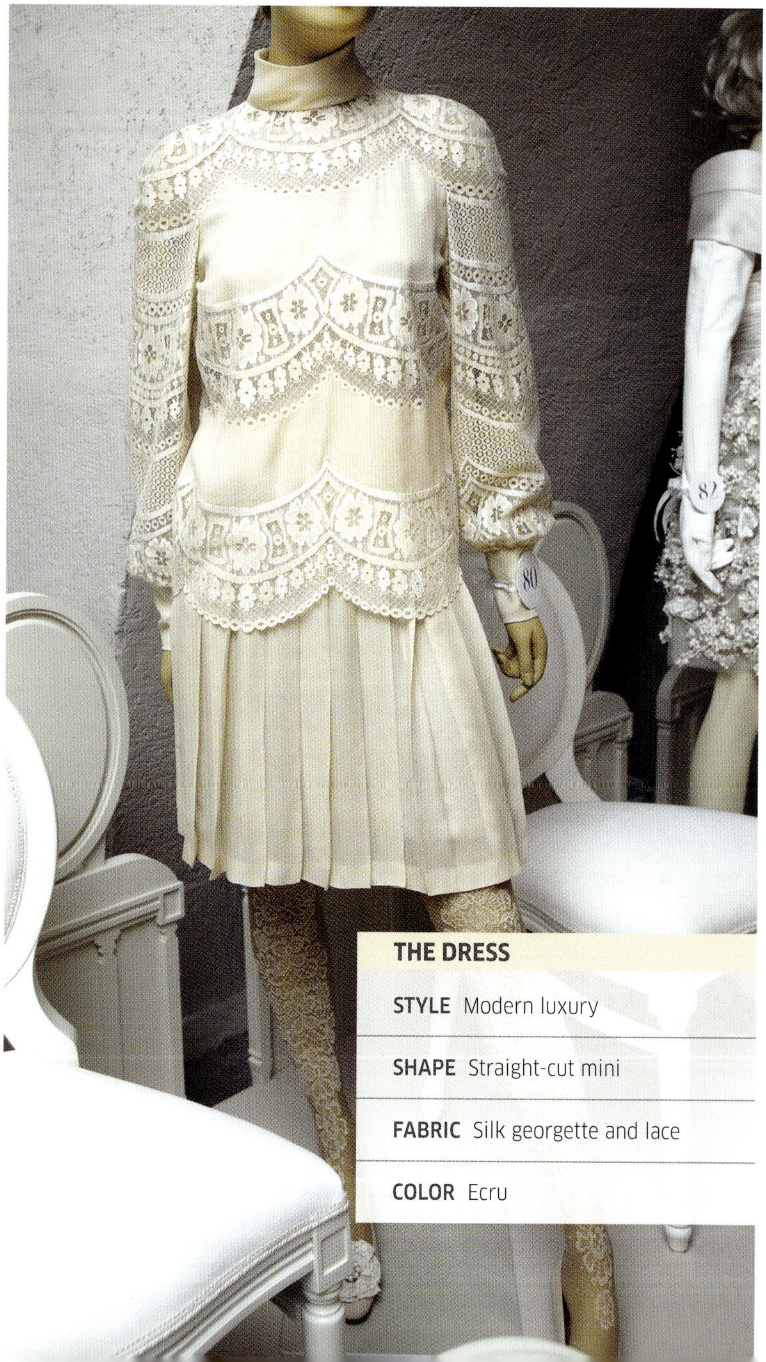

THE DRESS

STYLE Modern luxury

SHAPE Straight-cut mini

FABRIC Silk georgette and lace

COLOR Ecru

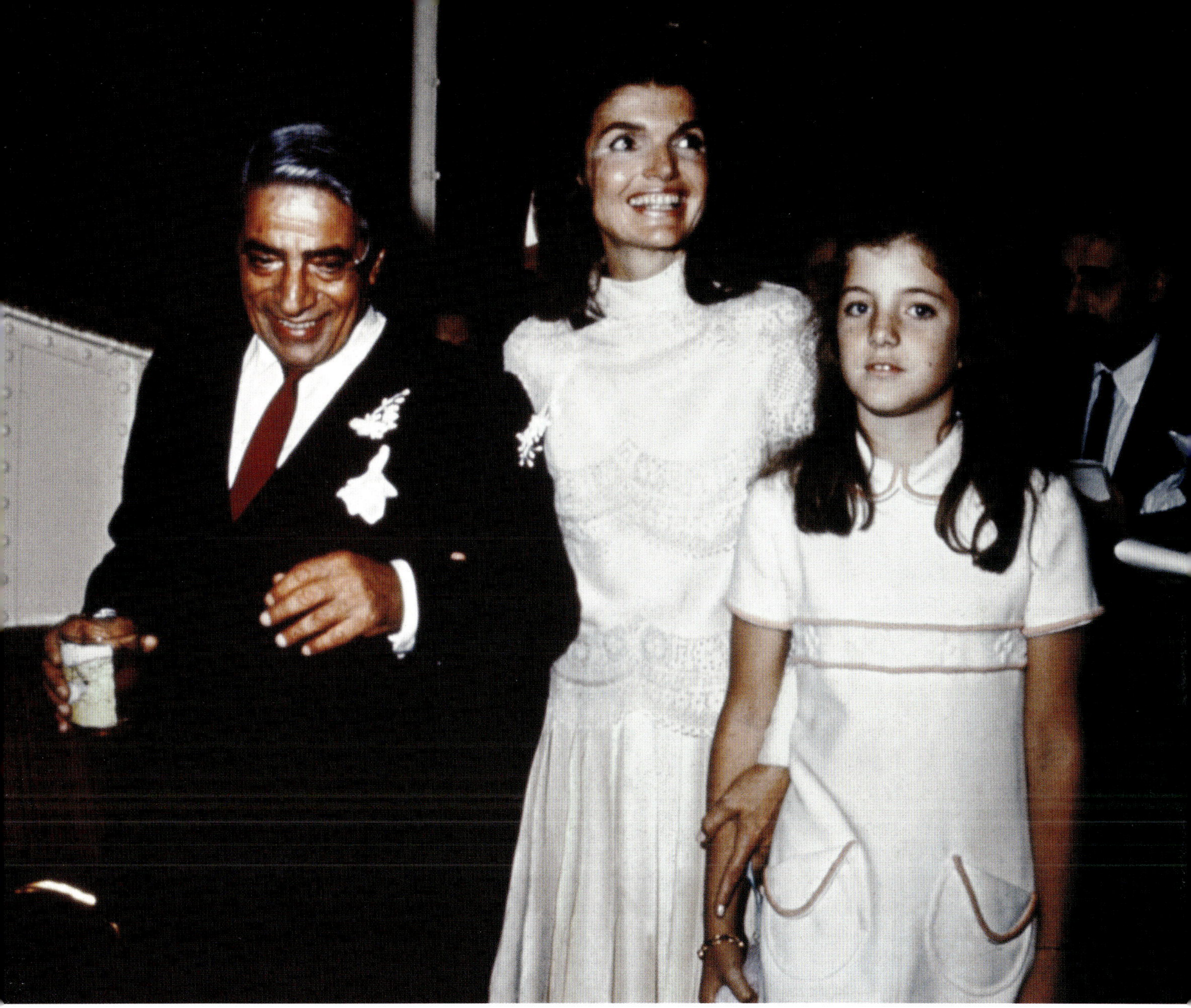

minidress-clad widow defied expectations of a second-time bride approaching forty. The look was completed by a tousled head of hair dressed with youthful ribbons. Although fashionable brides of the 1960s favored minimalist thigh-skimming shifts (see page 64), the miniskirt was nonetheless considered a phenomenon of the youthquake. Kennedy's choice of dress was timely, bridging the gap between old-world elegance and the modernity of the later 1960s. As a style icon to a generation of women, she sent the message that shorter lengths were also acceptable for the mature bride.

Kennedy's dress was reproduced on magazine covers around the world, sparking a flurry of orders that have been credited with making the dress the best-selling piece of couture produced by Garavani's atelier. (For more on Garavani, see page 81.) The intense interest in Garavani's design came at a critical junction for the couture industry. With society embracing ready-to-wear clothing, sales of couture were in steep decline, a situation at least temporarily reversed by the impact of Kennedy's wedding dress.

SECOND-TIME BRIDE
For her second wedding, Jacqueline Kennedy wore her dream wedding dress: a slim-fitting gown with firm lines to suit her tall, slender figure. (Shown at left at the designer's retrospective, 2012.)

22

Jean Muir

1969 For Pamela Talmey Colin

The minimalist gown designed by British dressmaker Jean Muir for Pamela Talmey Colin made a bold statement in its simplicity.

London's leading ready-to-wear designer, Muir created the cream, empire-line wool dress worn by the one-time London editor of *Vogue* magazine for her marriage to William David Ormsby-Gore, the 5th Baron Harlech and a former British Ambassador in Washington. The union of this influential and glamorous couple was described by Pathé News as the "society wedding of the year." From her choice of music—the bride walked down the aisle to Handel's *Solomon*, heralding the arrival of the Queen of Sheba, an in-joke with her friends about her Nefertiti-like profile—to her choice of dress, the wedding reflected Talmey Colin's clear-sighted, individualist vision.

Timeless and precise construction

Bucking the late-1960s trend for historical bridal styles, the bride commissioned her dress from a designer celebrated for her timeless aesthetic. Designed for a winter wedding, her fine cream wool dress was cut with a high waistline and a full-length, gently flared skirt. It had long puffed sleeves gathered into deep cuffs and a high neck with a stand-up collar. The perfectly balanced proportions of Muir's design—its purity of line, fluidity of movement, and softly rounded silhouette—were the hallmarks of the designer. The only decorative details to adorn the dress were understated and discreet. Couched cord, in the same shade of cream, was applied in a scrolling Celtic motif to the center of the chest, probably as a reference to the groom's Welsh title. Evenly and precisely spaced top-stitching around the cuffs and collar was typical of Muir's meticulous attention to detail and refined couture finish. Talmey Colin accentuated the clear, minimalist lines of Muir's design with her selection of accessories. Her dark hair was dressed with strips of matching cream braid created by the London milliner Graham Smith, and on her feet she wore a pair of cream court heels by the Italian firm Dal Co'.

Muir's design work, the first to blur the boundaries between couture and ready-to-wear fashion, inspired the term "wholesale couture." In the late 1960s and 1970s, many fashionable brides would follow Talmey Colin's example and select their dresses from the ranges of contemporary designers rather than patronize specialty wedding boutiques.

IN THE DETAILS
The dress was in the minimalist style, with fine attention to detail.

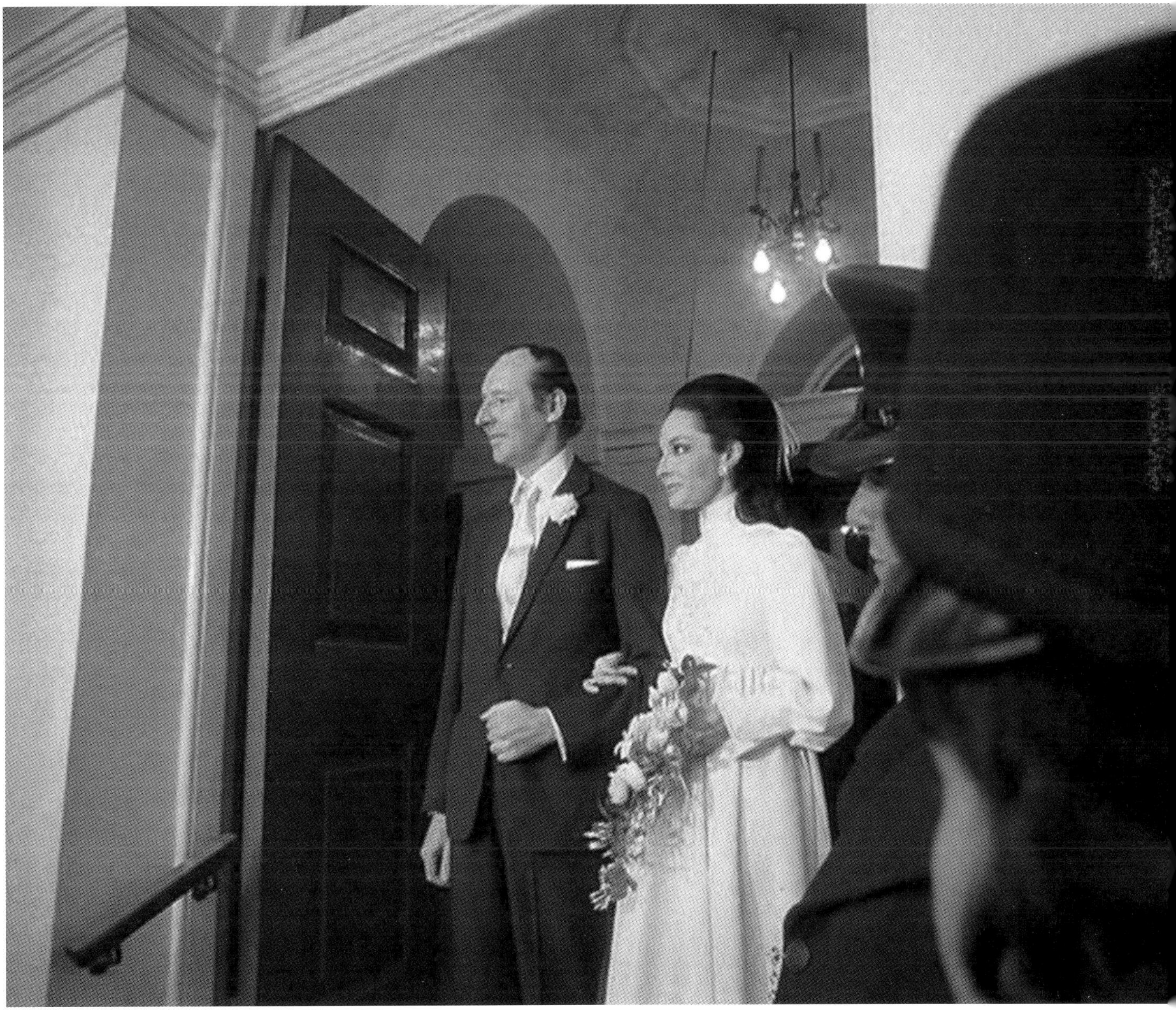

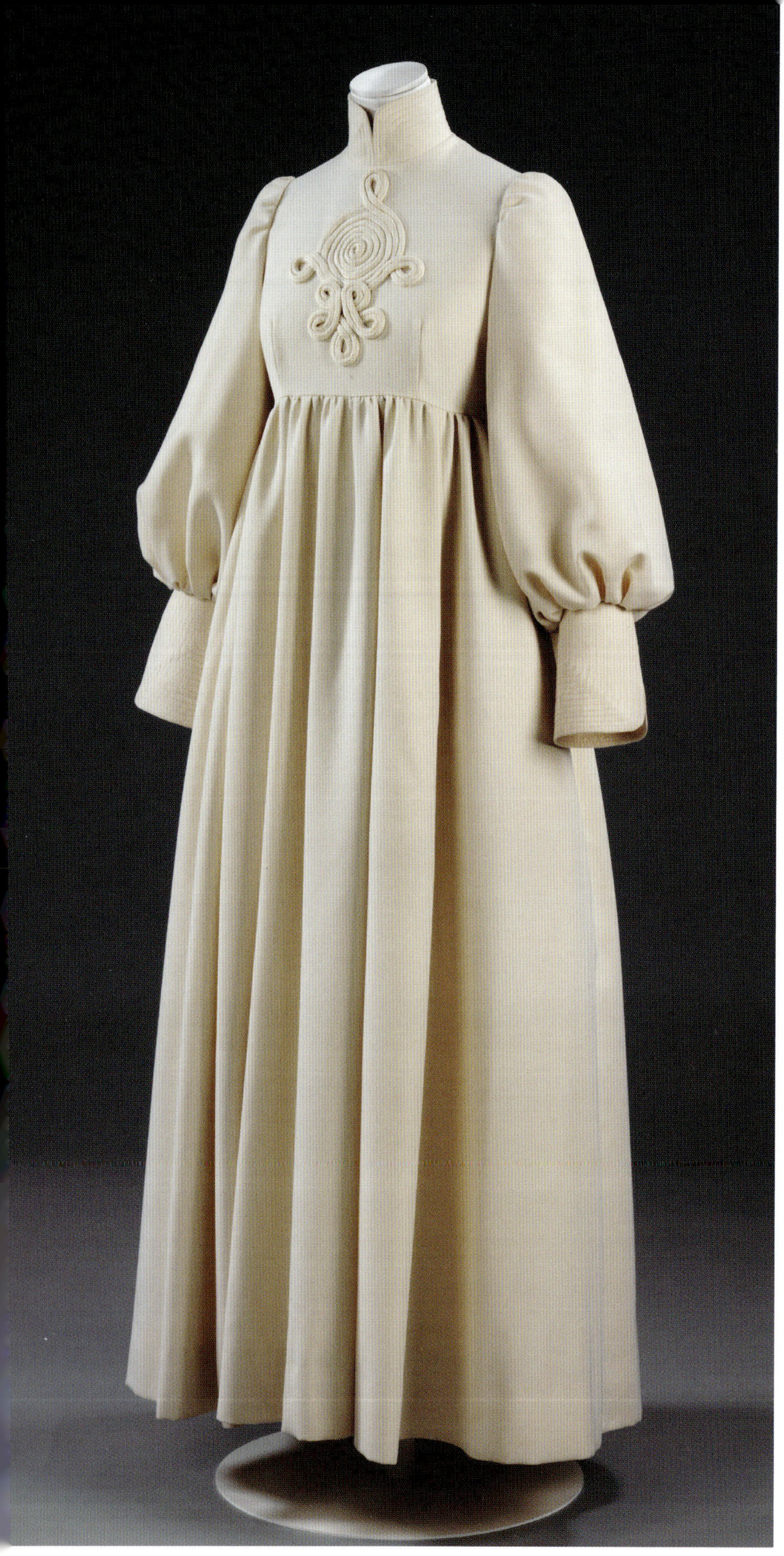

Crafted fashion

Compared to its contemporaries, Muir's design was radical in its simplicity. While many designers were plundering the dressing-up box of history, translating past fashions into faddy, frilly, flounced wedding dresses, Muir created an ensemble that managed to be fashionable, yet outside of fashion. Although the silhouette of the dress was vaguely Edwardian, it was a contemporary evolution of the style—stripped of extraneous details, pared down into a precise distillation. Muir, in her own estimation, transcended fashion. She infamously claimed that the word "fashion" would be better used a verb, as in "to fashion a dress," rather than as a reference to passing trends. This interpretation is evident in the value she placed on the construction process, which she described as "engineering with cloth." This wedding dress clearly demonstrates Muir's concern with craftsmanship—it is an icon of the exquisite tailoring and technical rigor for which Muir was hailed as "the world's greatest dressmaker."

EXPERT CRAFTSMANSHIP
The fine stitched detailing and clean finish are testament to the craft of couture.

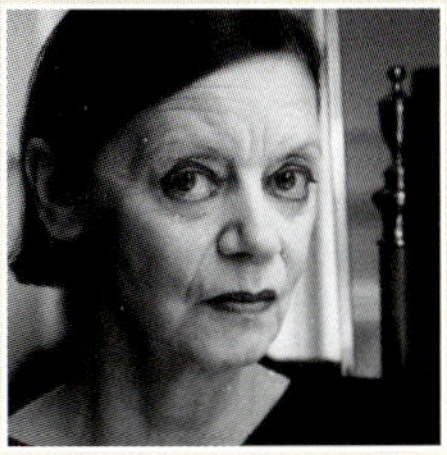

Jean Muir
1928–1995

Born in England to Scottish parents, the self-taught designer learned to draw, sew, and embroider at school. Muir's sketching skills were put to good use at the London department store Liberty, where she worked for six years before taking a job as a designer at Jaeger in 1956. In 1962 Muir launched Jane and Jane, a range of couture-quality clothing in a ready-to-wear line. Jean Muir Limited was established in London in 1966. Here the designer sealed her legendary reputation with exquisitely tailored and feminine clothing executed in supple, plain-colored fabrics.

THE DRESS

STYLE Celtic minimalism

SHAPE Empire

FABRIC Worsted wool twill

COLOR Cream

HIDDEN DETAILS

- A blue ribbon and silver horseshoe were sewn onto the inside hem.

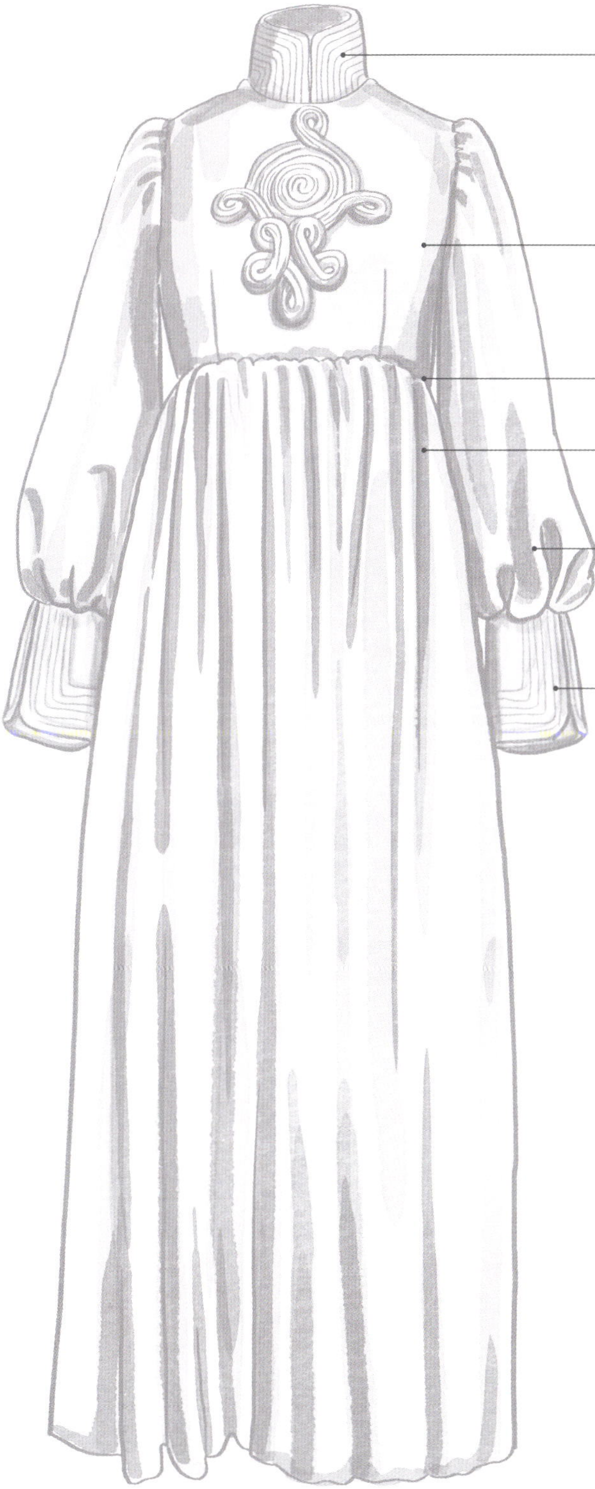

23

Yves Saint Laurent

1971 For Bianca Pérez-Mora Macias

When Bianca Pérez-Mora Macias wed rock star Mick Jagger in St. Tropez, the pregnant bride opted for an unconventional wedding outfit—a white linen skirt suit and wide-brimmed hat—that stands as an icon of effortless chic.

An instant classic, both chic and daring, Pérez-Mora Macias's wedding-suit ensemble set the bar for casual rock-and-roll wedding style. Although some sources attribute the suit to London's famous Savile Row designer Tommy Nutter, it is usually credited to Yves Saint Laurent. (For more on Saint Laurent, see page 63.) Breaking with tradition, the designer paired a plain and rather demure maxi skirt with a tuxedo-style jacket featuring wide lapels, pockets, and a single button fastening.

A certain attitude

Saint Laurent introduced his revolutionary tuxedo suit for women, Le Smoking, in 1967. Its reinterpretation of menswear for the female form caused something of a furor at the time. Le Smoking demanded a certain attitude that borrowed from typically masculine gestures—the hand-in-pocket slouch became the trademark pose of the Le Smoking woman. French actress Catherine Deneuve remarked of the garment: "The thing about a tuxedo is that it is virile and feminine at the same time. It really does make you feel different as a woman, it changes the gestures." By the 1970s, the sexual revolution of the 1960s had taken full effect and Le Smoking was identified with strong, liberated women. The characteristically sharp, austere lines of Pérez-Mora Macias's Saint Laurent jacket provided the perfect foil to her womanly curves. The designer had made a shirt for the bride to wear underneath, but by the time of the wedding she was four months pregnant and it no longer fitted. She opted to wear nothing underneath, a bold decision that exposed a deep expanse of cleavage.

Style endures

Wedding culture changed dramatically in the early years of the 1970s. Marriage was no longer intrinsic to the fabric of social life, and a less formal approach to weddings resulted in more casual bridal styles, as evidenced by Pérez-Mora Macias's pared-down look, replete with floppy sun hat and peep-toe sandals. In 1970, *Queen* magazine signaled the arrival of a new type of bride who was "not just a fashion cipher, part of a tradition but very much herself," a description that could have been written for Pérez-Mora Macias. Wedding fashions come and go, but this iconic Yves Saint Laurent suit looks as contemporary and stylish today as the day it was first worn.

TRADITIONS MAINTAINED
Although dressed unconventionally, the bride wore a hat that was trimmed around the crown with fabric roses and hung with a simple, shoulder-length tulle veil.

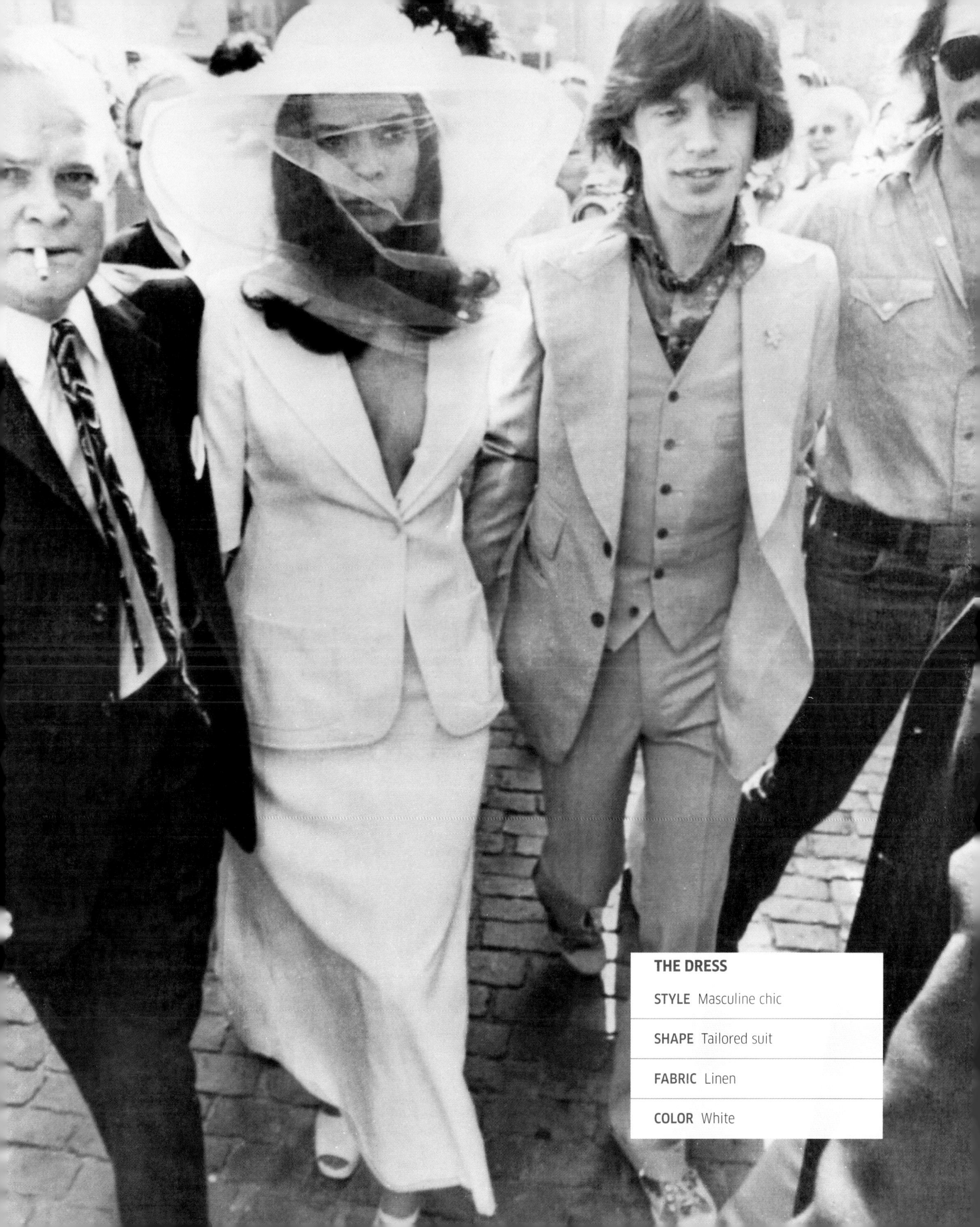

THE DRESS

STYLE Masculine chic

SHAPE Tailored suit

FABRIC Linen

COLOR White

24

Valentino Garavani

1973 Spring/Summer

Valentino Garavani's fluid chiffon and organza gown is an icon of "haute hippie" chic, channeling the free-spirited 1970s bride through the technical precision of haute couture.

Modele 248, a dress from Garavani's Spring/Summer 1973 collection, was described by *Vogue* magazine as "pleats, ribbons, ruffles galore." Created from delicate pale ivory chiffon, its lines flowed organically down the body, fitting closely to the torso, with oblique ribbed pleats from shoulder to waist and sewn-down pleats from waist to hips. Beneath the hips, the skirt fell freely to the hem, erupting in a frothy mass of organza volants, or wing-shaped frills. Rippling frills also surrounded the plunging V-neck, extending into short sleeves to balance the silhouette. A posy of purple silk cyclamens attached to a long satin ribbon caught around the waist completed the dress.

Many brides of the 1970s reacted against the severe formality of wedding gowns with princess lines and corseted bodices, adopting instead loose, layered designs in free-flowing fabrics. Caftans, and gypsy- or Celtic-inspired designs all became popular bridal styles. For brides wishing to retain some element of formality, Garavani's design was the perfect solution. This gown was chosen by society brides Pilar Crespi in 1973 and Christina Onassis in 1975. Unlike other, slightly more eccentric interpretations of hippie styling by designers of this period, Garavani's dress hasn't dated. Its organic form set a new standard of romantic bridal design, echoed by the sculptural waves and tumbling waterfalls of fabric seen in the twenty-first-century gowns of Alexander McQueen, Vera Wang, Marchesa, and Alice Temperley.

THE TEST OF TIME
Christina Onassis was one of many brides who fell in love with the Modele 248 dress.

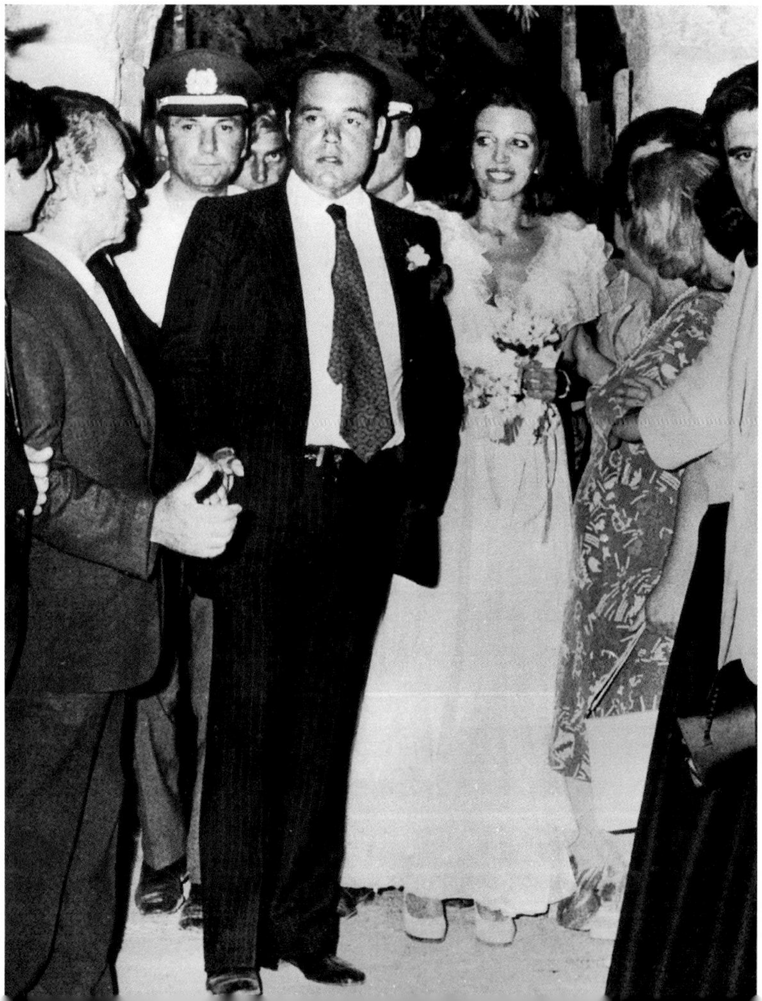

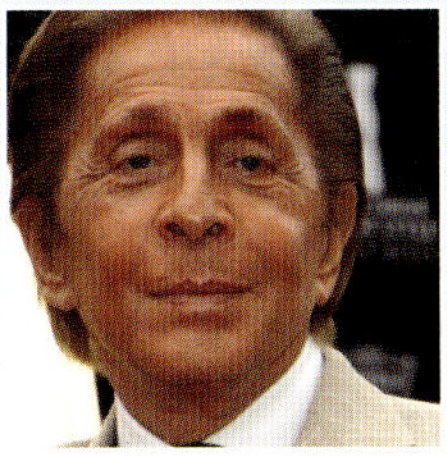

Valentino Garavani

1932–

Italian-born Valentino Garavani learned his haute couture skills in Paris during the 1950s, returning to Rome in 1959 to open his own atelier specializing in modern yet feminine styles. Since the 1960s, Valentino has been a byword for glamour, attracting an international clientele of women famed for their style and beauty. In 1967, *Time* magazine reported, "In a fashion world gone mad for mod, he designs clothes of great taste and elegance for women who prize beauty above eccentricity." The company, now owned by a private equity firm, has expanded into a lucrative international brand. In 2011, Garavani was honored with the Costume Council's award for artistry.

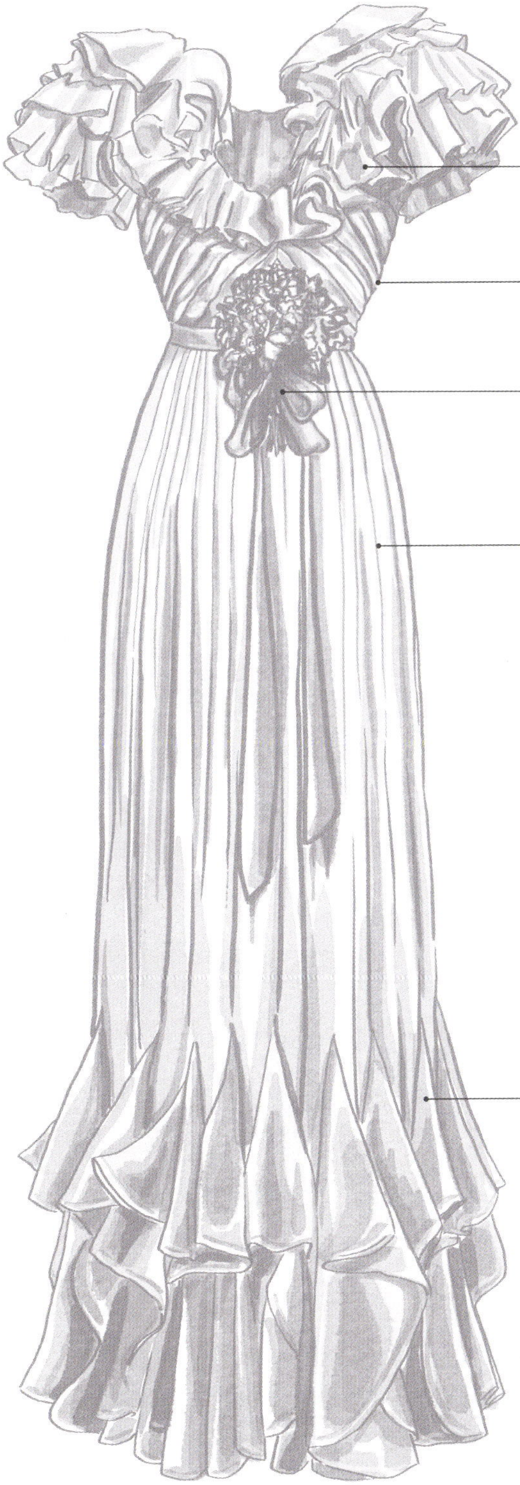

THE DRESS

STYLE Romantic hippie chic

SHAPE Fluid column

FABRIC Silk chiffon and organza

COLOR Pale ivory

25

Zandra Rhodes

1976 For Elizabeth Weiner

Zandra Rhodes's delicate hand-printed, pale yellow chiffon dress stood out as a beacon of subtle femininity in a bridal market saturated with novelty and absurdity.

Wedding dresses struggled to settle on a satisfactory form in the 1970s. Little in the plethora of styles found in contemporary mid-1970s fashion aligned with traditional bridal ideals of romance and femininity. Unable to find inspiration in the present, brides looked to the past, dredging up caricatured, historical looks, such as medieval chatelaines and Tudor maids, which allowed them to live out a fantastical identity for the day. In the year that Rhodes was commissioned to design Elizabeth Weiner's dress, Prudence Glynn, fashion editor of *The Times* newspaper, wrote with disapproval that "most modern wedding dresses are pure costume.... [They are] not so much a wardrobe investment as a chance for a once-in-a-lifetime chance to dream." Against this cacophony of confused costume, Rhodes channeled her independent and innovative approach to design, creating a subtle and modern bridal gown that was in accordance with the contemporary spirit of femininity.

The signature print

Rhodes's loose chiffon gown was rendered in the palest shades of creamy yellow and white. It was hand-printed in the same tones with a design inspired by her travels in exotic locations. Its fluid lines and pleated ruffles epitomized the designer's romantic style.

Printed textiles remain Rhodes's signature, around which her figure-flattering garments are constructed. The textile designer, trained originally in printing techniques and not fashion design, translated the narrative and aura of her two-dimensional prints into loose three-dimensional shapes. The structural foundation of this dress was developed from her best-selling 73/44 model, a pretty printed chiffon gown with a deep V-neck, large sleeves, and a full-length skirt gathered into the waist, bound with a satin sash.

Originally released in 1973, it was a style she revisited season after season, reinterpreting it in 1976 to reflect the movement and structure of her stylized exotic leaf and wave print. Fine pleating into the waistband of the skirt and down a panel on the center of the bodice echoed the rigid fanning anatomy of a palm frond. The defined lines of the pleats gave way to liquid folds as the fabric of the skirt and sleeves fell in gently rippling waves. The

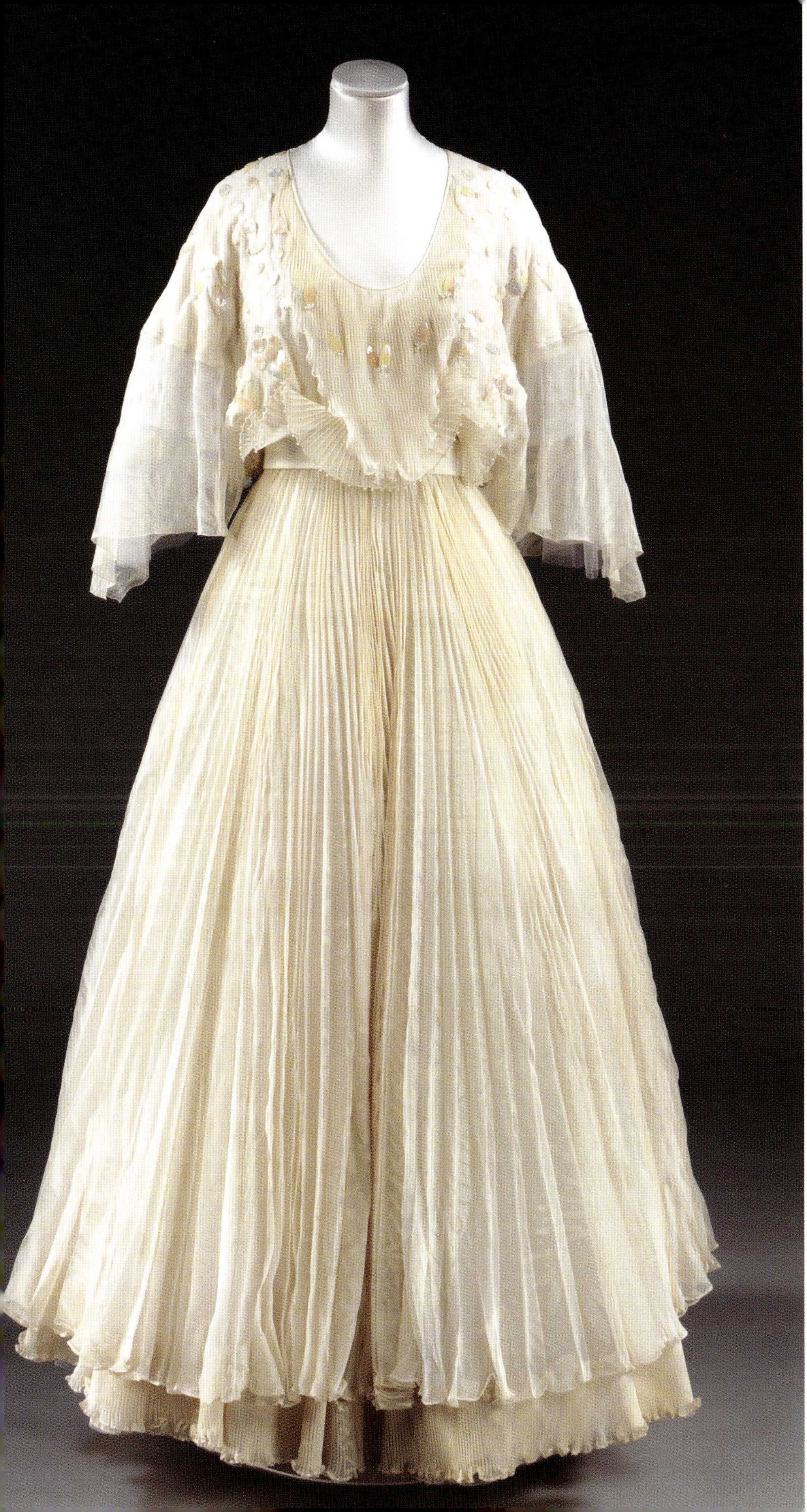

THE DESIGN FOR DESIGNERS

For her marriage to fellow designer David Emanuel, Elizabeth Weiner chose a dress by British designer Zandra Rhodes, who would become known as "the most original and fearless of British designers." Five years after their own wedding, the Emanuels were selected by Lady Diana Spencer to design her opulent wedding dress (see page 86).

undulating pleated frills around the top of the waistband and the hem of the petticoat, peeking out from underneath the skirt, amplified the rhythmic, wave-like quality of the dress. The aquatic spirit of the design continued in its surface decoration. Delicate, gleaming pearls sat around the waist, and iridescent, tinted plastic leaves and flowers were scattered across the matte chiffon bodice, resembling flecks of sunlight bouncing off the sea. When her contemporaries in the bridalwear industry were looking to the past, Rhodes strived to express a relationship between form and decoration that was in keeping with the moment.

THE DRESS

STYLE Fluid and organic

SHAPE Loose, circular

FABRIC Hand-printed silk chiffon

COLOR Pale yellow and white

HIDDEN DETAILS

- The dress was presented to the bride on a padded white clothes hanger with a blue hook, trimmed with ribbon and a silver horseshoe, with a protective cover decorated with silver angels—one on each shoulder.
- A satin sash wrapped tightly around the waist is tied at the back of the dress in a large bow. The ends of the sash are decorated with iridescent plastic flowers and leaves.

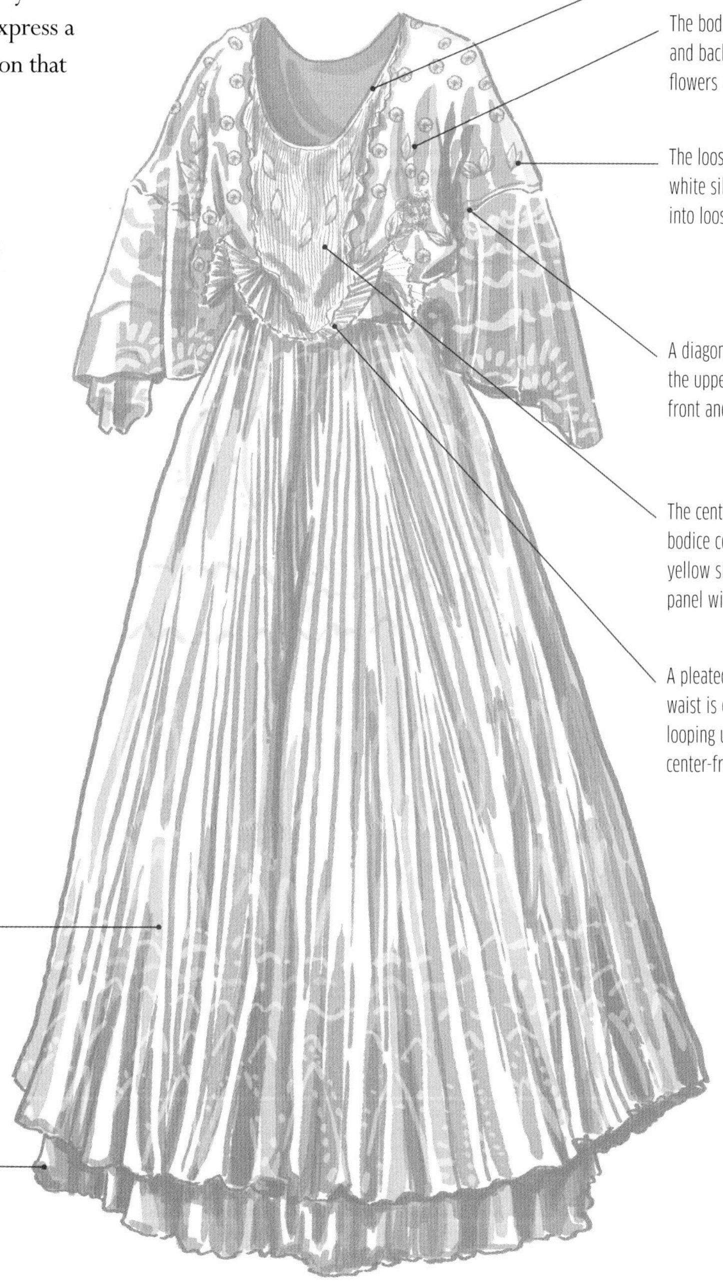

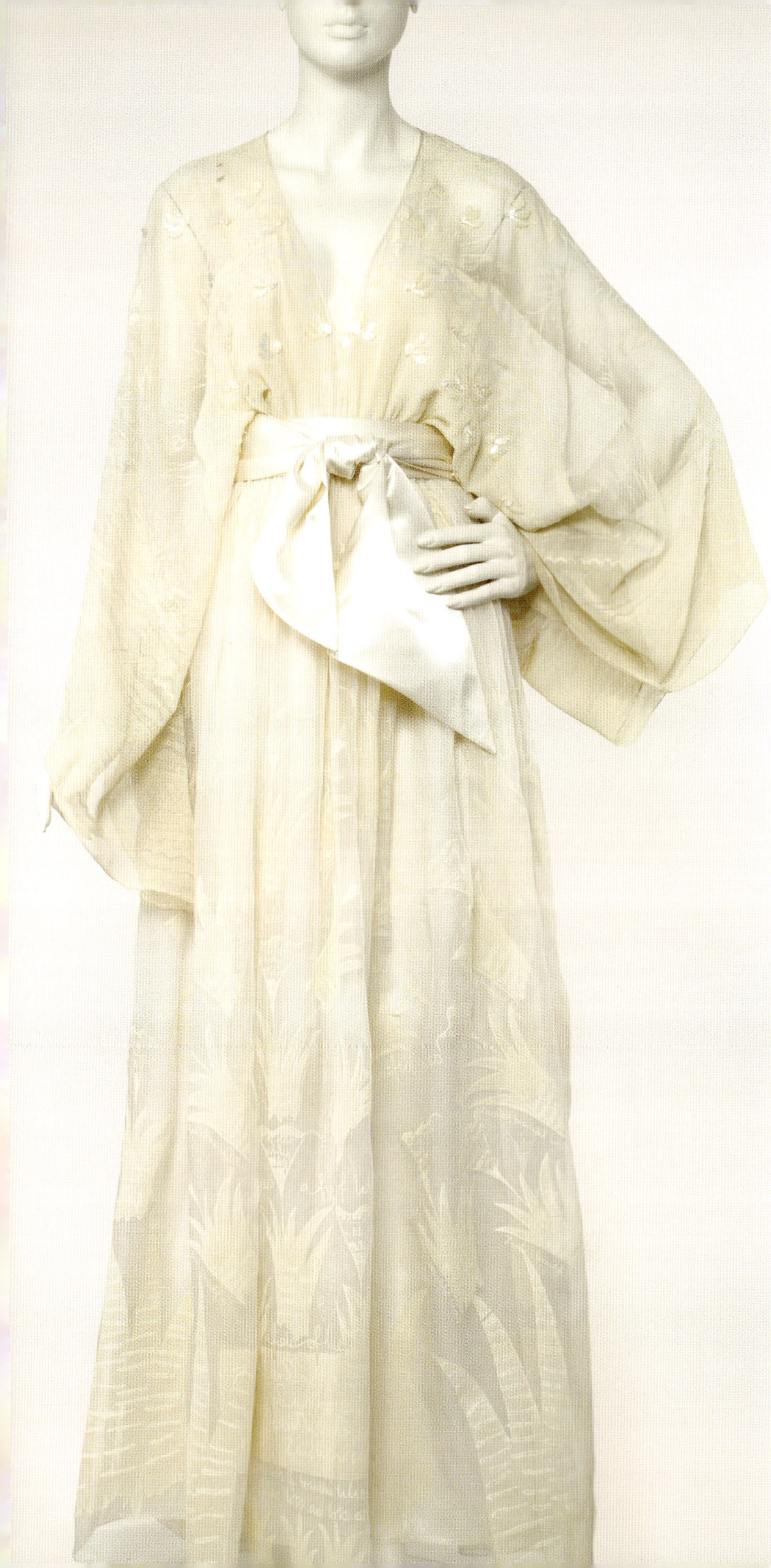

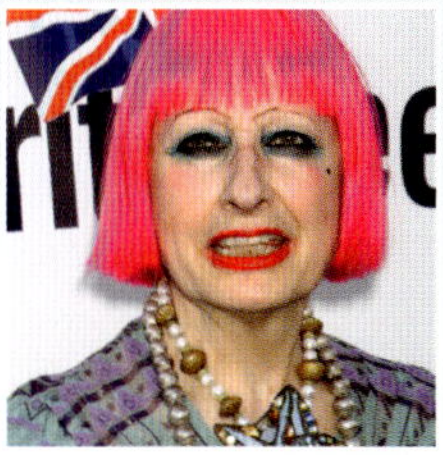

Zandra Rhodes
1940–

Rhodes trained in textile design, graduating from the Royal College of Art, London, in 1964. While teaching at art college, she opened the Fulham Road Clothes Shop in London with fashion designer Sylvia Ayton. Wanting full artistic control over her prints, she launched her first solo collection in 1969, the shapes of her prints dictating the designs of her clothes. Rhodes was at the forefront of a new wave of British designers in the 1970s, making a mark with her bold, unconventional designs and her equally memorable personal style and signature pink hair.

73/44 DRESS
Weiner's wedding dress was based on this design, first produced in 1973.

26

David and Elizabeth Emanuel

1981 For Lady Diana Spencer

Lady Diana Spencer's ivory silk wedding gown was the ultimate Cinderella dress. It set the standard for future royal wedding dresses and inspired a generation of brides.

In 1981, Lady Diana, a fresh-faced twenty-year-old bride, emerged from a glass coach in a cloud of airy paper taffeta, sparkling with the reflected light of more than 10,000 sequins and pearls. As she ascended the steps of St. Paul's Cathedral to meet her prince, a 25-foot (7.5-m) train unfurled dramatically in her wake. The bride's carefully orchestrated entrance was likened by one of the designers of her dress, Elizabeth Emanuel, to "a beautiful butterfly emerging from a chrysalis." This unforgettable moment was broadcast to an estimated 750 million television viewers worldwide, immediately embedding the image of Lady Diana in the public's collective imagination as the archetypal fairy-tale bride.

The fairy-tale dress

The dress incorporated all the aspects of an iconic princess wedding dress: frills, flounces and bows, sumptuous fabrics, jewels and embroidered lace, crinolines and corsetry, and a train to rival all trains. The defining features of the dress—its enormous skirt supported upon tulle petticoats, huge puffed sleeves, a wide double-flounce collar, and of course the sweeping train edged with sparkling embroidered lace—provided the proportions and perspective demanded by the occasion and setting. The grandiosity and retrospective romanticism of the design were offset by the youthful femininity and delicacy of its detailing, fabric, and color. The luminosity of the ivory silk fabric, the finely embroidered panels of antique lace, and the twinkling effect of tiny pearls and mother-of-pearl sequins gave the dress a magical soft focus.

A historic transformation

Royal wedding dresses enact spectacular performances that are designed to live on in history, but like all good wedding dresses they must please the tastes of the bride. It was the young Lady Diana's choice that the coveted commission to design her dress be granted to the relatively inexperienced designers David and Elizabeth Emanuel. Diana became enamored of their work after wearing a frilly collared blouse of their creation for a *British Vogue* photo shoot in 1980. The Emanuels said that they aimed to transform the bride into a "fairy princess," and their astute understanding of the public expectations for the wedding gown was reflected in its immense popularity.

FAIRY-TALE BRIDE
Diana's gown was the ultimate princess dress—the most iconic royal dress forever after.

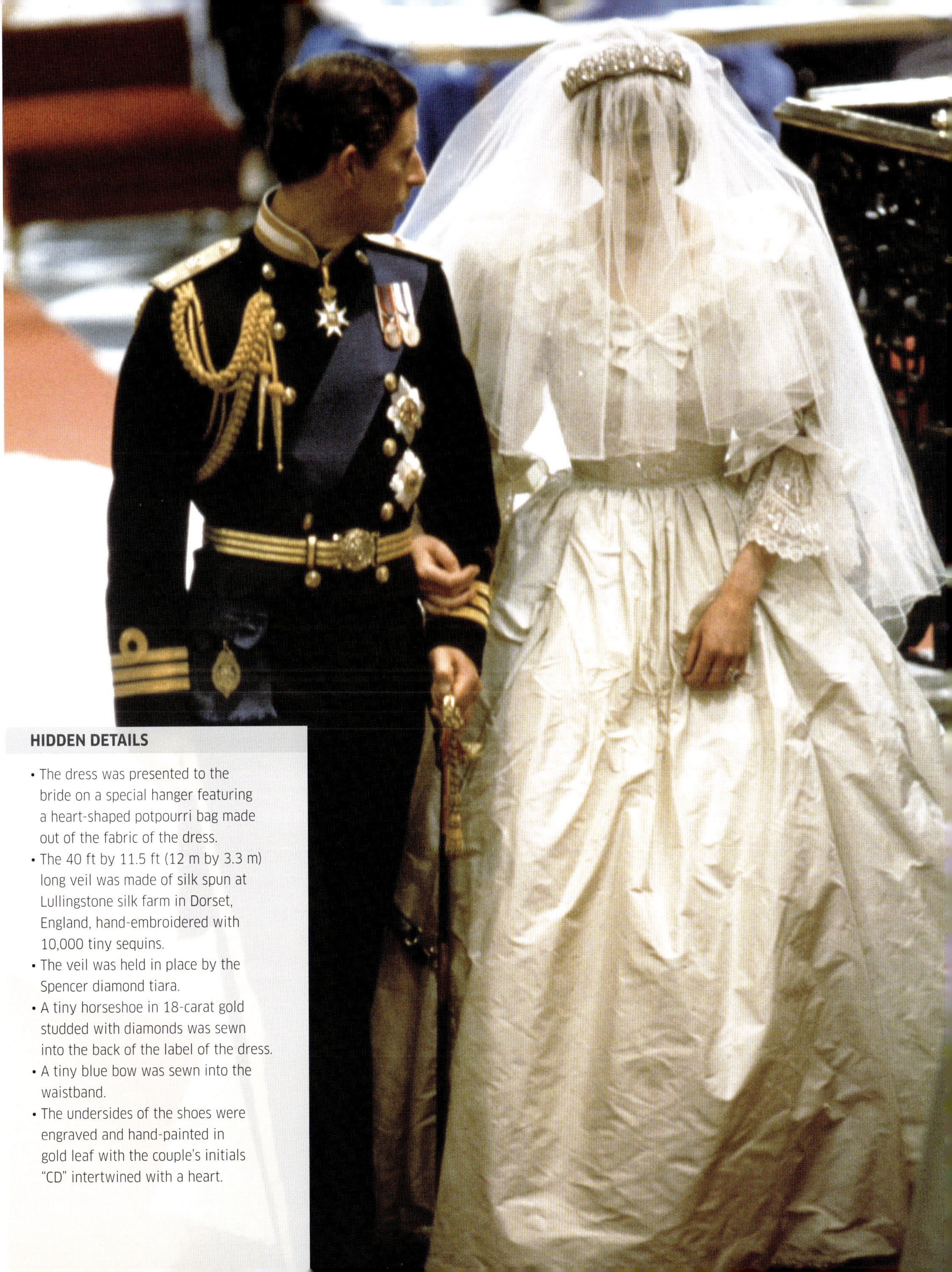

HIDDEN DETAILS

- The dress was presented to the bride on a special hanger featuring a heart-shaped potpourri bag made out of the fabric of the dress.
- The 40 ft by 11.5 ft (12 m by 3.3 m) long veil was made of silk spun at Lullingstone silk farm in Dorset, England, hand-embroidered with 10,000 tiny sequins.
- The veil was held in place by the Spencer diamond tiara.
- A tiny horseshoe in 18-carat gold studded with diamonds was sewn into the back of the label of the dress.
- A tiny blue bow was sewn into the waistband.
- The undersides of the shoes were engraved and hand-painted in gold leaf with the couple's initials "CD" intertwined with a heart.

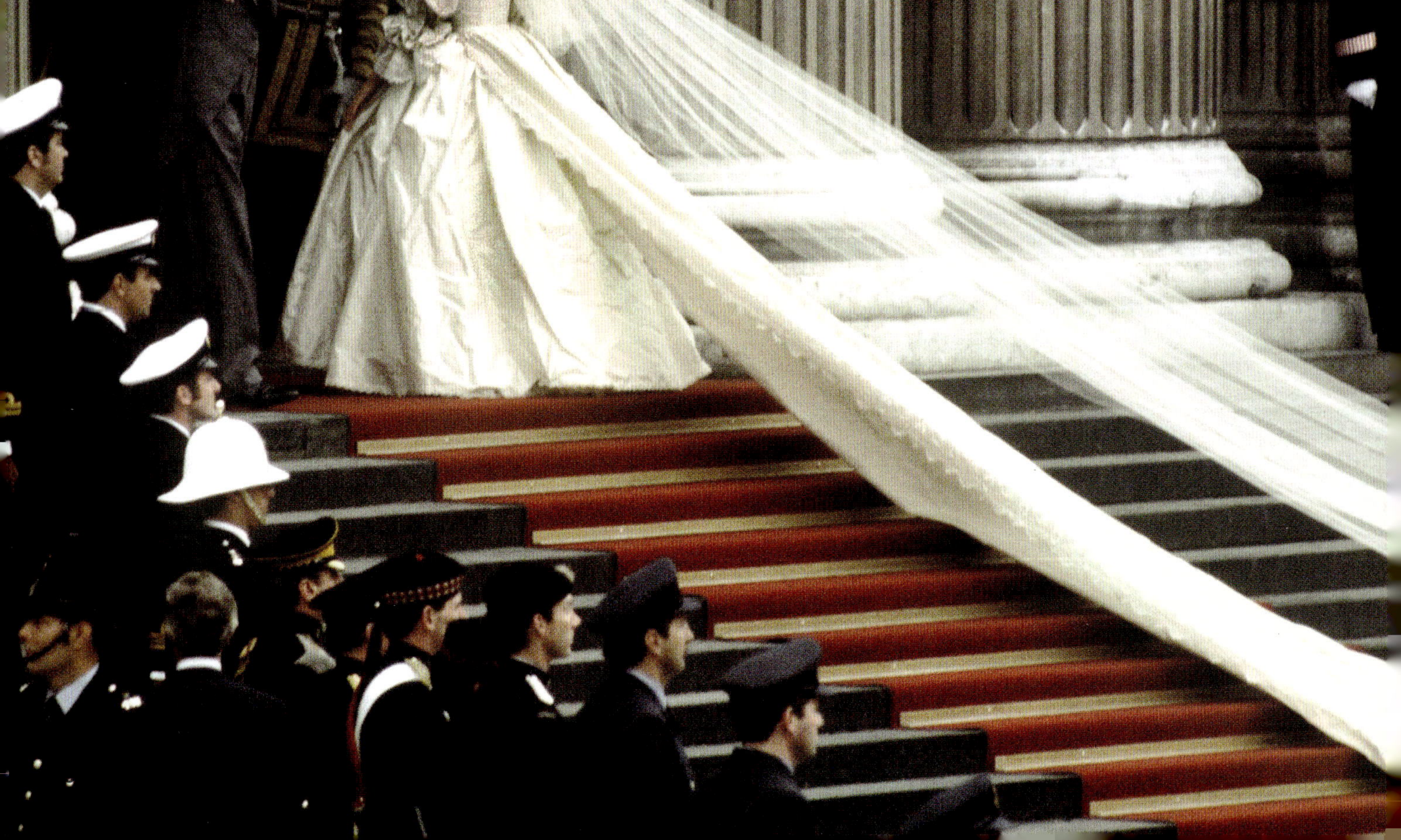

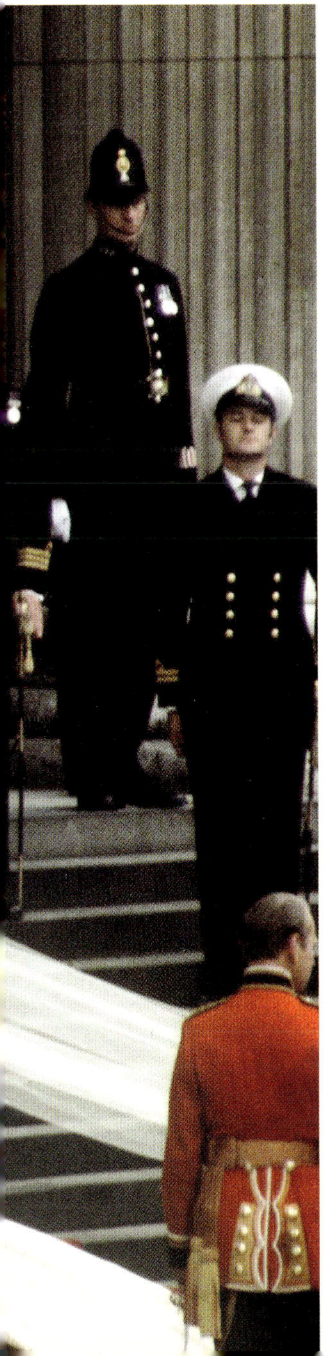

Bridal traditions sewn in

With no instructions or restrictions from the Palace about the commission, the designers were free to let their creativity roam. Research led them back to the romantic designs of historic royal bridal gowns, in particular to Queen Victoria's lace-trimmed wedding dress (see page 10).

The pair set out to make history with the longest and grandest royal bridal train. The train was so long that it had be fitted in secret at Buckingham Palace. The Emanuels produced around fifty designs for Lady Diana to choose from, all based upon the same silhouette—puffed skirt, full sleeves, and frills—in keeping with the New Romantic look of the early 1980s. Once the design was finalized, a pattern and a series of toiles were created to work out the details and sizing. Knowing that there was a limited amount of silk for the final dress, and no room for mistakes, the fabric wasn't cut until as late as possible. The couple were left with three months to make Lady Diana's dress and were still working on it right up until the evening before the wedding itself.

The Emanuels also made Lady Diana's second choice of design, in case details of the real dress were leaked in advance of the day. As it happened, the wedding dress remained a firmly guarded secret until the moment the bride stepped out of her coach, at which time sealed envelopes containing the much speculated-upon information about the dress were released. The price of the gown was not revealed, but newspapers valued it around £9,000 at the time, just under double the cost of a standard Emanuel wedding dress (the designers later revealed that they charged much less than this). Manufacturers rushed out their cut-price copies of the dress, with one Welsh company claiming to have produced a £465 version just one week after the nuptials. Realizing that Lady Diana's dress would generate worldwide interest, waxwork museum Madame Tussauds asked the designers to create a replica for their displays. In 2011, this near-identical dress was sold at auction to a museum in Chile for over $75,000.

THE TRAILING VEIL

A cotton bobbin-net lace veil with sequinned hand embroidery framed the bride's face with sparkling specks of light. The veil, fastened with the Spencer tiara, extended the full length of the train and hung to bouquet length at the front.

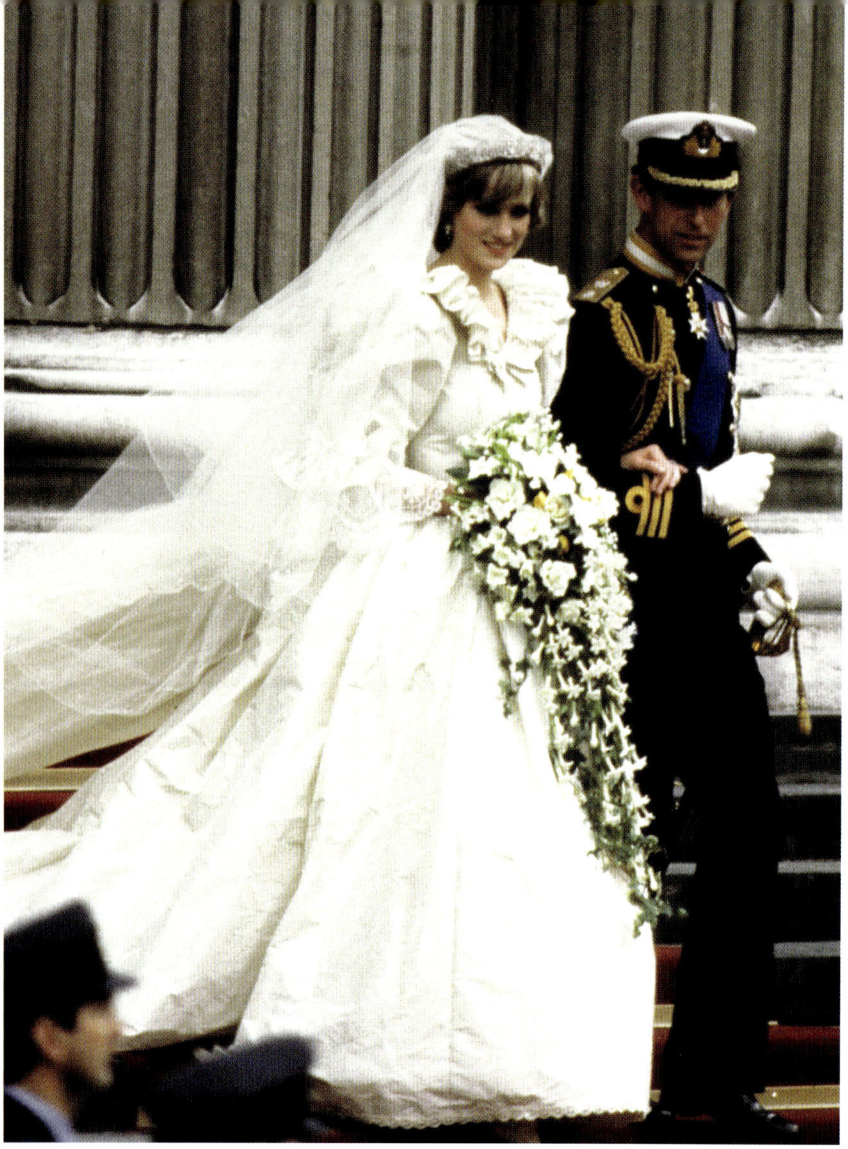

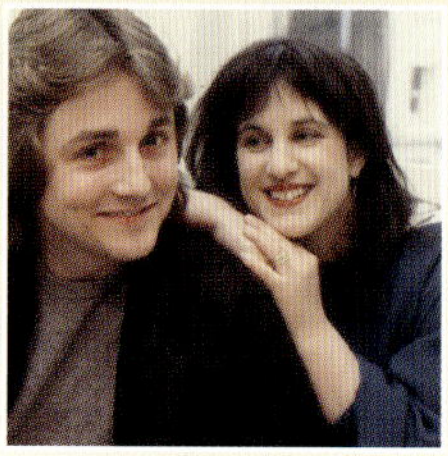

David and Elizabeth Emanuel
1952–; 1953–

Husband and wife David and Elizabeth Emanuel opened a dressmaking shop in London in 1977. In 1979, they closed their ready-to-wear business to concentrate on couture. Their style focused on contemporary reinterpretations of romantic historical references. Their success designing for Princess Diana's wedding brought the Emanuels international fame and a wealthy clientele. The couple divorced personally and professionally in 1990; both continue separate couture businesses.

THE LONGEST TRAIN
The 25-foot (7.5-m) detachable train fastened to the dress at the waist. It was bordered in its entirety with embroidered lace and trimmed down its length with three further bands of lace. The design of the lace was inspired by the Carrickmacross lace used in the bodice.

A touching testament

Lady Diana's dress had an instantaneous impact, shooting the Emanuels to fame and reigniting the popularity of romantic wedding gowns and the fairy-tale princess look. By the mid-1980s, bridal fashions had moved on, but the dress continued to resonate with emotional poignancy, a touching testament to the life of a doomed fairy-tale princess.

Following Princess Diana's death in a car accident in Paris in 1997, the dress toured internationally as part of the exhibition "Diana: A Celebration." It was later displayed in her family home and final resting place, Althorp Estate, England.

THE DRESS

STYLE Retrospectively romantic

SHAPE Crinoline

FABRIC Paper taffeta, lace, and tulle

COLOR Ivory

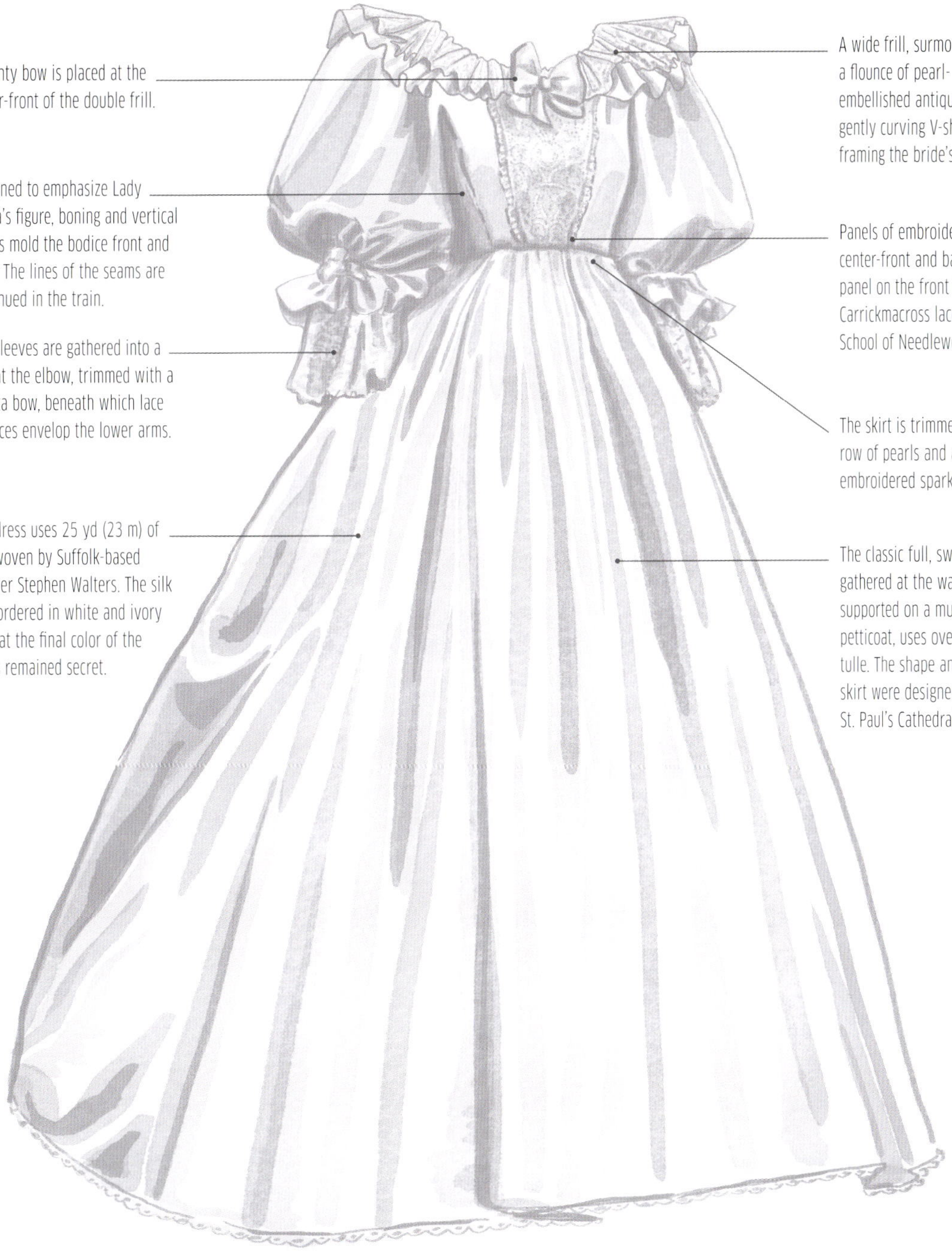

27

Carolina Herrera

1986 For Caroline Kennedy

The white organza, shamrock-embellished wedding dress Carolina Herrera created for Caroline Kennedy was a career-defining design for a couturier at the forefront of bridalwear.

Herrera began designing refined, meticulously tailored clothes in 1981, always ending her shows, according to *Vogue* magazine, with a "spellbinding wedding dress." But it was not until 1986, when Kennedy—daughter of Herrera's most famous client, Jacqueline Kennedy Onassis—commissioned her to create her wedding gown, that she received international recognition.

Embellished with memories

Kennedy requested that her wedding dress feature shamrocks in memory of her father, John F. Kennedy. Shamrocks were said to be a favorite of JFK, America's first Irish-Catholic president, who was assassinated in 1963. Herrera's design incorporated the emblem of Ireland into her signature broad-shouldered silhouette. The motif was appliquéd onto the fitted bodice of the short-sleeved white silk organza gown, all around the hem of its full crinoline skirt—which extended into a 25-foot (7.5-m) train—and scattered over the tulle veil. Herrera recalled that "the only people involved in the design of Kennedy's dress were the two of us."

The dress was an instant sensation. Buoyed by its critical success and inundated with requests for bridalwear, the designer developed a full bridal collection the following year, which hit the stores in January 1988. Nearly three decades later, Herrera remains as popular as ever with brides as the go-to designer for elegant and sculptural silhouettes combined with romantic, restrained embellishment.

Herrera has never exactly replicated Kennedy's much-coveted dress, recognizing that it was the personal expression of one woman and should remain sacrosanct. When creating her custom-made wedding gowns, the designer works with the individual brides to realize their particular dreams and aesthetic vision: "Whether it is a touch of color, or a certain fabric, they always want a dress that is unique."

While it would be counterintuitive for the designer to reproduce a couture design, Herrera recognizes the enduring appeal of Kennedy's dress nonetheless, and has returned to its silhouette and appliqué detailing on more than one occasion, updating these elements to keep pace with contemporary trends. In 1996, a full decade after Kennedy's wedding, she extracted the essence of her design into a paper pattern for the mass market. Following the Carolina Herrera Vogue Bridal Original sewing pattern (number 1776), brides could sew their own floral-embroidered gown with a high, round neck, gently puffed and padded shoulders, cap sleeves, a dropped waist adapted

ENDURING MOTIFS
Following the popularity of this design, scattered motifs became a signature of Herrera.

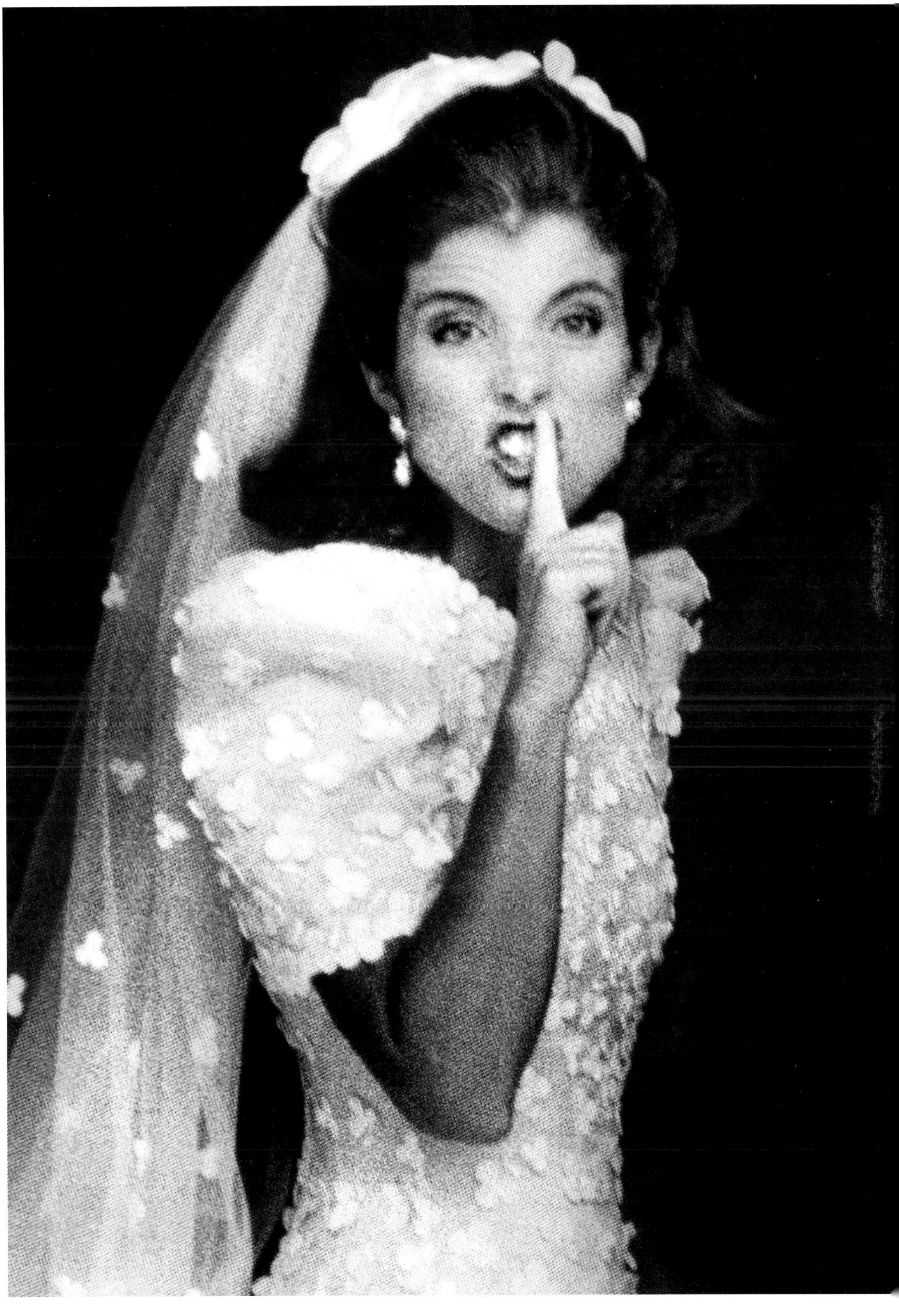

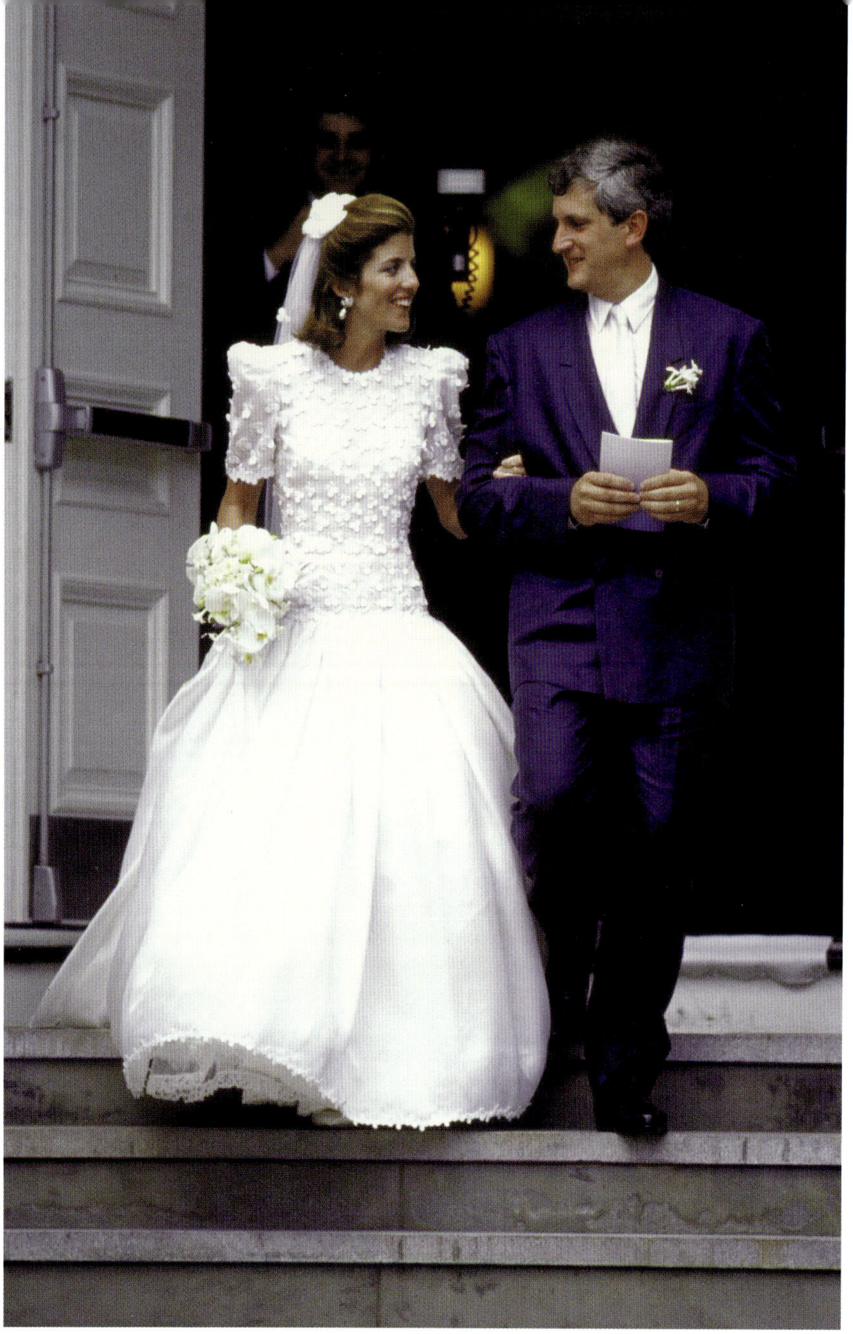

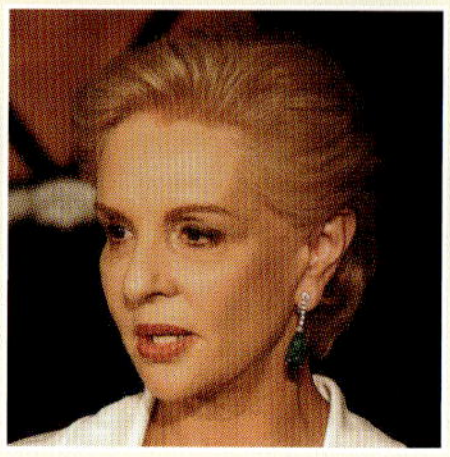

Carolina Herrera
1939–

Born into a family of Venezuelan aristocrats, Herrera was a famed beauty and New York socialite before turning to fashion design in 1980. "I prefer clothes that are simple, well cut, but with one major extravagance," she told *Vogue* magazine in 1987, the year in which she launched her bridal collection. The designer has dressed numerous celebrity brides, including Barbie, creating a collector's edition of the doll in 2008. The same year, she hit the headlines by designing a wedding dress for the film *Twilight*, and her achievements were recognized with a Lifetime Achievement Award from the Council of Fashion Designers of America.

1980s SILHOUETTE
The strong shoulders of the design are carefully balanced by the skirt and bodice.

with a scalloped edge, and a full flared skirt extending into a train edged with floral-embroidered braid.

Herrera, who created wedding dresses for all four of her daughters, paid tribute to her most famous design in her creation for Patricia, her youngest child. In 2002, she dressed her willowy, dark-haired, dark-eyed daughter in a long-sleeved, slim-fitting gown of white crepe satin scattered with tiny white appliquéd blossoms. Her picturesque snood was embellished with the same design.

Kennedy's shamrock-strewn wedding dress proved to be Herrera's own lucky charm, launching her career in bridal dress design and defining a winning formula. The strong silhouette and appliquéd floral details drawn from Kennedy's dress have become Herrera's enduring hallmarks.

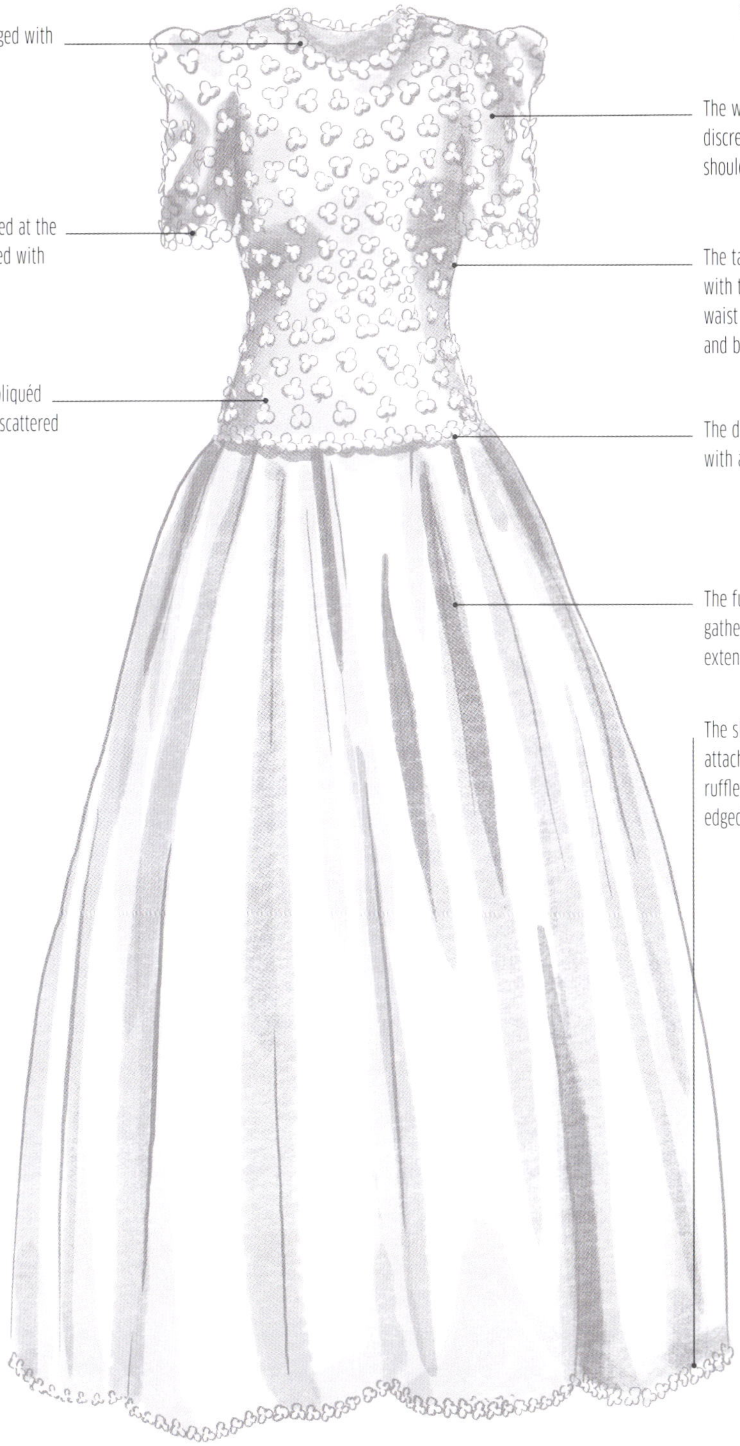

THE DRESS

STYLE Romantic

SHAPE Broad-shouldered

FABRIC Silk organza

COLOR White

28

Joe Casely-Hayford

1992 For Liberty

Fusing luxurious materials with a ragged DIY punk aesthetic, Joe Casely-Hayford exposed a surprising parallel between traditional bridalwear and countercultural style.

In 1992, Casely-Hayford was commissioned by Liberty department store in London to design a dress for their exhibition of contemporary British wedding fashion. Identified by *The Independent* newspaper in 2007 as one of the "Fabulous Fifty" most influential fashion creatives in London, Casely-Hayford made his name with an original combination of Savile Row tailoring and street style. His highly technical and precisely tailored clothes, peppered with witty and original detailing influenced by club culture, drew on the two pillars of British fashion: heritage and anarchy. Casely-Hayford's exploration of the relationship between alternative and conventional design underscored his bridal commission for Liberty.

Punk style meets tradition

Casely-Hayford produced a full-length ivory silk dress decorated with pearls. Luxurious silk is a traditional material for a wedding dress, but instead of the usual lustrous varieties, Casely-Hayford selected raw silk, which he treated in a most unconventional manner. Fraying the fabric, piecing it together in a patchwork formation, and further embellishing it with metal chains and rivets, Casely-Hayford mimicked an aggressive punk aesthetic.

The design of the dress followed the slender, feminine lines of a column, but deviated from this popular bridal style by introducing elements of the construction and styling of a leather jacket—an emblem of renegade rebellion. Many subcultural groups have made the leather jacket their calling card, using studs, hand-painted slogans and symbols, patches, frayed fabric, badges, and safety pins to express who they are and what they believe. Casely-Hayford cleverly combined this practice of customization with the bridal tradition of placing interesting detailing on the rear of the dress to entertain the congregation who can see only the bride's back during the ceremony. The back of this dress was decorated with a large, metal-studded heart motif, pierced by an arrow and surrounded by the embroidered slogan "Farewell My Sweet Liberty," alluding to the loss of personal freedom symbolized by a wedding ceremony.

The antifashion wedding dress

Casely-Hayford's dress also drew on Liberty's alternative design heritage. When Sir Arthur Lasenby Liberty opened his first shop in 1875, he was at the forefront of the artistic movement that rejected prevailing Victorian tastes in the quest for improved standards of design. Artistic dress was adopted by independent-minded British women who

PUNK DETAILING
The back of the dress is decorated with metal rivets in a pierced heart motif, and the slogan "Farewell My Sweet Liberty" is worked in embroidery and studs.

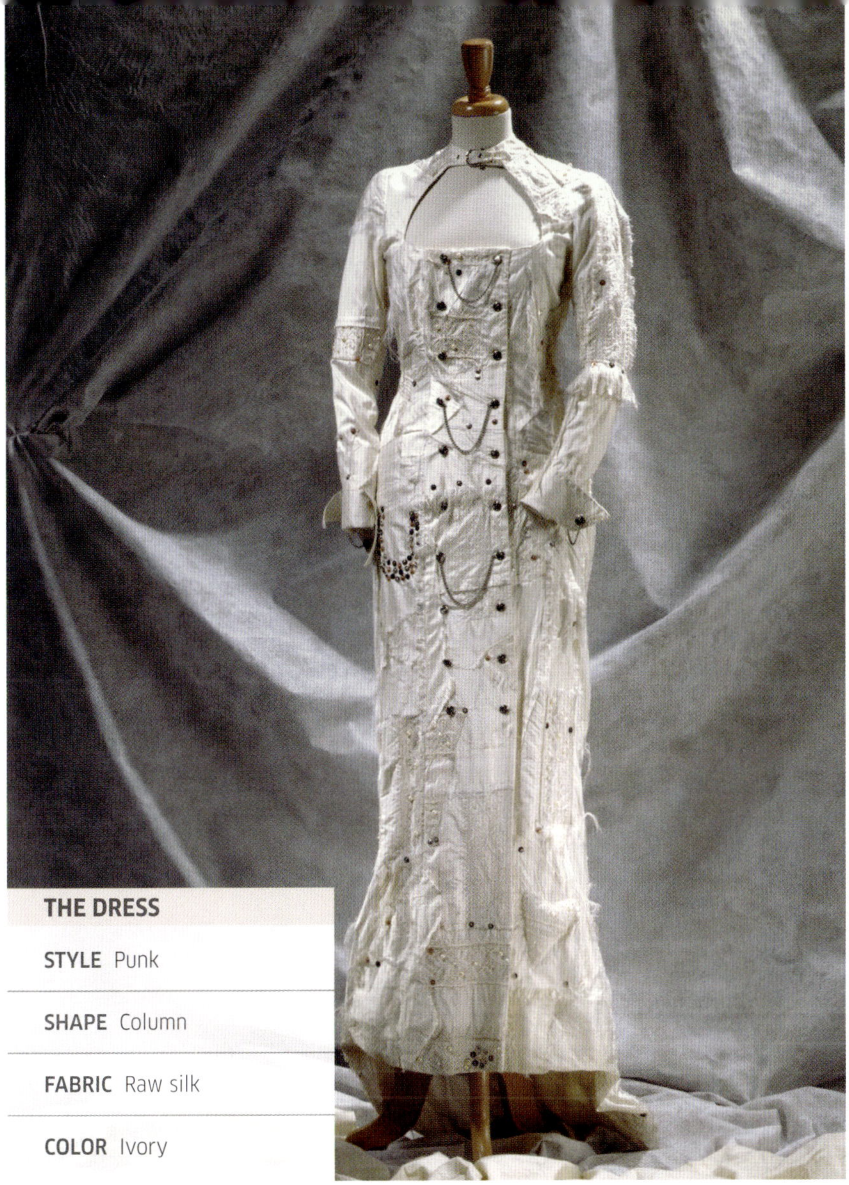

THE DRESS	
STYLE Punk	
SHAPE Column	
FABRIC Raw silk	
COLOR Ivory	

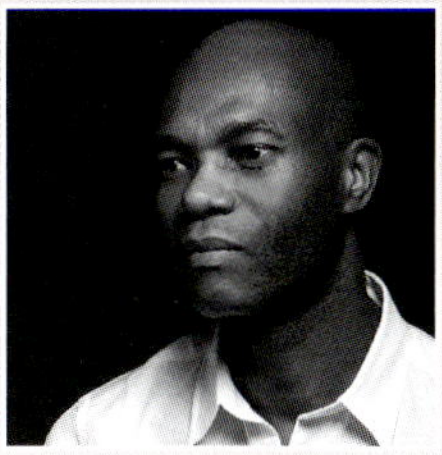

Joe Casely-Hayford
1956–

Born in Ghana, Joe Casely-Hayford came to London with his family as a child. In the early 1970s he worked as an apprentice on Savile Row and studied fine tailoring at the Tailor & Cutter Academy. From the late 1970s he produced performance clothes for rock groups. In 1984 Casely-Hayford launched his menswear label, followed in 1986 with a womenswear collection, and in 2009 with a new luxury menswear range that he designed with his son. These collections, which were sold worldwide, now have a strong following in Japan. Casely-Hayford, who was nominated for the British Fashion Council's Most Innovative Designer award in 1991, has produced various collaborations with mass retailers.

refused to accept the dictates of restrictive couture fashion. Liberty fabrics, produced in collaboration with the dyer and printer Thomas Wardle, were popular with artistic brides who cut and draped the fabric into unconventional wedding dresses. In 1884, Liberty set up a costume studio specializing in free-flowing quasi-medieval gowns made from Liberty fabrics, marketed as "never out of fashion." Liberty's wedding dresses were worn primarily by bohemian brides who were attracted by the store's reputation for alternative dress.

Countercultural styles and traditional bridalwear are in many ways at opposite ends of the sartorial and cultural spectrums. Alternative dress is resolutely antifashion, an expression of identity and group-belonging outside the mainstream culture. In contrast, the white wedding dress, in its most traditional form, represents established customs and social structures. However, it too can stand outside of fluctuating fashion trends and ideally it represents the personality and style of individual brides. Casely-Hayford's post-punk wedding dress stood between these two polarities, highlighting their surprising similarities. As an iconic alternative design it also drew attention to the rebellious history of the antifashion wedding dress.

29

Catherine Walker

1992 For Lady Helen Windsor

With its distinctive arching neckline, the wedding dress Catherine Walker created for Lady Helen Windsor was a defining highlight of the designer's illustrious career.

This uniquely structured embroidered gown is testament to the intelligence, consummate craftsmanship, and refined aesthetic of one of Britain's most celebrated couturiers. When Lady Helen, daughter of the Duke and Duchess of Kent, became engaged to art dealer Timothy Taylor, she commissioned her wedding gown from her mother and Princess Diana's favorite designer: Catherine Walker. Walker's discretion and understanding of the requirements of her clientele won her a dedicated following of stylish celebrities and society ladies in the UK.

Drawing on history and tradition

Preparing for her prestigious commission, Walker displayed her characteristically rigorous approach to the design process. The venue for the nuptials was to be St. George's Chapel at Windsor Castle. Here, Walker says, she spent many hours studying its sixteenth-century architecture in order to develop a sympathetic language for the design of the dress. She found her inspiration in the chapel's Gothic windows, going on to echo their structure in the dress's deeply curved neckline, sculptural collar, and upwardly curving capped sleeves with turned-back cuffs. The design of the pearl and diamanté embroidery that framed the neckline and formed a pendant to the collar was arrived at after the designer had studied the pattern of the diamonds in the Kent family tiara that Lady Helen was going to wear. Walker also undertook detailed research into variations of embroidery forms before settling on the final design of the collar.

Walker's pearl-white wedding dress was a distinctly modern interpretation of its historical reference points, free from nostalgic revivalism. Constructed from ten full-length panels of silk zibeline, the dress flared out in the clean fluid lines that were Walker's signature, falling into a soft skirt and a 6-foot (1.8-m) train—proportions the designer based on her extensive investigation of the chapel's layout and proportions.

A labor of love

The construction of the dress was so complicated that Walker quipped in her autobiography that she nearly had to bribe her team of seamstresses to work on it. Getting the fit exactly right was the key to its success. When the bride lost a little weight leading up to her wedding day, Walker entirely recut the bodice so that it held its crisp lines. Demonstrating her customary delicacy, the designer made this last-minute alteration unbeknownst to the bride. Walker's dedication to her craft is most evident in the

IN CONTEXT
The design of the dress was carefully based on the Gothic architectural details of the wedding venue.

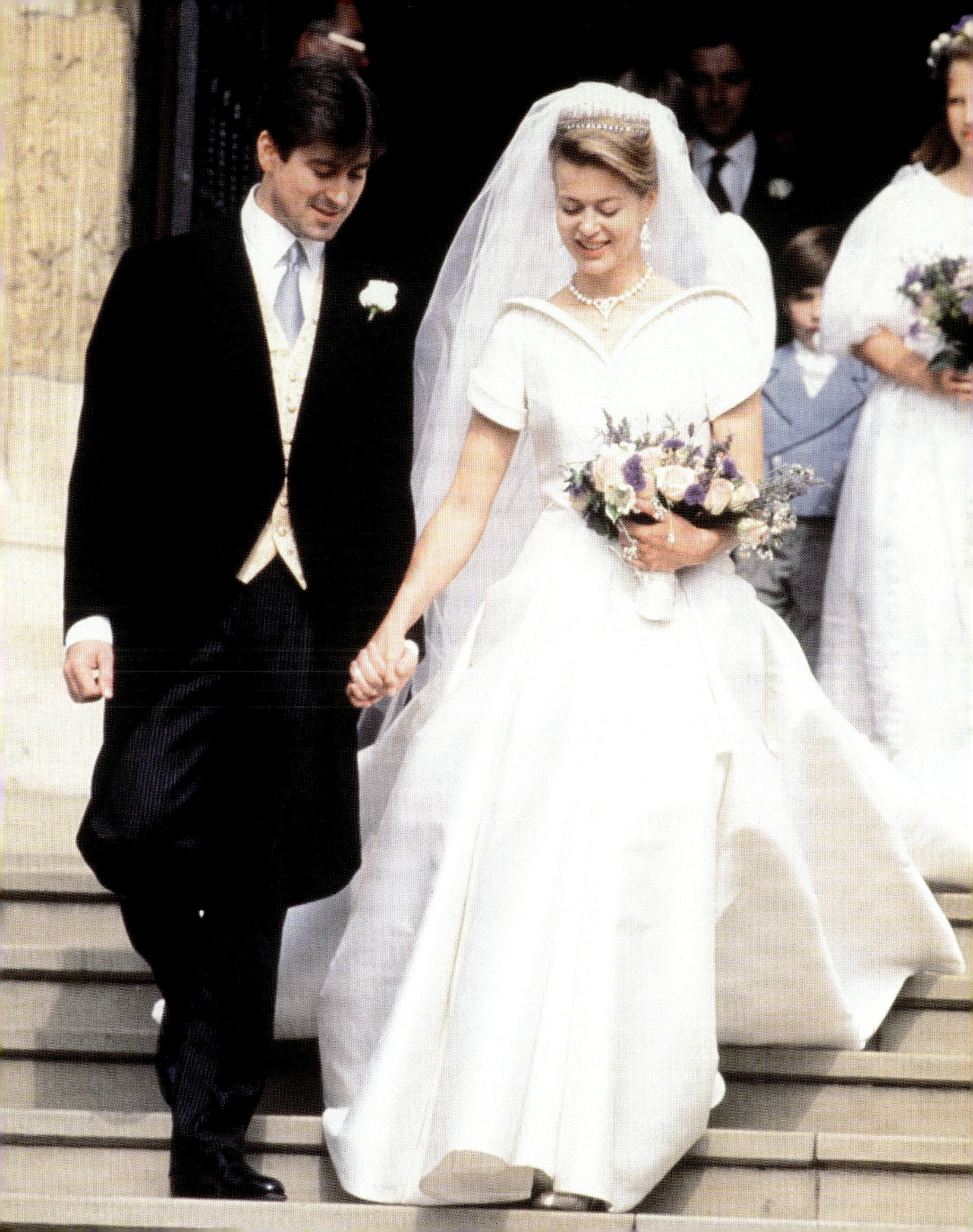

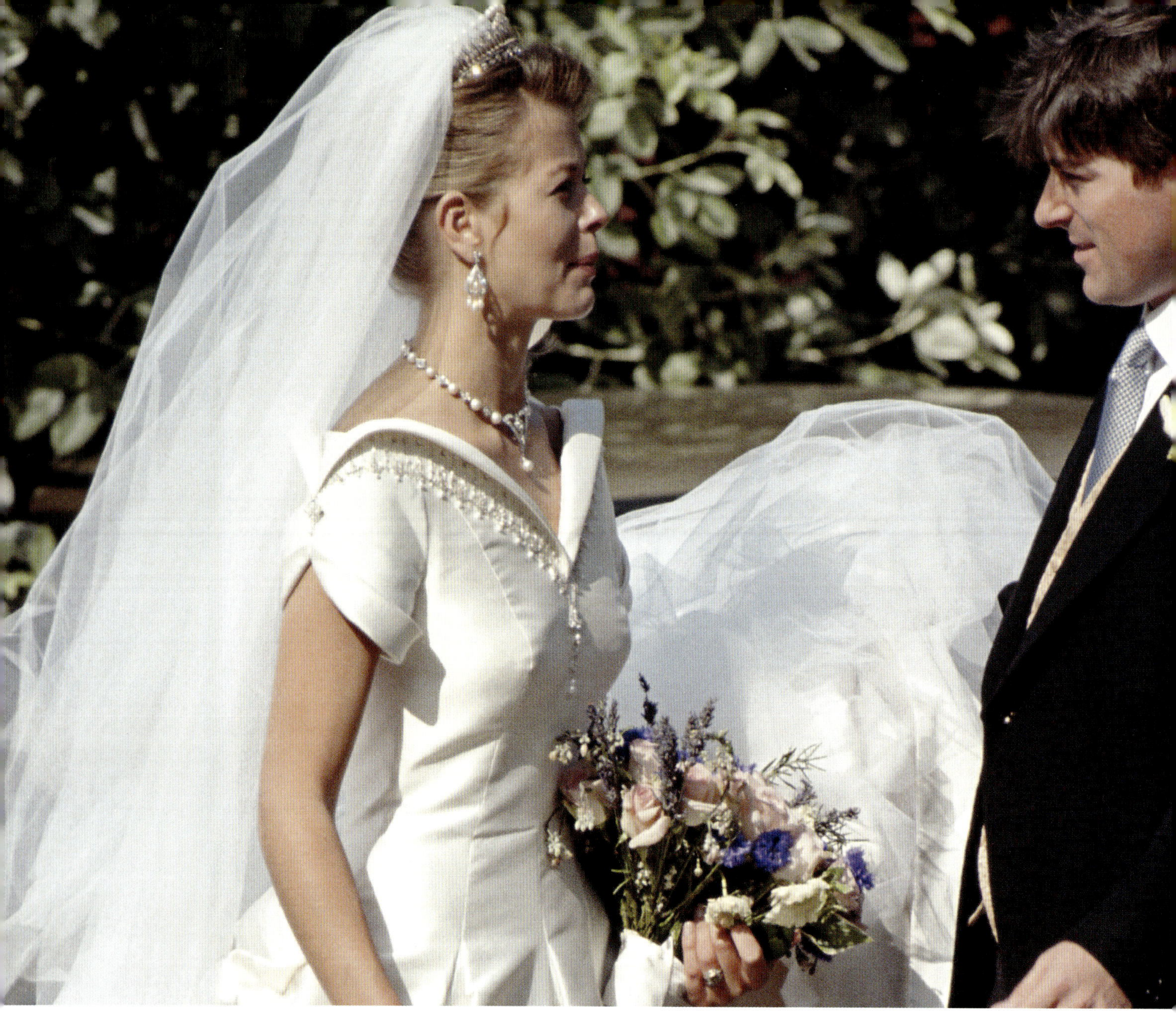

dress's defining feature—the folded collar that projected over the curved neckline in a seemingly smooth and seamless arc, its two sides dovetailing with exact precision in the center of the dress.

The design is testament

In her autobiography, Walker wrote of this gown: "When Lady Helen Windsor walked down the aisle, I knew I had given her my best." Walker was an anomaly in the fashion world: known as "composed, quiet, and reserved," she preferred her creations to speak for themselves, which this design did admirably. Following Walker's death in 2010, Lady Helen's wedding gown was frequently cited as one of the crowning achievements of Walker's career. Catherine Walker & Co. continues to create wedding dresses in the style of Lady Helen's gown: pure-cut patterns fashioned from luxurious fabrics and enhanced with sparing surface embellishment.

TIARA TOPPING
The folded neckline is trimmed with pearl and diamanté embroidery based on the pattern of diamonds in the bride's tiara.

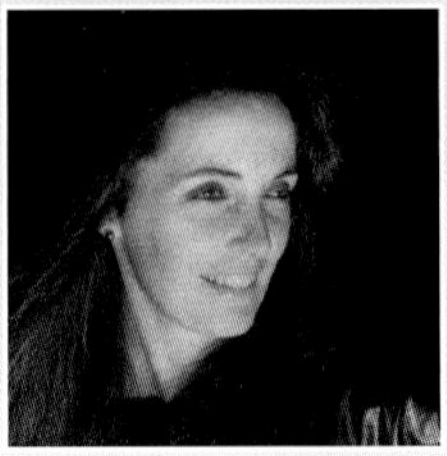

Catherine Walker
1945–2010

French-born Catherine Baheux studied aesthetics and philosophy at university. While researching her PhD, she moved to England, where she married and settled. In 1977, after studying fashion at night school, she founded the Chelsea Design Co. with her second husband. The firm was rebranded Catherine Walker & Co. in 1994. The London-based company follows the model of a traditional Parisian atelier, with workshops for tailoring, dressmaking, and embroidery. Walker was honored with awards for the British Fashion Council's Designer of the Year for British Couture in 1990 and Designer of the Year for Glamour in 1991.

THE DRESS	
STYLE	Modern Gothic
SHAPE	Fluid and full-skirted
FABRIC	Silk zibeline
COLOR	Pearl white

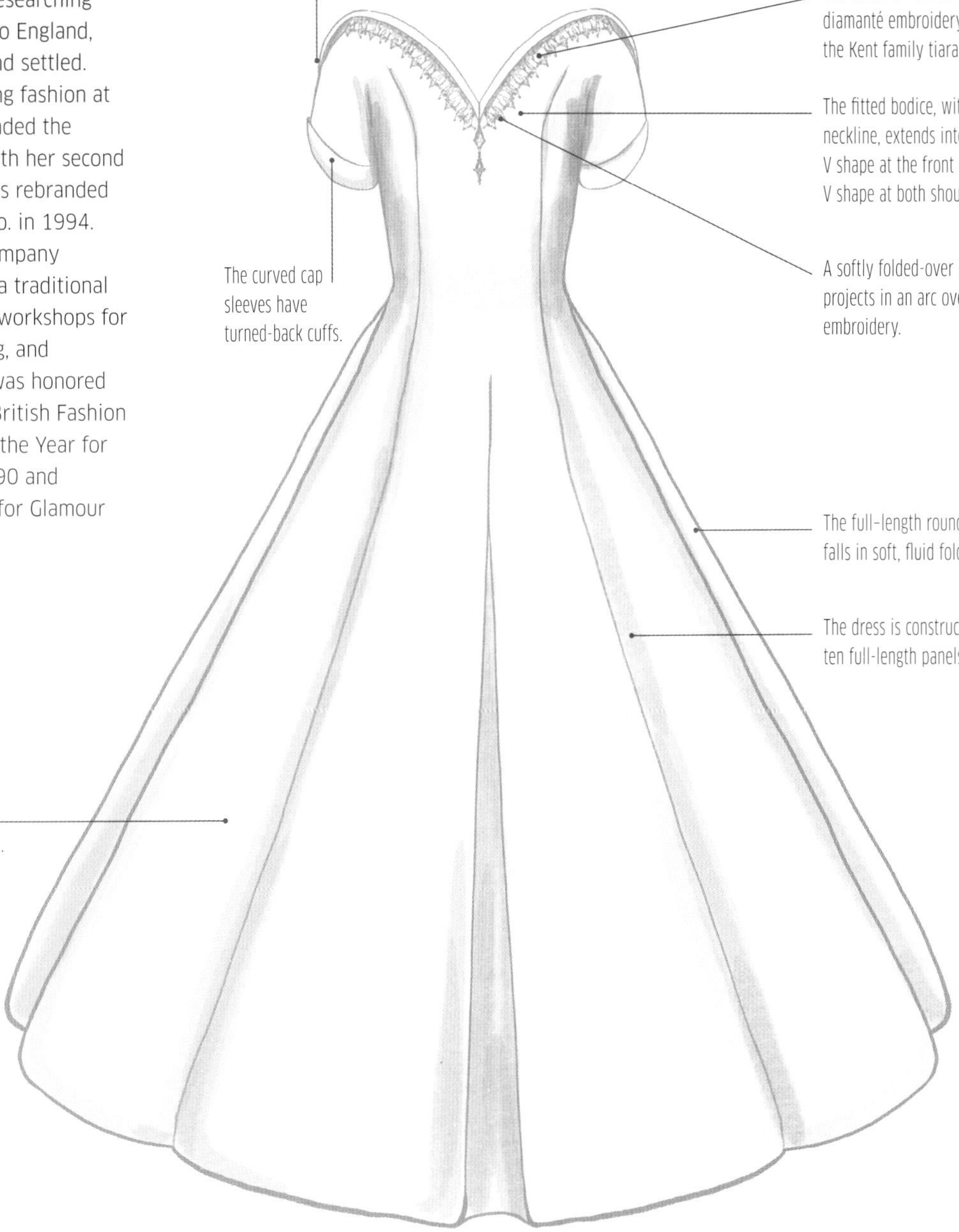

30

Christian Lacroix

1992 Fall/Winter

Christian Lacroix's lavishly embroidered black satin wedding dress made an elaborate aesthetic and cultural statement.

In 1992, Lacroix, acknowledged by *Vogue* magazine as "the master of fantasy and fashion as entertainment," concluded his Fall/Winter 1992–1993 haute couture collection with a provocative black wedding dress. Typifying the designer's unrestrained creative process, its striking silhouette, overlaid with rich texture, exuberant ornamentation, and bold colors, was a celebration of excess. A complex construction, the dress was composed of four parts: a black net body, under a long-sleeved corseted black bodice, a full black skirt, and an asymmetrically swagged off-white overskirt. Each component was decorated with hand embroidery realized by the famous Lesage atelier. Gold leaf, looping figure-of-eight gold threads, and a "necklace" of multicolored paste gems and gold beads adorned the high neckline. The deep cuffs of the bodice, along with its low round neckline curving over rigidly puffed shoulders, were encrusted with heavy, scrolling, gold-filigree-style embroidery, gold baubles, beads, and purple paste gems.

Floral motifs on the front of the corset were worked in vibrant red, pink, purple, and green silk chenille threads, while garlands of flowers in the same combination of chenille threads were swathed across the front of the underskirt. Two large paste cocktail rings, worn one on each hand over black net gloves, and a black tulle veil, attached to jeweled hair ornaments worn on a high chignon, completed the ensemble.

Flamboyant and dramatic

Lacroix's design melded the historical and Spanish influences that recurred throughout his career. The corseted bodice and swagged skirt gave a nod to the structure of eighteenth-century and Renaissance designs, while the embroidery distilled the grandiosity and luxury of Baroque ornamentation. The bold combination of bright colors and black, the rich floral embroidery, and the mantilla-style headpiece spoke of his interest in flamenco culture. It drew on a profusion of sources synthesized by the designer's contemporary sensibilities, described by *Vogue* magazine as being "perfectly calibrated to appeal to Nouvelle Society."

When Lacroix established his salon in 1986, he was hailed as the latest "savior of couture." His fantastical creations revived the haute couture industry and were bought with relish by "the monied proponents of 1980s conspicuous consumption." It was the opinion of *Vogue* magazine's then editor-in-chief, Grace Mirabella, that Lacroix was a designer for "women who dream of grand spectacle."

WHO HAS THE RIGHT?
Lacroix's black gown questions whether it is appropriate for contemporary brides to wed in white, a color symbolic of virginal purity.

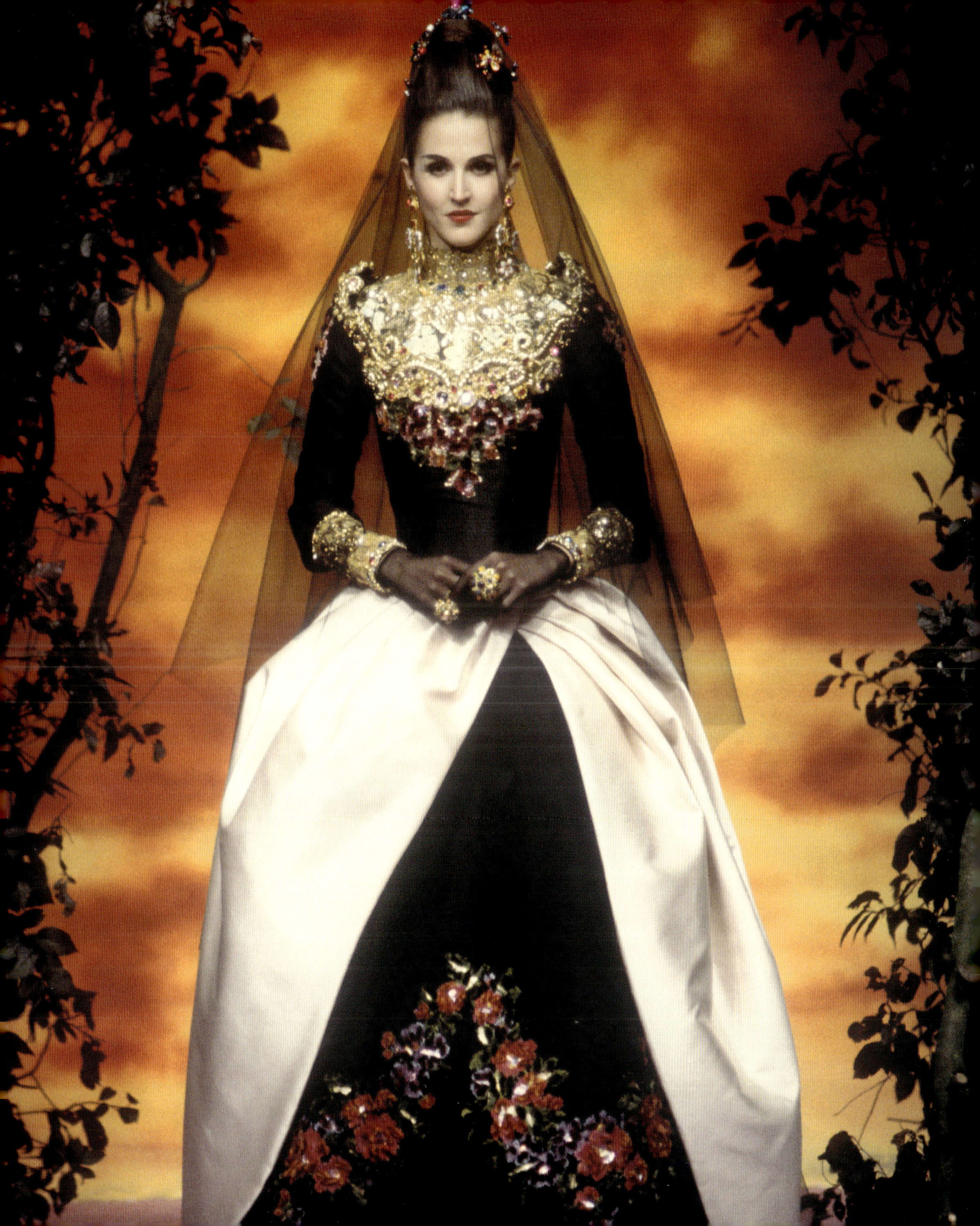

Where better to showcase a Lacroix design than the grandest of contemporary spectacles: the wedding ceremony. Bridalwear was central to Lacroix's business. Lacroix's designs, which cost between $23,000 and $92,000, accounted for 40 percent of his orders. In 1992 alone he received eighteen commissions, and twelve the following year, primarily from Middle Eastern, Asian, and European clients. Lacroix recognized that, for his clientele, "a wedding dress is one woman's dream of being center stage, as though it were theater or ballet." In making wedding dresses, the designer said he acted as "an assistant to the imagination" of wealthy young women. "The girls who come here, they have a certain story in their mind about their wedding. ... It's more about playing a certain character than about fashion."

Lacroix's black wedding dress, titled Qui a le Droit?, represents the theatrical, unorthodox approach to bridalwear that attracted brides-to-be to the designer. This particular dress wasn't worn by a bride but was created for the catwalk, from whence it was donated to the Victoria and Albert Museum in London. This unusual and extreme take on the wedding dress was made as a comment on the relevance of the traditional "virginal" white gown in contemporary society. "Who has the right?" Lacroix asks—via the dramatic medium of black silk satin—to be wed in white?

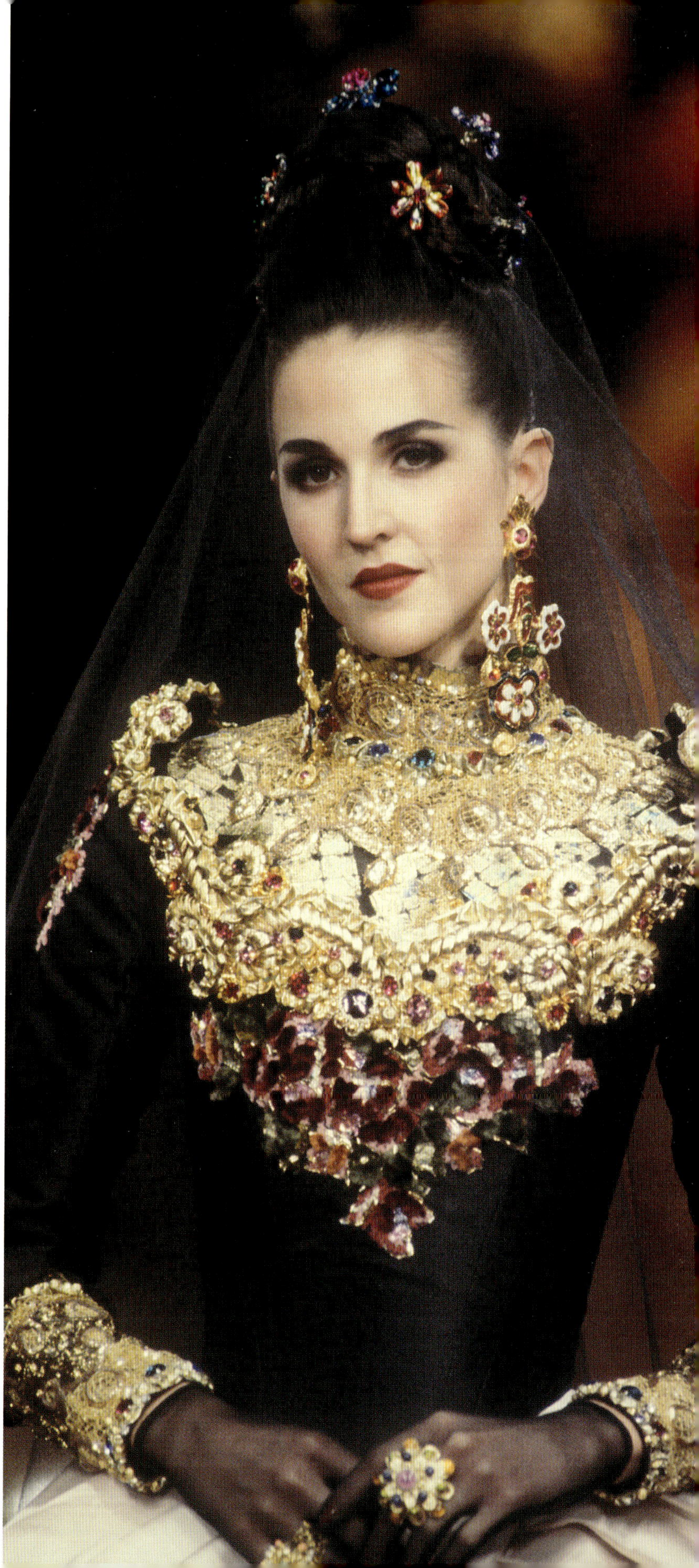

EMBELLISHED DESIGN
The neckline is trimmed with heavy, twisted, scrolling gold-thread embroidery, pink paste jewels, and gold-thread-covered baubles.

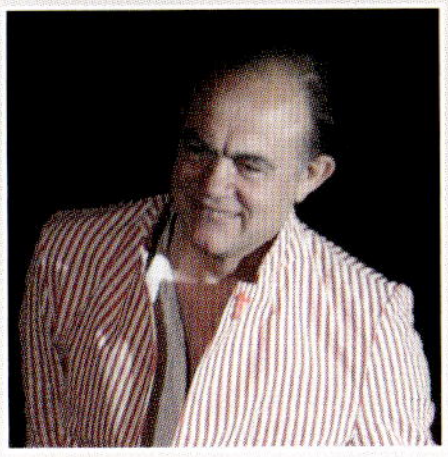

Christian Lacroix

1951–

Born in Arles, France, Christian Lacroix studied history of art with plans to become a museum curator. Instead, he joined Hermès as a design assistant in 1978. In 1981 he moved to the House of Patou, where he learned the intricacies of haute couture, establishing his own salon in 1987. In 2005 he created Christina Aguilera's flamenco-inspired wedding dress. Failing to find the balance between "the needs of art and business," Lacroix was forced into bankruptcy in 2009 and severed all ties with his namesake house in 2010.

THE DRESS

STYLE Pseudo Spanish and Baroque

SHAPE Corseted and full-skirted

FABRIC Silk satin

COLOR Black and off-white

HIDDEN DETAILS

- The low, wide neckline, scooping over the shoulders, extends into a V shape at the back.
- Inverted pleat at the center-back of the waist; deep, dropped, V-shaped waist at the front and back.

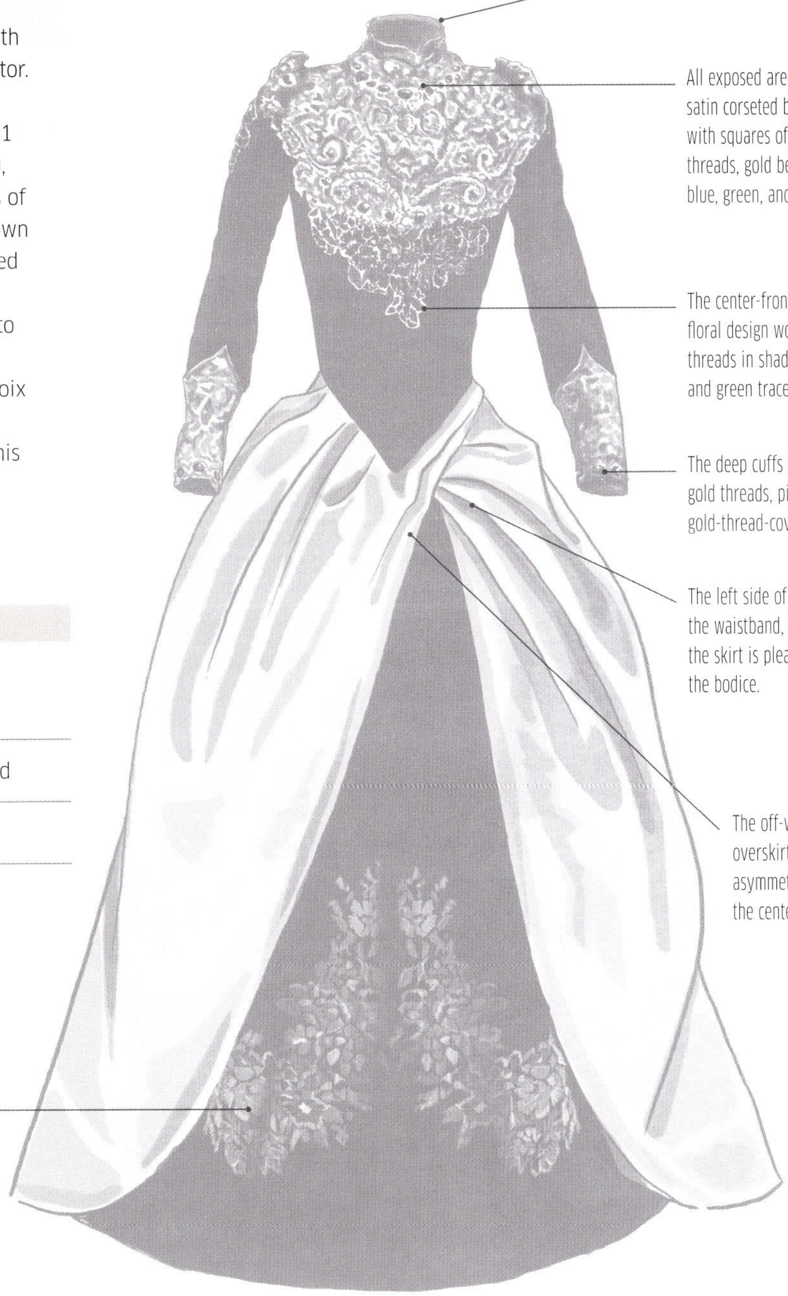

31

Gianni Versace

1997 Atelier Versace Fall/Winter

Brash and super-sexy, the silver micro-mini wedding dress worn by Naomi Campbell as the finale of Gianni Versace's haute couture Fall/Winter 1997–1998 collection proved to be the designer's swan song.

Described by *Vogue* as "fashion's rock star," the designer had a flair for capturing the media's attention with high-octane glamour and provocative gestures. Versace dominated the fashion industry in the 1980s and 1990s with his unmistakable designs. Sparkling micro-minidresses, skin-tight jumpsuits, plunging necklines, vivacious top-to-toe prints, and risqué bondage details became instantly recognizable signatures. The designer capitalized on the drama of his collections with fashion shows produced like rock concerts and sensational advertising campaigns that brought his designs to the attention of an international audience. Versace's flesh-baring, bottom-skimming wedding dress, epitomizing his world-famous aesthetic, made a fitting statement to cap his career.

Short, striking, and seductive

Composed of double-layered silver Oroton—a light metal mesh invented by the designer in 1982—and embellished with beaded Byzantine-inspired crosses, the dress shimmered and swung seductively upon the body of the celebrity supermodel as she stalked down the runway. Upon turning to head back along the runway, the model dramatically exposed a glittering silver cross that marked the length and width of the short tulle veil she wore. Suzi Menkes of the *New York Times* later called Versace's reworking of the Byzantine cross motif "ominous inspiration." As the show concluded, Versace appeared onstage to receive his applause. To the soundtrack of British electronic group The Prodigy's most controversial hit, "Smack My Bitch Up," he thanked his famous bride with a kiss. Less than a week later, the designer was shot dead on the steps of his home in Miami Beach.

The future

Donatella Versace took over the responsibility of designing for her brother's brand following his death. In 2012 she recalled for the first time in public the moment that made history: "I can look at it now with a smile," she told the *New York Times*. "I remember my last moments with Gianni, the rehearsal, the show. But finally I have freedom. I am not afraid." Her Fall/Winter collection of 2012–2013 was the first spectacular presentation of the Atelier since her brother's death. In this emotional collection, Donatella Versace revisited the Byzantine crosses and metal mesh fabric of her brother's signature wedding dress, reworking those details into her new designs.

THE MINIDRESS
Designers have raised hems on wedding gowns for decades, but Versace's dress stands out for being overtly sexy, even by today's standards.

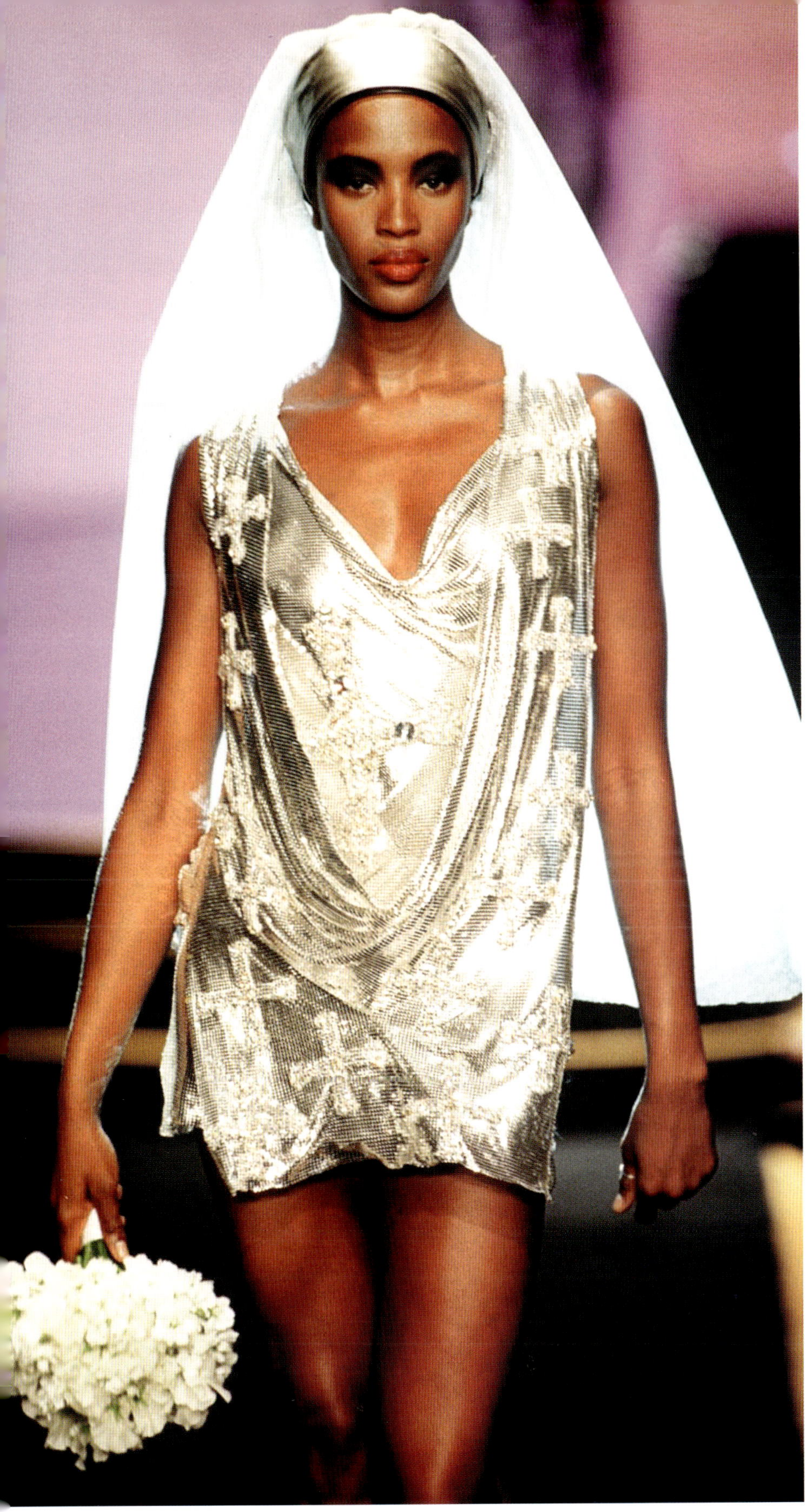

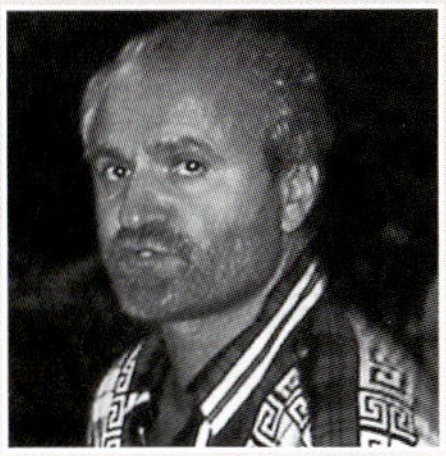

Gianni Versace
1946–1997

Gianni Versace founded the Gianni Versace Company in 1978. Assisted by his brother, Santo, and sister, Donatella, the designer built his company into a hugely successful international brand empire. Versace's exuberant Atelier haute couture collection, launched in Paris in 1989, was aimed at the mega-rich and the red carpet, but the designer reached a broader section of society with his diffusion ranges.

In the early 1990s, Versace was credited with launching the supermodel phenomenon, their glamour and celebrity being the perfect representation of the brand. However, crucial to Versace's success was his skill. As *Vogue* magazine noted: "Were his clothes less well made, his daring mixes of high art and popular culture might have descended into the tawdry or tacky." The designer was killed in 1997. His sister, Donatella, took over the reins as chief designer.

THE DRESS

STYLE Über-glam

SHAPE Micro-mini

FABRIC Oroton

COLOR Silver

32

Yohji Yamamoto

1998 Fall/Winter

Yohji Yamamoto's oversized costume gently mocked the traditional statement value of a white wedding dress.

The wedding dress is traditionally the finale of a couture fashion show. Usually, this show-ending dress is a spectacular gown that captures the essence of the collection in an extreme form. The vast crinoline wedding dress and hat ensemble that concluded Yamamoto's Fall/Winter 1998–1999 presentation defined the designer's anarchic experiments with volume, structure, and movement. Model Jodie Kidd was sent onto the runway in a hoopskirt dress with a circumference measuring more than 39 feet (12 m). The garment extended so far from the model's body that it looked like a separate structure—almost like a wedding marquee—out of which emerged her slender frame, clad in a simple streamlined bodice. The "palanquin" hat echoed the proportions of the skirt, being so large that four poles, carried by attendants, were required to support it. The fragility of the model's body contrasted with the monumental size of the ensemble, leading some fashion historians to interpret the dress as a protective barrier or fortress.

Finding absurdity in tradition

Made of fluid white silk supported upon hoops of bamboo, the dress caricatured extravagant crinoline wedding gowns. Yamamoto has said of his approach, "With my eyes turned to the past, I walk backwards into the future." The crinoline, first fashionable in the mid-nineteenth century, continues to be used for traditional wedding gowns as the foundation upon which the rich surface of silk is shown to its best advantage. Yamamoto's monstrous crinoline satirizes the excesses and extravagance of the form and, he claims, plays up to mainstream society's perception of the vanity and stupidity of fashion. But, with his customary dexterity, Yamamoto transformed this absurd creation into an object of beauty. Once set in motion, the dress defied its apparent bulk and floated with grace and weightless ease down the runway.

The iconic finale

Finale wedding dresses are rarely worn by real brides; their iconic status derives from their cultural cachet. Yamamoto's oversized dress is perhaps the most outstanding example of the finale wedding dress, whose impact resonated far beyond the initial and inevitable publicity it received after it was first shown. It has remained an abiding source of fascination for fashion historians, emblematic of the practices of avant-garde design that succeeded in elevating the intellectual status of fashion. Images of Yamamoto's dress continue to circulate online, in print, and in exhibitions.

STRANGE TRANQUILITY
Despite its size, the dress floated down the runway.

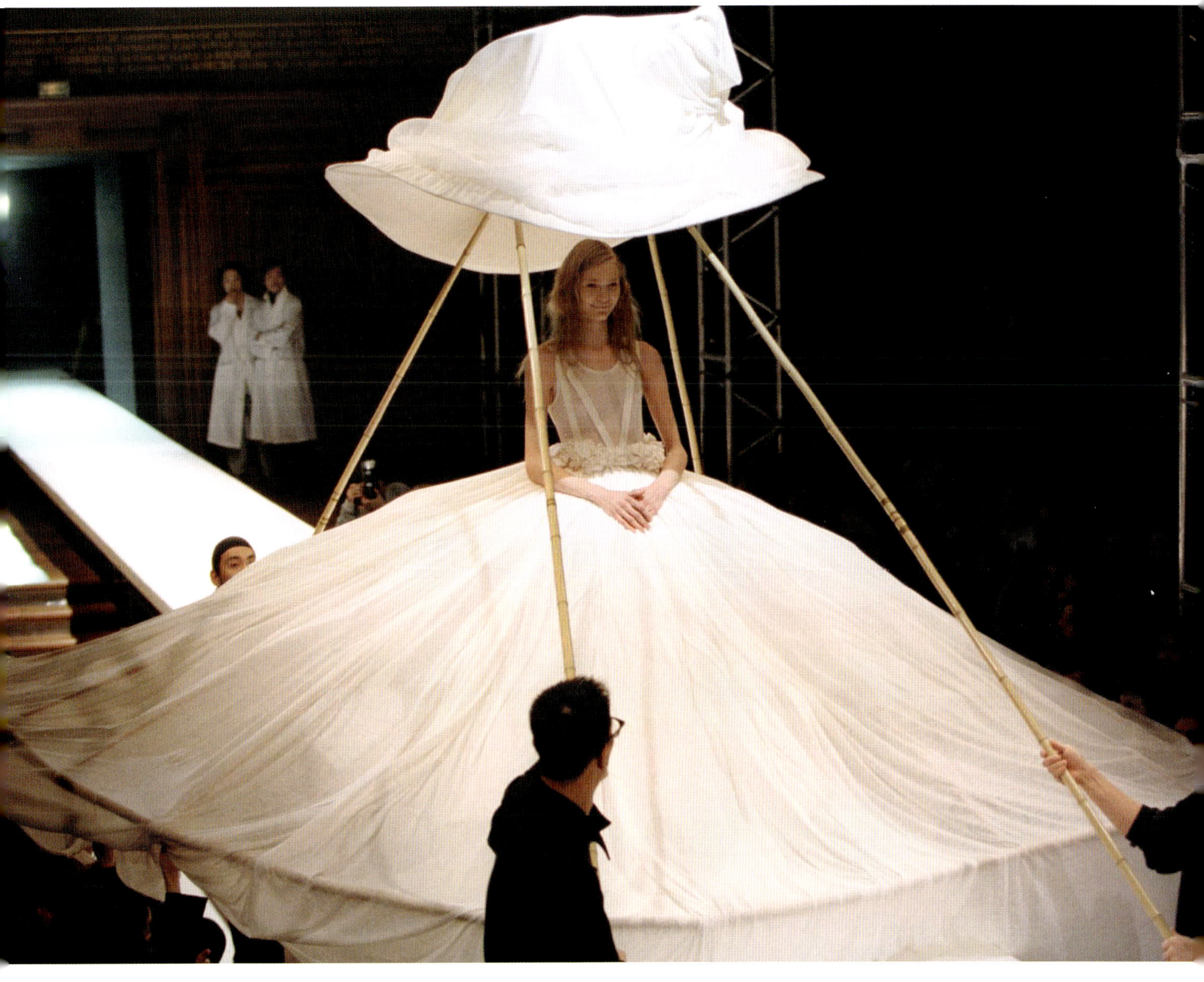

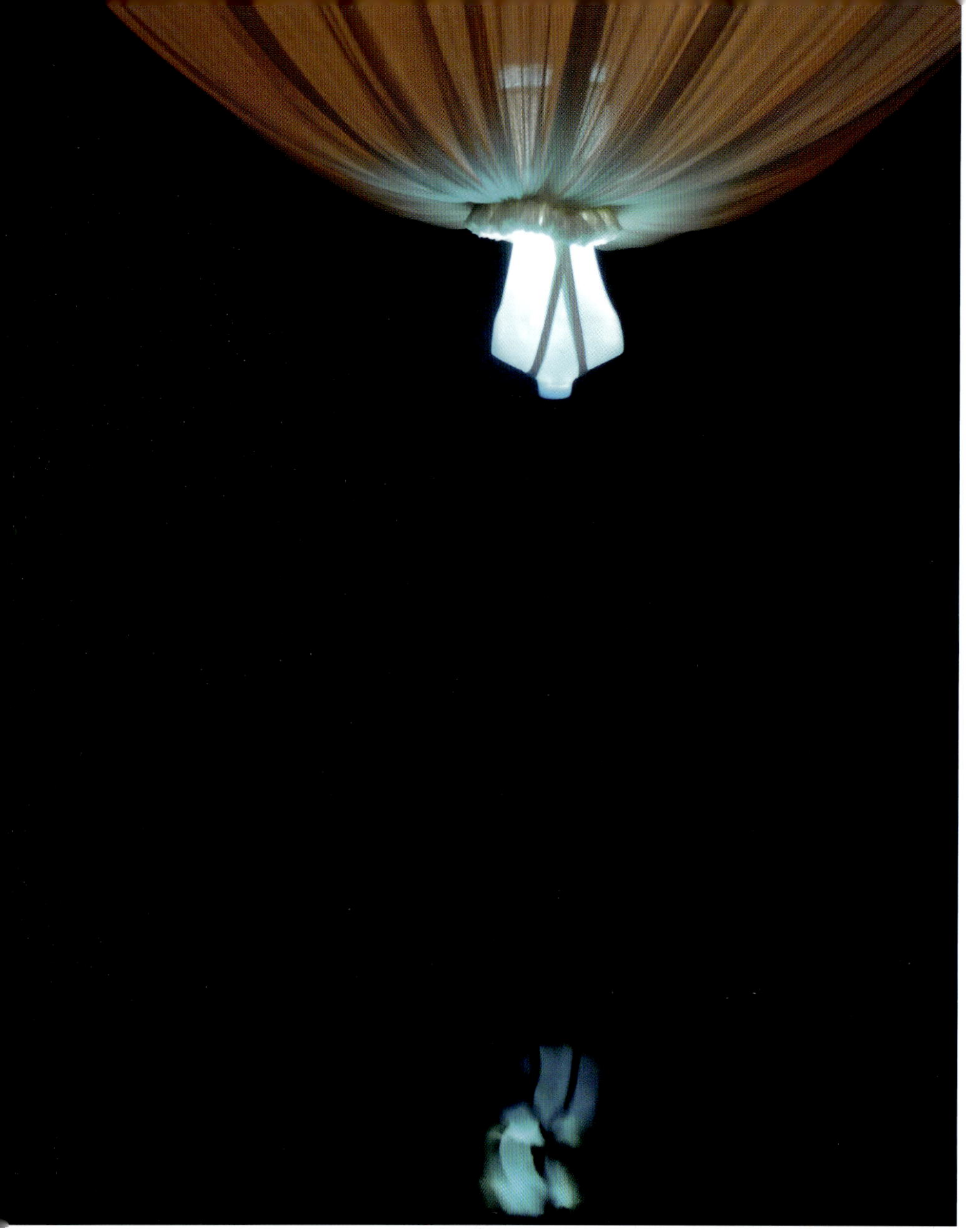

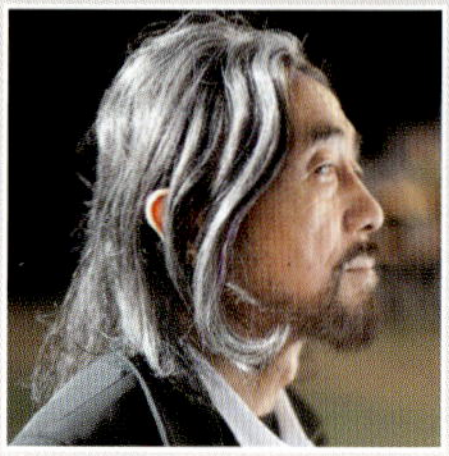

Yohji Yamamoto
1946–

Japanese designer Yohji Yamamoto began his fashion career in 1966, working in his mother's clothing shop in Tokyo. In 1972, he established Yamamoto Inc. and launched Y's, a womenswear line that made its Paris debut in 1981, the same year he launched the more experimental Yohji Yamamoto label. Yamamoto has gained a cult following of avant-gardists valuing his severe, deconstructed aesthetic. His sphere of influence continues to increase with designs produced for other mainstream brands. With every step, *Vogue* says, Yamamoto remains constant in his passion for "achieving anti-fashion through fashion."

SUSPENDED BEAUTY
The dress is hung upside down, reflected in the water beneath.

Making waves

In 2011, the crinoline dress was resurrected as a piece of installation art entitled "Yohji Making Waves." Spectators were rowed across a reflective artificial lake to make closer inspection of the dress, which was suspended over the black water. Waves blew across the presentation space, created in the middle of a cavernous hydraulic power station in Wapping, East London.

HIDDEN DETAILS

- The dress has a separate underskirt.
- The hat cannot be worn without the assistance of four attendants, one for each of the poles that support it.

THE DRESS

STYLE Architectural

SHAPE Crinoline

FABRIC Silk georgette

COLOR White

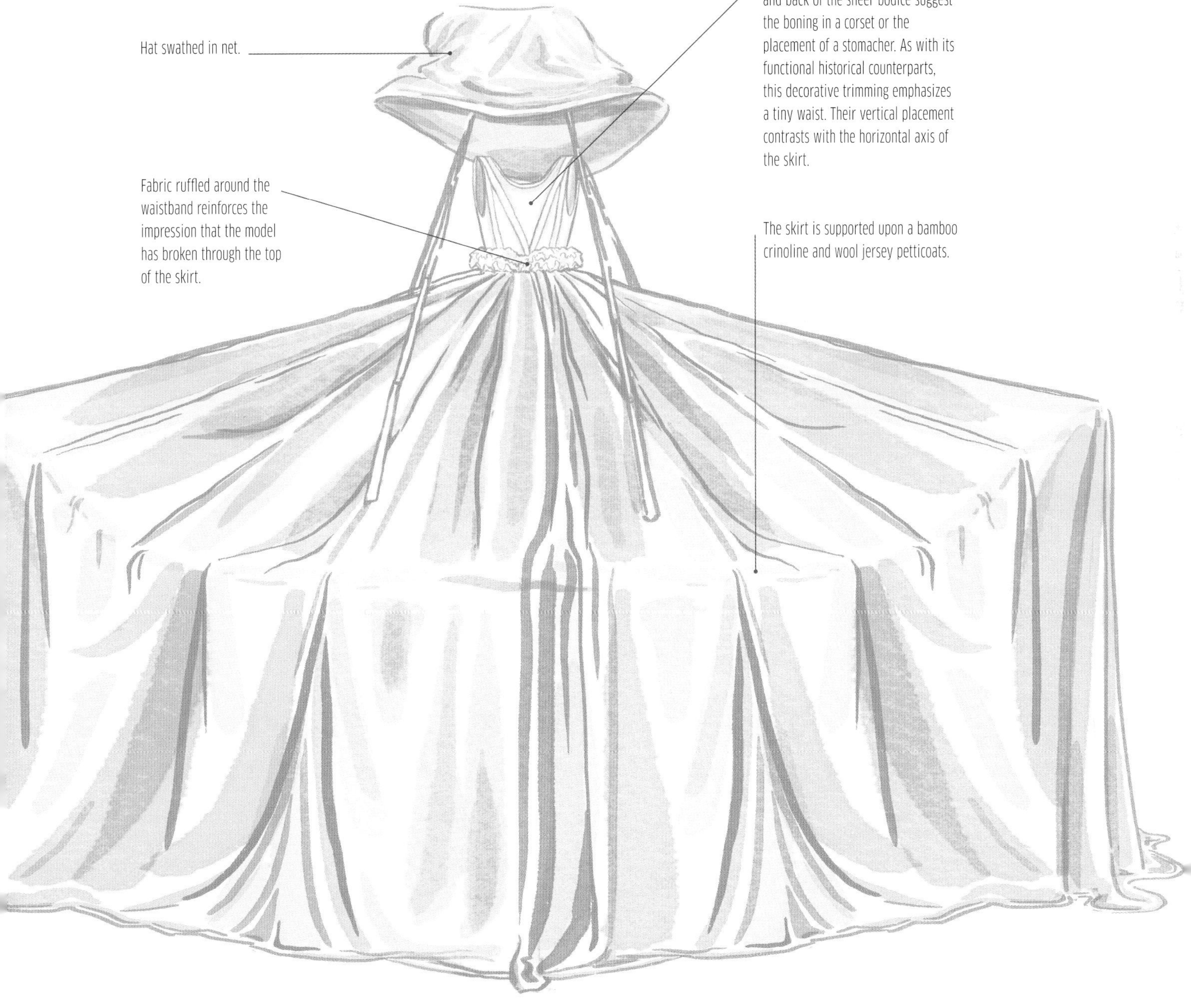

33

Vera Wang

1999 For Victoria Adams

The elegant champagne-colored satin ball gown created for Victoria Adams is an iconic example of Vera Wang's aspirational designs.

Before she was a respected fashion designer and one half of the Beckham empire, Adams was known as one of the pop band the Spice Girls, and the chief "WAG" (the label given to the wives and girlfriends of England's national soccer team). The marriage of Adams to her soccer-star fiancé, David Beckham, marked the beginning of the multi-million Beckham brand. The event set the gold standard for lavish celebrity weddings at the turn of the millennium. British gossip magazine *OK!* reportedly paid £1 million at the time for exclusive coverage of the wedding (the reason no photographs of the bride may be reproduced here).

A pseudo-royal occasion

The wedding, which took place at Luttrellstown Castle in the Republic of Ireland, was an extravagantly stage-managed spectacle fed to the public in three successive issues of *OK!* magazine. Illustrated interviews with the couple detailed every aspect of their pseudo-royal fairy-tale wedding: the purple flag initialed with VBD (for Victoria, baby Brooklyn, and David) raised above the castle after the couple recited their vows; the notorious gilded red-velvet thrones upon which they posed during the reception; and, of course, the bride's sumptuous couture wedding dress made from the finest Italian Clerici duchesse satin, worn with a diamond and gold coronet.

Princess aspirations

Adams asked Vera Wang—the fairy godmother of wedding dresses—to realize her regal aspirations. "I wanted to look quite virginal on my wedding day," said the bride, who already had a child with her husband-to-be. Veering from her usually sexy image, Adams selected a stately, structured design that emphasized her tiny frame. A suitably grand impression was created by a majestic 20-foot (6-m) train and a formal floor-sweeping skirt, its immense volume eased into a dropped waist with inverted pleats. Rising out of the skirt from an S-shaped seam was a long, tightly fitted strapless bodice sculpted into Wang's famous "crumb-catcher" neckline.

The bodice of Adams's dress was constructed from panels of satin connected from top to bottom hem with vertically mirrored curved seams. These visually narrowed and lengthened the bride's slender torso, working with the gently curving horizontal waist seam to draw attention to her hand-span waist. The line of the waist was echoed in the eye-catching design of the neckline, whose sculptural folds, standing away from the chest, enhanced a small bust. Under the dress, Adams wore structural foundation

HIDDEN DETAILS

- The tulle petticoat is stiffened with horsehair.
- Corset by Mr. Pearl.
- The dress fastens center-back with a zip.
- Separate 20-ft (6-m) train.
- The bride wore a diamond-set coronet created by the jeweler Slim Barrett.

THE DRESS

STYLE Regal and romantic

SHAPE Ball gown

FABRIC Silk duchesse satin

COLOR Champagne

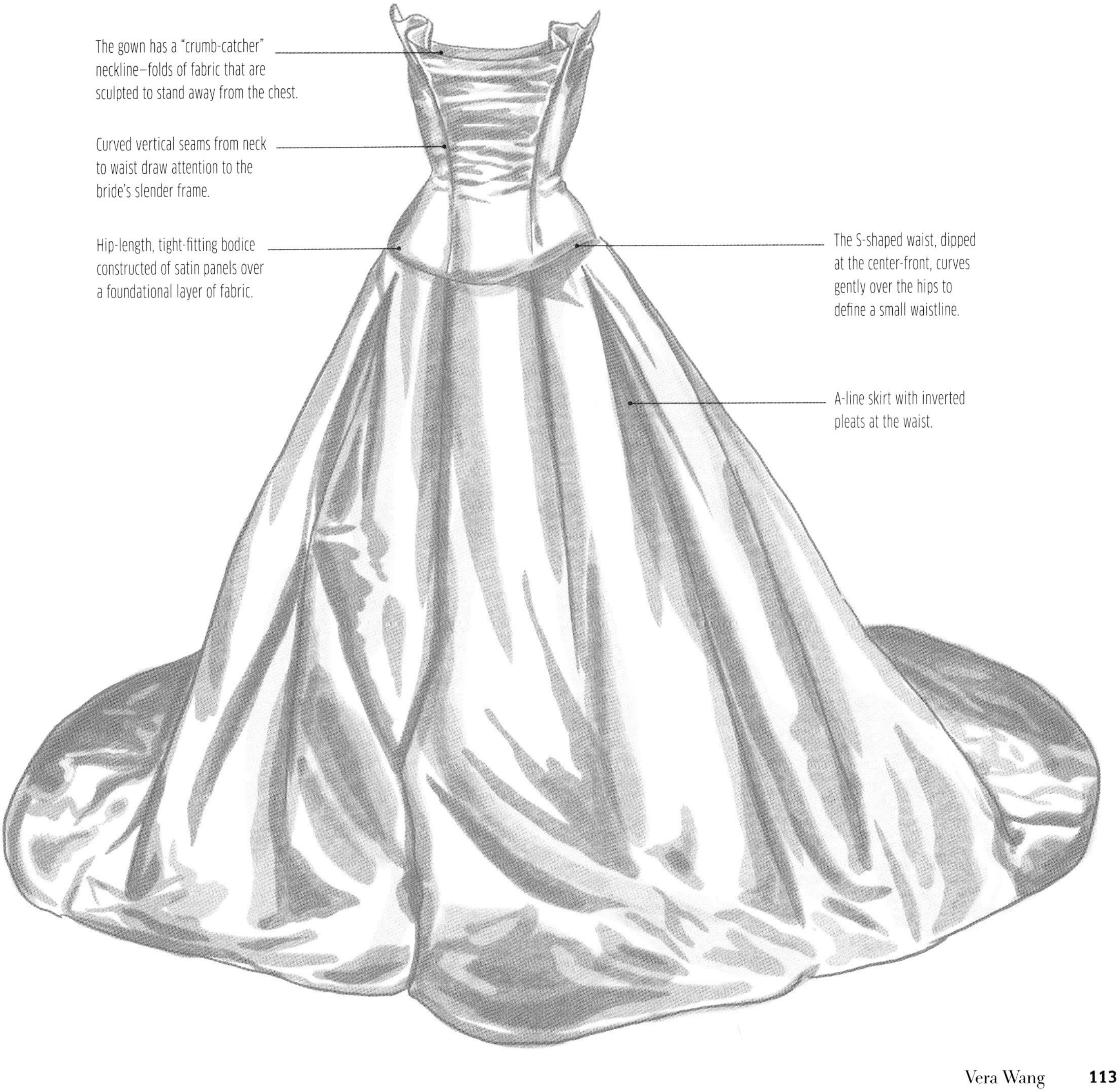

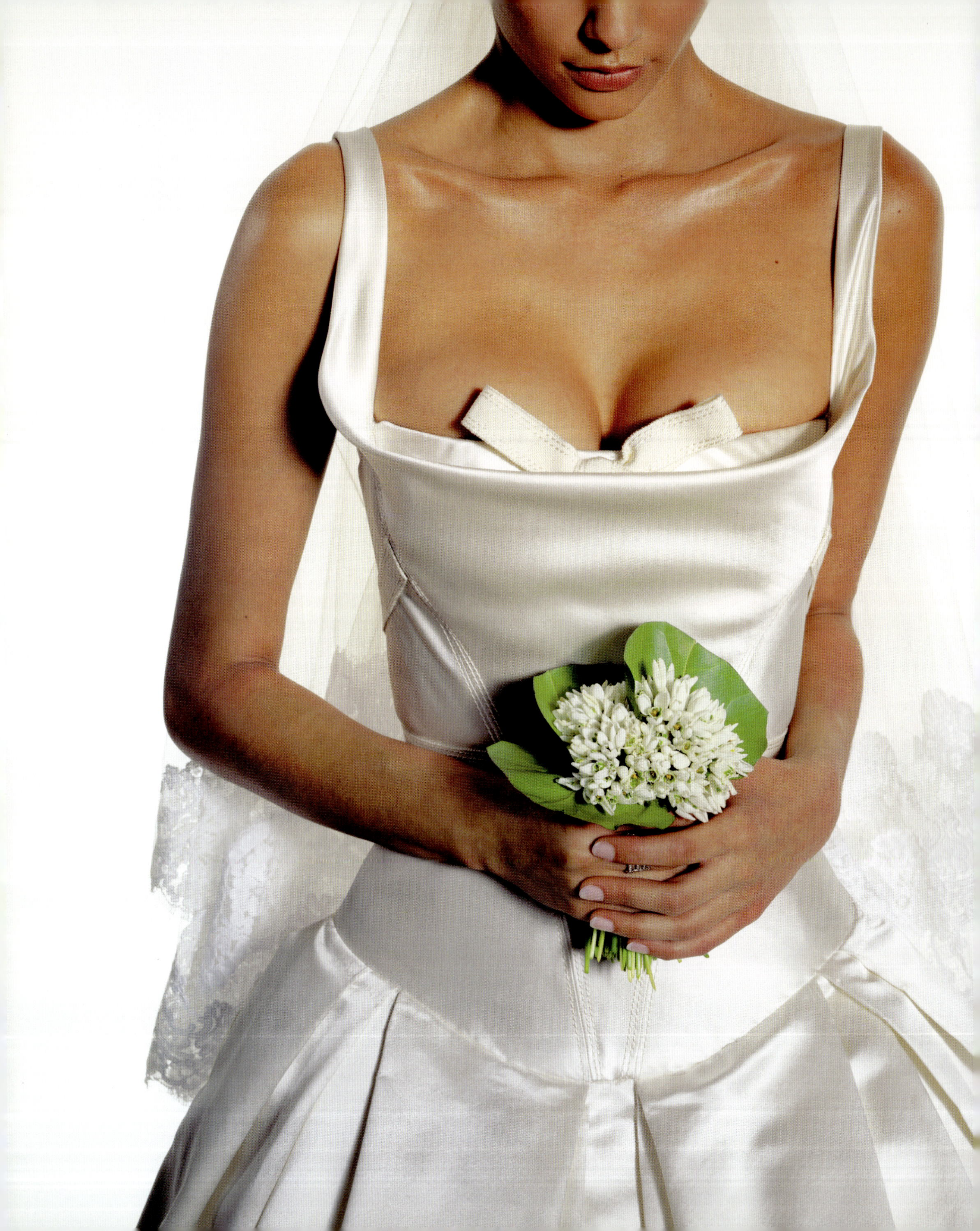

garments. A petticoat made from 164 feet (50 m) of tulle, stiffened with horsehair, supported the skirt's A-line silhouette, while a corset by English corsetier Mr. Pearl molded her torso into the smooth curves that held the strapless bodice in place.

Transatlantic design

It took two preliminary consultations, six fittings, and fifteen months to make Adams's dress at an estimated cost of $100,000. In order to perfect the corseted waist, the dress was sent between New York and London, leading Wang to quip that it was truly a "transatlantic dress." At the time of the wedding, it was reported that Wang made just six to ten couture wedding dresses a year and that they each had six to eight people working on them. Wang's design for Adams personified her aspirational brand, marking it out as a source for sophisticated, exclusive wedding gowns. Wang revolutionized the way brides viewed wedding culture by elevating the wedding dress into "a state of mind" and the expression of a desirable lifestyle. As Wang tells it, "I'm trying to channel who [the bride] is and who she wants to be."

Prior to the Beckhams' nuptials, high-profile celebrity brides such as Mariah Carey, Uma Thurman, and Sharon Stone wore Vera Wang creations at their weddings, but none had as great a public impact as Adams. Her gown has been credited with the subsequent ubiquity of strapless styles and the beginning of a marked increased in spending on bridalwear, as women strived to emulate the dream embodied in the celebrity wedding dress.

STORE FOUND, THEN STYLED
Adams was inspired to request Wang to design her gown after spotting a corseted design with a "crumb-catcher" bust, as shown here, at a Vera Wang store. Adams's design was made strapless, creating an enduring bridal trend.

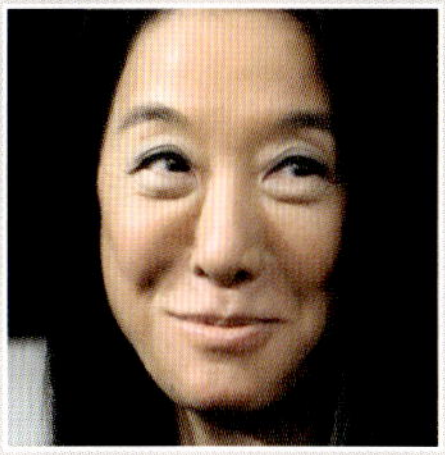

Vera Wang
1949–

Wang founded her bridal boutique, offering ready-made and custom dresses, in 1990, a year after her own nuptials and following a successful career at *Vogue* magazine (1972–1987) and Ralph Lauren (1987–1990). Drawing on the frustration she'd felt trying to find her own wedding gown, Wang told *Vogue* that she "readdressed the whole industry of bridal" by attending to the styling of every detail of a wedding. She was the first American designer to make an impact on the European market. In 2011 Wang launched the lower-cost White by Vera Wang range at David's Bridal. After the brand expanded into homeware, fashion, and fragrance, its sales income was estimated at $700 million in 2011.

34

Yohji Yamamoto

2000 Spring/Summer

Although experimental, this quietly rebellious dress is beautifully wearable and elegant.

Mainstream wedding gown designers respond to fashion in the silhouette and detailing of their designs but rarely stray far from the bridal ideal of femininity and luxury. In his Spring/Summer 2000 collection, radical designer Yamamoto again deconstructed the sartorial conventions of the traditional wedding gown, rebuilding it in the model of his avant-garde aesthetic. Yamamoto's approach to this wedding dress is emblematic of his challenge to the traditional norms of clothing and gender and his analytical interrogation of the sculptural possibilities of dress. Twisted drapery, voluminous forms, unusual pattern-cutting, and inexpensive fabrics replace figure-enhancing tailoring and rich silks and satins. (For more on Yamamoto, see page 110.)

Utilitarian poetry

The dress was executed in cotton muslin, a utilitarian fabric confounding the high-status expectations of wedding couture. Cotton muslin is usually employed to create toiles—the preparatory model of the finished dress—in which the designer works out ideas and plays with the fit of a gown. The hasty, work-in-progress associations of the toile were amplified in this gown by the exposure of raw frayed edges and selvedges, the application of large basting stitches, and the fluidity of the silhouette. It was with great skill and poeticism that Yamamoto fused the unfinished aesthetic of the dress with couture detailing and construction. The dress appears to have literally been dissected by the designer before being pieced back together in a bafflingly complex fashion—an impression reinforced by the decorative basting stitches, which suggest the lines of a plastic surgeon's marker pen intersecting the garment. The stitches revealed the grain lines of the fabric and alluded to the placement of real seams. Applied decoratively, these stitches indicated Yamamoto's intriguing design process.

Playing with proportion

Typically, wedding dresses are molded to highlight the femininity of the bride—their forms often define small waists or reveal elegant décolletages. Yamamoto subverted sartorial clichés of bridalwear by creating an elegantly feminine form that simultaneously masked the lines of the female body with voluminous shapes. The designer's millennial dress freed the torso from corsetry and restrictive shaping. All rigidity in the design was transferred up to the right shoulder, where a cantilevered sculptural neckline extended above the collarbone and snaked around the edges of the body to cascade down the sides and back. Rather than reduce the silhouette

SCULPTING SPACE
The space between the wearer and the dress becomes fundamental to the silhouette of this gown.

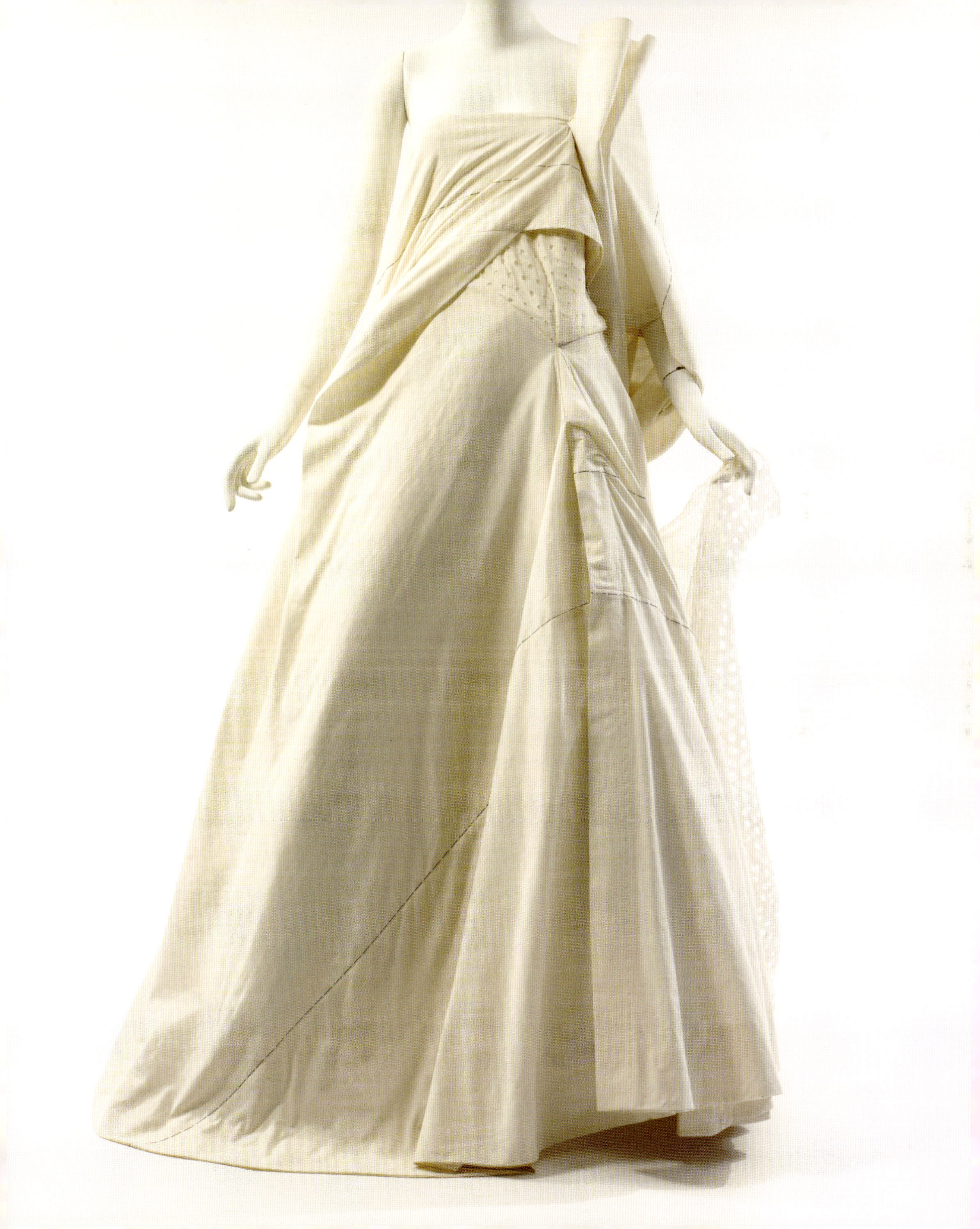

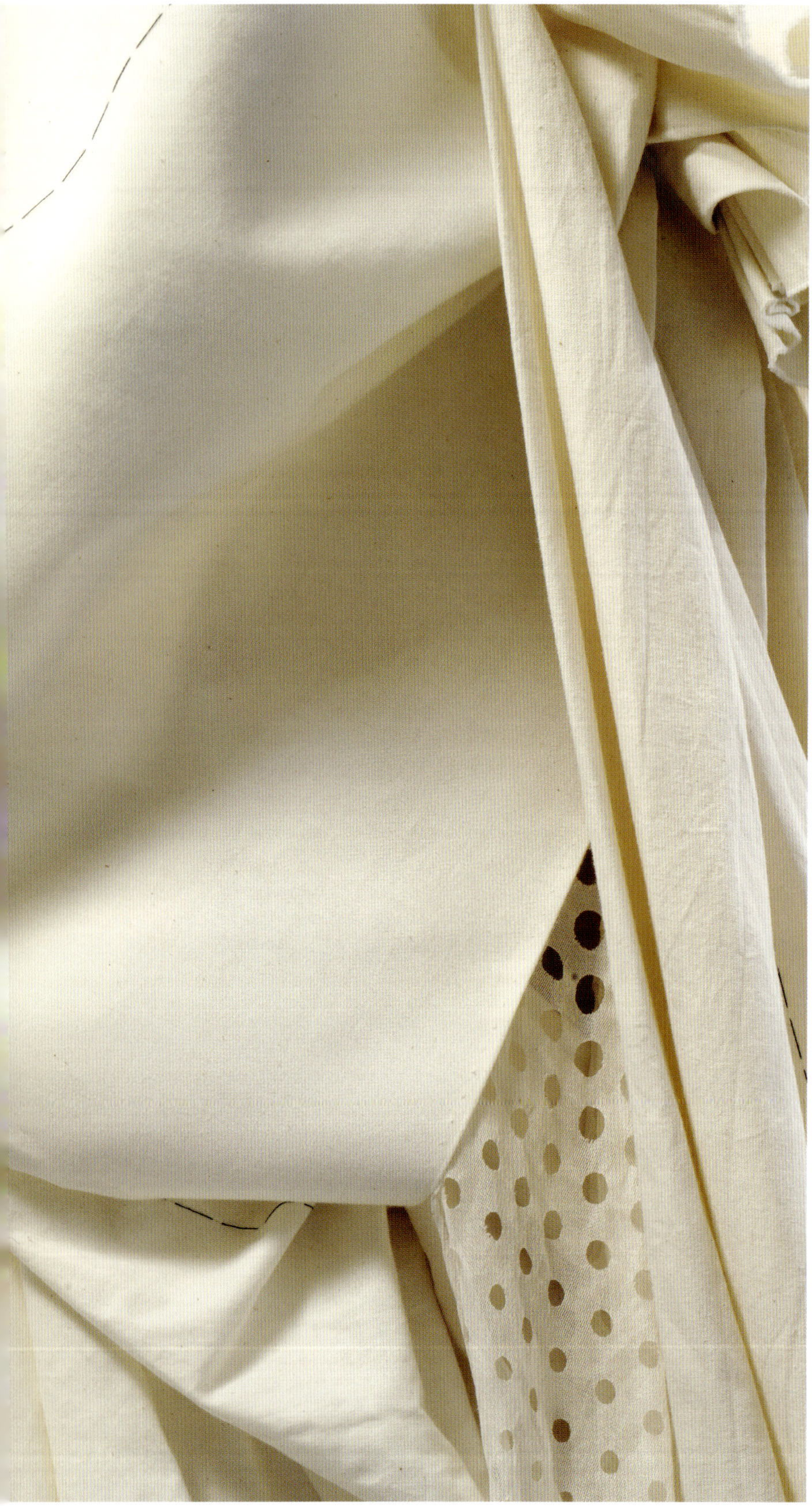

into neat proportions, Yamamoto extended it beyond the mass of the body. The area between the garment and the body was of great importance to the designer, who has said of his motivations: "What interests me is the 'space' between the person wearing the clothes and the clothes themselves—the airiness, the movement, the silhouette." Unusually for a wedding dress, drapery emanated from points dropped below the bust and waist. Fabric, roughly pleated to the top of the back of the dress, created a three-dimensional body of billowing fabric—a quasi-train more suggestive of the informal eighteenth-century "sack back" gown than the predecessor of the traditional wedding train, the court train.

Beauty that is imperfect by nature

The unique structuring of this wedding dress, implying the relaxed codes of dishabille, undermined the rigidity of formal wedding attire. The loose, energetic fluidity of the gown's silhouette also testified to the Japanese aesthetic of wabi-sabi. Wabi-sabi is a transient state of beauty, accepting imperfection and incompleteness. Yamamoto embraced this principle in his work, once stating that "perfection is the devil." Yamamoto's gown had no true precedent: alternative designer wedding gowns tend to be the outré designs of the couture catwalk. Yamamoto's dress managed to be both avant-garde and wearable, revealing the possibilities for brides seeking a beautiful, intelligent, and cutting-edge alternative to mainstream wedding fashion.

MAKING HIS MARK
Yamamoto's design was studded with exposed elements of construction: dressmaker's marks, basting stitches, and raw hems.

THE DRESS

STYLE Avant-garde

SHAPE Deconstructed

FABRIC Natural cotton muslin and silk jersey

COLOR Unbleached white and ivory

HIDDEN DETAILS

- Gathered fabric at the back of the dress creates a sweeping skirt, given volume by an underskirt.
- Ivory silk jersey with large laser-cut holes threads through the dress at the front and hangs over the right shoulder to suggest the form of a veil.

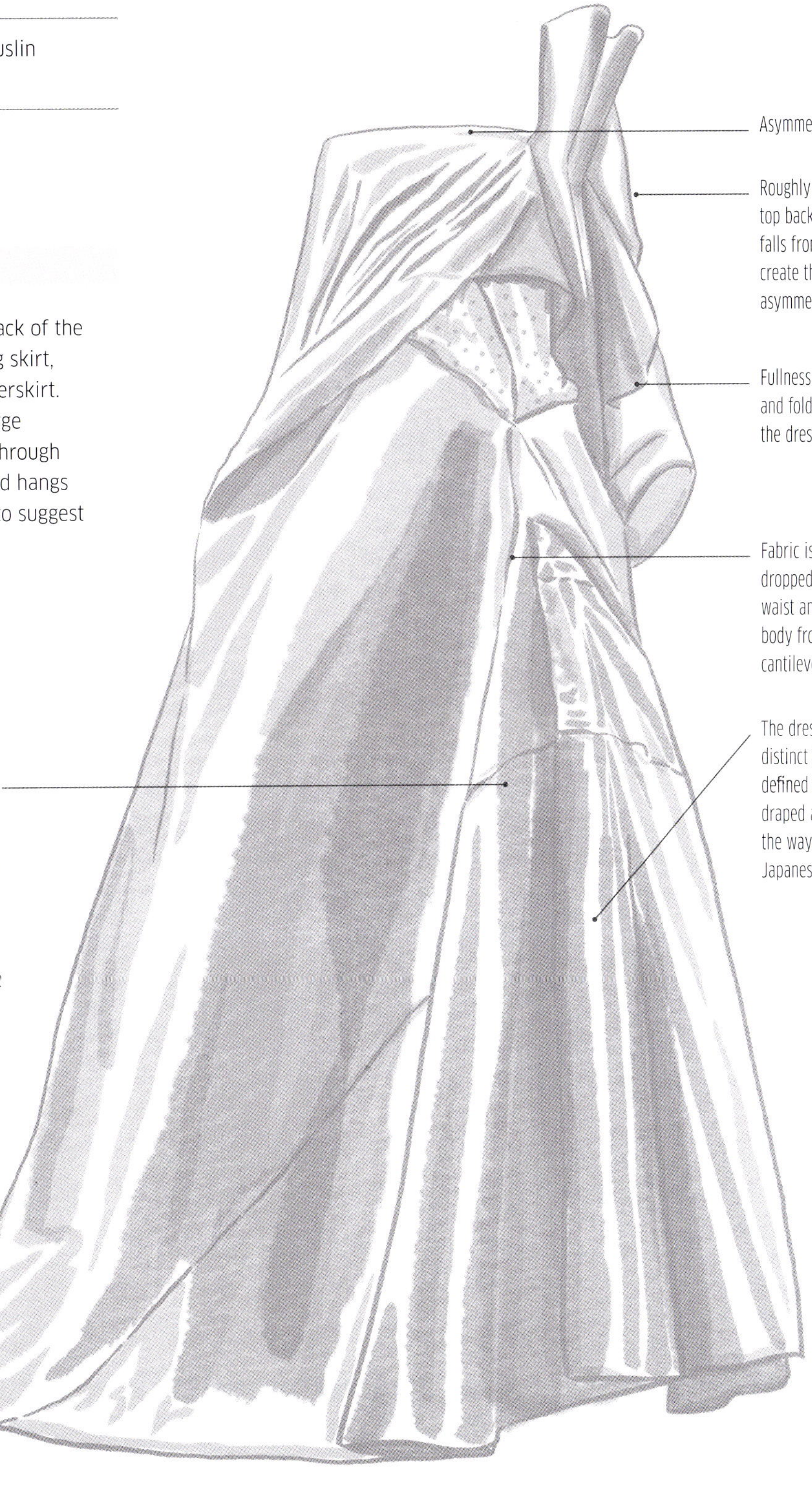

35

John Galliano

2002 Christian Dior for Gwen Stefani

When couture collided with a "punkette superheroine," the result was a striking hot-pink ombré wedding dress.

Singer Gwen Stefani turned to flamboyant designer John Galliano to design the wedding gown she wore for her marriage to rock star Gavin Rossdale in 2002. *Elle* magazine reported that the bride told the designer: "I wanted it to be over the top, but not traditional—I wanted it to be everything." Stefani enthused that the "genius" designer translated her ambiguous request into "an amazing, perfect" design. Galliano's creation, simultaneously bold and subtle, fused couture craft and irreverent styling. Equal parts pretty and punk, it was a celebration of the singer's personal style.

Pulled apart

The dress, fabricated from silk faille, was spray-painted bright pink around the hem, fading into white above the knee. The hue was a reference to Stefani's one-time signature hot-pink hair color. The dramatic coloration of the gown distracted from its more provocative transgressions of the sartorial norms of bridalwear. Full-length, trained, draped, and corseted, the gown seemed on first impression to conform to the classic structure of a white wedding dress. However, these elements and expectations were skewed by its asymmetrical cut and construction. On close inspection, the gown was seductively dishevelled. The cut of the gown made it appear as though it had been pulled around and apart, implying the eager, preemptive hand of the groom. The trained skirt was constructed to present the illusion that it had been forced around to the front; the soft cascades of drapery that typically fall from the waist, over the hips, and to the train displaced into twisted lengths of fabric at the front of this unusual wedding dress.

Seductive details

This conceit was echoed in the oblique placement of metal corset hooks down the front of the bodice, suggesting that it had also been hastily yanked out of place. The low-cut boned corset, its neckline festooned with white tulle, extended on one side into a shoulder strap that slipped seductively over the upper arm, radiating an air of sexual nonchalance. The allusion to partial undress was continued in the back of the design, where the bodice was "ripped" apart to expose the bride's corset lacings. The suggestive imagery implied by Galliano's design inverted a convention common to many cultures—that of ritually dressing a bride before her wedding. In the process, Galliano subverted the traditional image of the demure, chaste bride.

FADE TO WHITE
The dress cleverly referenced the bride's punk persona while maintaining couture standards.

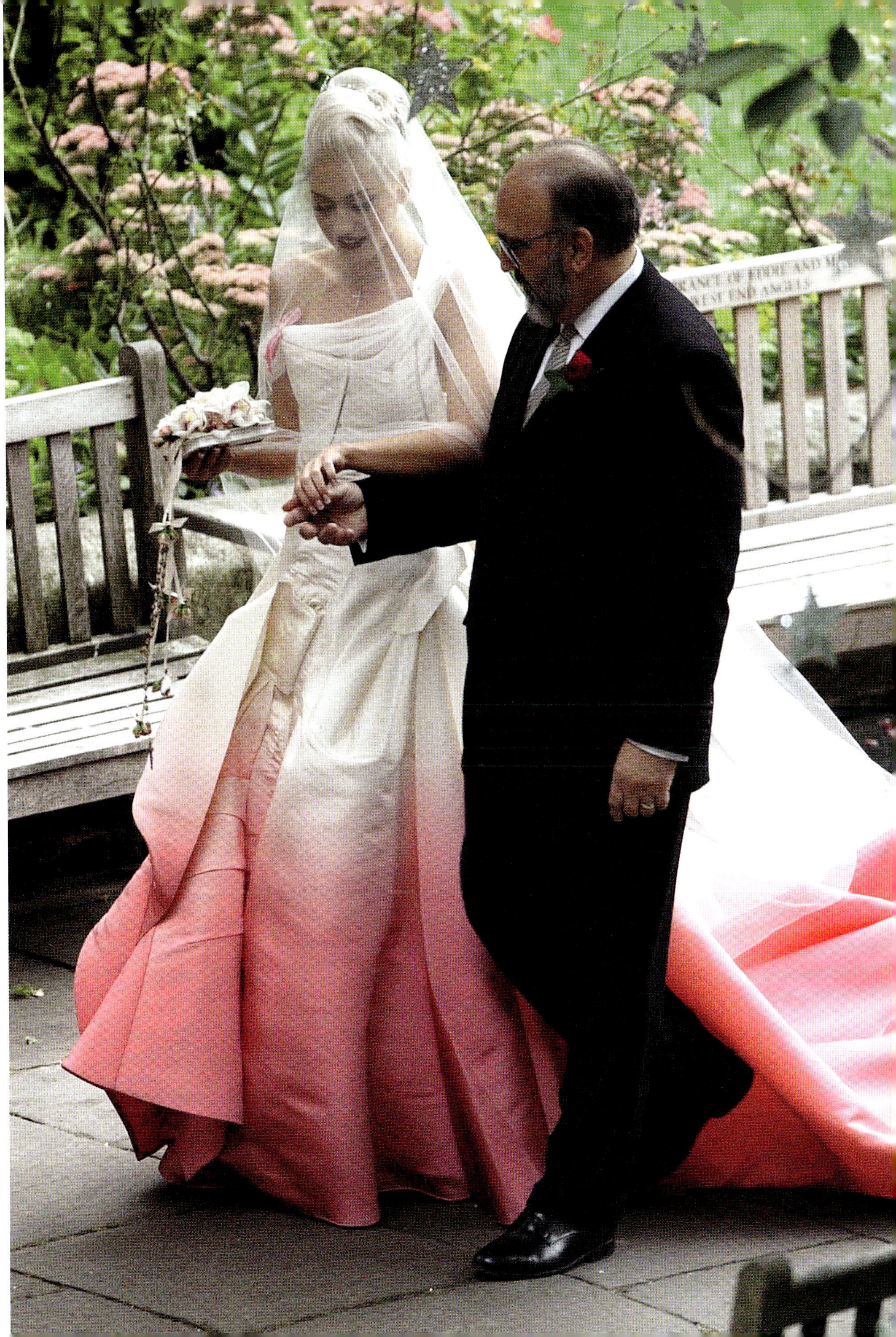

Fun and subversive

Galliano's unconventional wedding dress accorded with Stefani's persona, described by *Vogue*, as a "tough-girl sex symbol with nice-girl appeal." Stefani is the front woman of rock ska band No Doubt, a solo artist, and the designer of her own fashion label, L.A.M.B. The singer has a striking aesthetic matched by an equally powerful voice, speaking to and for women through songs that riff on career advancement, bad breakups, sexism, and marriage.

Stefani wore her Galliano gown twice: first for her nuptials in St. Paul's Church in London's Covent Garden, accessorized with a full-length veil trimmed with appliquéd antique lace, vertiginous hot-pink sandals, rosary beads, and her grandmother's Catholic prayer book; and then again to renew her vows witnessed by friends in Los Angeles. For its second outing, the dress was paired with a Georgian pendant of pink tourmaline, peridot, and diamonds by Neil Lane. When asked by *Elle* magazine in an interview in 2011 what the last piece of clothing she wore that made her feel amazing was, Stefani answered: "my wedding dress." It was, she continued, "a work of art," and for that reason she donated it to London's Victoria and Albert Museum, because "it needed to be seen."

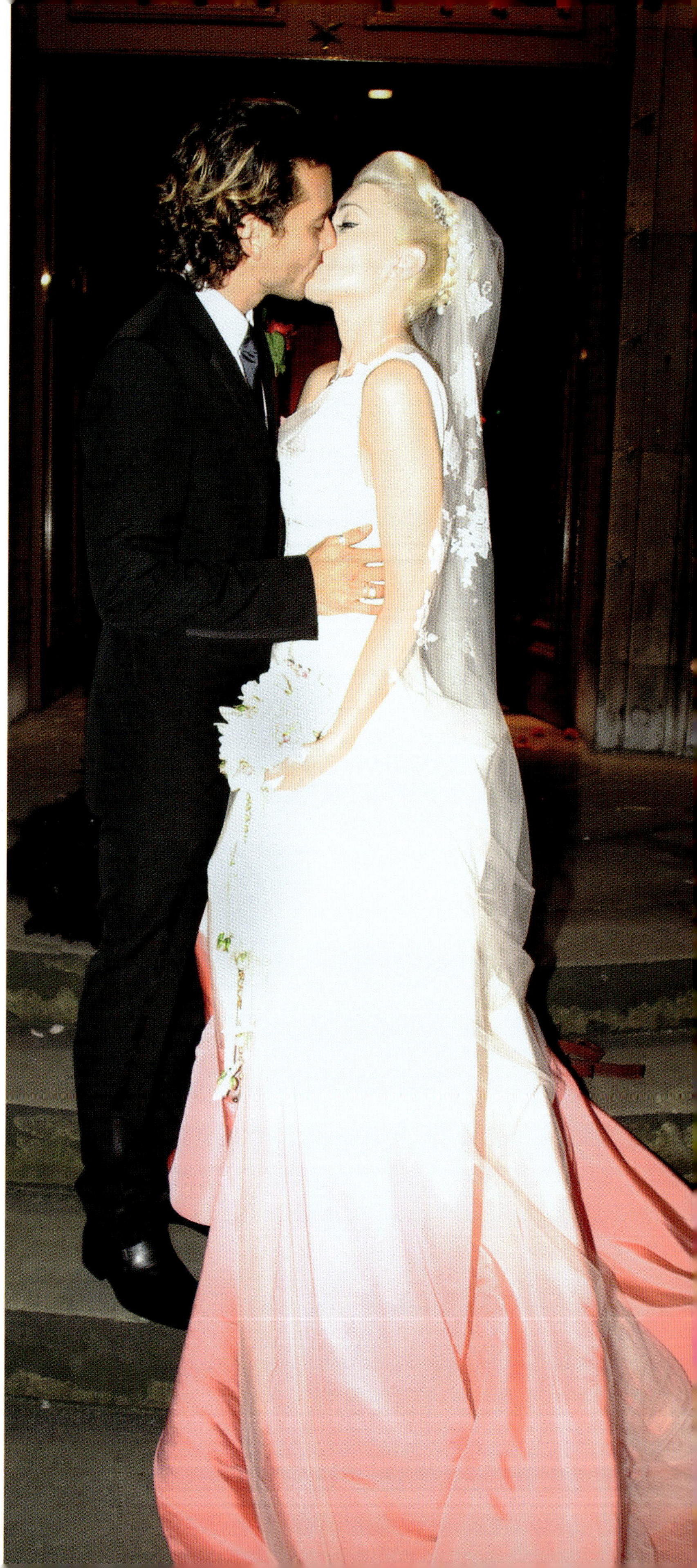

DELIBERATELY DISHEVELED
The floor-length trained skirt, spray-painted pink, faded to white above the knee. The detailing of the design was off-kilter, as if it had been pulled aside by the groom.

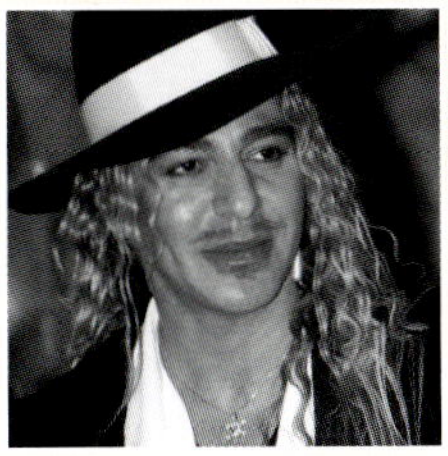

John Galliano

1960–

The Gibraltar-born British designer is known as the showman who spectacularly fell from grace. Galliano's graduate collection, Les Incroyables (1984), established his reputation, but critical acclaim in London did not equate financially, prompting the designer's relocation to Paris in 1992. His breakthrough collection (1993) led to his appointment as Head of Design at Givenchy (1995) and a promotion to revive the house of Dior (1996). In the 1990s and 2000s the designer was prolific, but at the height of his success, in 2011, he was embroiled in a scandal that resulted in his being dismissed from all his positions (see page 166).

THE DRESS

STYLE Punk

SHAPE Asymmetric

FABRIC Silk faille

COLOR White and hot pink

HIDDEN DETAILS

- The fabric is overlapped over the back of the bodice in a V formation, exposing the corset laces beneath.
- The skirt lies flat at the back.

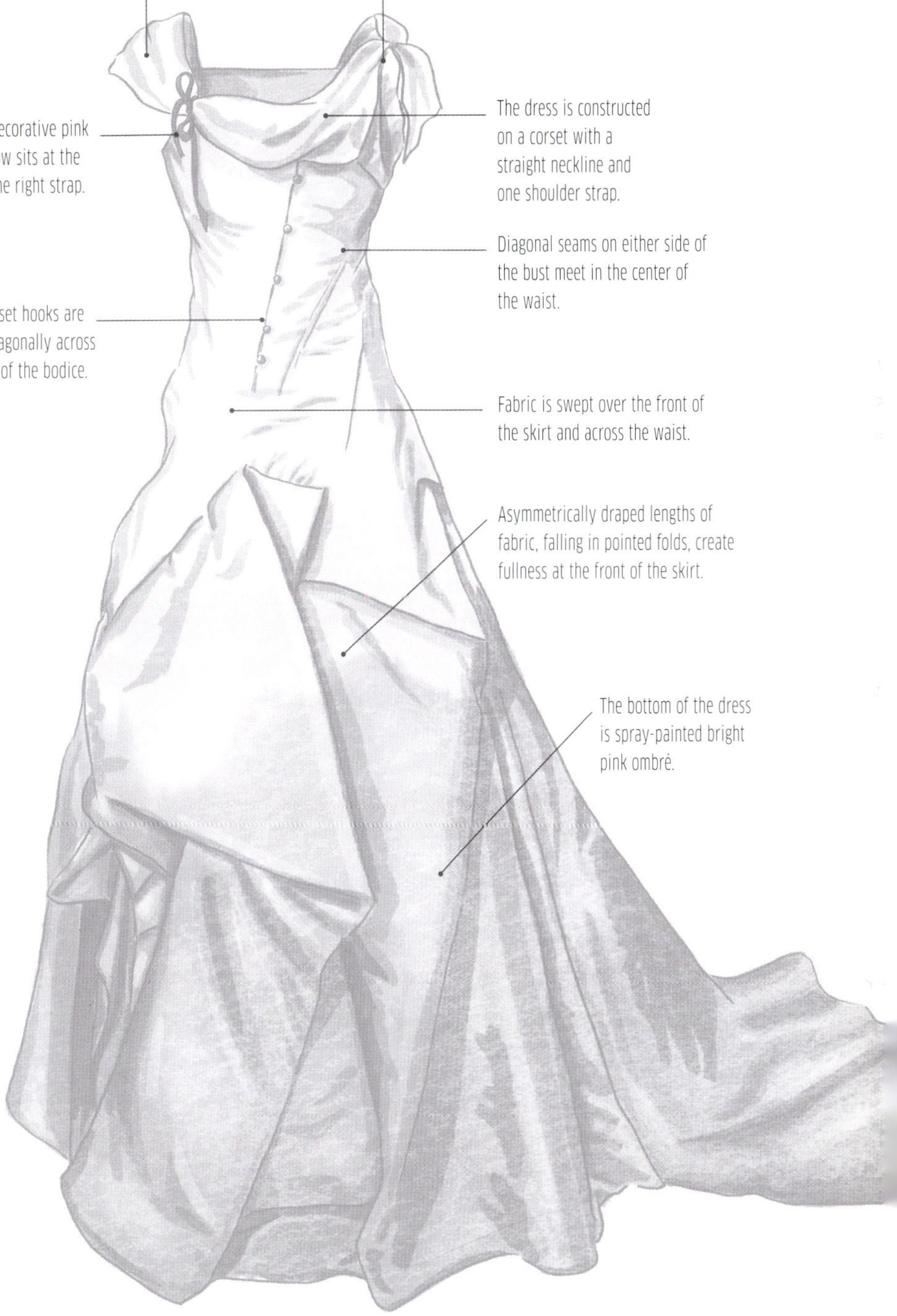

36

Viktor & Rolf

2004 For Mabel Wisse Smit

Viktor & Rolf's bow-covered wedding dress married a conventional silhouette with embellishments that made a visual, tongue-in-cheek comment on the standard aristocratic wedding gown.

Dutch designers Viktor & Rolf are known for their playfully subversive approach to the fashion industry. When human rights activist Mabel Wisse Smit married Prince Johan Friso of Orange-Nassau, second in line to the Dutch throne, she challenged the design duo to apply their avant-garde outlook to the tradition of the wedding dress. The designers later said that the bride requested a memorable dress and dismissed designs if she considered them too conventional. For a wedding that forced the groom to renounce his succession to the throne, Viktor & Rolf's design made an appropriately ironic statement about the spectacle of society weddings.

A perspective trick

From the front, the pure-white, duchesse satin dress was a flattering, traditional design featuring modest long sleeves, a boat neckline, and a floor-length skirt leading into a 10-foot (3-m) train. The entire surface of the dress was covered, in the designers' words, with "a profusion of bows" placed on a trelliswork. The diamond-shaped trellis was matched across the seams and armholes so that it appeared as if the dress was cut from one piece of cloth. The scale of the pattern grew incrementally from the top of the dress to the bottom—the smallest bows along the neckline and the largest at the hem. Bows, which the designers said were "very much part of our idiom," symbolized "longevity, commitment and permanence." The trelliswork appeared to reference the romantic medieval styling popular with early twentieth-century brides.

While the front of the dress appeared to adhere to the sartorial conventions of the white wedding dress, the back of the dress parodied them, dramatically ramping up the scale of the motif so that the train trailed with gargantuan bows at its edge. As the back of the dress is the congregation's primary view of the bride while she makes her vows, it has historically featured bold decoration, a feature taken to absurd proportions in this design. The extreme contrast between the smallest and largest bows, in partnership with the rigid straight lines of the train, created a false sense of perspective, amplifying the visual impact the train made as the bride passed up and down the lengthy cathedral aisle.

The wedding of Wisse Smit to Prince Friso took place in the Old Church in Delft, the Netherlands, with the usual pomp and ceremony of a royal wedding. But, as with the bride's dress, this royal marriage was not all it seemed on first appearance. The televised

A PROFUSION OF BOWS
The iconic oversized bows made a reappearance in the designers' collaboration with retailer H&M (see page 136).

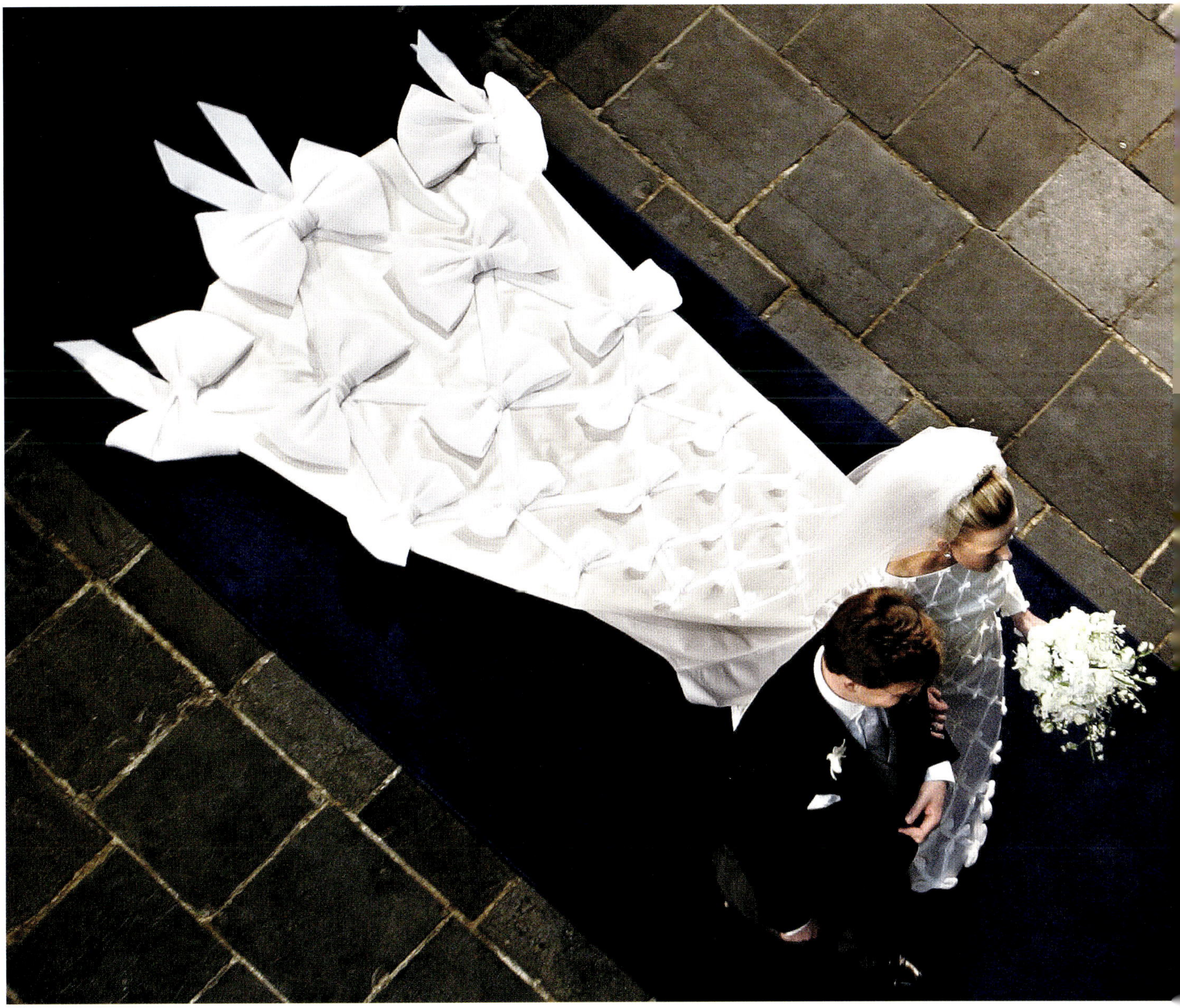

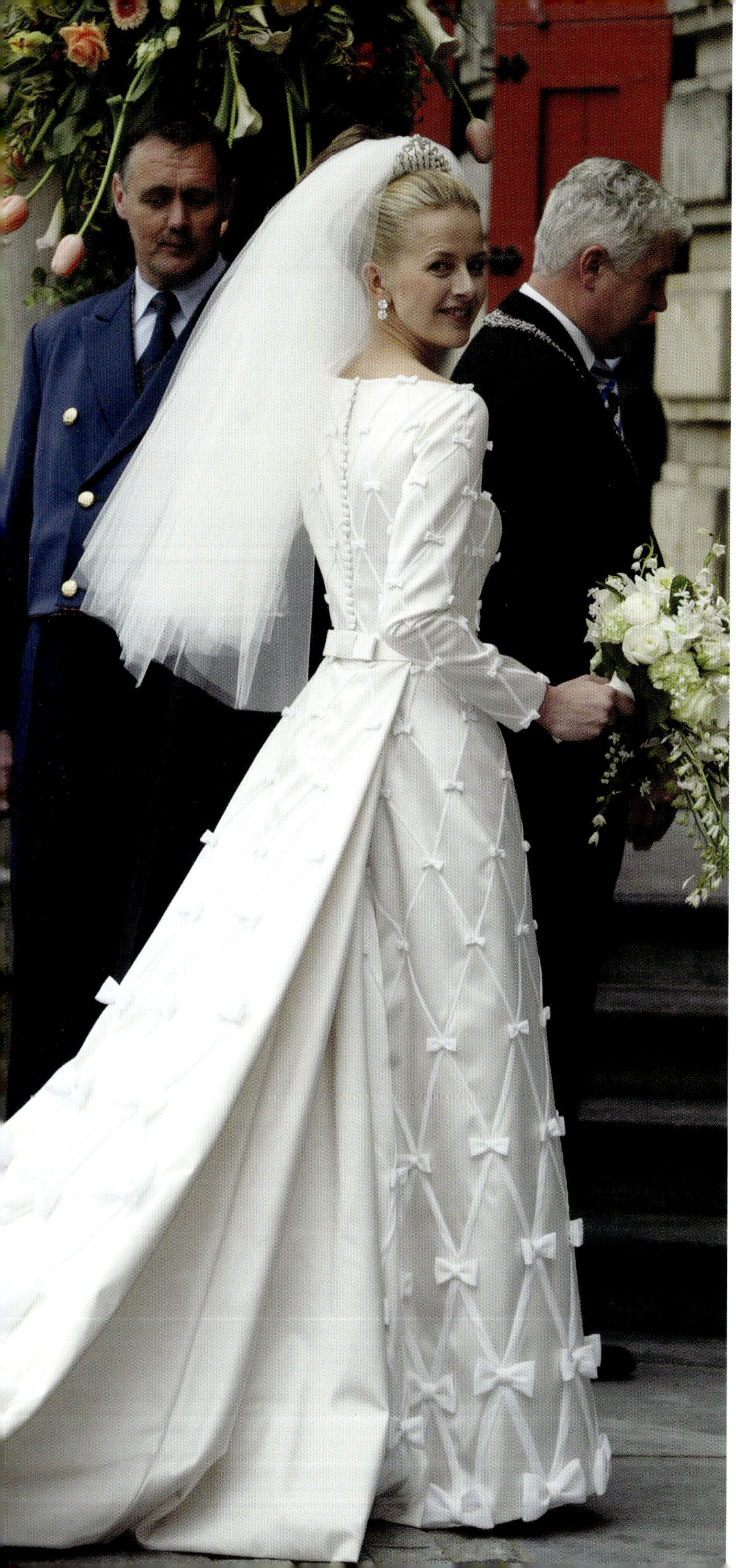

event incurred considerable interest because of what the press dubbed Mabelgate. The Dutch Government refused to ask Parliament to give permission for Prince Friso to wed Wisse Smit on the grounds that the couple had supplied "incomplete and incorrect information" about her relationship with a Dutch drug lord. Prince Friso continued with the marriage regardless, but as a consequence lost his membership in the Dutch royal house.

Fashion as comment

No other designers have a better understanding of the impact of image in a media-driven society than Viktor & Rolf. The designers' knowing distortion of the symbolism and imagery of bridalwear testifies to their accolade as "semiotic tacticians." Viktor & Rolf's wedding dress took its place in a lineage of experimental and avant-garde practice: the play of size and perspective was a nod to Schiaparelli's surrealist strategy of disjunction (see page 36) and to Yohji Yamamoto and Comme des Garçons' interrogation of sartorial expectations (see pages 108, 116, and 168). As with all challenging design, Viktor & Rolf's wedding gown met with mixed reactions. Some critics saw it as disrespectful to the supposed solemnity of the marriage ceremony and thought it visually overpowering, while others appreciated the caricature and understood the dress as an intelligent piece of design.

CLASSIC DESIGN, TWISTED
The dress played on romantic medieval traditions favored by twentieth-century society brides, loosely referencing the 1920s interpretation of the historical style.

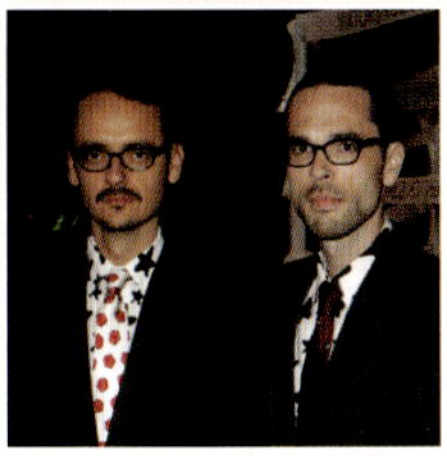

Viktor & Rolf

Both 1969–

Viktor Horsting and Rolf Snoeren's work defies categorization, encompassing performance art, couture, and global branding. The pair, who met at Arnhem Academy of Art in the Netherlands, moved to Paris in 1992, where they produced fashion and art installations and ephemeral "collections" that preempted their entry into the fashion scene. The pair said of fashion, it "is an aura, an escape from reality… a glossy fairy-tale world made real." Their often surreal, self-referential designs play on notions of opposites and contrasts.

HIDDEN DETAILS

- The lattice and bow pattern is matched around the armholes and covers all the seams, giving the impression that the dress is cut from one piece of cloth.
- 128 bows on the skirt, 85 on the bodice, and 35 on the train.
- The dress fastens at the center-back with covered buttons.

THE DRESS

STYLE Avant-garde

SHAPE A-line

FABRIC Double-faced duchesse satin

COLOR White

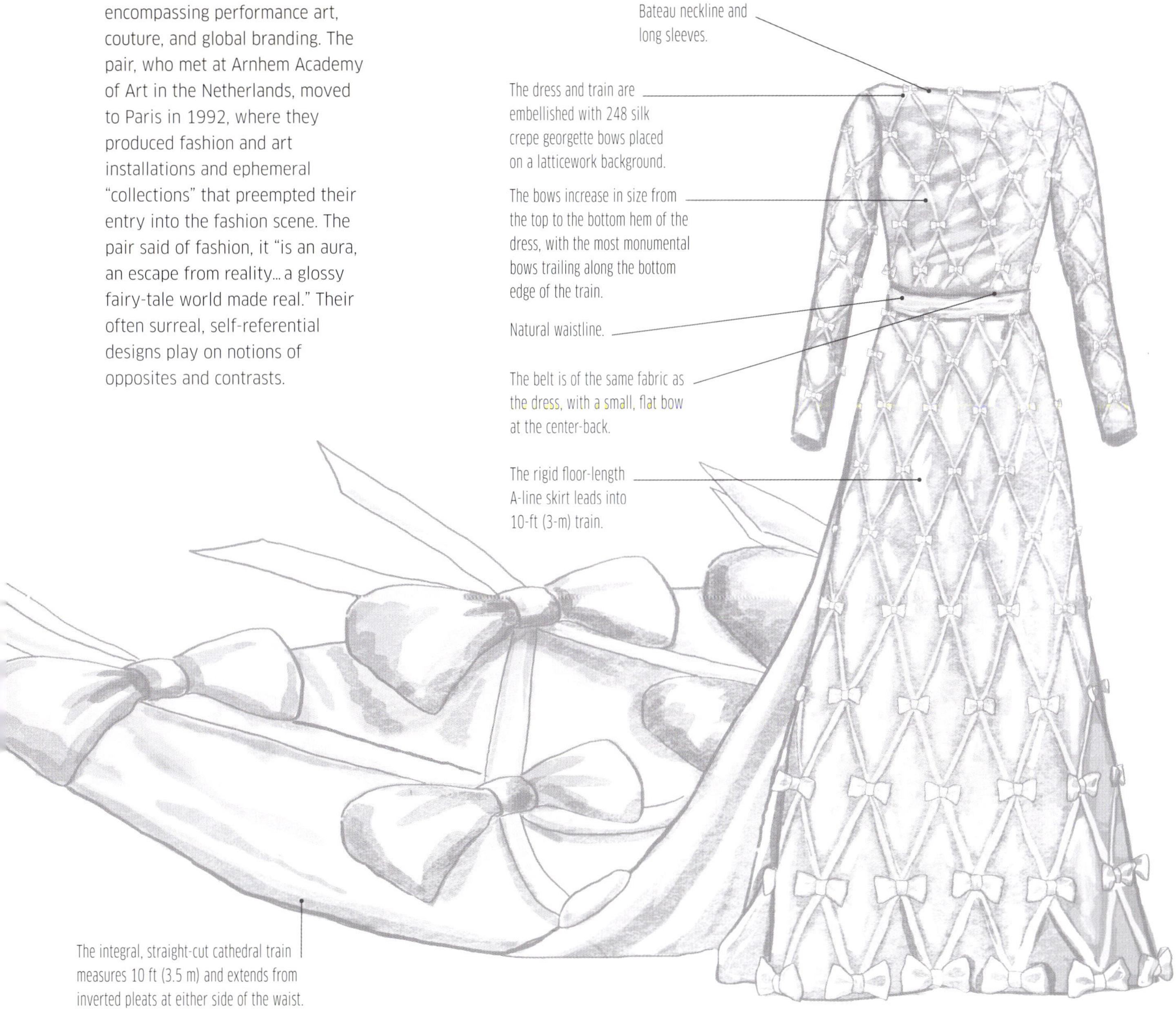

37

Alexander McQueen

2005 For Victoria "Plum" Sykes

Alexander McQueen's breathtaking "Madame X"-styled wedding gown was made for an English rose with a taste for the avant-garde.

New York socialite and *Vogue* contributing editor Victoria "Plum" Sykes was lucky enough that on becoming engaged, her good friend McQueen, the "enfant terrible" of British fashion, offered to make her an unforgettable wedding gown. The resulting immaculately fitted dress, spiraling into a 5-foot (1.5-m) train, was a model of classic elegance and craftsmanship; it reputedly later persuaded royal bride Catherine Middleton to select this visionary design house to create the dress she wore for her wedding to Prince William in 2011 (see page 158).

The design process

The designer and bride's friendship extended back over a decade. The pair met while they were both embarking upon their careers in the fashion industry. Sykes, who had modeled for McQueen, written about the designer in *Vogue*, and worn as many of his designs as she could beg, borrow, or steal, knew his creation would be unique. But when she requested a "vaguely trendy, avant-garde wedding dress," it was the designer himself who ordered her to think again, telling his friend that on her wedding day she had to look "impeccable, exquisite." McQueen played on Sykes's image as the quintessential English rose, but, characteristically, the designer underscored this hazy romantic representation with a design that was also strong, provocative, and sensuous. His fitted dress for Sykes testified to his assertion: "I want to empower women."

The design of Sykes's dress was the result of about ten fittings, made over six months, in which the designer worked in his customarily direct approach. Eschewing muslin toiles, McQueen slashed into and drew upon the crisp white paper taffeta until he perfected his vision of a modern-day, soft-focus version of *Madame X* (see also page 42). The bride recalled the designer's creative process in *Vogue*, telling the magazine, "at each fitting, I would try the new version on and Alexander would appear with a black marker pen and draw all over the silk and then take his scissors to it. He could literally cut a dress by eye—I never saw him use a pattern." McQueen designed the dress, but Sarah Burton often oversaw the fittings and, according to Sykes, likely sewed much of the gown, which Sykes valued in the region of £30,000 ($45,000).

Structure and shape

The foundation for the dress was a thigh-length corset that tightly molded the bride's willowy frame into a statuesque silhouette, echoing that of infamous American socialite Virginie Gautreau in John Singer Sargent's portrait,

ROMANTIC EMPOWERMENT
McQueen's design was both alluring and provocative, designed to empower the wearer.

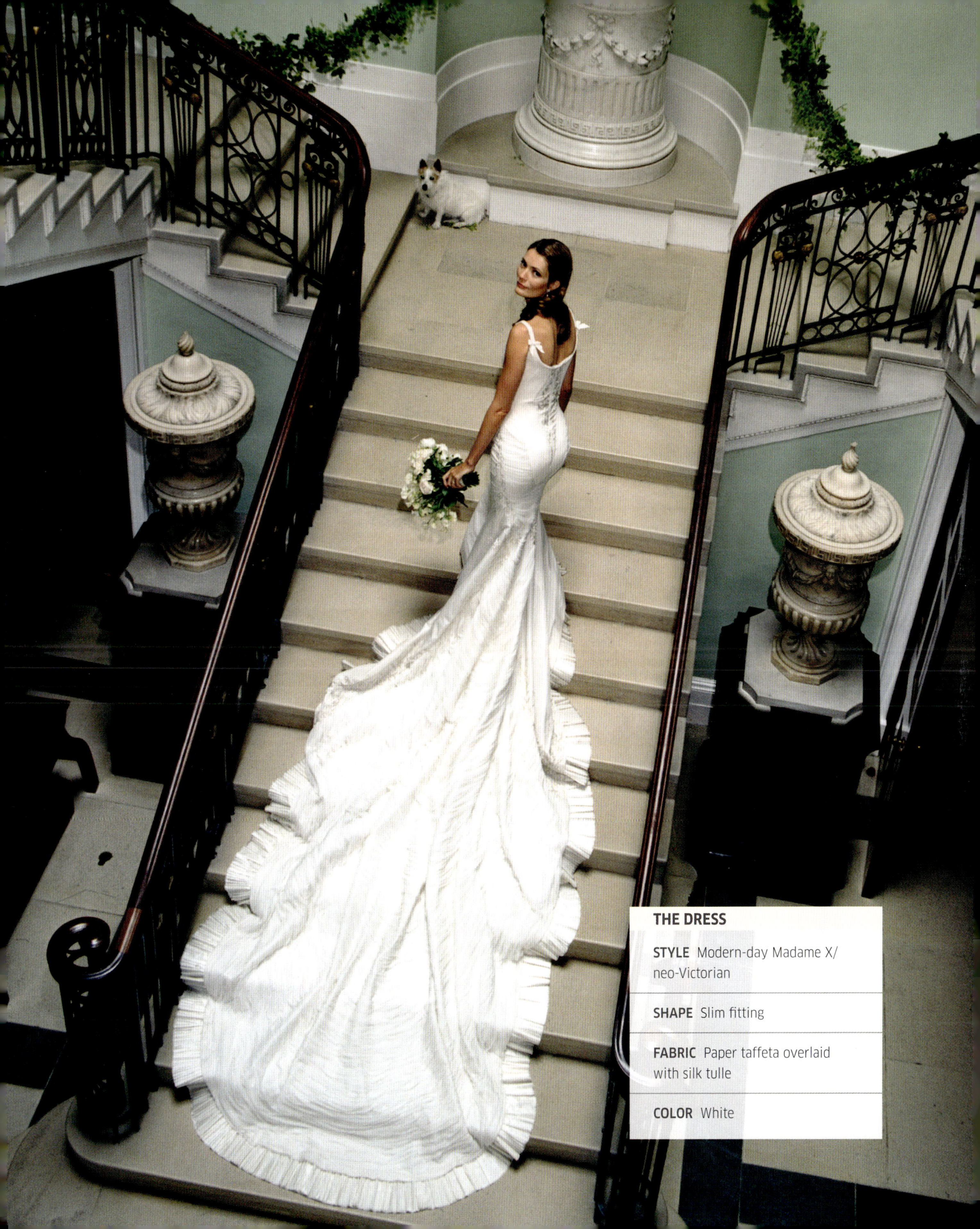

THE DRESS

STYLE Modern-day Madame X/ neo-Victorian

SHAPE Slim fitting

FABRIC Paper taffeta overlaid with silk tulle

COLOR White

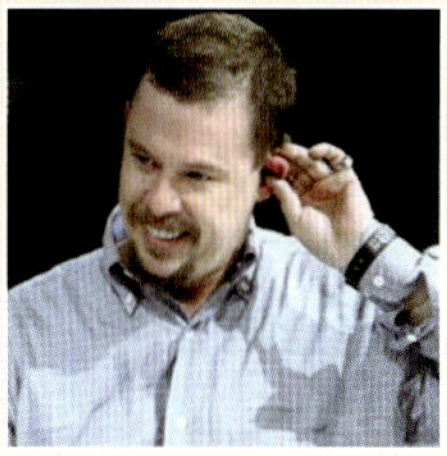

Alexander McQueen
1969–2010

Born Lee McQueen, the designer dubbed the "enfant terrible" of the fashion world grew up in working-class East London. Upon leaving school, McQueen apprenticed in London's tailoring heartland, Savile Row. In 1992, he graduated with a masters in fashion design from London's Central St. Martin's college. His thesis collection established his design credos: strict tailoring fused with dark romanticism. McQueen was appointed chief designer at Givenchy in 1996 but left the house in 2001, saying it was "constraining his creativity." The designer committed suicide in 2010. He is remembered for his spectacular collections and dramatic style of presentation.

Madame X. Beneath the corset fell a slim skirt, swirling at the hem into a long rippling train edged with a deep, knife-pleated dust ruffle. The taffeta dress was overlaid with fine silk tulle; McQueen's decorative treatment of the fabric harking back to historical dressmaking techniques. Upon the train, the tulle was ruched using a Victorian technique. At either side of the bodice, the layers were stitched together in narrow diagonal rows, referencing the contouring compartments of eighteenth-century stays (boned corsets), through which dresses achieved their smoothness of profile and firmness of form. This structural feature was brought to the surface to draw the eye across the bride's curvaceous torso. At the front of the dress, the rows tapered to a pointed V shape, articulating a narrow waist. At the back, the stitching altered direction at the waist, extending down to meet in the middle of the bride's derriere, creating an elongated diamond shape at the center of her back suggestive of an open, unlaced corset. Delicate hand-embroidered traceries of silver roses curling around the sides of the dress counteracted the hard lines of the stitching, and echoed the curve of Sykes's hips and thighs. The final dress wasn't ready until the day before the wedding, when it was delivered to the bride at her wedding venue, the Sledmere family estate in Yorkshire, by the corset maker.

McQueen was, as this dress testifies, a master of his craft. His collaborator and successor Sarah Burton recalls that McQueen "knew everything about how to construct a garment." (For more on Burton, see page 162.) It was, Sykes told *Vogue*, "the ultimate wedding dress, truly a work of art and a testament to the incredible talent of Alexander and the workmanship of his seamstresses, who were devoted to him. McQueen was a true original."

INSPIRING DESIGN
This dress was reportedly a key factor in Catherine Middleton's choice of dress (page 158), shown at right, on display at Buckingham Palace.

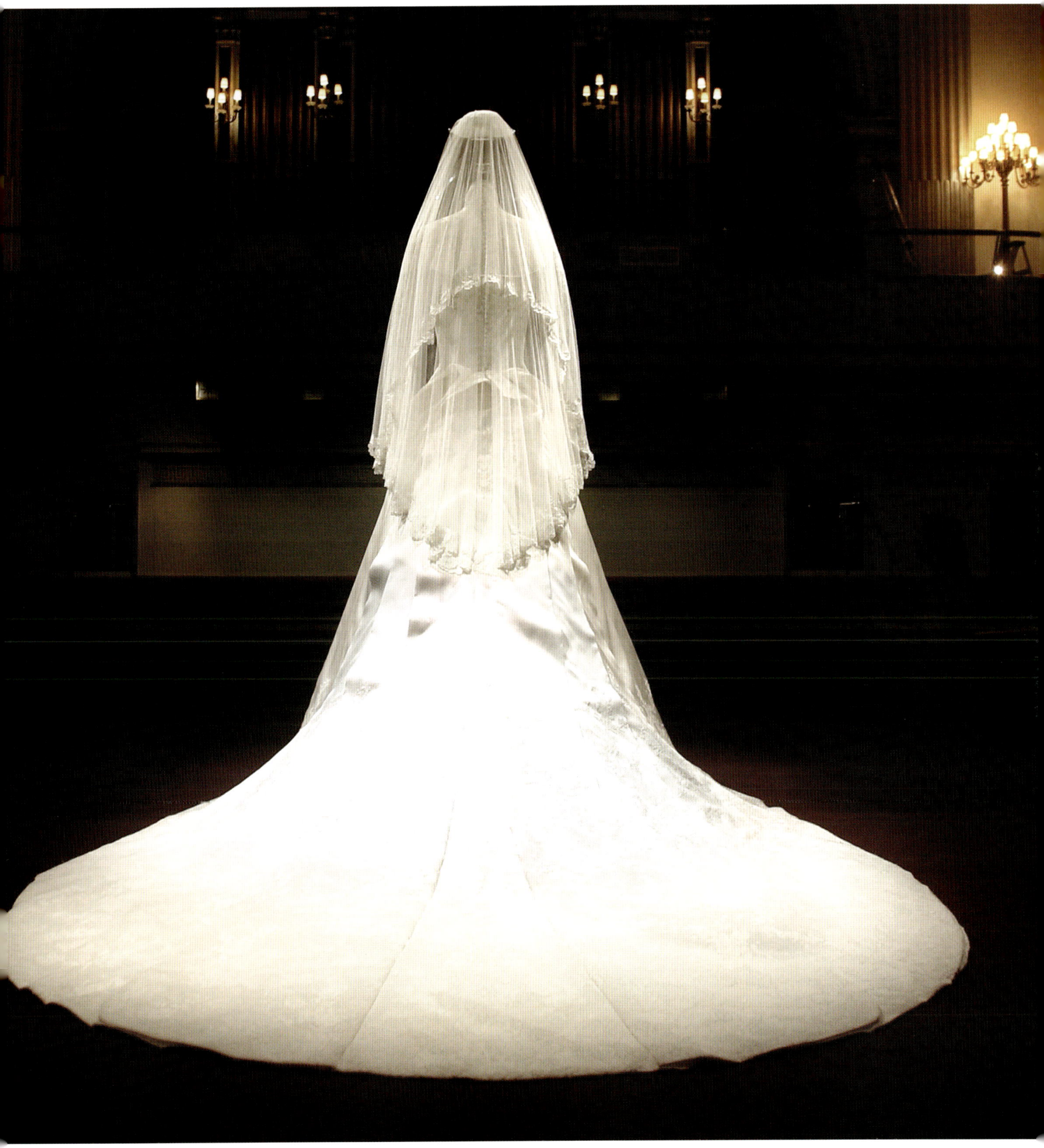

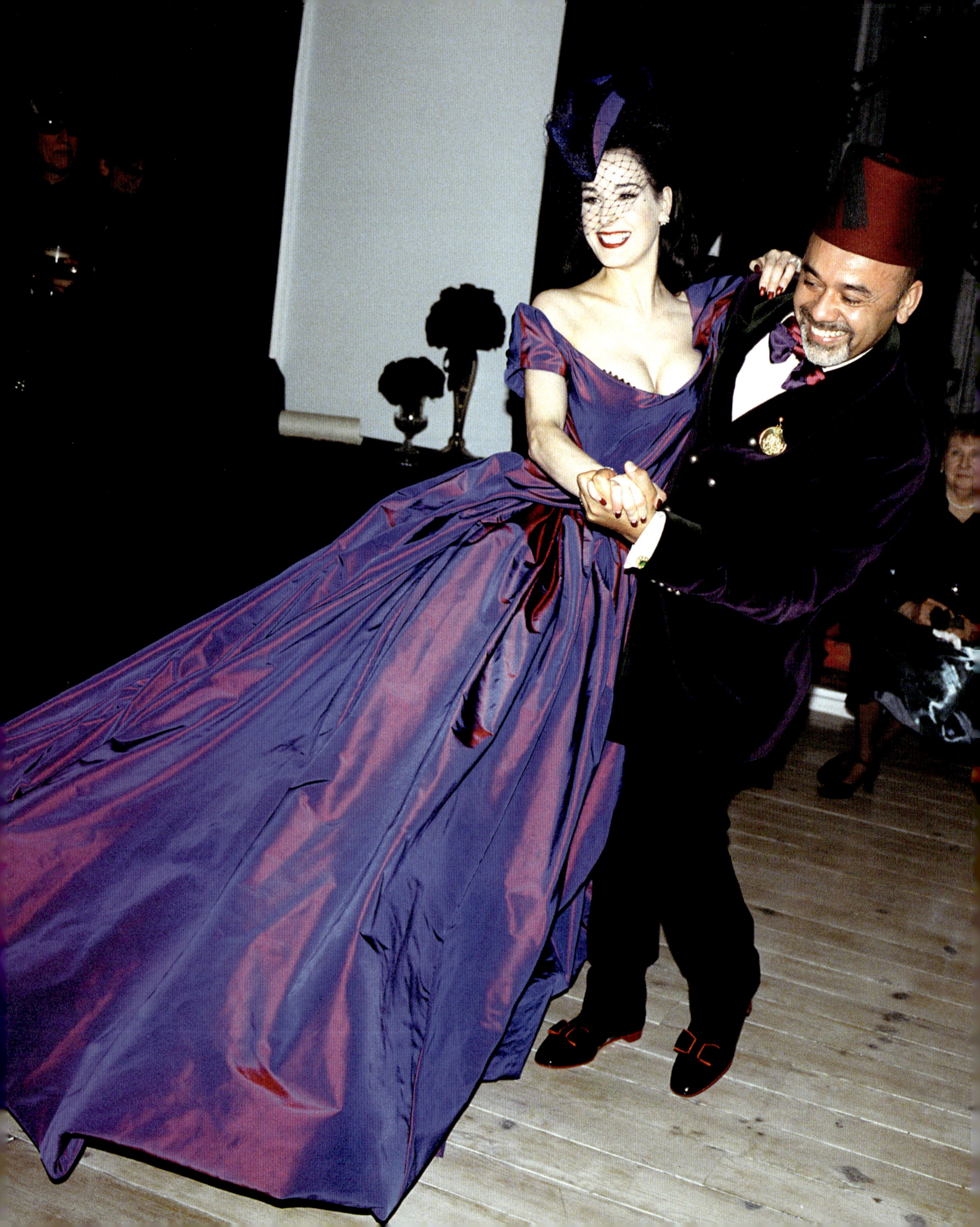

38

Vivienne Westwood

2005 For Dita Von Teese

The iridescent violet shot-taffeta wedding dress created for Dita Von Teese (née Heather Renée Sweet) by Vivienne Westwood was a study in "high drama and high style."

The "international queen of burlesque," Von Teese, married shock-goth rocker Marilyn Manson in 2005. Reporting on their wedding, *Vogue* magazine's international editor at large, Hamish Bowles, observed that the couple's "big day was never going to be a conventional." The icons of alternative culture married at midnight in their home in Los Angeles, later affirming their vows with an extravagant ceremony at Gurteen Castle in Tipperary, Ireland. Officiated by Chilean art-house film director Alejandro Jodorowsky, the event was beautifully decadent. The house was decorated with 4,000 black and blood-red roses and gold and black skull-shaped candles. Windows were dressed with black lace and heavy black velvet curtains. The tables were covered with custom-woven black Irish linen set with towering candelabras and cascades of burgundy grapes. The magnificent neo-Gothic castle exuded a dark romanticism reminiscent of an Edgar Allan Poe story.

Splendid opulence

In flickering candlelight, the bride made a dramatic entrance, her gown shimmering in a restless spectrum of rich purples that offset her striking porcelain complexion and jet-black hair. Swiss shot taffeta, amounting to a total of 56 feet (17 m), had been loosely draped by the expert hand of Westwood. Over a tight-fitting corset, the fabric swirled around the bride's tiny waist. Spreading from gathers and pleats into a voluminous trained skirt, the design undulated with soft folds that Von Teese's every movement reconfigured into eddying pools, royal-purple-shadowed valleys, and magenta-highlighted peaks.

Historical glamour

Westwood artfully manipulated the fabric into shapes reminiscent of the formally structured pannier and crinoline gowns of the past. "An exquisite, eighteenth-century Dresden figurine come to life" is how Hamish Bowles described the bride. Von Teese wore her gown with a little tricorne hat by milliner Stephen Jones, trimmed with black mink pompons and a black net veil. This was color-matched to delicate Christian Louboutin high-heeled sandals.

The dress unleashed the bride's Scarlett O'Hara fantasies. Like the heroine of the film *Gone with the Wind*, Von Teese has a miniscule waist, reputedly measuring 17 inches (43 cm) when corseted. This and her swelling cleavage were molded by a champagne-colored satin and black-lace corset, commissioned by the bride from the renowned English corsetier Mr. Pearl. Von Teese's infamous, feminine physique was emphasized by Westwood's design, which

DRAMA AND COLOR
As the bride dances with her shoe designer, Christian Louboutin, her dress swirls larger than life, in beautiful cascades.

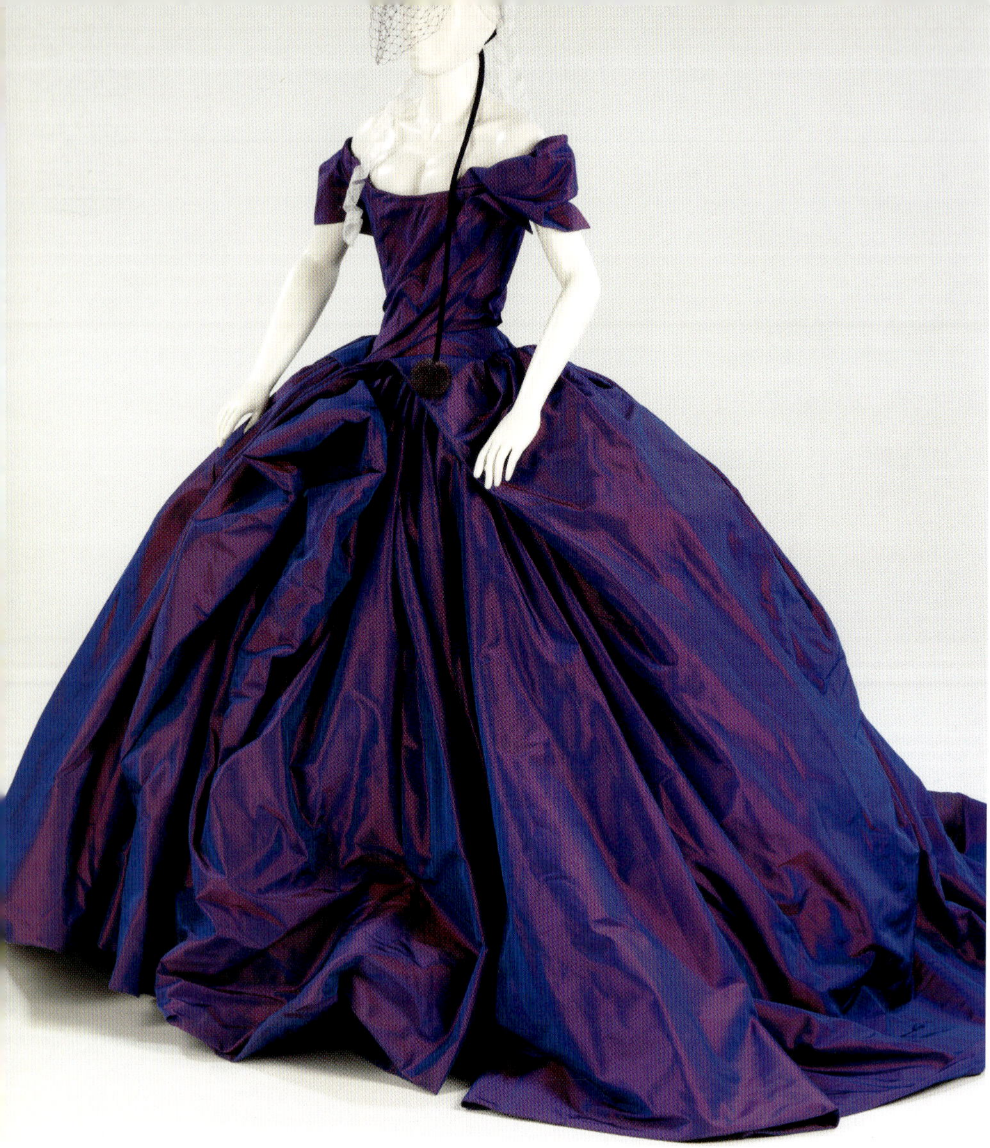

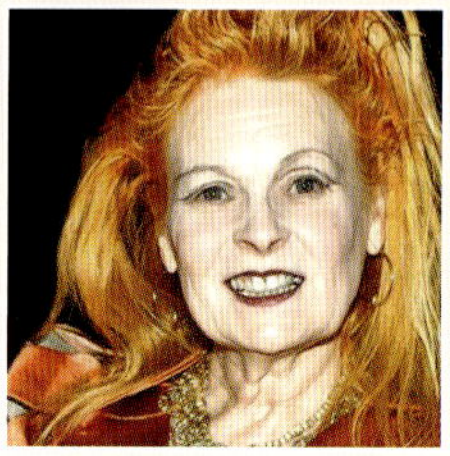

Vivienne Westwood
1941–

English designer Dame Vivienne Westwood personifies the creativity and subversive originality of British fashion. Her introduction of corsets as outerwear in 1985 filtered into bridalwear during the 1990s. In 1992, Westwood introduced wedding dresses to her collections and in the following year she produced her first bridal range for Liberty of London, launching her own made-to-measure bridal collection in 1996. Bearing her classic hallmarks of corsetry, swathed skirts, drapery, and tailoring, Westwood's wedding dresses bring an avant-garde edge to the bridal industry.

ANTEBELLUM BODICE
Skimming the bride's chest and shoulders, the bodice artfully exposed the elegant lines of her neck and a sensuous expanse of décolletage.

contrasted its huge skirt, supported upon a separate crinoline, with a tight, low-cut bodice.

Historic style, contemporary techniques

If the silhouette of Westwood's design was historical, then the techniques by which she achieved these lines—her cut and loose handling of the fabric—were entirely contemporary. "My clothes have a scent, a feeling of ... a certain type of nostalgia which, for me, is how I would define glamour," said Westwood, continuing: "even though it's all references to the past, they are synthesized to a point where they couldn't have been done at any other time."

On her wedding day, Von Teese's heady glamour, a combination of her signature 1940s pin-up-girl looks and nineteenth-century romanticism, transcended niche categorization, crossing the boundaries of mainstream and alternative style. "I didn't want a white wedding or a Gothic wedding," said the bride and, true to her word, her dress was somewhere in between. Von Teese's couture Vivienne Westwood dress, fitted on a mannequin made exactly to the bride-to-be's measurements, and eased onto her body on the wedding day by Westwood's chief couturier, fueled the contemporary bridal ideal of a uniquely personal gown.

THE DRESS

STYLE Gothic romanticism

SHAPE Neo-Victorian crinoline

FABRIC Shot taffeta

COLOR Purple

HIDDEN DETAILS

- Blue and red bows are sewn inside the dress.
- The dress fastens center-back.
- The bride wore a red and black jeweled garter and a champagne-colored satin and black lace Mr. Pearl corset.

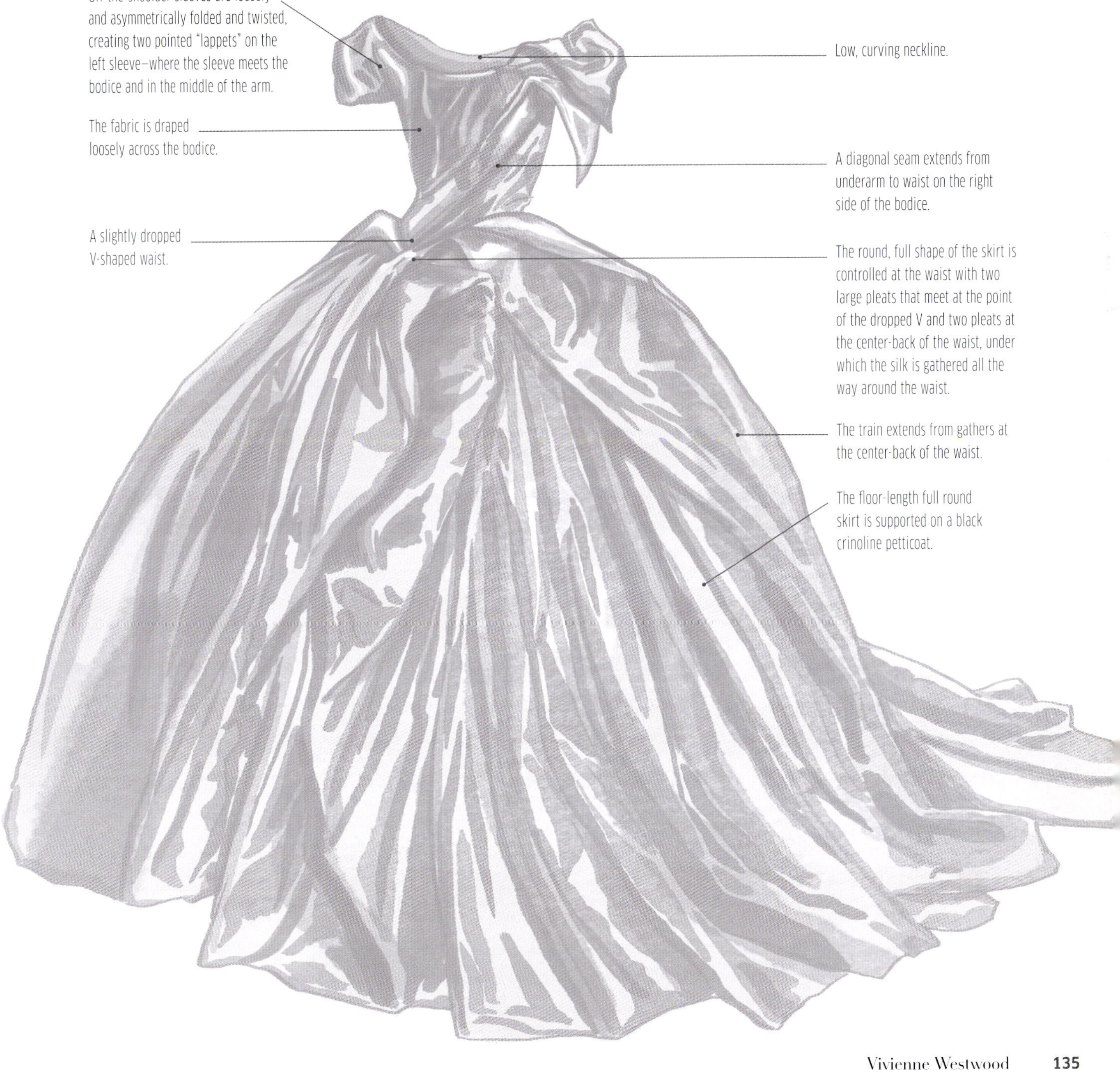

39

Viktor & Rolf

2006 For H&M

Viktor & Rolf's wedding dress for the international retail chain H&M was a crossover success, blurring the boundaries of cerebral, conceptual design and mass-market fashion.

Swedish retailer H&M's collaborations with famous designers Karl Lagerfeld (2004) and Stella McCartney (2005) were wildly successful. Following the release of their collections, stampedes broke out in H&M's stores as customers fought to snap up designer bargains. When, in 2006, H&M selected obscure Dutch designers Viktor Horsting and Rolf Snoeren to a create a limited-edition capsule collection, the fashion press considered it an intriguing choice. The pair had a strong following in the fashion community for their challenging, cerebral designs but were less known by the general public.

Viktor & Rolf developed their highly anticipated collection around the concept of a "fashion love story"—the surprising union of a conceptual design house with an affordable mass-market retailer. This ephemeral marriage was embodied by typical Viktor & Rolf designs—their twisted take on fashion classics—at a low price point. The star of the collection was a white silk duchesse wedding dress decorated with a deep ruffle and huge bow. Bows are a signature feature of Viktor & Rolf. Symbolizing love and commitment, the associations of the bow are often distorted by the designers' play on scale and their surrealist strategy of dislocation. The oversized bow on this dress was a subtle allusion to their treatment of its iconic form in Mabel Wisse Smitt's wedding dress (see page 124). However, if the bow proved too overpowering then the bride could detach it, leaving a pretty if unremarkable dress. The advertising campaign played up the designers' unconventional approach by presenting the wedding dress as the subject of a surreal double wedding. The Brazilian model Raquel Zimmermann was pictured as a bride with the designers as mirror-image grooms.

The dress, costing $349 dollars, was the runaway success of the collection. Just 1,000 were produced and all sold out within hours. People reportedly queued up outside H&M's flagship Fifth Avenue New York store from two o'clock in the morning to secure their purchase. British newspaper *The Daily Mail* ran an article titled "Yes, We Got That Viktor & Rolf Dress," telling the stories of four women who braved the frenzy and wore the dress on their wedding day. One woman, a single fashion designer from London, bought three dresses—despite the fact that she wasn't getting married.

Viktor & Rolf's wedding dress brought a version of their avant-garde design to the mass market and has now entered popular culture as a cult fashion item.

A COMMITMENT TO FASHION
If the bride chooses, she can reject the conceptual feel of the design and remove the oversized bow from the front.

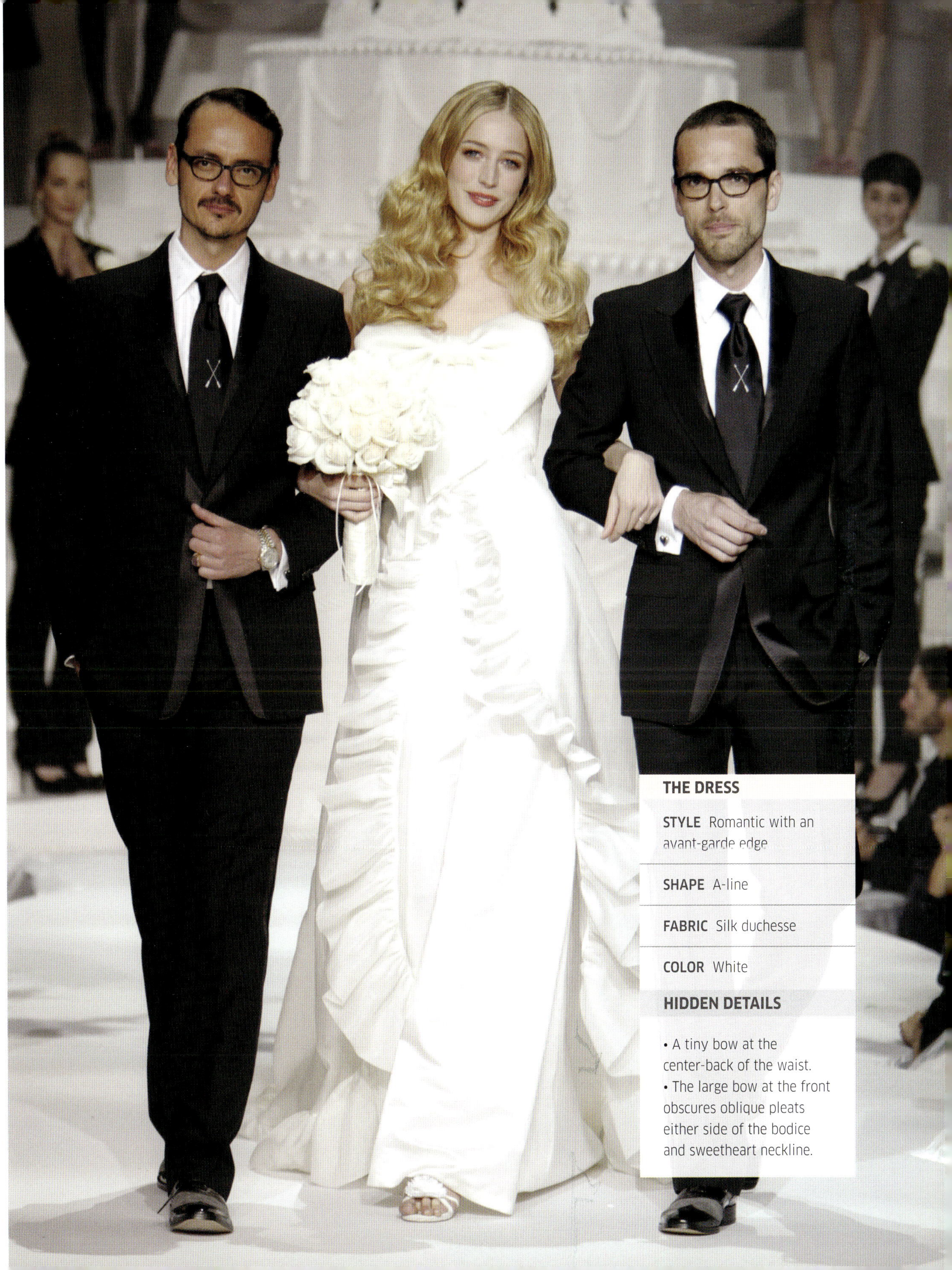

THE DRESS

STYLE Romantic with an avant-garde edge

SHAPE A-line

FABRIC Silk duchesse

COLOR White

HIDDEN DETAILS

- A tiny bow at the center-back of the waist.
- The large bow at the front obscures oblique pleats either side of the bodice and sweetheart neckline.

40

Alexander McQueen

2006 Fall/Winter

Alexander McQueen's antique lace gown defined his provocative Widows of Culloden collection—yet hidden in its ruffles was another story.

McQueen's Fall/Winter 2006–2007 Widows of Culloden collection was inspired by the 1745 massacre of the Scottish Jacobites at Culloden by the British government's army. McQueen was passionate about his Scottish ancestry, which was uncovered by his mother, and Widows of Culloden communicated a defiantly political statement. In McQueen's words, "What the British did there [at the Battle of Culloden] was nothing short of genocide." His collection of romantically melancholic garments summoned the ghosts of the slaughtered Scottish army's widows.

The finale wedding dress, which summed up the aesthetic of the collection, was made of beautiful antique lace, fitted close to the body until the hips, at which point it fell in softly cascading ruffles to the ground. Its elongated silhouette was based on dresses from the 1890s. Explaining its shape, McQueen said: "I was interested in the idea that there are no constraints on the silhouette. I wanted to exaggerate a woman's form, almost along the lines of a classical statue." Underscoring the soft, mournful quality of the dress was an austere edge, evoking in McQueen's imagination "the nip of the ice on [the] end of your nose." This discordant sensation was worked out in McQueen's design process through his treatment of the dress's veil, which swept upward from the neckline and caught on a headdress of white resin antlers. McQueen recalled that "when we put the antlers on the model and then draped over it the lace embroidery that we had made, we had to poke them through a £2,000 piece of work. But then it worked because it looks like she's rammed the piece of lace with her antlers." Sharp-pointed antlers piercing delicate, virginal, lace-appliquéd tulle brought a note of masculine aggression to the gentle femininity of the design, endowing the vulnerable widowed bride with strength and force: "I want people to be afraid of the women I dress," McQueen had told *Vogue* ten years earlier. (For more on McQueen, see page 130.)

A legacy and an inheritance

Just as McQueen's mother had passed on her knowledge of their family's past to her son, so the designer intended his exquisitely handcrafted, one-off couture creation to be a valuable heirloom worn by generations of brides. The fiercely political narrative informing the creation of the dress hid a lesser-known but no less significant story: that of the master craftsman handing over his skills to his friend and successor, Sarah Burton. When Burton married in 2004, McQueen created

A FEARSOME BRIDE
The design forced the bride to destroy her veil, endowing her with an aggressive edge.

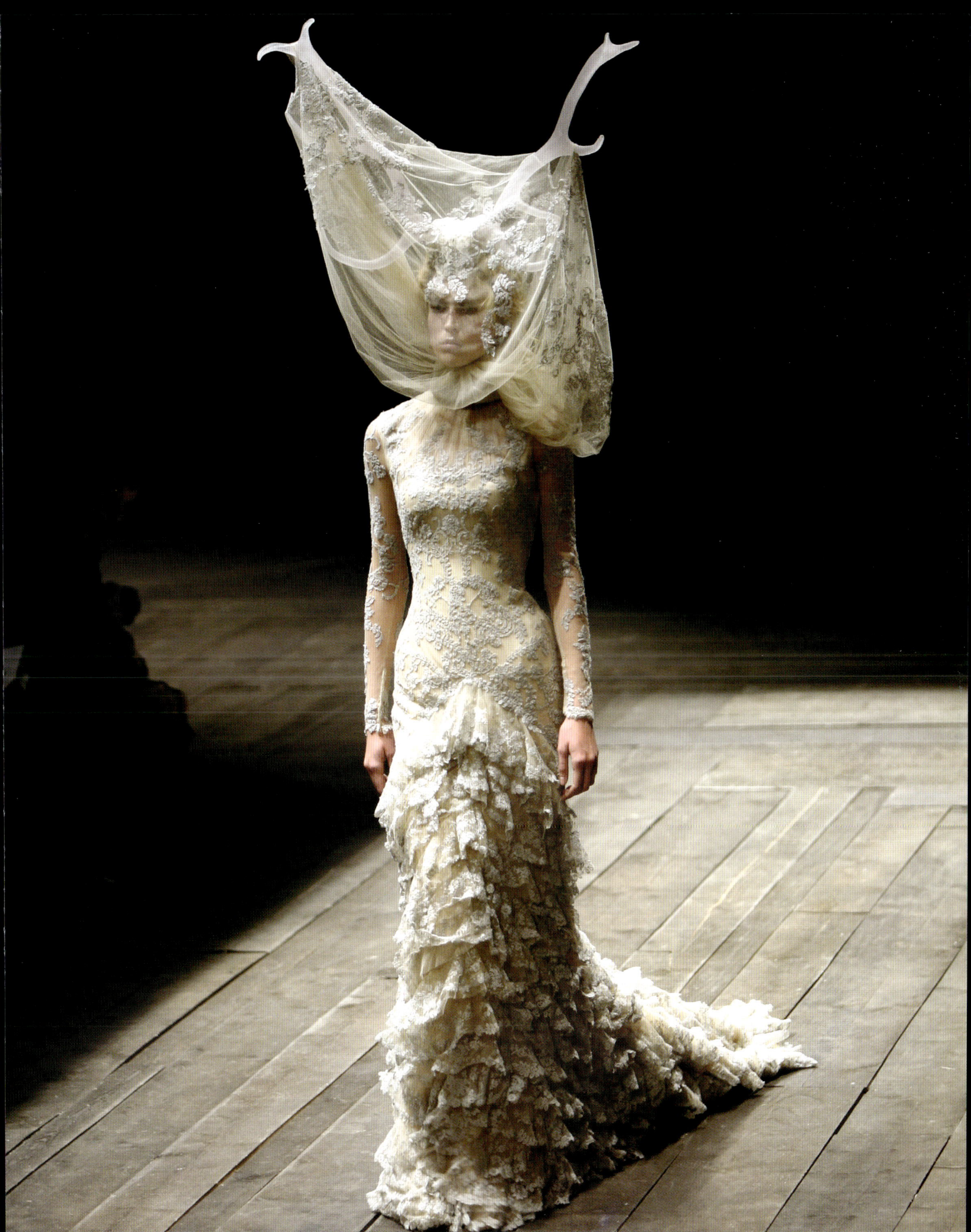

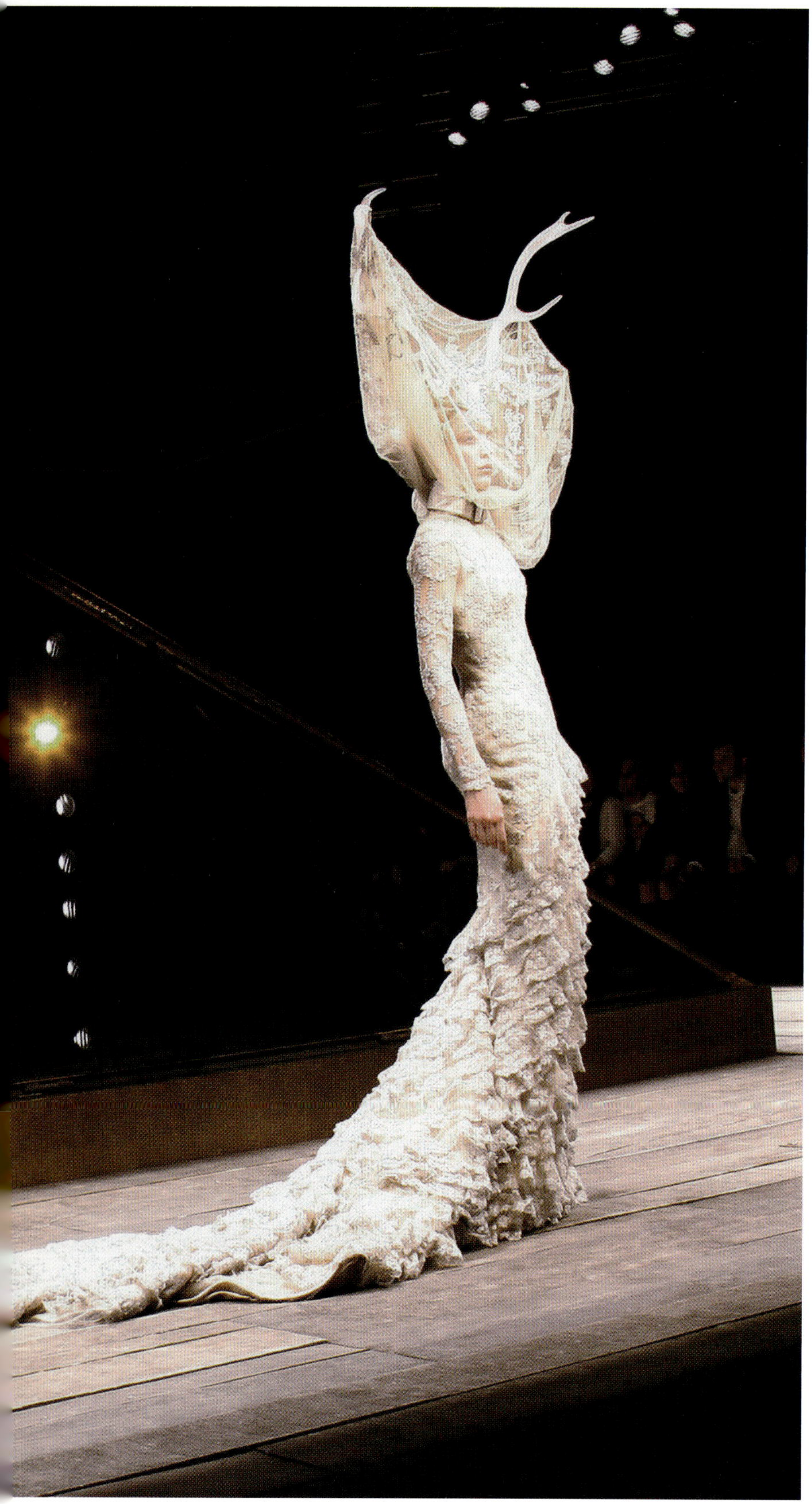

her wedding dress. This was the design he reworked two years later to create the Widows of Culloden wedding dress. Burton recalled that while McQueen was working on her own dress, he had pushed her to perfect the Carrickmacross-lace overlay technique: "Lee wanted the lace to lie flat; he hated gathers," Burton said. "We had to figure out how to make lace work in the round with those ruffles. … So we cut out all of the flowers from the lace and reappliquéd [them] on tulle to make our own fabric."

An armory of design knowledge

The rigorous execution of McQueen's vision equipped Burton with the skills she would later use to create one of the most beautiful wedding dresses of the century: the lace-appliquéd gown she designed for Catherine Middleton in 2011 (page 158; for more on Burton, see page 162).

The Widows of Culloden dress bridged the gap between McQueen's famously anarchic, anti-establishment designs and the less well-known private commissions undertaken by his house for brides as diverse as his former stylist, Katy England, and actress Kate Winslet. Following McQueen's tragic suicide in 2010, Burton took over as creative director of his brand. *Vogue* observed that McQueen's legacy continues to shine through Burton and the "incredible wedding dress she made that astonished the world in his name." Between the McQueen-designed wedding dress Burton wore and the one she went on to design for the future Duchess of Cambridge lies the Widows of Culloden wedding dress—an emotional treasury of the histories, relationships, and stories closest to McQueen.

STATUESQUE DESIGN
The dress's elongated silhouette was based on dresses of the 1890s.

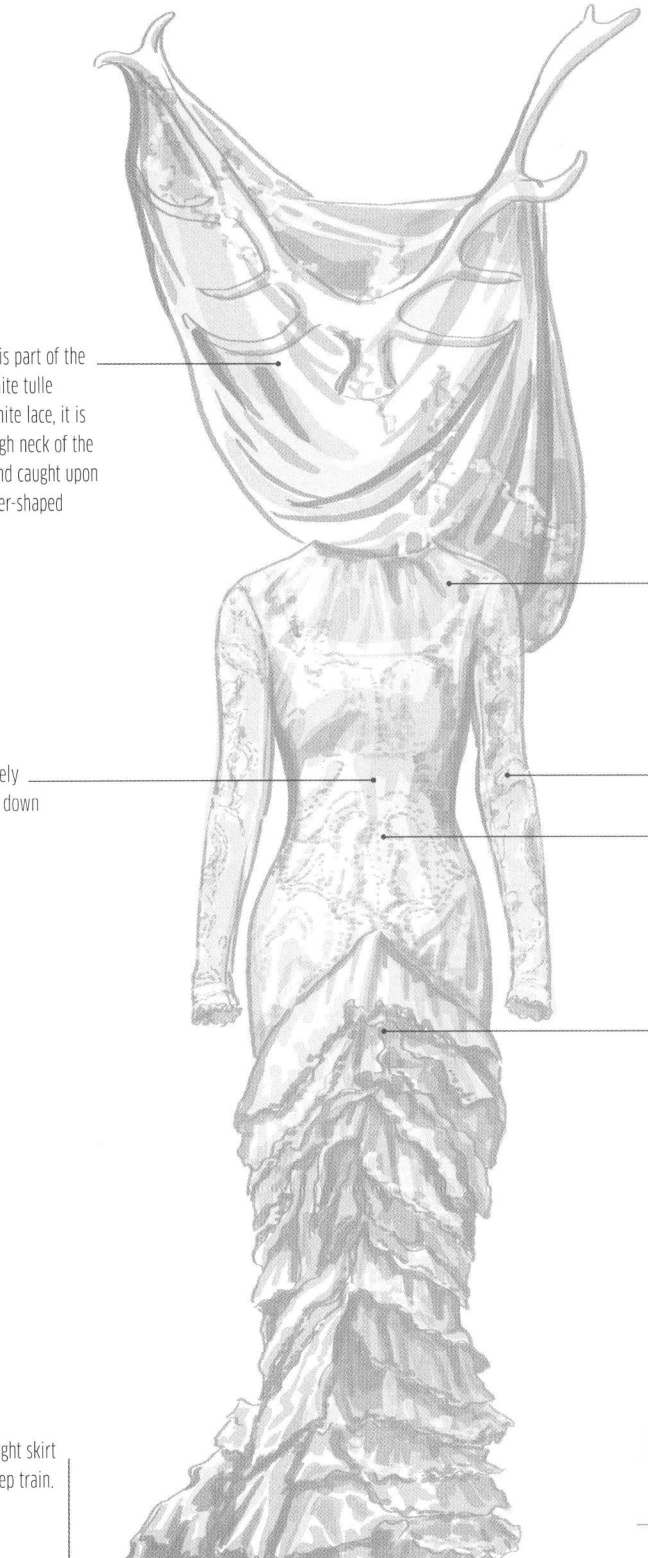

THE DRESS

STYLE Melancholy romantic

SHAPE Column

FABRIC Silk tulle and antique lace

COLOR Cream

THE DRESS

STYLE	Neo-Victorian
SHAPE	Origami
FABRIC	Silk satin and silk tulle
COLOR	White and silver

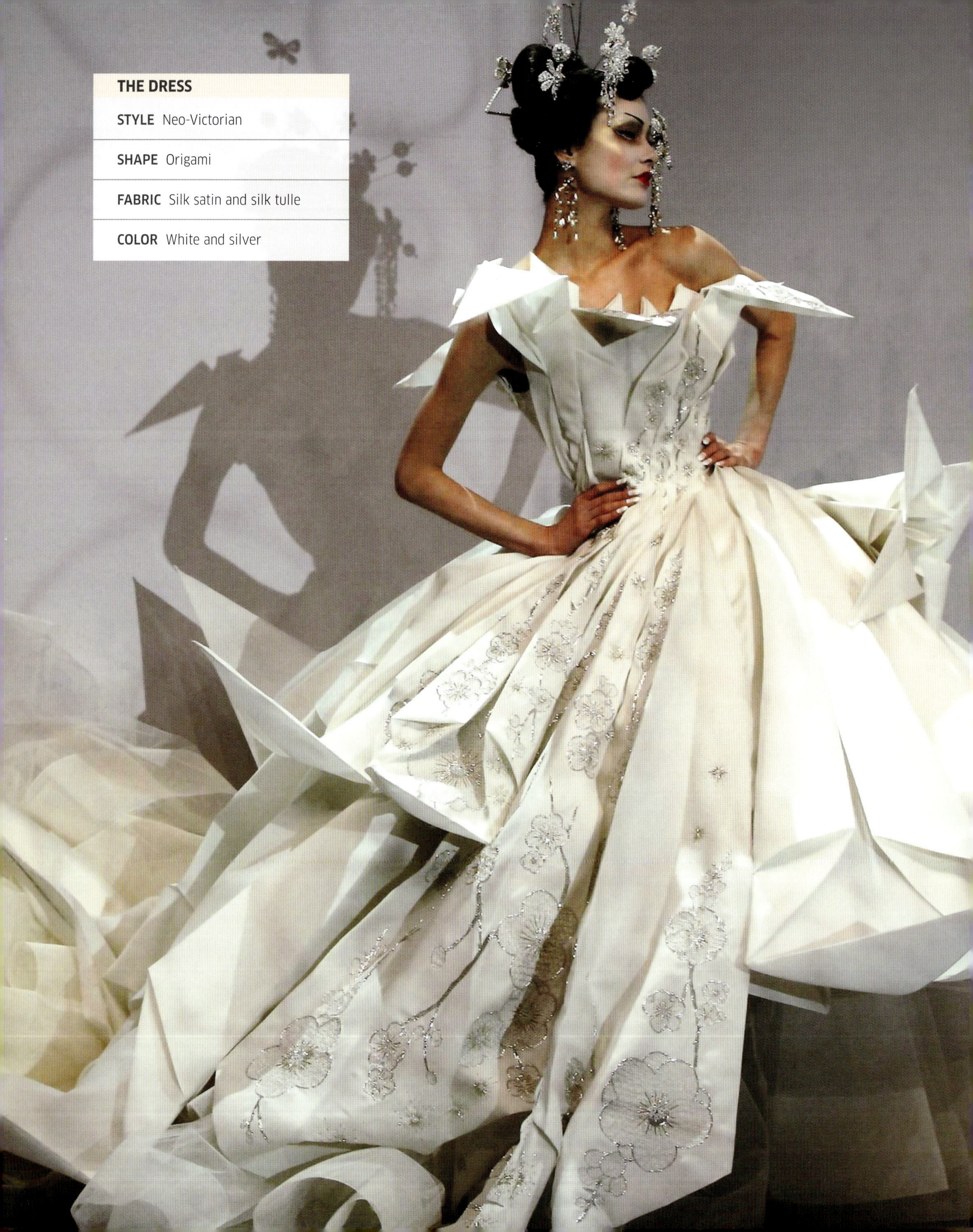

41

John Galliano

2007 Christian Dior Spring/Summer

Christian Dior's Spring/Summer 2007 show, crafted by John Galliano, concluded with an intricately pleated and folded wedding gown, like a living origami crane crafted from embroidered satin and clouds of silk tulle.

Galliano's research for the collection took him back in time to a Japan populated by teahouses, cherry blossoms, and graceful geishas. From there he delved into the archives of the Dior salon, distilling the elegant tailoring and romantic eveningwear of Christian Dior's seminal 1947 New Look collection. The 2007 show's succession of beautifully tailored suits and breathtaking evening gowns told a tale inspired by Cho-Cho-San and her romance with Lieutenant Pinkerton in Puccini's opera *Madame Butterfly*. The suitably theatrical finale wedding dress was Madame Butterfly personified.

Sculpting a masterpiece

The fabrics and shaping of a traditional wedding dress were, in this master couturier's skillful hands, magically sculpted into an entirely novel form. Layers of silk tulle formed the foundation of the dress. Bursting out at the rear, the train appeared to be emerging from a chrysalis in soft, ribbonlike folds. Over this softly structured stratum, planes of stiff white satin were folded into sharply defined geometries ending in gravity-defying peaks. A frosting of cherry blossom embroidery, rendered in silver thread, sparkled diagonally down the length of the gown. Around the neckline, the folds opened out like a flower, framing model Shalom Harlow's masklike face, painted in Kabuki-style makeup. Crowning her head was a Stephen Jones headpiece dripping with trembling diamond flowers and topped with, of course, a butterfly.

The press were unanimous in their praise for this dress. It was, they said, Galliano at his finest. The collection, marking his ten-year anniversary at Dior, was a return to form—to the extravagant, intricately engineered, and meticulously tailored clothing for which Galliano was best known. An arch storyteller, Galliano used his collections to weave narratives that drew on an eclectic range of historic and exotic sources, peopled by female characters loosely based on reality, famous fictional women, and stereotypes. Galliano said of his approach, "It's a dialogue between past and present. The starting point is usually factual, but we allow our imaginations to run riot." (For more on Galliano, see page 123.)

In Japan, there is an ancient belief, now part of common folklore, that folding 1,000 cranes makes a wish come true. Galliano's origami folded gown evoked the emotions, sensitivity, and wish fulfillment of every bride's dream white wedding dress.

UNFINISHED SYMPHONY
Panels of satin running the length of the dress were folded into origami-like shapes. Each panel suggested the paper craft in progress.

42

Vivienne Westwood

2007 Fall/Winter

Fictional bride Carrie Bradshaw's Vivienne Westwood wedding dress became a real-life bridal icon.

Despite its inauspicious backstory, the ivory silk wedding dress worn by jilted bride Bradshaw in the movie *Sex and the City* is enshrined in bridal legend. In the film, the newly engaged fashion writer and columnist, played by Sarah Jessica Parker, is featured in *Vogue* magazine modeling a series of wedding dresses from the real-life recent collections of leading bridal couturiers, including Dior, Carolina Herrera, Christian Lacroix, Lanvin, Vera Wang, and Vivienne Westwood. From this dazzling panoply of luxurious confections Bradshaw falls in love with Westwood's billowing, strapless design. Bradshaw describes the dress from Westwood's Wake Up, Cave Girl! collection, as "so special it would bring a wedding tear from even the most unbelieving of women."

Westwood's collection of swirling, tumescent forms with exaggerated darts and pointed details realized her sculptural vision of Stone Age woman. In this, the finale piece, the Cave Girl silhouette was taken to the extreme, with a contemporary interpretation of a polonaise-style dress. The gown featured a voluminous skirt of ivory radzimir taffeta under a bunched, champagne-colored, silk duchesse satin overskirt, which sat beneath a tight strapless bodice with a sharply pointed, plunging neckline. By simultaneously enlarging and reducing the silhouette, Westwood maximized a powerful impression of femininity, underscoring the effect with the dramatic luminosity of silk fabrics. Westwood's gown was so grand and artful that it could have stepped out of the Van Dyck or Thomas Gainsborough portraits to which she frequently turned for inspiration. (For more on Westwood, see page 134.)

The dream wedding

In the movie, Westwood gifts Bradshaw a slightly different version of the made-to-measure gown, costing $23,780. The provocatively low neckline, which allowed glimpses of the model's nipples on the runway, was replaced for the actress with a more structured bodice. The neckline was also trimmed on one edge with sparkling crystals. Bradshaw's dress, worn with a vertiginous bird-of-paradise headpiece, tulle veil, and customized Dior "Gladiator" heels, was at the center of her fairy-tale wedding.

Although Bradshaw's wedding day doesn't go to plan, the movie and the dress were huge hits. For those who could afford it, Westwood's floor-sweeping confection could be custom-ordered in the bride's choice of fabric and color, taking between three and six months to make. The popularity of Bradshaw's dress prompted Westwood to launch a ready-to-wear cocktail-length version for the online retailer

FROM CATWALK TO SILVER SCREEN
Westwood's Fall/Winter 2007–2008 dress was later made famous by its inclusion in the *Sex and The City* film of 2008.

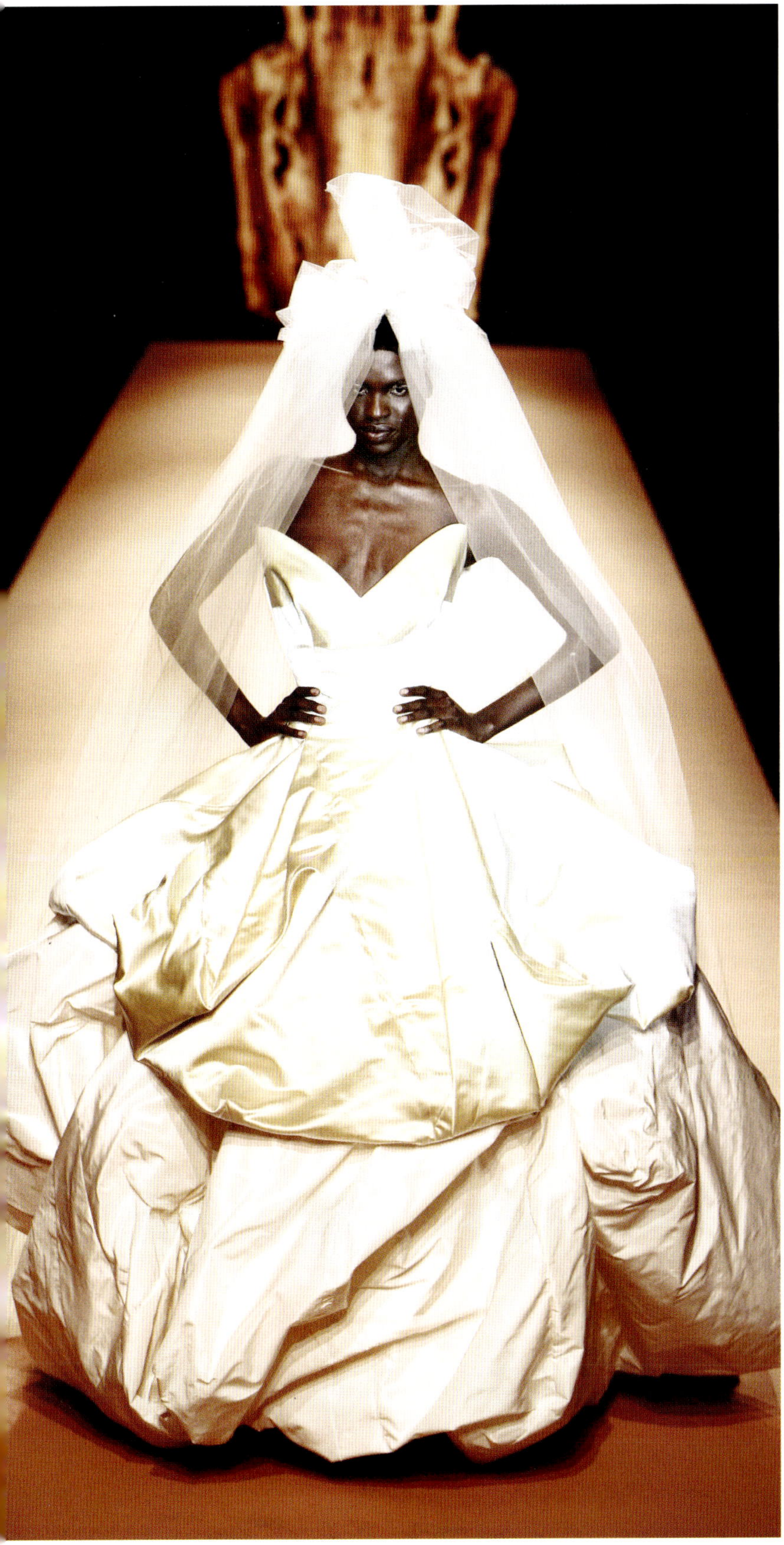

Net-A-Porter in spring 2009: the "Lily" dress, costing $9,875. Like its Cave Girl counterpart, the dress was a commercial success despite the global recession that had hit months after the release of the movie. The Lily dress sold out within hours of appearing on the website, prompting British *Glamour* magazine to wonder, "I can't think of a single other fictional character who could sell $10,000 wedding dresses in the middle of a recession, can you?"

Life imitates art imitating life

Bradshaw was, as the fashion press recognized, a style icon to real women. Her slippery status as a fantastical character with a substantial presence in the real world was perpetuated by *Vogue*, who followed the fictional wedding-dress feature with a real fashion shoot of Parker and Chris Noth on an imaginary honeymoon in New York for the June 2008 edition, published to coincide with the film's premiere. *Vogue* magazine's images epitomize the appeal of Bradshaw's fictional existence in New York, marked by a seemingly unending disposable income to spend on designer fashion. Westwood's wedding dress distilled the illusion of the *Sex and the City* lifestyle into a tangible object that could be purchased in reality. Making the transition from catwalk to silver screen to real life, the dress embodied the aspirations of a generation of successful, style-conscious brides.

THE DRESS

STYLE Glamorous and romantic

SHAPE Polonaise-style skirt and strapless bodice

FABRIC Silk duchesse satin and radzimir taffeta

COLOR Ivory and champagne

43

Olivier Theyskens

2008 Nina Ricci for Lauren Davis

When *Vogue* contributing editor Lauren Davis got married, the bride wore not one but two dresses, creating a third look at two o'clock in the morning by cutting the hem of her second gown to make a flirtatious minidress.

For the nuptials that took place in the Iglesia Santo Domingo, Cartagena, Colombia, Davis began her three-day wedding odyssey wearing a reverential ball-gown-style dress and matching coat. Marrying Colombian Andres Santo Domingo, heir to a fortune measured in billions, the bride's suitably grand ensemble was fashioned from 65 yards (60 m) of silk jacquard woven with peony blooms. The coat, made in the same fabric, was embroidered with tinsel paillettes, silver threads, vintage lace, and tufts of clipped white feathers. Craftsmen working in Nina Ricci's ateliers worked for 1,200 hours to assemble the outfit, after which it was taken to the legendary Lesage embroiderers to be finished—a process that took an additional 800 hours to ensure that the beading, in the words of Monsieur Lesage, "did not look like a Christmas tree, but like something washed away, swept away in the detail of the dress." *Vogue* estimated that a Parisian couture wedding dress of the quality of Davis's would have cost in the region of $200,000, a figure that, according to *Vogue*, even Madonna balked at when she approached Olivier Theyskens to design the dress for her marriage to Guy Ritchie.

Dressing for the occasion

For the designer, Theyskens, Davis's marriage was the perfect opportunity to create the ultimate wedding dress, a dream he had harbored since childhood. Theyskens's design responded to the couple's wedding venues: a sixteenth-century Roman Catholic church, the location for the evening ceremony; the Santo Domingo's house, where the reception was held; and a seventeenth-century fort overlooking the sea, the venue for the late-night after-party. Theyskens reportedly told the bride: "For your wedding you want to be respectful of the occasion and the historic church. This is a special day, you need a special dress." The spectacular ceremony dress certainly fulfilled Theyskens's aspirations. Accompanied by Mendelssohn's "Wedding March," Davis swept down the aisle past the 500 gathered guests.

On arrival at the reception, the bride changed into a fitted dress encased in spiraling tiers of weightless feathers, a subtle homage to the discreet decorative trim applied to her ceremony coat. Its strapless bodice mimicked the sweetheart neckline of the formal

FITTED TO PERFECTION
The ensemble took 1,200 hours to assemble, plus an additional 800 hours for the embroidery.

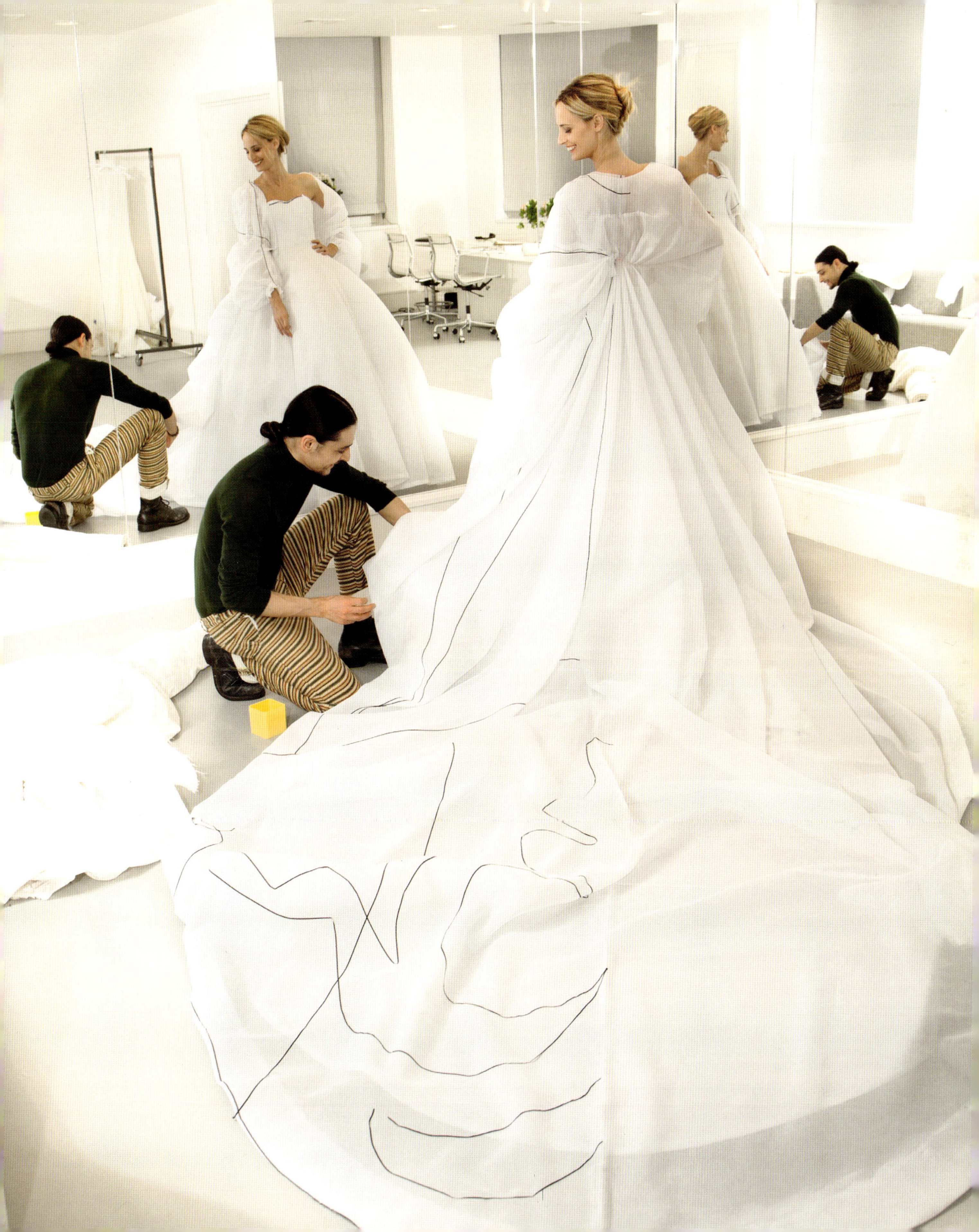

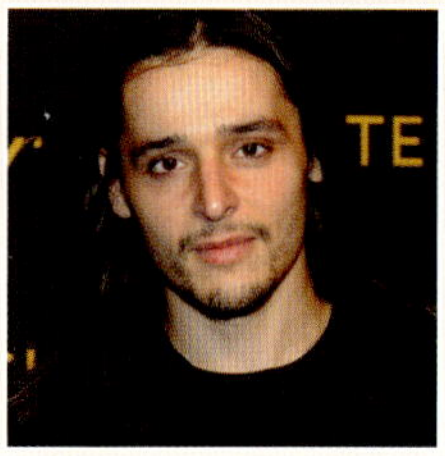

Olivier Theyskens
1977–

Flemish designer Olivier Theyskens was identified by *Vogue* magazine in 2000 as one of the "Generation Next," describing his work as "the height of youthful haute-Goth cool." After producing an eponymous line, Theyskens was brought in to revive couture houses Rochas in 2002 and Nina Ricci in 2006. Unfortunately, his approach of combining streetwear and couture craftsmanship failed due to issues with pricing, and he was dismissed from Ricci in 2009. Theyskens began designing under his own name at Theory, and in 2010 was promoted to artistic director for the entire company.

ceremony dress, and the gentle shell-like folds of the skirt were a nod to the illusion of a tidal wash of embroidery on the train of the coat. The complementary styling of these two gowns, so different in their structure, wove a thread of aesthetic continuity through the wedding. At two o'clock in the morning, Theyskens, with surgical precision, sheared off the bottom half of the feathered dress, metamorphosing the gown into an asymmetric minidress channeling the spirit of 1920s and Latino fringed dance dresses. Thus attired, Davis and her groom led their guests up a ramp lined with ceremonial dancers to the fortress, where the newlyweds partied into the early hours of the morning.

The pinnacle of society weddings

Vogue magazine featured a lush photographic spread of the wedding accompanied by a first-person account of the extravaganza. No details were spared in the description of the event and the making of the dress, enabling readers to partake vicariously in the luxury of a no-expense-spared wedding. Davis's couture wedding dress marked a moment in time of wedding culture. It was the epitome of the monumental society wedding dress of the 2000s, surpassing even the most expensive wedding dress to date: Melania Knauss's crystal and pearl embroidered Christian Dior wedding dress, reportedly costing $100,000 and taking 1,000 hours to create, which she wore to marry Donald Trump in 2005.

In 2008, the world was plunged into a global economic crisis. In such circumstances Davis's wedding dresses might have seemed excessive, but the groom's parents explained their hope that the publicity from the event would attract tourism to Colombia. Another potential point of controversy was the mid-event restructuring of Davis's reception dress, which Theyskyens cut in half to create a flirty minidress. To willfully cut a couture gown would be viewed by some as sacrilege, but throughout bridal history wedding dresses have been repurposed following the event. More wasteful is the "trash the dress" phenomena that occurred in the early part of the 2000s, in which brides were photographed destroying their dresses by running into the sea or even setting them alight.

The train is subtly embroidered with tinsel paillettes, silver threads, and tufts of clipped white feathers, giving the impression that the trimming is ingrained into the details of the jacquard fabric.

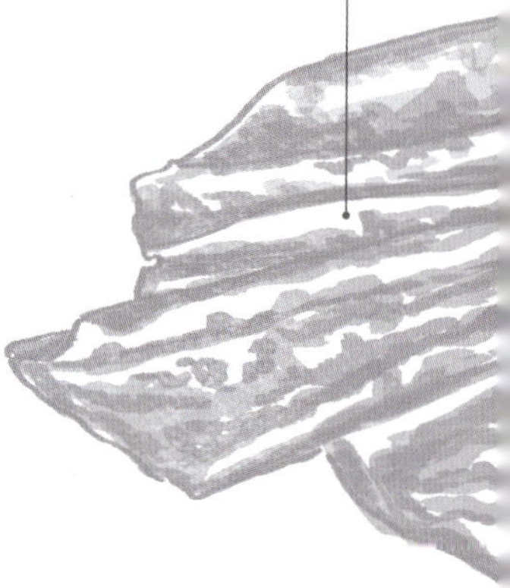

HIDDEN DETAILS

- Lace yoke extends to a V shape at the back of the coat, with the train falling from just below the shoulder blades.

THE DRESS

STYLE Traditional and romantic extravagance

SHAPE Ball gown

FABRIC Silk jacquard and feathers

COLOR White and silver

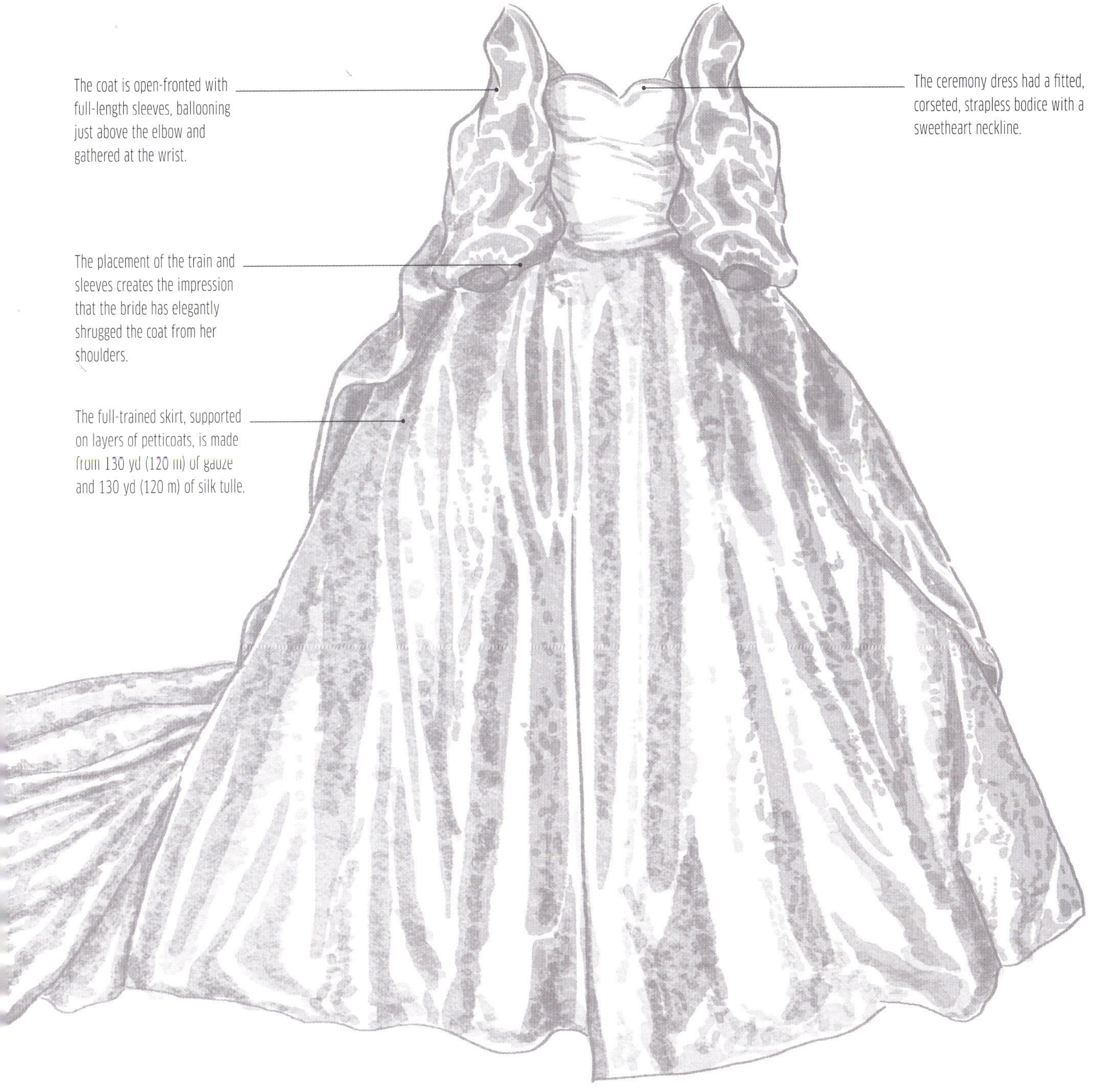

44

Jean Paul Gaultier

2009 Spring/Summer

Jean Paul Gaultier's wisp of a white wedding dress—juxtaposing the overt sexuality of his infamous corset dresses with the iconography of the Madonna—was a witty play on the traditional image of the chaste bride.

Gaultier frequently uses his finale wedding dress to make a tongue-in-cheek comment on societal and aesthetic codes, drawing attention to the discrepancy between the associations of the white wedding dress and the lives being led by most twenty-first-century brides.

The Virgin Mary brides

In 2001, Gaultier created a contemporary retelling of the sixteenth-century devotional painting *The Madonna and Child Playing with the Veil* by Jan Gossaert (circa 1520). Gaultier's 2001 bride appeared in a simple white strapless dress, with a babe-in-arms partially wrapped in the tulle veil hanging over her shoulders. A decade later, the designer alluded to the now commonplace presence of a bride and groom's children at their nuptials, ending his Spring/Summer 2013 show on a humorous note with four children emerging from beneath the bride's skirt.

Prior to the 2009 show, the Virgin Mary was first used as a controversial muse in Gaultier's Spring/Summer 2007 Les Vierges (The Virgins) collection, which concluded with an androgynous bride in a sheer white, loosely ruffled robe and a high tulle headdress fashioned into a halo. Carrying a single lily, the bride appeared to reference the Madonna in Dante Gabriel Rossetti's painting *The Annunciation* (1849–1850). Of his intentions in the Les Vierges collection, the designer said: "It is not about using Christianity as much as it is about the beauty of religious icons." The iconography that Gaultier explored in 2007 set the stage for his most powerful and provocative exploration of the Madonna bride.

Dispensing with an actual wedding dress, Gaultier sent the bride of his Spring/Summer 2009 collection down the runway in what appeared to be her lingerie and a light tulle veil arranged into a halo shape. The ensemble fused his Madonna iconography with one of his most enduring sartorial signatures: the corset worn as outerwear. The "dress" was composed of a transparent white corseted body attached to glossy nude stockings and covered with layers of sheer tulle fashioned into a skirt that split open at the bride's thigh, like a frothy peignoir, and extended upward into a veil that surrounded her face with fanning pleats. The design was an almost identical version of a black-lace ensemble that had preceded it in the show.

An assertion of women's power

With her strong sexual aura and subtly virginal undertones, Gaultier's bride stands

REVEALING DESIGN
Gaultier's confection was founded on his sartorial signature, the corset as outerwear.

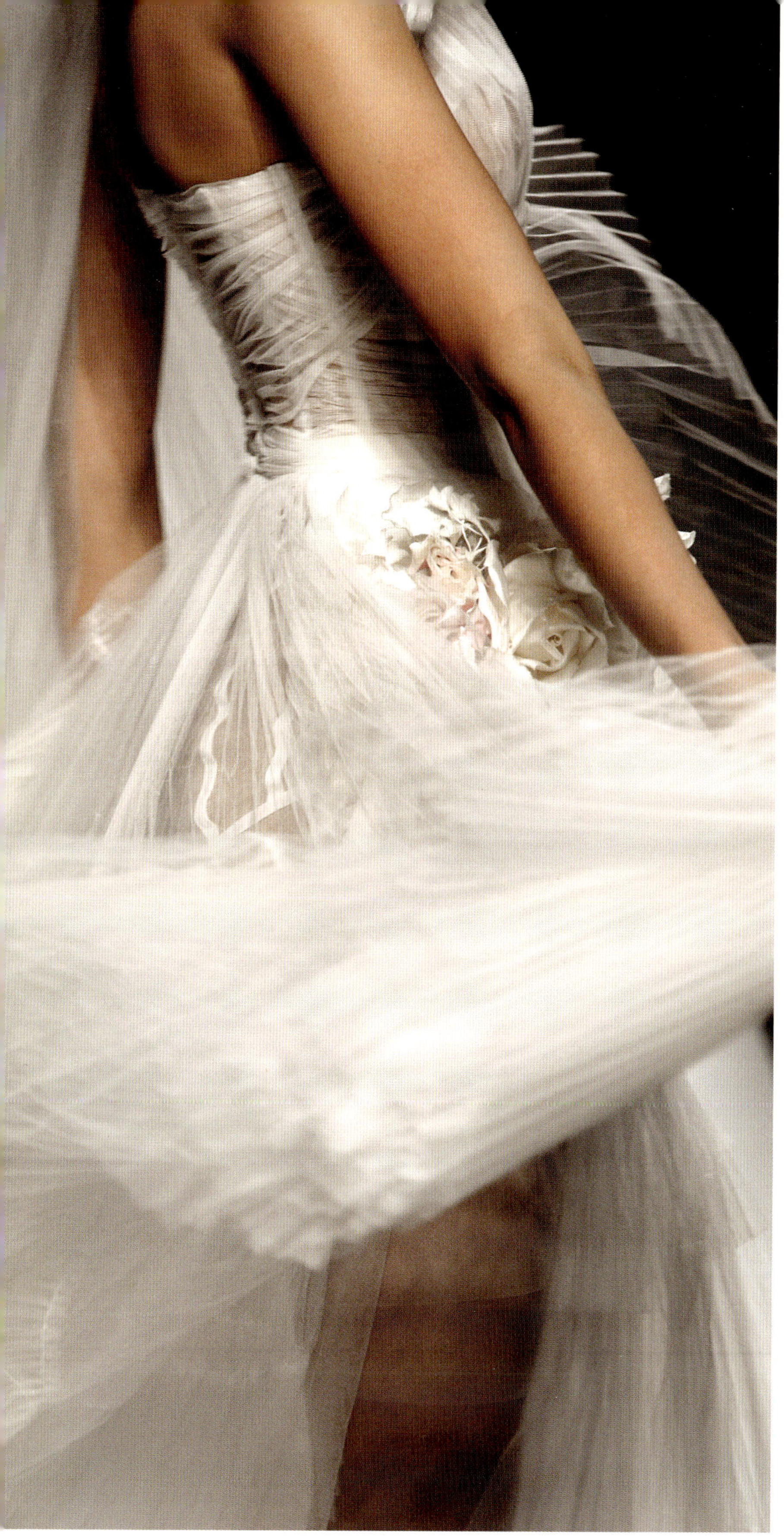

to be interpreted as an embodiment of the psychoanalytical Madonna/whore complex, with its conflicting expectations of sexual desirability and virtuousness. However, with typically derisive humor, Gaultier subverts the notion of a female body imprisoned by society's norms.

In Gaultier's version, the corset is an assertion of the power of women's bodies. Marie, Gaultier's maternal grandmother, instigated his career-long obsession with the corset when she asked her young grandson for help in lacing her up. "I found the instrument so fabulous and beautiful," said the designer. "From that moment I became fascinated by the idea of transforming one's body with clothes, and the idea that certain garments can accentuate something you want and hide something you don't want." Gaultier's corseted bride may have seemed like the negation of the feminist struggle, but in fact the corseted bride can be read as a powerful post-feminist statement of the emancipation of appearance.

Sexual politics were not the only contemporary issue to be addressed by the 2009 gown. The curlicue cord that trimmed the veil, a continuation of the scrolling motifs worked into embroideries and prints elsewhere in the collection, was—as fashion journalist Sarah Mower observed—reminiscent of paper money. This decorative detail was a light-handed pun on the global economic crisis, which prompted other designers to send out safe, commercially friendly finale dresses that year.

Gaultier's corseted wedding dress, drawing on the iconography of the Madonna and commerce, holds up a mirror to contemporary social issues. It is in itself an icon of the designer's limitless imagination.

CORSETED FREEDOM
In Gaultier's interpretation, the corset liberated the wearer.

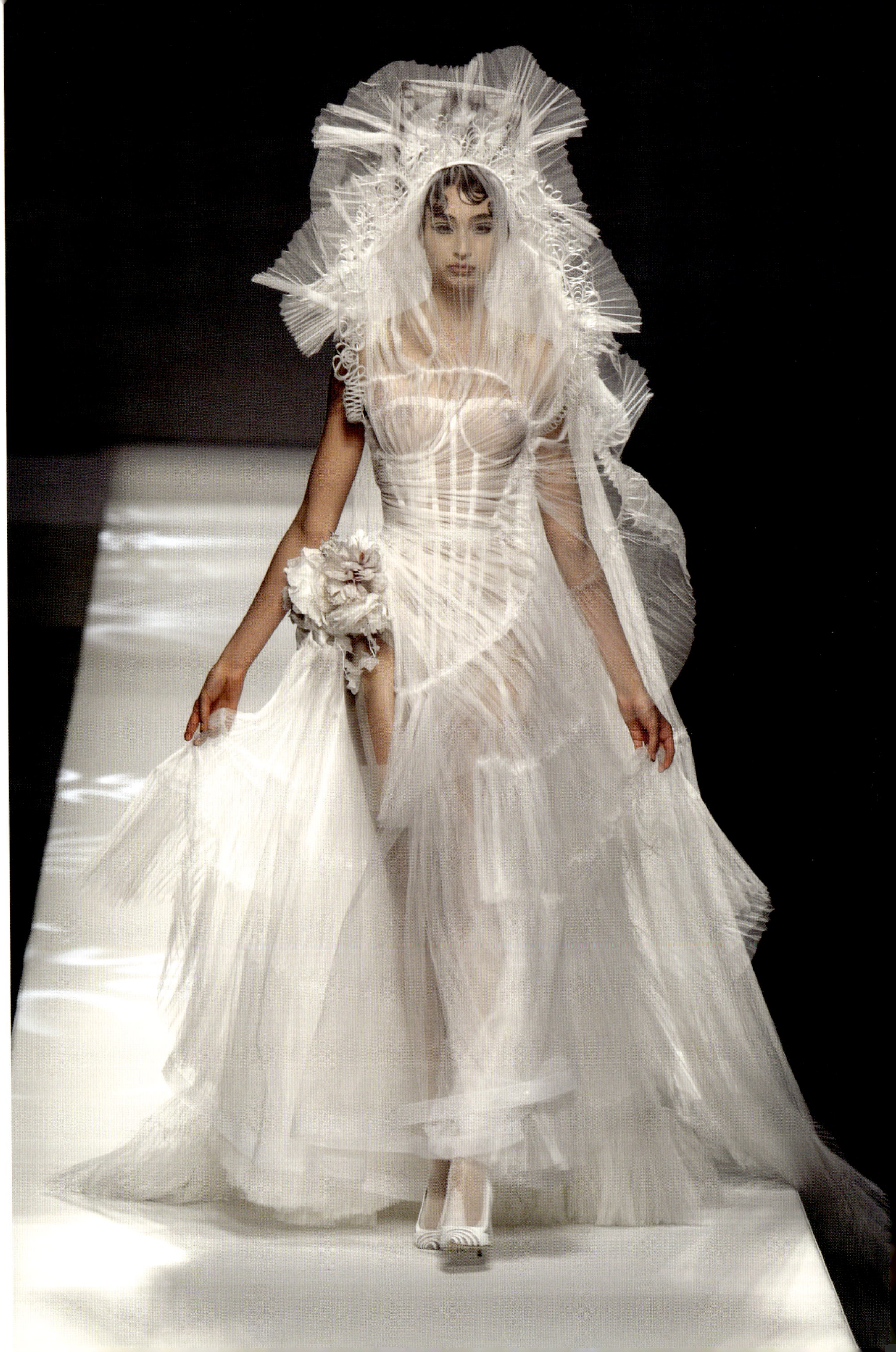

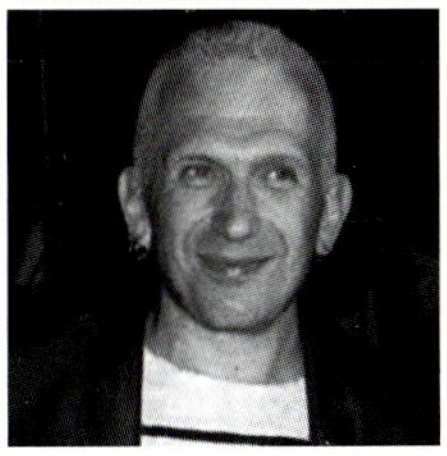

Jean Paul Gaultier

1952–

The self-taught French designer created the first of his iconic conical bras at age seven for his teddy bear. Between 1970 and 1975 Gaultier discovered the craft of couture with stints working for Pierre Cardin and Jean Patou. He established his own women's prêt-à-porter label in 1976, branching into haute couture in 1997. Gaultier launched his infamous corset dress in 1983 and in 1990 designed the coned bustier worn by Madonna on her Blond Ambition tour. Along with Vivienne Westwood, he has been credited with the assimilation of external corsets into bridalwear.

THE DRESS

STYLE Lingerie

SHAPE Corseted peignoir

FABRIC Silk tulle

COLOR White

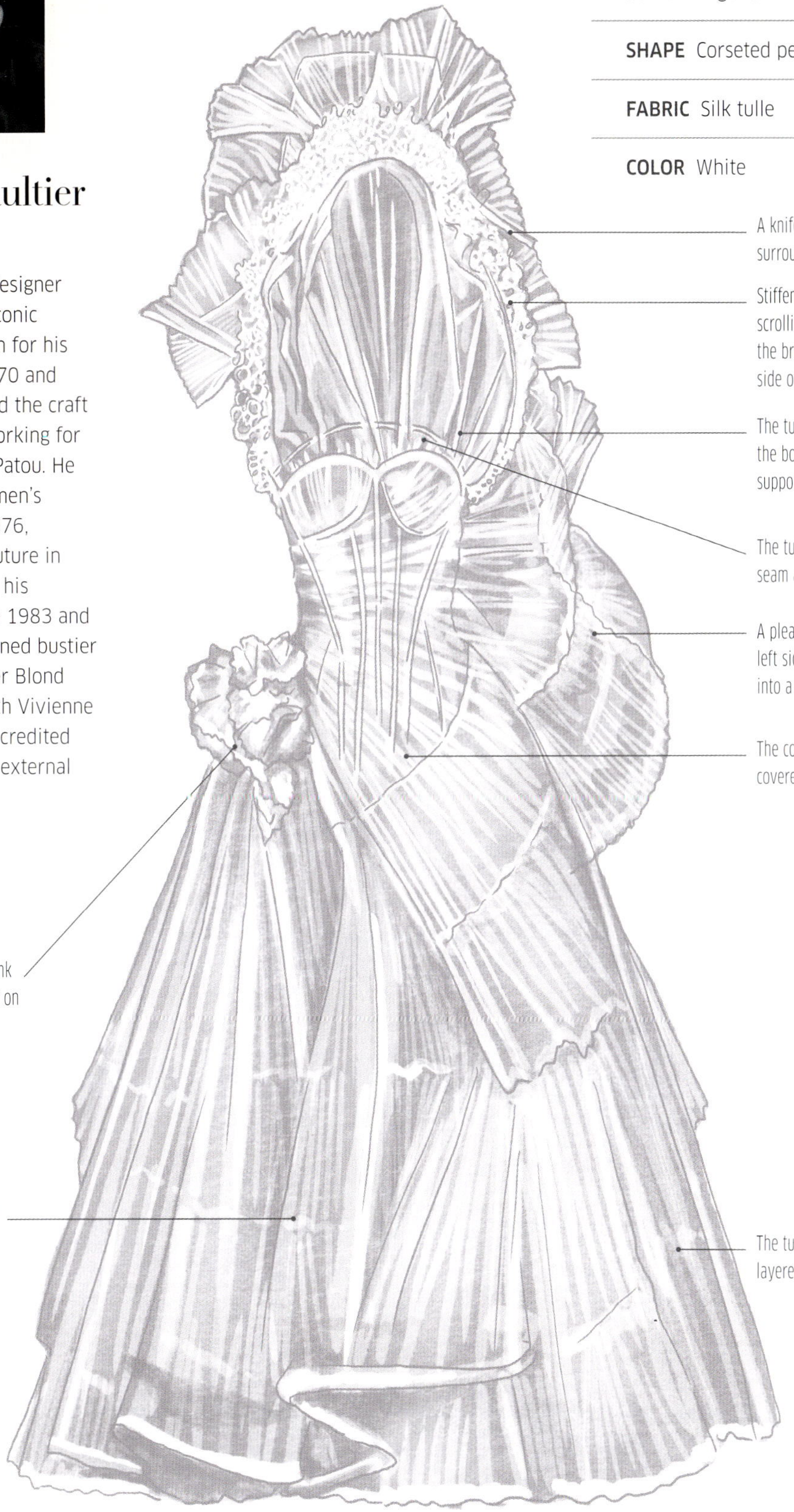

45

Giambattista Valli

2010 For Charlotte Dellal

Giambattista Valli's wedding dress for Charlotte Dellal was "a confection of seemingly endless cascades of tulle" that transformed into a sleek mermaid silhouette.

When shoe designer Dellal married investment banker Maxim Crewe, her fashion designer friend Valli created a show-stopping wedding gown that transformed into a dance-ready reception dress. At the nuptials, which took place at the bride's parents' home in the English countryside underneath a chuppah formed out of trees and flowers, Valli dressed the bride in a frothy, off-the-shoulder tulle dress. Dellal accessorized the gown with a pair of signature leopard-print high-heeled pumps from her Charlotte Olympia label. Derek Blasberg, editor-at-large of British *Harper's Bazaar* magazine, attended the wedding and tweeted, "The sun set just as Charlotte Dellal entered the tent in a tiered extravaganza of gorgeous wedding dress. Wouldn't fit in a church anyway!"

Hollywood glamour and abundance

The dress's enormous skirt was a mille-feuille of tufted ruffles mounted upon a stiff fabric foundation. It fell from the waist into a terrain of deep ridges that leveled out into a wide, round train. Out of this mountain of tulle emerged a fitted bodice swathed in organza that was twisted into a wide band swirling around the bride's shoulders. The architectural lines and voluminous form of the gown harked back to Dior's structured New Look silhouette and the glamorous sirens of 1950s Hollywood. "I love pieces when you don't know whether they are from the past, the future, or right now," Valli has said. It was a style that suited the aesthetic of the London-based British-Brazilian heiress who was celebrated by *Vogue* magazine for her "Vargas curves, bright-red lips, and fiery Rita Hayworth hair." When interviewed by the magazine about her style, the bride defined it as "Old Hollywood glamour with a sense of humor."

The beauty of metamorphosis

Dellal revealed to *Vogue* that it was clear to her that the Italian designer, whom she first met while interning at Ungaro, would be the one to create her wedding dress. She entrusted its design entirely to her friend, saying: "When you ask someone like him to make your wedding dress, you let him work his magic. We had very few fittings, so it was a fantastic surprise."

The Italian designer, who shows in Paris, excelled at high-drama dresses marked by strong silhouettes and immense volume, balanced with irrepressibly feminine details—ruffles, drapery, and bows. "At Ungaro," Valli told *Vogue*, "I discovered the flou [soft drapery]

STRAIGHT FROM THE RUNWAY
Dellal's wedding dress was based on the designs Valli created for his 2009 collection (pictured here).

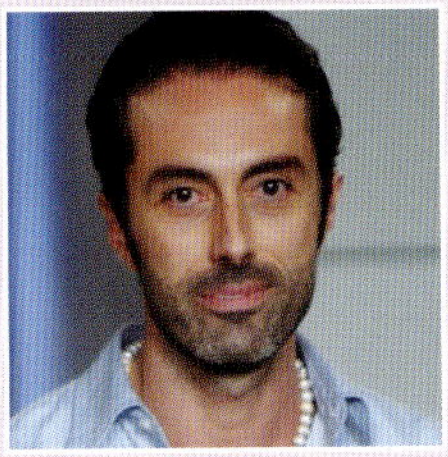

Giambattista Valli
1966–

The Italian designer has been called the Valentino of his generation. After studying in London and Italy, Valli landed a job with Roberto Capucci. He moved to Paris in 1997 to work for Emanuel Ungaro, becoming the designer's successor as creative director the following year. Valli debuted his own label in 1995, aimed, he said, at "the international jet set." After receiving many personal requests for wedding dresses, Valli released a bridal capsule collection in 2008, with prices ranging from $11,000 to $16,000.

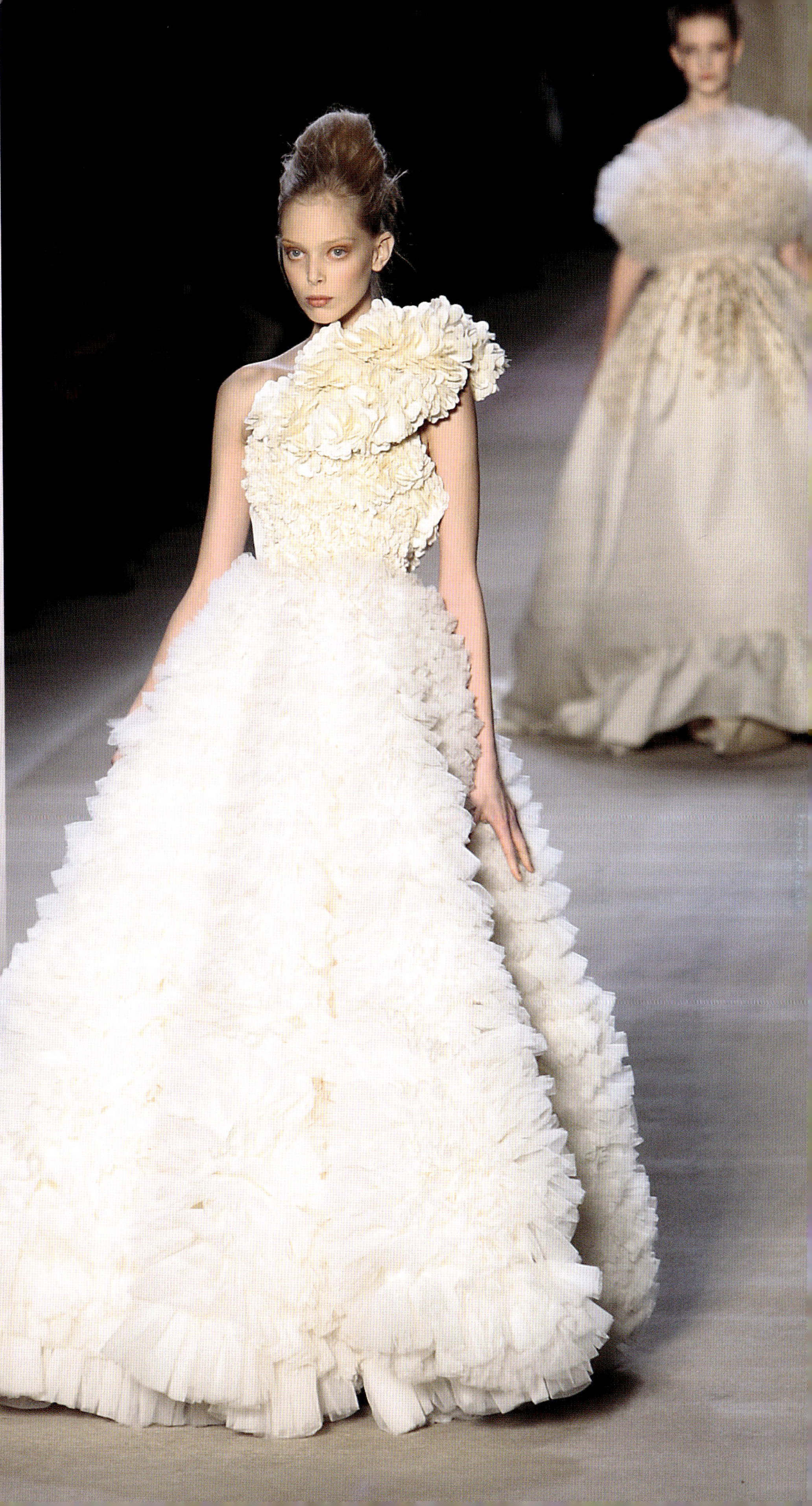

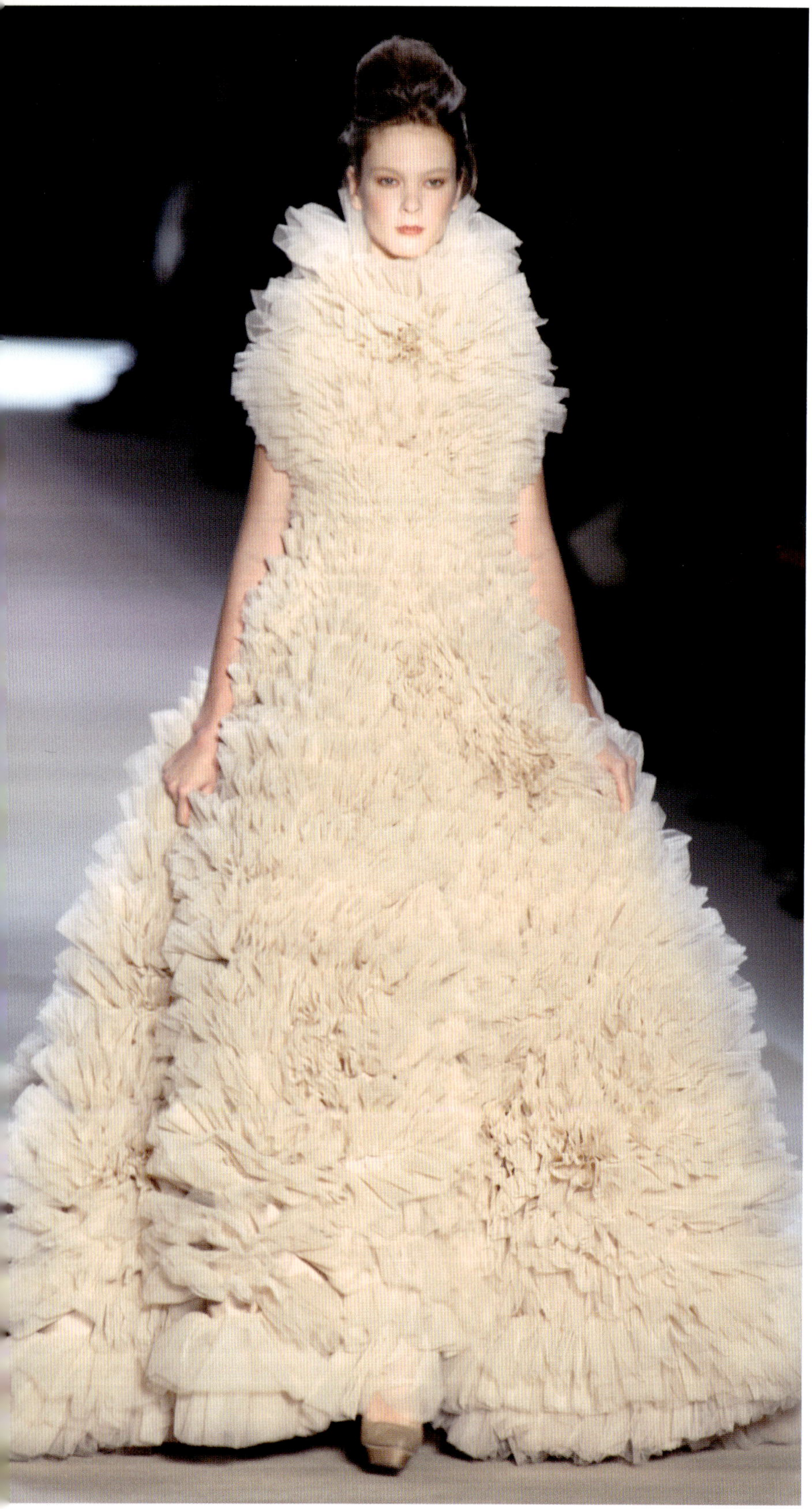

and the language of Paris." Valli's design for Dellal was a continuation of the "thousand-meter" multi-tufted tulle gowns he debuted in his Spring/Summer 2009 collection. The show concluded with a dress layered in ruffles from its high neck to floor-sweeping hem. The collection, the designer told the fashion press, was "about metamorphosis," a concept he translated most literally into the design of Dellal's convertible wedding dress, which shed its ruffles to become an entirely different style and shape of garment.

When the time came for dancing, the bride simply slipped off the overskirt, revealing a fitted sheath continuing out of the bodice's drapery, flaring at the knees into a floaty mermaid hem. To this outfit, the hat-loving bride added another personal touch: a white satin "cat hat" designed by her favorite milliner, Marie Mercié, that matched the straw versions worn by her young bridesmaids. Dellal described her evening transformation as "like stepping out of a wonderful cake."

Following Dellal's example, many brides now opt for two looks, often a classic and romantic dress for the ceremony and something a little more fun for the reception. So-called convertible wedding dresses, where a portion of the dress is removed, smooth the switch from day to night without the fuss of an outfit change. In recent years, designers who have caught on to the trend for removable overskirts include Anne Barge, Reem Acra, Monique Lhuillier, and Oscar de la Renta, who in 2013 inventively reused a tiered tulle skirt as a dramatic cape.

RUFFLES GALORE
The frothy ruffles took the world by storm when they were revealed at the 2009 show.

THE DRESS

STYLE Old Hollywood glamour

SHAPE Ball gown over mermaid

FABRIC Silk tulle and organza

COLOR White

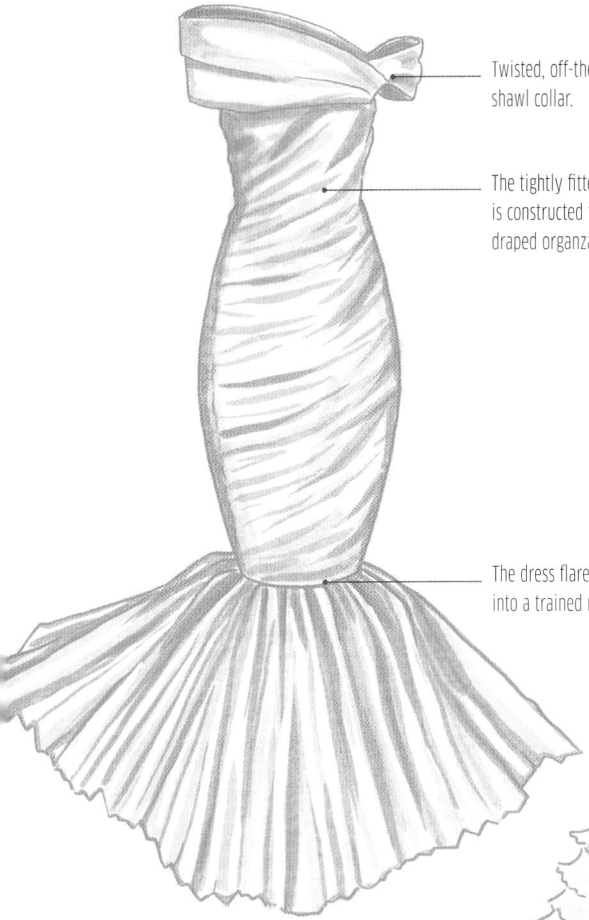

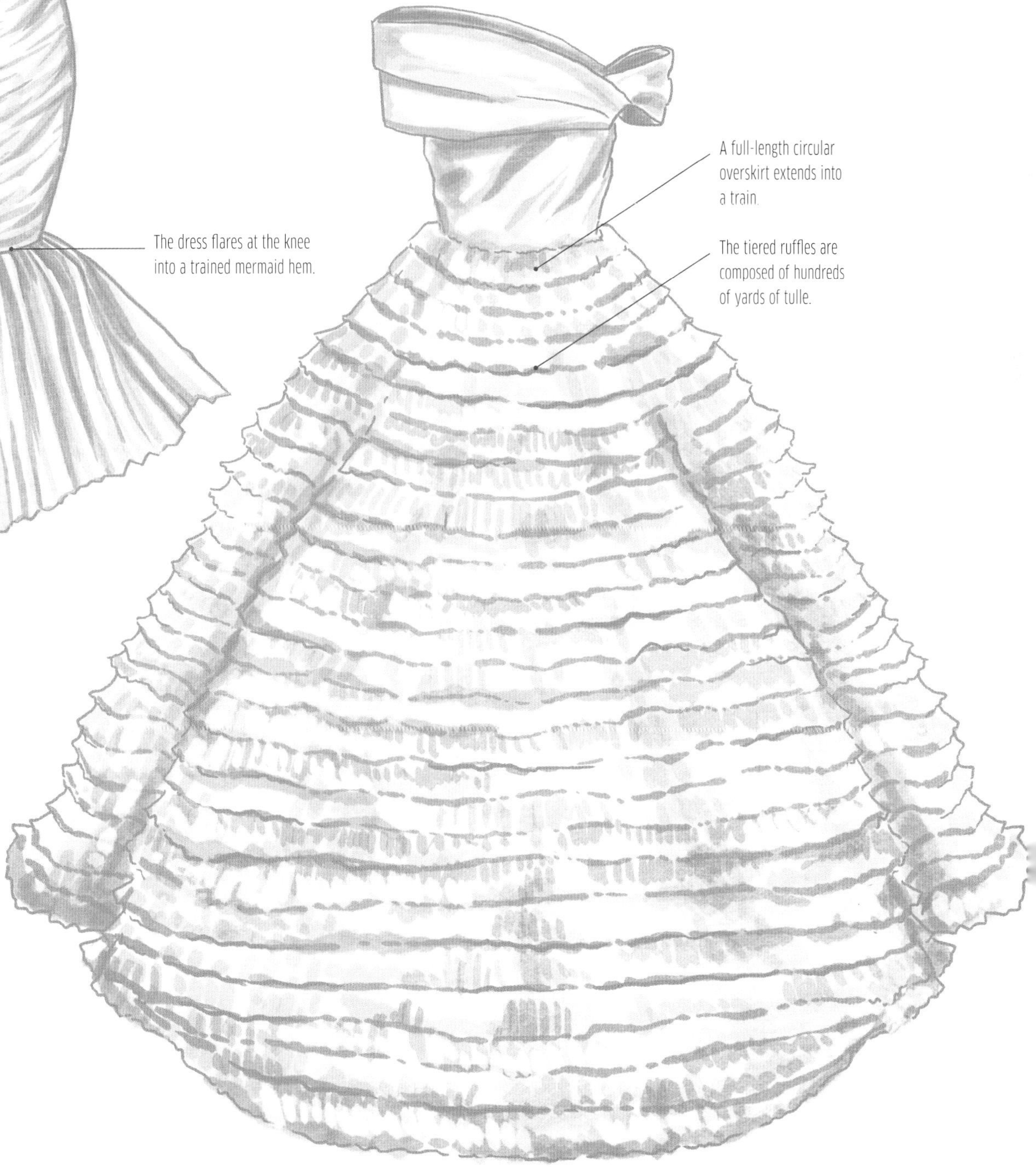

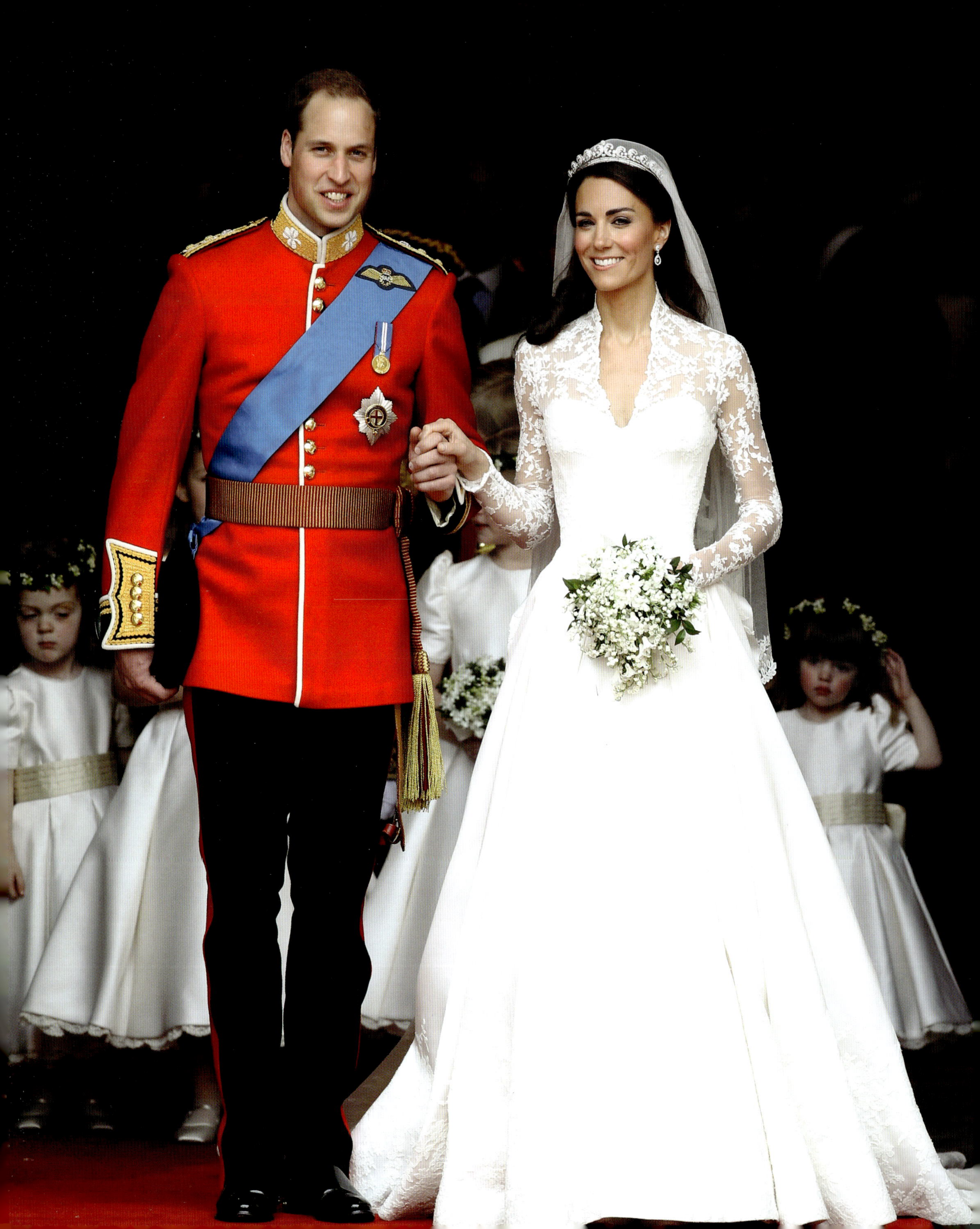

46

Sarah Burton

2011 For Catherine Middleton

Capturing the traditions of 200 years of royal weddings in a distinctly contemporary design, Sarah Burton's wedding dress for Catherine Middleton reflected the vision of a new generation of the British monarchy.

Conferring the coveted commission to create her royal wedding gown upon Britain's most avant-garde fashion label was, in the opinion of *British Vogue* magazine's editor, Alexandra Shulman, "a bold and brilliant decision" on the part of the future queen consort. Middleton's selection of a design house renowned for its radical aesthetic and artisanal methods, showed sensitivity to both tradition and contemporary fashion.

Burton's creation, a stunning sweep of ivory satin gazar hand-appliquéd with lace, epitomized the heritage of British couture. Drawing upon skills and fabrics from across the United Kingdom, the designer, reflecting the bride's wishes, paid tribute to the arts and crafts movement. Originating in the nineteenth century, this design movement advocated truth to materials, traditional craftsmanship, attention to detail, and simplicity of form. The pure lines and romantic detailing of Burton's dress respectfully interpreted that tradition through a unique cut, contemporary techniques of construction, and modern fabrics.

Burton's signature strong-yet-feminine silhouette had the strength of presence befitting a state occasion. But in its scale and subtle embellishment, the dress retained the sense of modesty requested by the bride. The dress fitted closely to Middleton's torso with a strapless corset, overlaid with an engineered lace bodice. The nipped-in waist and padded hips, hallmarks of the late McQueen, recalled Victorian corsetry. These elements, together with the late-nineteenth-century-inspired bustle, transformed the dress into a streamlined structure. Composed of arches rising out of the back of the waist, the bustle unfolded like an opening flower into soft pleats flowing organically into the train. The graceful lines of the skirt were comparable to Queen Elizabeth II's 1947 dress (see page 38), while the severity of the bodice evoked the wedding dress of the Queen's modernist sister, Princess Margaret, who married in 1960. Many observers commented on the similarity of Middleton's lace-covered wedding bodice to that worn by Princess Grace in 1955 (see page 54). Both were created using the Carrickmacross technique, developed in Ireland around 1820, whereby individual lace motifs are cut out and incorporated seamlessly into the overall scheme.

A celebration and a collaboration

Burton described the dress as "a real feat of engineering," an acknowledgment of her three-dimensional process of creation. The designer began by determining, with the bride,

PURE WHITE LACE
Embroiderers working on the lace washed their hands every thirty minutes to keep the lace and threads pristine.

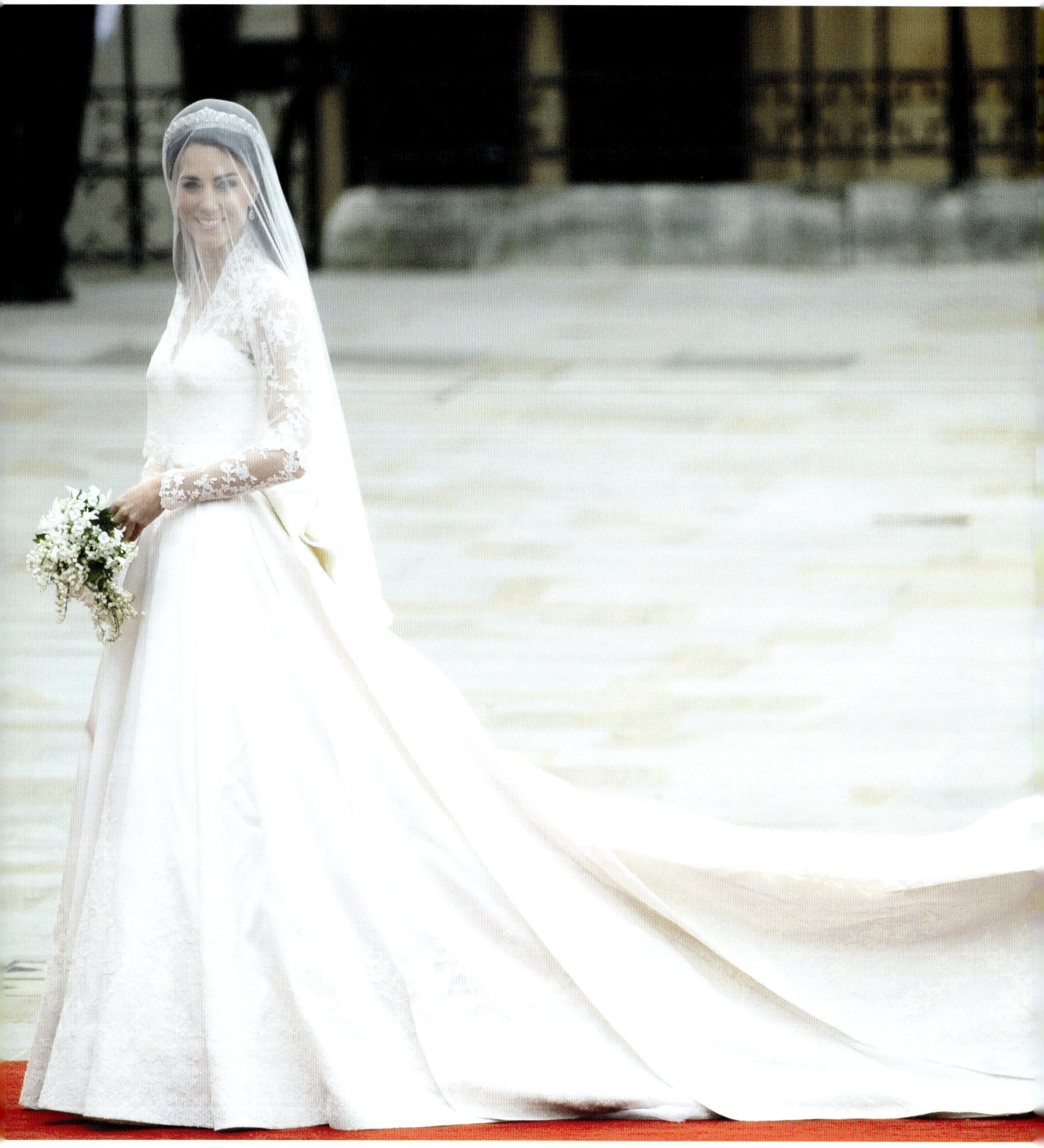

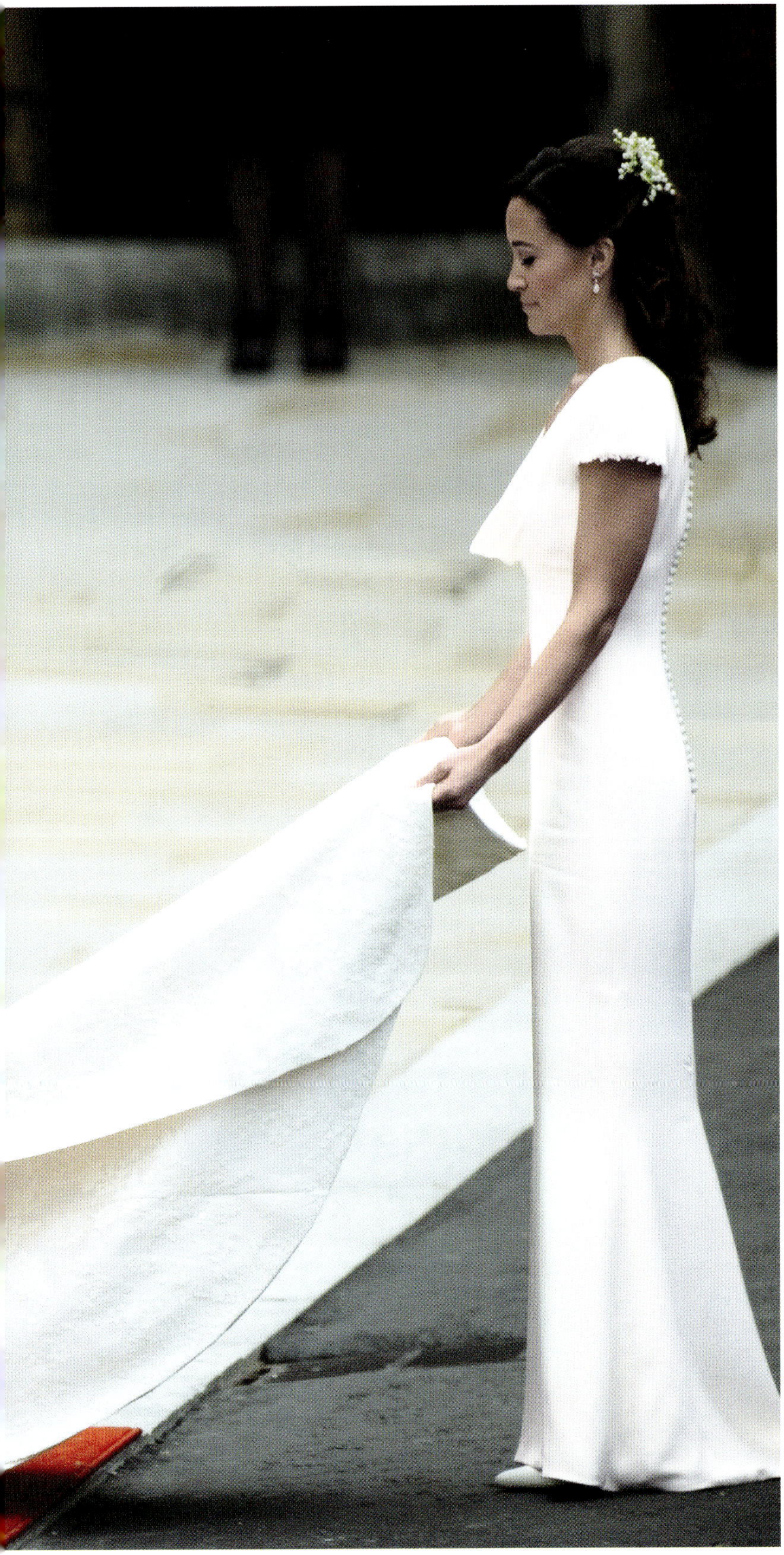

the shape, proportions, and scale of the dress, working out the details in a series of toiles. Once finalized, a paper pattern was cut. The next stage was the creation of the unique lace design incorporating the four emblems of the United Kingdom: the rose, daffodil, thistle, and shamrock. The motifs, cut from six different kinds of lace, were arranged into a new design upon the paper pattern, which was then copied and laid on the toile to check that the design matched perfectly and symmetrically all around the dress. The finished lace was then pinned to lengths of silk tulle, one for each panel of the dress, and sent to the Royal School of Needlework. Here, embroiderers hand-sewed the lace to the ground with intricate and precise stab-stitching around each motif. When the panels were completed, the lace was cut away from the tulle and sewn onto the satin gazar by the McQueen seamstresses. Sarah Mower at *Vogue* deemed the dress, with its weighted train and hidden supports, "technically faultless," noting that it "allowed the bride to move with ease, carrying all the weight of British history and expectation without the slightest wrinkle or hitch."

The dress expressed a truly modern collaboration between a bride and a designer; a partnership, in Mower's words, "in which the individual wishes of a young woman have been expressed and enabled by another young woman of vast talent." Guided by Middleton's clear vision, Burton created a wedding gown that was patriotic—blending tradition and modernity—and majestic, yet modest. Over half a million visitors went to see the dress, produced at an estimated cost of US $434,000, when it was displayed at Buckingham Palace following the wedding (see page 130).

EYES ON THE BRIDESMAID
Burton later created a sell-out version of Pippa Middleton's bridesmaid dress for the online retailer Net-A-Porter.

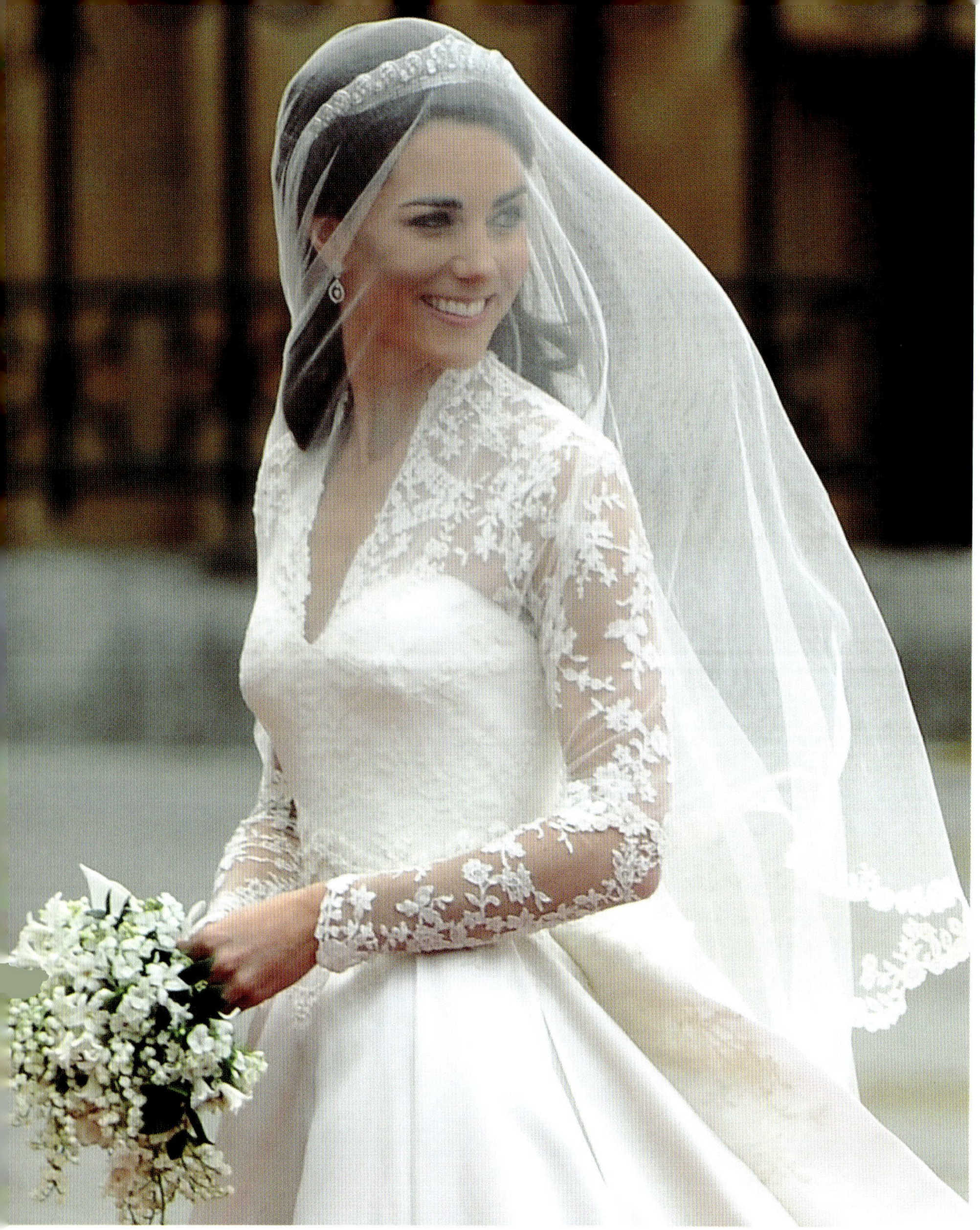

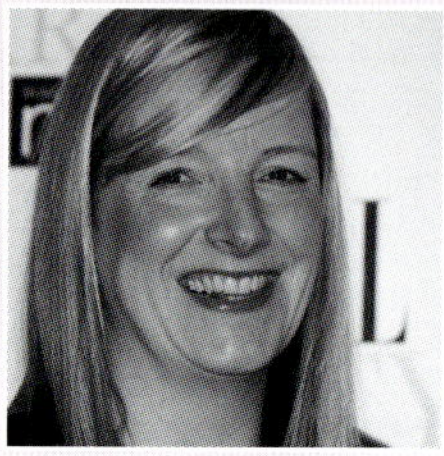

Sarah Burton

1974–

In 1996, while a student at Central St. Martin's College, London, Burton began interning for Alexander McQueen and never left, becoming his right hand and head of womenswear in 2000. Burton stepped out of McQueen's shadow when she took over as creative director following his death in 2010. Burton uses the same cutting and tailoring techniques that define the label but has a softer aesthetic than her mentor.

EMBLEMATIC
The dress's lace design incorporated a rose, a thistle, a daffodil, and a shamrock—the four floral emblems of the United Kingdom.

HIDDEN DETAILS

- Hand-stitched silk tulle underskirt trimmed with Cluny lace.
- The bottom part of the dress, in particular the middle part of the train, is weighted with canvas, so that the train falls back into exactly the same position when lifted.
- The arches at the top of the train are supported upon a hidden bustle.
- A blue ribbon is sewn into the hem.
- Down the back are fifty-eight gazar- and organza-covered buttons fastened by rouleau loops.
- The veil, which falls to just below the bride's waist, is made of layers of soft ivory silk tulle decorated with a trim of hand-embroidered flowers. The bride wanted the veil to be virtually unadorned, to give the ensemble a "romantic feel."
- Middleton's shoes were hand-crafted by the Alexander McQueen team.
- The bride wore a Cartier "halo" tiara from 1936. Loaned by the Queen, it was Middleton's "something borrowed."

THE DRESS

STYLE Regal and restrained

SHAPE Hourglass

FABRIC Silk satin gazar and lace

COLOR Soft ivory

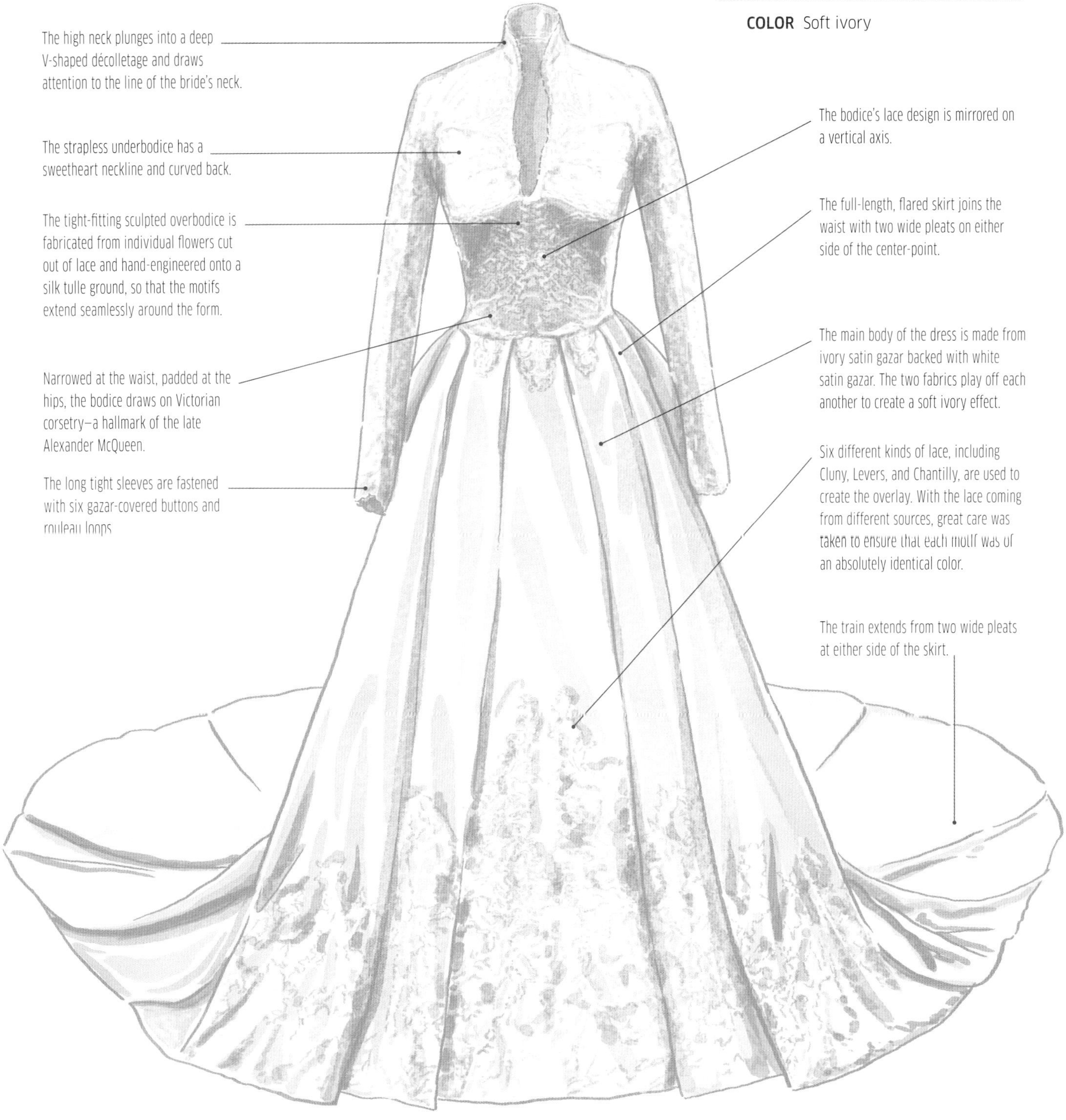

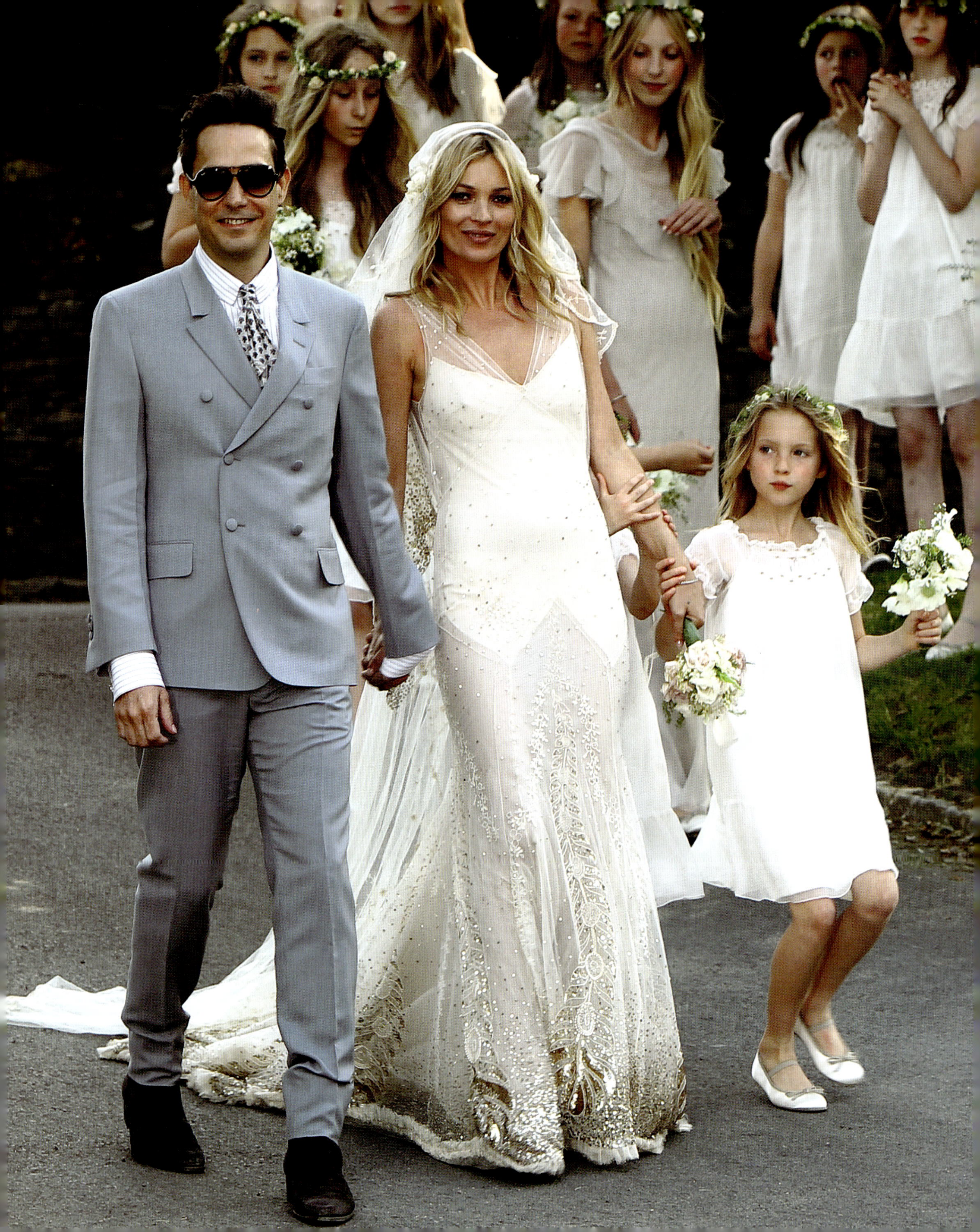

47

John Galliano

2011 For Kate Moss

Kate Moss's ethereal slip of a wedding dress, discreetly embroidered with glittering gold phoenix feathers, was simultaneously understated and provocative.

The wedding of the British supermodel to musician Jamie Hince was the fashion world's equivalent of a royal extravaganza. "Mosstock," as the press labeled the weekend-long festival-style celebration at the bride's Cotswolds home, was produced and attended by leading lights of the fashion and music industries. With the whole of the fashion world at her disposal, speculation was rife as to who would dress the bride. Moss chose to acknowledge a twenty-year friendship by bestowing the honor upon the disgraced and beleaguered fashion designer John Galliano. (For more on Galliano, see page 123.)

"Rock-n-roll Great Gatsby"

The cream-colored, slim-fitting gown sprinkled with golden paillettes was a classic Galliano design. Bias-cut and nostalgic, it utterly encapsulated the bride's laid-back, vintage-inspired aesthetic. *British Vogue* magazine concluded that the gown returned Moss to the "waif we know and love." As with his most celebrated collections, a fantastical narrative—inspired in this instance by photographs of Zelda Fitzgerald, Moss's personal icon—led Galliano's design process. Moss told the designer that she wanted the dress to be "kind of dreamy and 1920s, when everything is soft-focus. ...That light and that kind of fun decadence. It's rock 'n' roll Great Gatsby!" The 1920s style was reflected in the treatment of her light-as-air embroidered tulle veil, worn like a cap, set either side of her head with fabric flowers. As it billowed in the air, it drew to mind an observation of Moss by Hamish Bowles, *Vogue*'s European editor at large: "How do you catch a cloud and pin it down?"

The styling of the dress was closer to 1930s fashions, featuring an opaque thigh-length bias-cut silk slip overlaid with sheer chiffon panels, merging into a translucent floor-length skirt, through which the silhouette of Moss's slender legs were just visible. The sequins dusted around the hem of the skirt were, in Galliano's imagination, as though "the scullery maid had picked up milady's fallen sequins to spangle her own dress." Rising from these sparkling "ashes," beaded phoenix plumes licked, flame-like, up the front of skirt. In Galliano's words, the embellishment was "Delicate and defiant, like Kate."

Like the mythological phoenix, Moss's career was reborn from the ashes of a drug scandal in 2005 that caused the model to be dropped as the face of fashion houses Burberry and Chanel. Moss emerged from the scandal stronger and more in demand than ever before.

The symbolism of the beading also resonated with the recent firestorm

PHOENIX RISING
The dress's subtle phoenix feather embellishment alluded to the troubled histories and creative resurrection of both designer and bride.

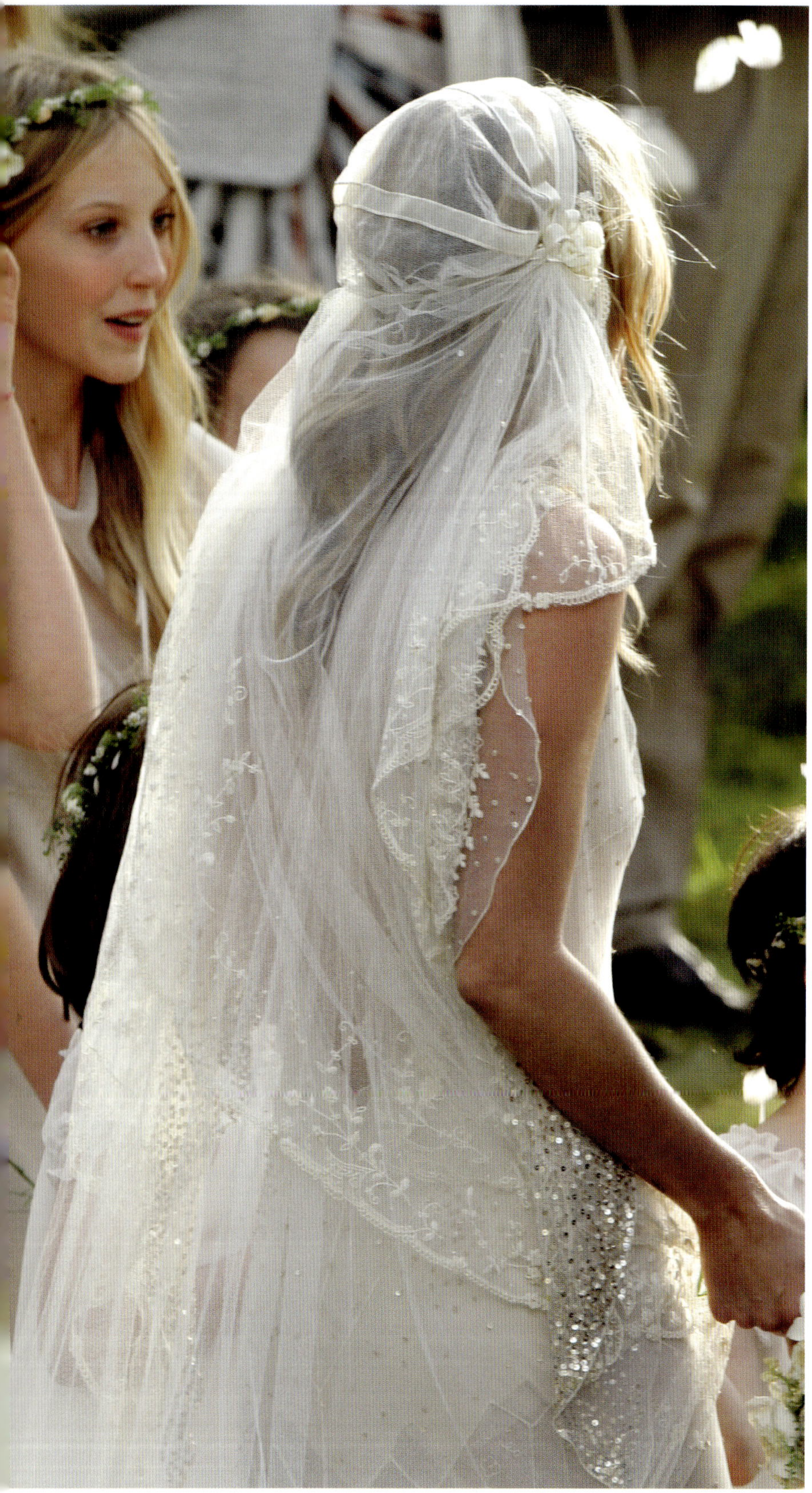

surrounding Galliano. At the time of the wedding, the designer's glittering career had been entirely overshadowed, destroyed by the designer's vicious anti-Semitic assault on a couple in a Parisian bar. The incident resulted in his being dismissed from his job as creative director of Christian Dior, fired from his own label, and prosecuted in the French courts. He later received a guilty verdict for the attack.

An act of friendship

Moss's decision to commission her wedding dress from Galliano was an act of friendship rather than a political or symbolic statement. She was an old and close friend of the designer, who, fashion journalist Robin Givhan noted, "must surely have a better sense of what is in his heart than those who can only judge him by what he said and what he did while in the haze of addiction." Givhan speculated, "for a man who was once hailed as a creative genius, who has seen his professional life destroyed by his own hand, [the commission to design Moss's dress] must be a sweet salvation." Galliano himself admits that designing this dress was the first step in his creative and professional rehabilitation. He reported to *Vogue* that the model '"dared me to be John Galliano again." In true Galliano style, he sent the bride to her nuptials with some stage direction: "I told her, 'You have a secret—you are the last of the English roses—and when he lifts your veil he's going to see your wanton past!'"

VINTAGE BOHEMIAN CHIC
Moss is synonymous with vintage style. Galliano's wedding gown perfectly captured the bride's English-rose glamour and simultaneously created a major bridal trend for vintage-inspired looks.

THE DRESS

STYLE Informal, vintage inspired

SHAPE Bias-cut slip

FABRIC Silk, silk chiffon, and embroidered tulle

COLOR Cream and gold

HIDDEN DETAILS

- Manolo Blahnik customized a pair of his Godichefac sandals with crystals and blue insoles for the bride. Blahnik later told *Women's Wear Daily* that they had been reworked five times before the bride was satisfied.
- An antique rosary is hidden in the dress as a tribute to Galliano's late partner-in-design, Stephen Robinson. In Galliano's words: "So Stephen is watching, nestled in the back of the bow."
- The full length of the gown, the veil is edged all around with trailing floral embroidery and gold sequins. It was held in place like a cap with three bands of ribbons, secured at either side with flowers made from fabric ribbons.

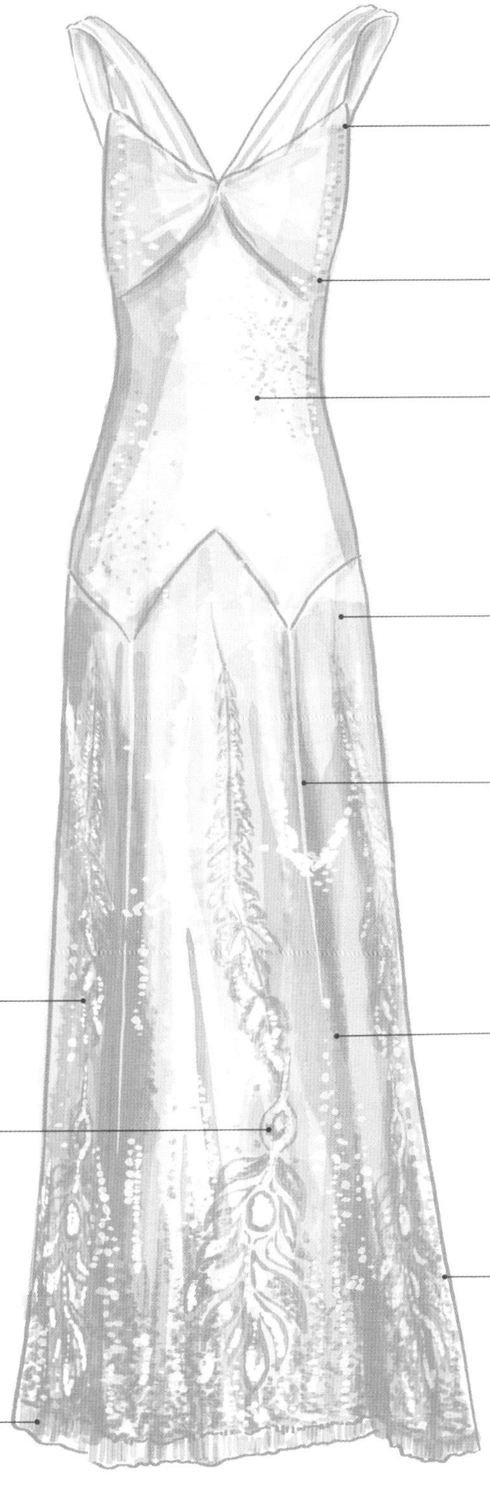

48

Rei Kawakubo

2012 Comme des Garçons Spring/Summer

"With creation as [her] sword," Rei Kawakubo cut through the craft of bridal couture, unpicking every nuance and texture of the traditional white wedding dress in a collection aptly titled White Drama.

In this collection for Comme des Garçons, Kawakubo picked up the threads of a dialogue begun by Yves Saint Laurent's 1965 cocoon wedding dress (see page 60). Kawakubo expanded Saint Laurent's statement into an entire bridal collection full of subversive twists: voluminous satin dresses, tailored frock coats with disproportionately long sleeves, heavy crinoline cages sitting over ensembles, capes like heavy monastic robes, jersey tubes smothered with clusters of giant flowers, and somber handkerchief veils. Bulging wigs fashioned from ballooning white rubber and clouds of insulating foam distorted the models' heads into monstrous forms of elephantine proportions. Kawakubo's troupe of surreal brides presented a complex reading of the white wedding dress driven by cultural and feminist ambiguity.

Subverting traditions

The first bride appeared on the runway in a crisp ivory duchesse satin long-sleeved shift with a curving puffed overskirt: a classic 1960s look complemented by Courrèges-inspired white go-go boots. Except that in place of a bouquet, a large satin bow shackled her wrists together. As the collection progressed, the brides became increasingly physically disempowered. Hands were submerged within the folds of skirts and whole arms were lost within the cavernous expanse of exaggerated trumpet sleeves. Curving seams on capes and tunics lashed the body, and, in their most extreme form, extended the garments up and over the models' faces. Peaked white hoods with oblique gashes slit across the front and sometimes the back resembled menacing versions of 1960s futuristic headpieces, or *tsunokakushi*—the traditional bridal headwear worn in Japanese Shinto weddings. Bulky hooped skirts, referencing nineteenth-century crinoline petticoats, insidiously encroached upon the body until they took on the alarming structure of cages, trapping the bride within by pinning her arms to her sides. Veils of guipure lace, heavily layered silk, and bunches of fabric flowers utterly obscured the brides' visages, blotting out the individuals beneath, their heavy forms closer in tone to Victorian widow's weeds than the levity of contemporary bridal veils.

On approaching the finale, Kawakubo's garments recaptured the same physical form and obscure symbolism as Saint Laurent's 1965 cocoon: narrow jersey tubes encased the brides from head to foot, their upper bodies weighted down under a crust of fabric, paper, and crocheted flowers; vertical slits at hip level enabling hands to make a brief

WHITE DRAMA
The collection, simultaneously free-spirited and sobering, stands as the most innovative renovation of wedding traditions in fashion history.

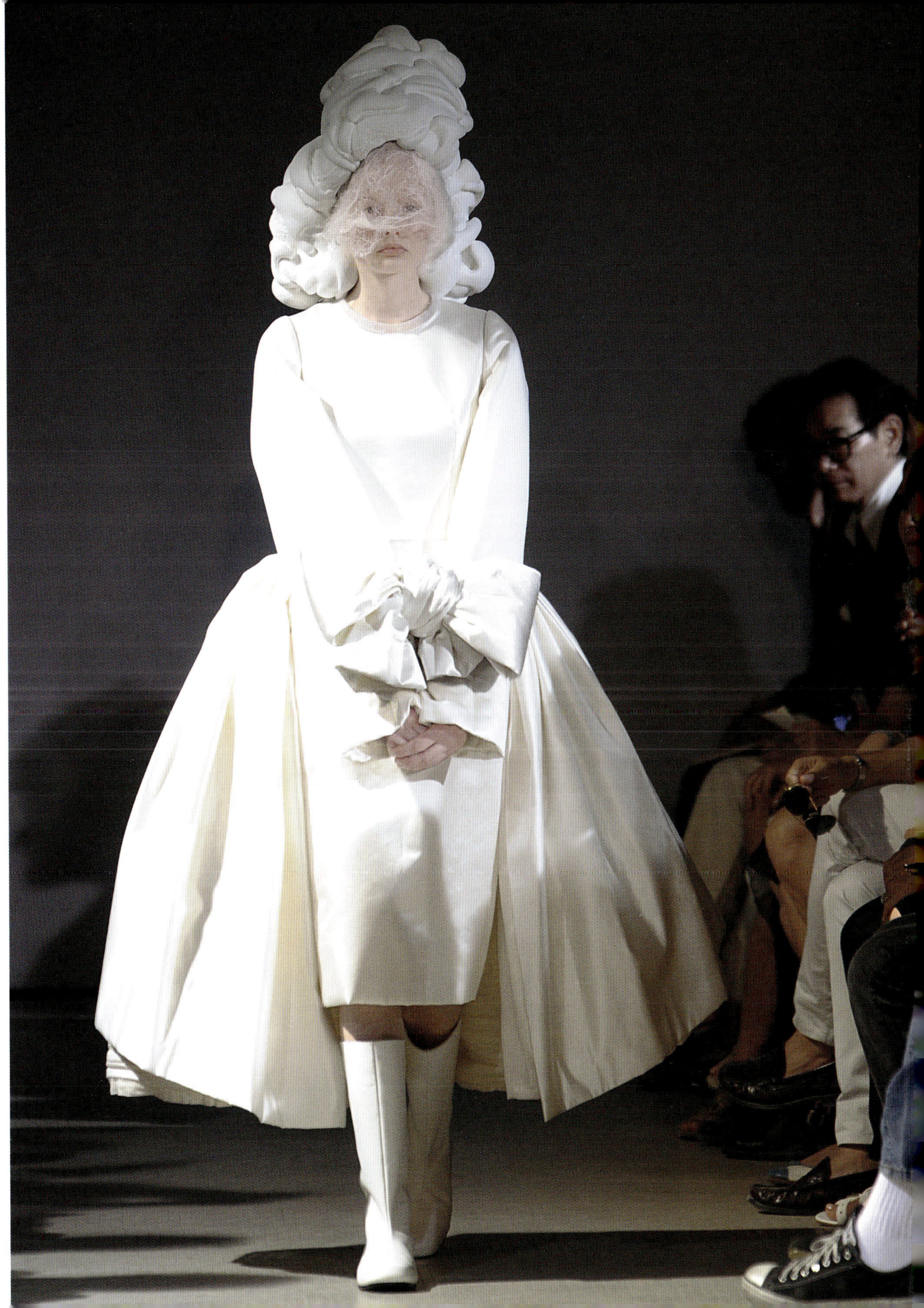

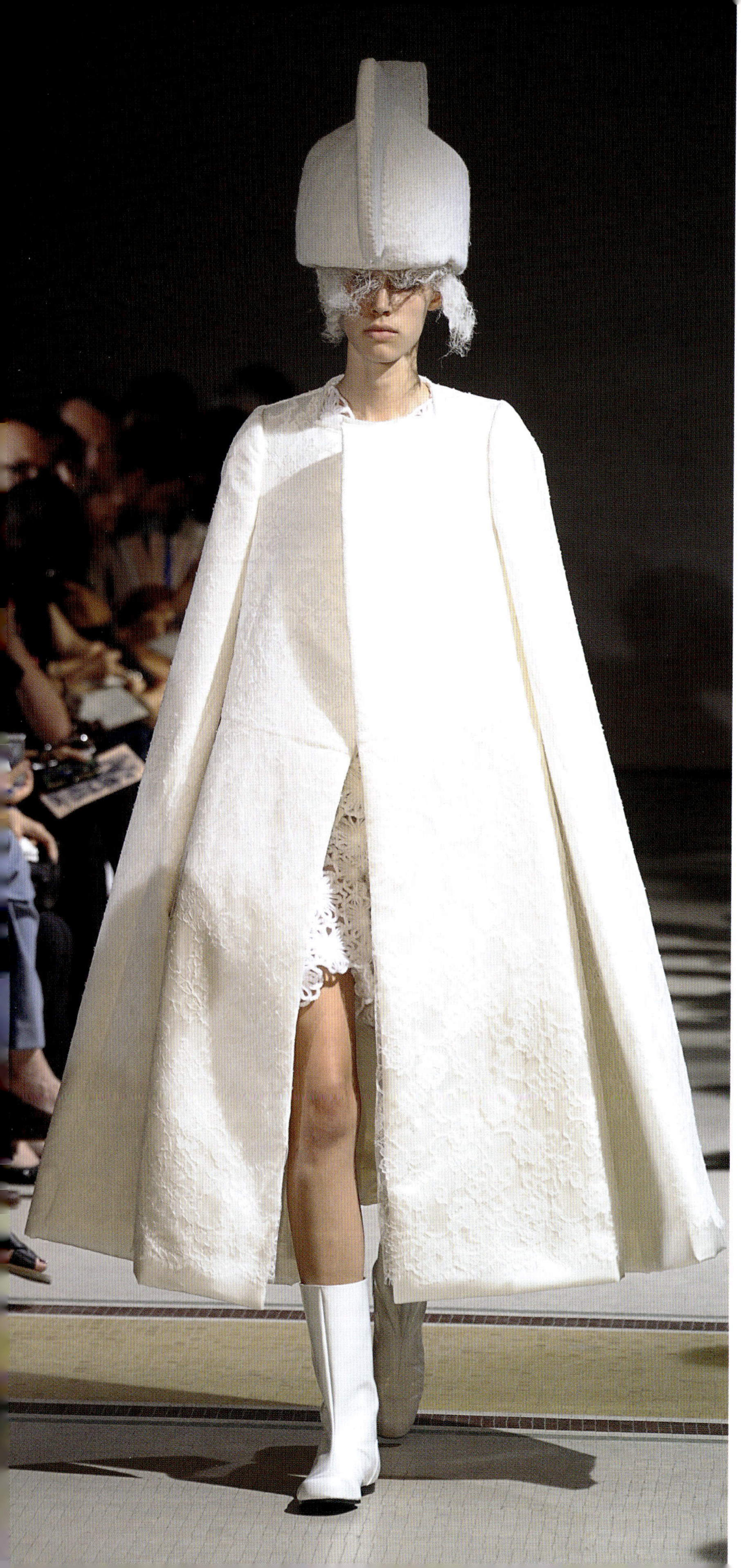

reappearance. Recalling the commentary surrounding Saint Laurent's cocoon dress, *Vogue* magazine concluded that with these forms "the symbolical imagery of women willingly walking towards ritualized helplessness became inescapable." There was also something funereal or mummified about the models—the smooth jersey shrouding their bodies a reminder that in Japan white is the color of mourning.

Dual symbolism

As Kawakubo reminded us in this collection, white is a color synonymous with two of life's major rites of passage: marriage and death. In her masterful treatment of fabric and form, the designer balanced this duality of meaning. Contrasting treated and refined fabric, opaque and sheer, shiny and matte, heavy and light, White Drama was simultaneously oppressive, somber, and "joyously ravishing." It was, Kawakubo's husband, Adrian Joffe, remarked, "everything that makes you happy and sad in life."

INSPIRATION FOR FASHION-FORWARD BRIDES
Although seemingly shocking, Kawakubo's designs offer an abundance of inspiration—dramatic capes softened with pretty roses, sharp tailoring, pure white emboldened by graphic black decoration, layered textures, crisp shifts, and sculptural skirts.

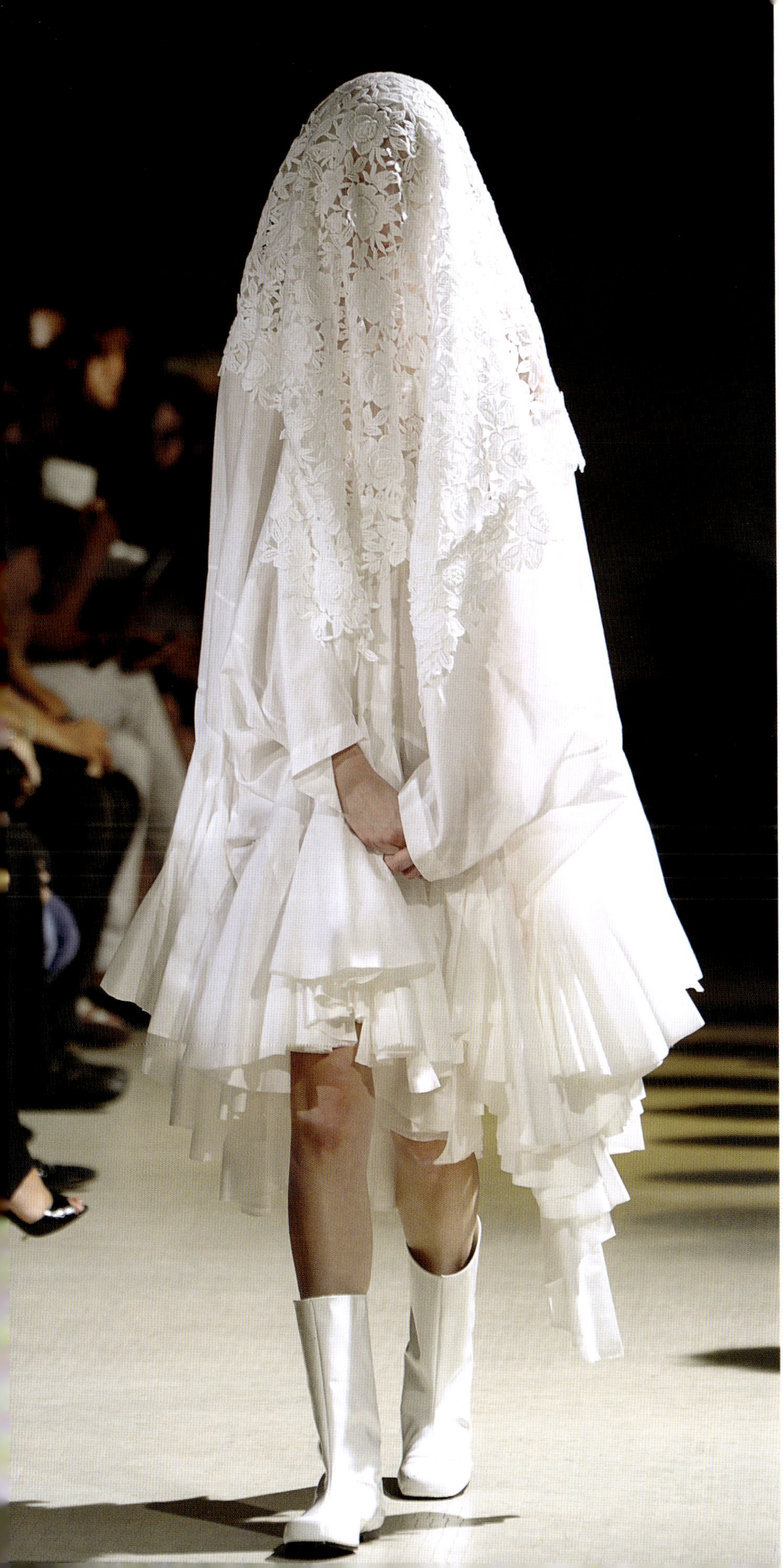

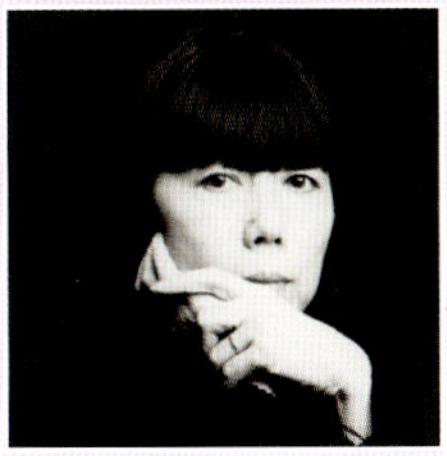

Rei Kawakubo

1942–

Comme des Garçons is a Japanese fashion label founded by designer Rei Kawakubo and her husband, Adrian Joffe, in 1969. Kawakubo is ranked as one of the most innovative and influential designers of all time. Her non-conformist garments—often asymmetrical, destroyed, or deconstructed—are, *Vogue* says, "a passionate cauldron of ideas, feelings and emotions." In 1997, Kawakubo produced her infamous Dress Meets Body, Body Meets Dress collection. Featuring garments with disfiguring lumps of padding, the collection shocked the fashion world.

Comme des Garçons is based in Tokyo but shows its main collections from Paris. Kawakubo managed to build the company into an international brand while maintaining complete creative freedom without financial backers.

THE DRESSES

STYLE Avant-garde retro

SHAPE Shifts, crinolines, and cocoons

FABRIC Silk, guipure lace, jersey, and foam

COLOR Shades of white

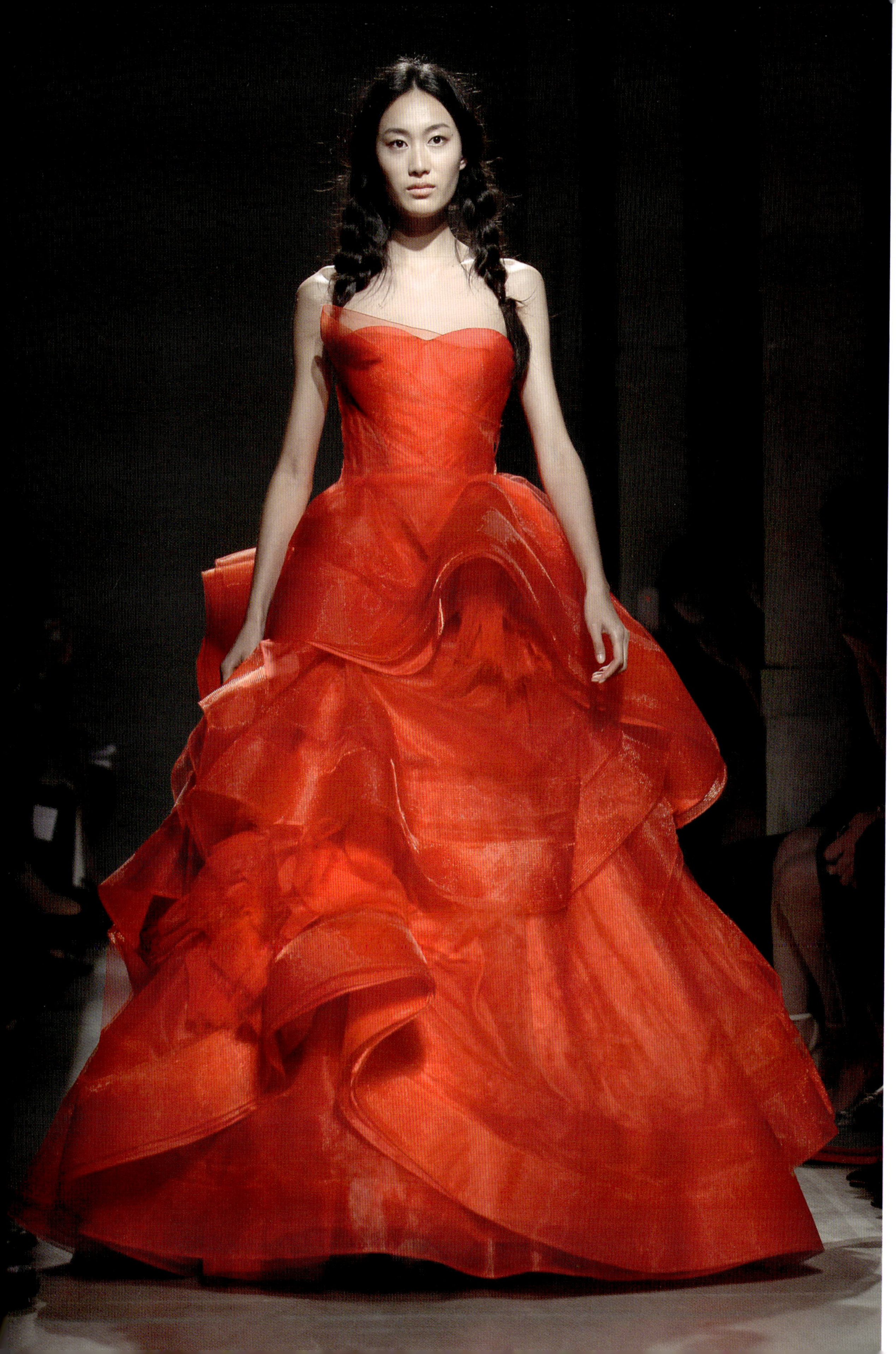

49

Vera Wang

2013 Spring

Vera Wang's red wedding gowns marked a monumental shift in her aesthetic that some interpreted as foreboding change in her personal life.

In 2012, white gave way to red when Wang, the designer famed for her dreamy romanticism (page 114), presented a dramatic bridal collection that spanned a spectrum of reds. Monochromatic dresses in bright crimson and vermilion gave way to richer cardinal and dahlia hues before climaxing with dramatic dark berry and grape shades. The collection consisted of fifteen dresses in classic ball gown and mermaid silhouettes, given an entirely modern makeover.

An abundance of form and color

Corsets wrapped in complicated arrangements of tulle, embroidery, and horsehair exploded into skirts arranged into asymmetrical tiered flanges, soft swirls, cascading pleats, ragged strata, and frothy tails. Intriguing details—oversized corsages, sparkling scarlet jewels, crystal embroidery, tiny chevron pleats, delicate lace, and pleated ruffles veiled with curtains of tulle—gave the designs a "collage effect" that encouraged the eye to move restlessly, picking out these minutely worked subtleties. Sculpting and layering fabric, Wang exposed the depths and nuanced shades of her chosen dramatic hue.

The voluminous dress that Wang named "Katherine" exemplified the drama and attention to detail that characterized the collection. "The first thing that hits you with Katherine is the grandeur of the ball gown," said Wang. Its visual impact was achieved entirely by the designer's modern and sculptural treatment of fabric. The tightly fitting strapless bodice was swathed obliquely with horsehair mesh, bold brushstrokes cutting a line to the gown's nipped-in waist. Beneath the bodice the skirt erupted into enormous, surging waves of fabric. Wang created volume without weight by winding multiple lengths of organza, edged with rigid horsehair, around the skirt, lifted up with tacking stitches into irregular, undulating tiers. This construction did away with the need for separate foundation garments, so beneath the fabric "there's nothing but air," Wang explained. "As the dress moves, and the shadows and tones become lighter, or darker, through those waves of fabric—you get a magnificent ballet of color and shadow."

At the back of the dress, Wang heightened the visual effect by increasing the density of the waves so that they appeared like the "gatherings of [a] bustled crinoline, creating asymmetrical figures in the line of the gown." At the front of the dress, oversized flowers fashioned from eyelash organza peeked out, the designer imagined, as if "from a neatly wrapped bouquet," drawing attention to the shadowy depths of the skirt. It was Wang's own opinion

CRIMSON BRIDE
Famed for romantic, white wedding dresses, Wang painted the runway red with her Spring 2013 collection, which included this dramatic "Katherine" model.

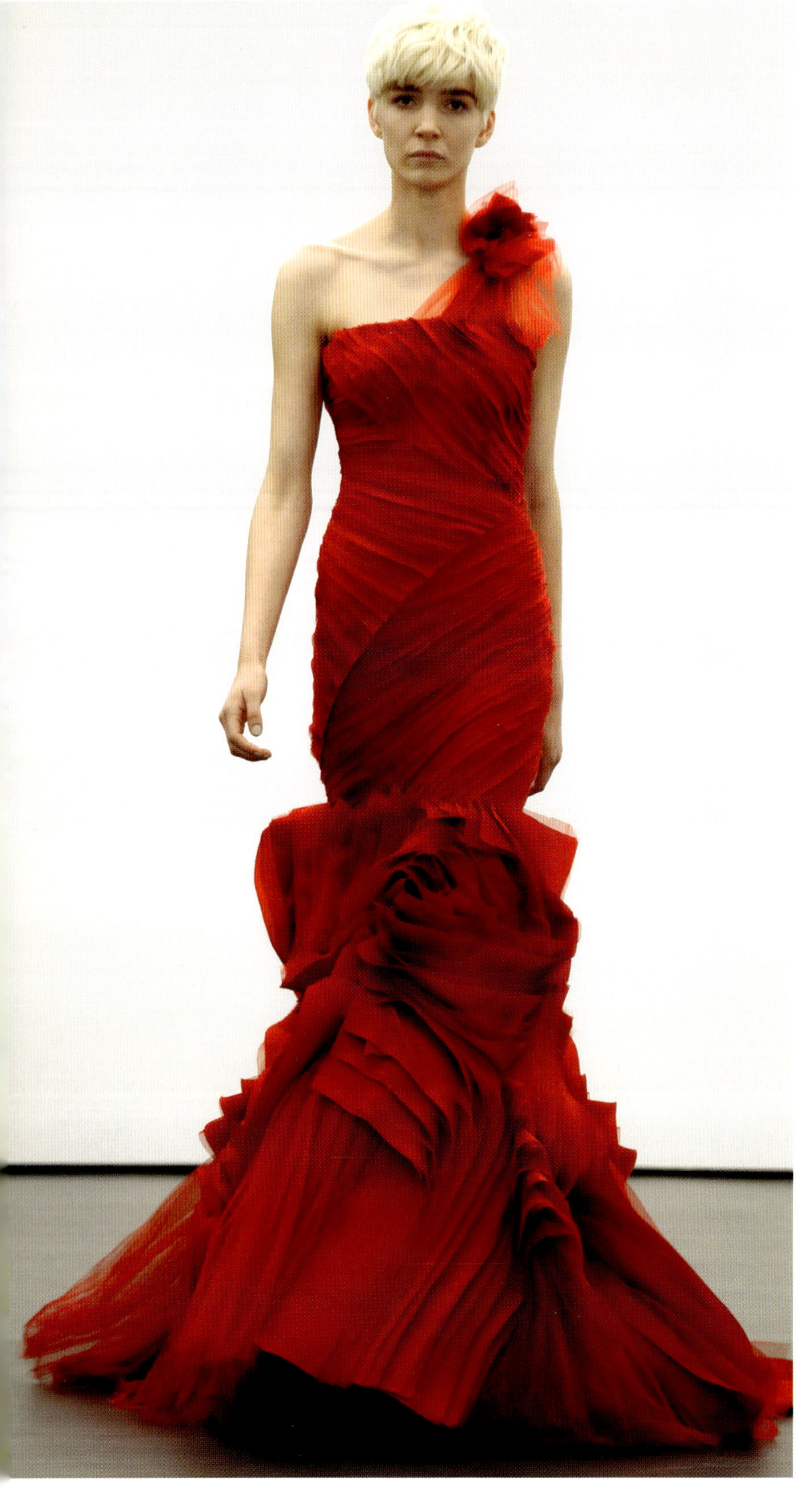

that Katherine was "a consummately couture presentation." Reflecting the craftsmanship of their construction, the cost of gowns from this collection started at around $5,000.

What prompted the designer to take such a radical change of direction with this collection, which was enigmatically entitled "Beautiful dream. The symbolism of Red"? Some commentators suggested that the fiery gowns, coming off the heels of a series of black designs, foretold Wang's own marital woes. Months after debuting the collection, the designer separated from her husband of twenty-three years. Tamara Albu, associate professor of fashion at Parsons The New School for Design, observed that the collection was "in a way a symbolic gesture. Creative people do take their inspiration from everywhere, including their own personal life."

However layered with symbolism, the color red will always conjure up powerful, passionate emotions, including joy, and is symbolic of happiness in Wang's Chinese cultural heritage. Wang called this emblem of bridal auspiciousness, when translated into her contemporary wedding dresses, "Boldly romantic, charming, protective, and a celebration of love" perfect for the ambitious, independent, successful women targeted by the Wang brand. (For more on Wang, see page 115.)

For those brides who preferred their wedding dresses a little less feisty, all the gowns from the collection could be ordered in white. But Wang's red gowns drew attention to the designer's position as the bridal industry's premier trendsetter, prompting the question: what will Vera Wang do next?

SHIFTING SHADES AND MERMAID SHAPES

As the collection progressed, the colors changed and the shapes evolved.

THE DRESS

STYLE Boldly romantic

SHAPE Ball gown

FABRIC Silk organza, silk tulle, and horsehair mesh

COLOR Crimson

HIDDEN DETAILS

- The waves of fabric dramatically increase in density at the back of the dress.

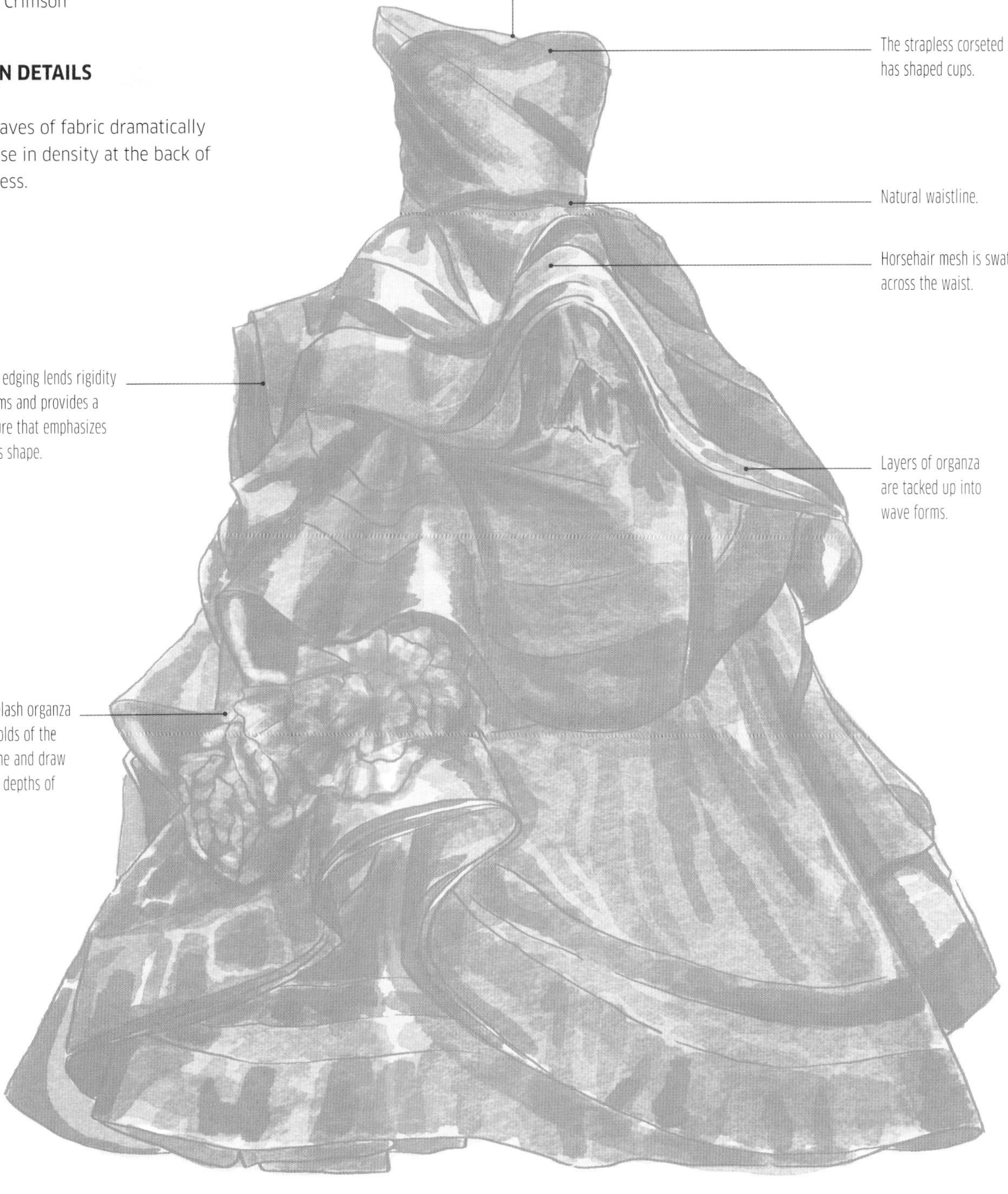

50

Karl Lagerfeld

2013 Chanel Spring/Summer

In a watershed moment for fashion, Karl Lagerfeld sent a pair of matching brides down the runway as a statement of support for the legalization of gay marriage in France.

Chanel's Spring/Summer 2013 haute couture collection was shown in Paris the week after hundreds of thousands of protesters descended on the city to oppose French President François Hollande's plans to allow same-sex couples to marry. For the presentation, Lagerfeld converted Paris's Grand Palais into a mystical forest scene inhabited by fanciful nymphs costumed in feathered, embellished, and embroidered garments. At the end of the show, Lagerfeld offered his riposte to the protest: twin brides walked out hand-in-hand with a young pageboy in tow. The girls were uncanny mirror images of each another. Their identical white gauze, spiky feathered, and zigzag embroidered dresses were worn with slim-fitting slacks beneath—a subtle allusion to the duality of lesbian brides' gender identities.

It appeared as if the sumptuous feathered wedding gown concluding Chanel's previous season's collection had been shredded into two equal halves. More obviously, fashion journalists noted, there was a touch of Miss Havisham about the girls' raggedy skirts and frothy, feathered fascinators that partially obscured their gothically made-up black eyes. These details echoed Charles Dickens's portrayal in *Great Expectations* of a jilted bride, forever dressed in disarrayed veil and decaying heaps of lace.

A political statement

The complete equality of image presented by Lagerfeld's brides reflected the wording of Barack Obama's inauguration speech made less than twenty-four hours previously. In his speech, the reelected American president related the drive for same-sex marriage to the quest for gender equality. Lagerfeld, who had never been slow to grasp maximum publicity for his work, was quick to affirm that his collection was aligned with the gay rights agenda. When asked if his unconventional bridal gowns were a statement in support of Hollande's legislation, he answered, "Of course." The press immediately picked up on Lagerfeld's fashionable portrayal of a political issue, though some were less than convinced by the depth of his spectacle. Fashion journalist Stephanie LaCava proclaimed: "Don't say it's the 'modern family.' It's just girls looking great, keeping in sentiment with the rest of the show. Couture's about atmosphere and beauty, no need to analyze."

Whether intentionally or not, Lagerfeld's twin brides made a timely and poignant statement that captured the zeitgeist. In the twenty-first century, the culture of weddings is rapidly diversifying, and the symbolism of the white wedding dress is changing to keep pace with contemporary developments.

DISTRESSED TWINS
Following Gaultier's lead (page 150), Lagerfeld used his finale white dresses to comment on twenty-first-century brides.

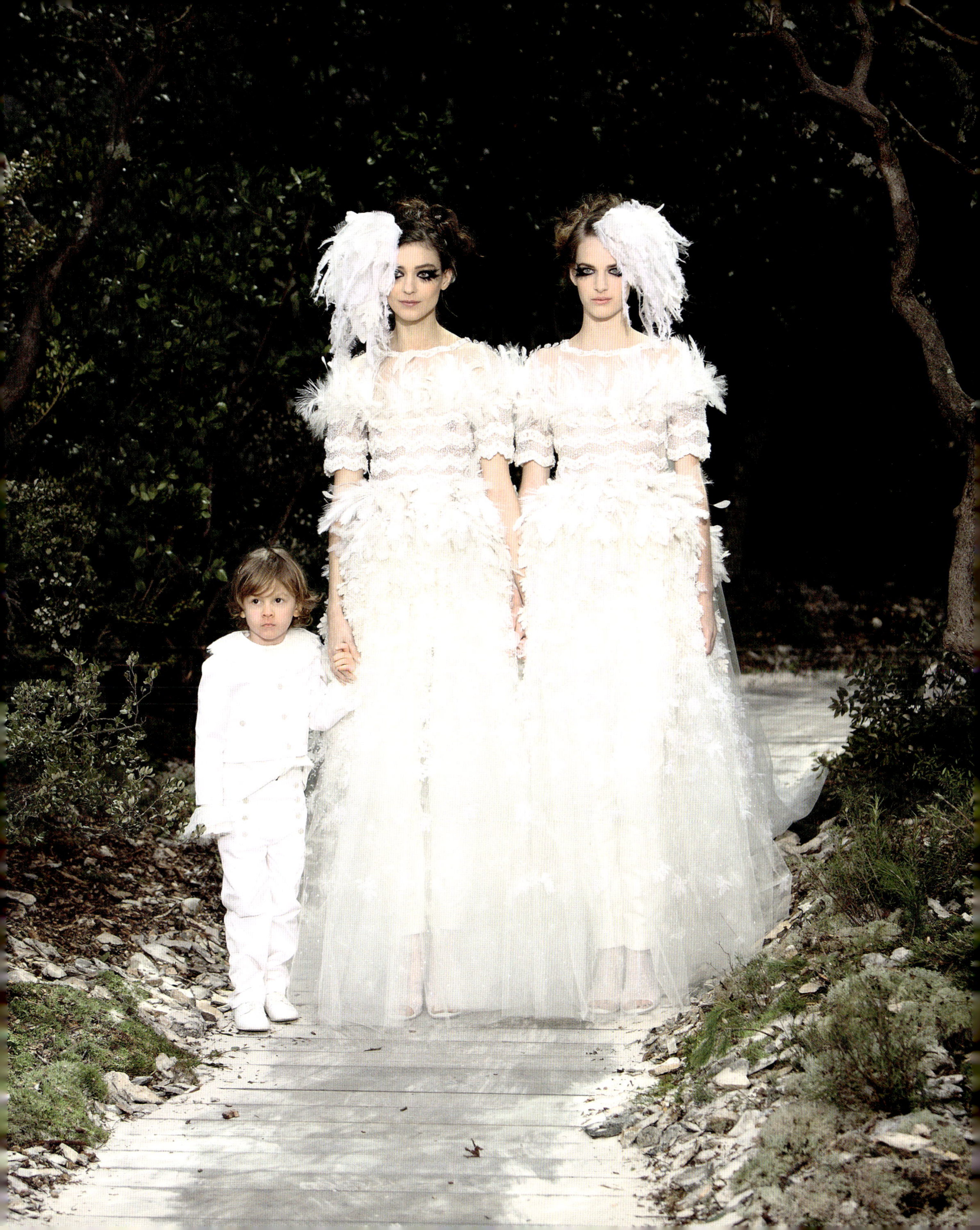

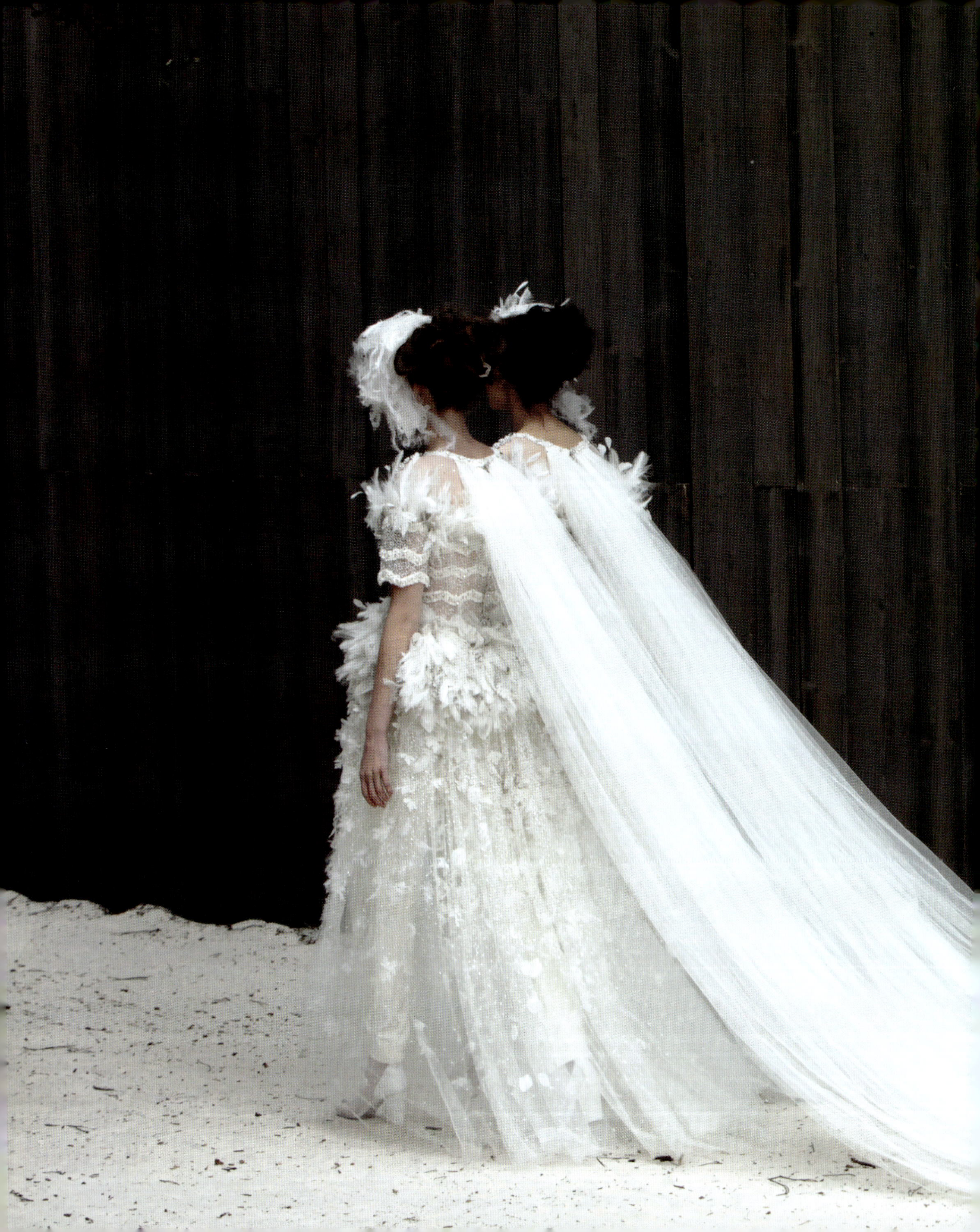

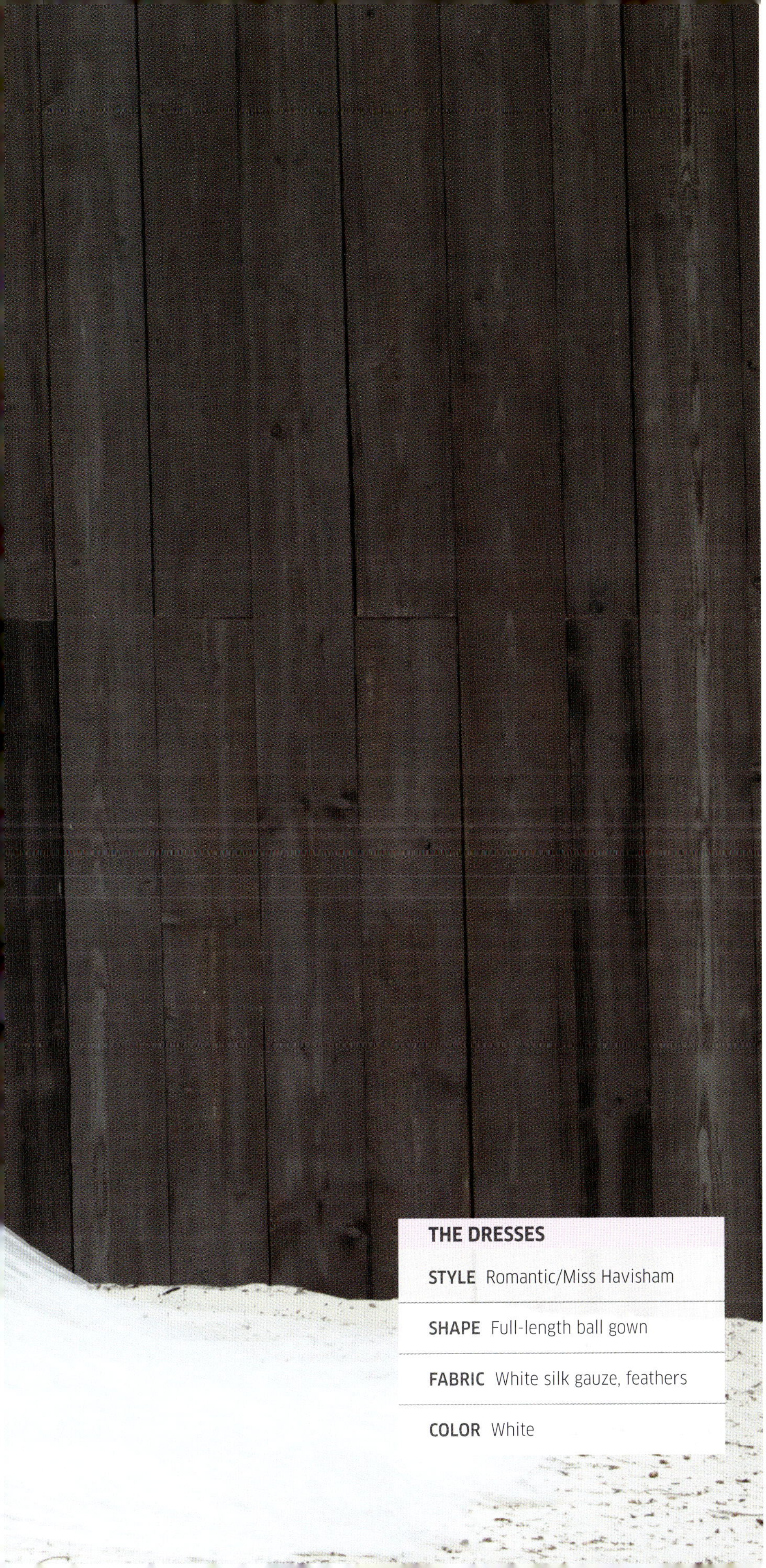

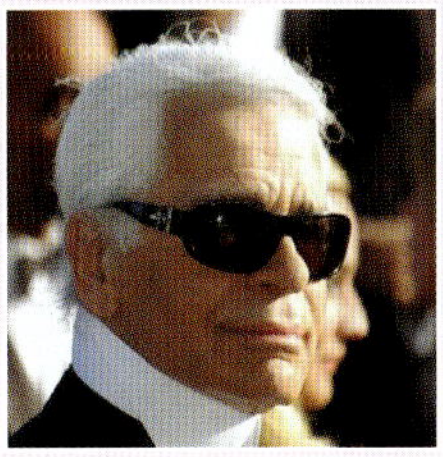

Karl Lagerfeld
1935–

The brand that is synonymous with luxury and restraint, Chanel revolutionized fashion in the 1920s with modern, pared-down style. Karl Lagerfeld became chief designer in 1983. His designs play with the brand's signature elements, injecting them with an element of subversion and wit. Prior to his reinvention of Chanel, Lagerfeld held prestigious roles as assistant to Pierre Balmain (from 1955) and head designer for Chloé (from 1965–1983 and 1992–1997). He has also designed for Fendi and Jean Patou, among others.

THE DRESSES

STYLE Romantic/Miss Havisham

SHAPE Full-length ball gown

FABRIC White silk gauze, feathers

COLOR White

STRONG SILHOUETTES
The brides wore trailing Watteau trains of tulle attached at the shoulders and slim-fitting white slacks underneath their skirts.

Designers Brides Should Know

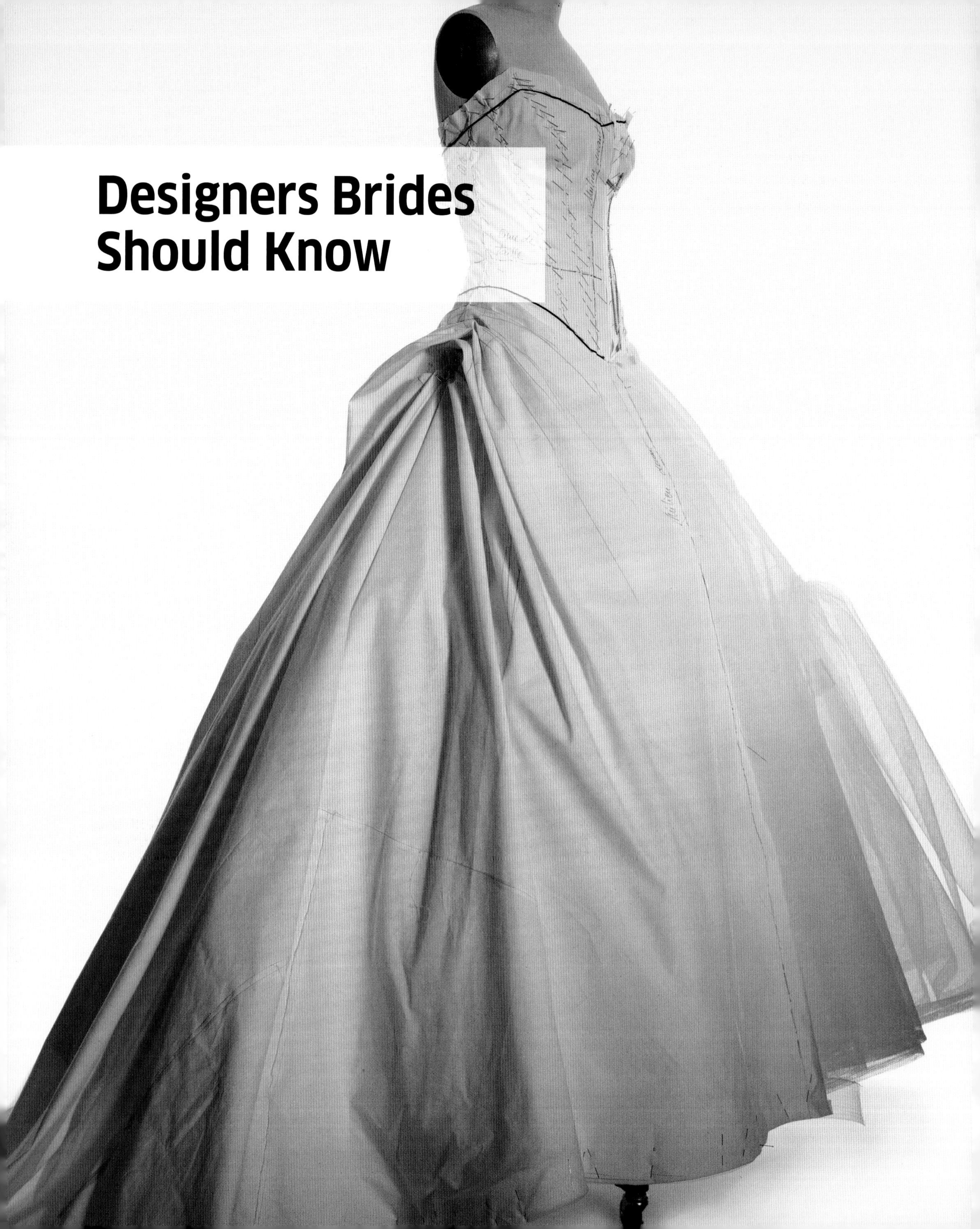

Although many fashion designers occasionally create wedding dresses, these are the world's premier designers of bridal collections who are not featured elsewhere in the book.

Reem Acra

Reem Acra designs for the modern woman, reimagining timeless bridal styles with her glamorous aesthetic and customizable ensembles.

Lebanese-born Reem Acra launched her eponymous bridal line in 1997 in New York. The designer's collections reflect her design philosophy, which she states "combines her appreciation for the traditional and classic with the modern fashion needs of today's woman of style." Acra revealed to the *Wall Street Journal* that she immerses herself in the interests and lives of young women, and that the concepts for her collections are driven by her understanding of their mindset. "I'm hearing the bride, I'm listening to her," Acra said. Her dresses achieve drama through volume, balanced by a lightness of the garments that is essential to the modern bride. Femininity comes in the form of delicate, contemporary applications of lace, illusion necklines, and marabou feather trimmings, while the all-important bridal magic and sparkle comes from her signature beadwork and embroidery.

Each season, the designer challenges herself to develop her collections in response to her clientele, finding new ways of expressing a contemporary bridal vocabulary. For 2012, she played with the possibilities of fabric, developing a unique laser-cutting technique that offered a fresh, light take on lace. In spring 2013, Acra aimed "to redefine the way modern women reveal their strength." She presented a collection composed of mix-and-match pieces that enabled brides to customize their style. For the finale, models removed overlays, feather-light tulle capes, boleros, bodices, and skirt tiers from their gowns, transforming floaty, dreamy designs into sexy formfitting columns, sparkly micro-minis, and a multitude of styles in between. With up to five looks in a single ensemble, brides could seamlessly transition from ceremony to reception to after-party. Understanding the shifts in the landscape of contemporary wedding culture has enabled Acra to redefine wedding dress design in a truly innovative way.

Oscar de la Renta

"The guru of glamour," Oscar de la Renta is the powerhouse of the bridal industry.

For over fifty years, Oscar de la Renta has been producing designs that are, in the estimation of *Vogue* magazine's editor-in-chief, Anna Wintour, "feminine, romantic, and appropriate"—a combination of qualities perfectly matched to the aspirations of mainstream bridalwear. Since the early days of his career, the designer has created couture wedding gowns for family and private clients. The unique dress he produced in 2009 for landscape architect Miranda Brooks typifies these special custom creations. Inspired by Sofia Coppola's filmic vision of Marie Antoinette, de la Renta conjured up an elaborate tiered and pin-tucked white cotton broderie anglaise dress with a huge bustled overskirt

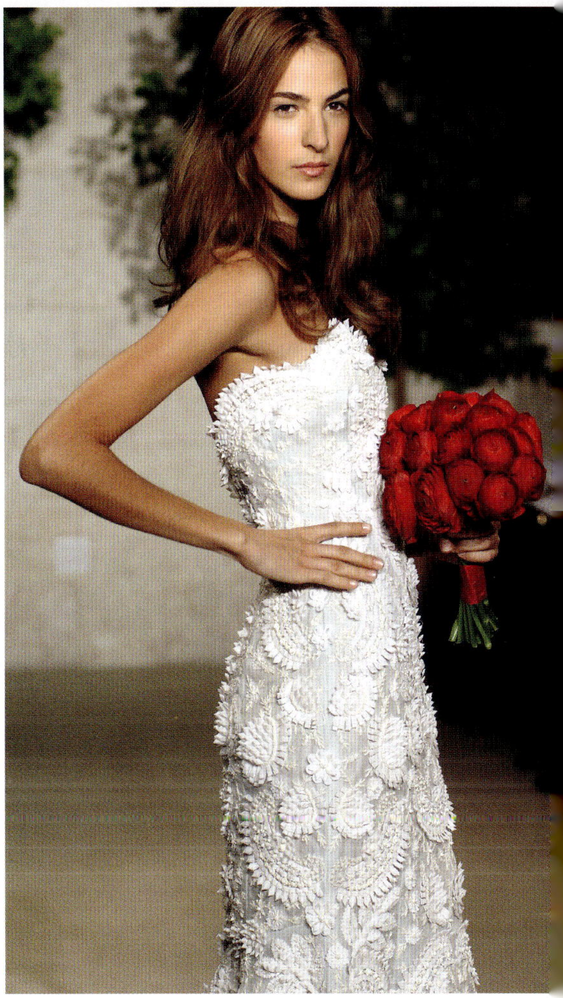

LEFT: VERA WANG TOILE
This mock-up of a strapless gown reveals the complex construction and creative process of Vera Wang, probably the best-known wedding dress designer in the world (see pages 112 and 172).

ABOVE: OSCAR DE LA RENTA
Dress from the Spring 2008 Oscar de la Renta bridal collection, shown in New York.

embroidered with poppies and violets (an allusion to the bride's two daughters, named after the flowers).

De la Renta began producing dresses for the bridal market through a licensee, but as demand rose for his designs he officially began his own bridal business in 2006, telling *Vogue* that he wanted to ensure all aspects of production met his high standards. Every one of his bridal gowns is precisely constructed using couture techniques in the most luxurious fabrics. Discussing his aesthetic with *Vogue*, the designer explained, "I design gowns that are extremely feminine. I think lace and embroideries are very special for a wedding." The formalities of the wedding ceremony appeal to the designer: "I have always loved the traditional aspects of a wedding—I love the idea of a father walking his daughter down the aisle and lifting her veil in front of the altar." While retaining an old-fashioned, romantic approach, de la Renta promotes contemporary interpretations of traditional bridal styles. For his Spring 2013 collection, the designer combined classic silhouettes with striking blue ruffled tulle and satin-faced organza trains.

De la Renta has remained at the top of his profession by responding to change. In 2011, he embraced the principles of eco-fashion, designing his first 100 percent organic wedding dress. In 2013, the company led the bridal industry's engagement with online media, posting live coverage of its Spring 2013 collection to the virtual moodboard Pinterest, allowing brides and fans worldwide a near real-time reveal of the latest styles.

Lanvin

Fashion-forward and little bit tongue-in-cheek, Lanvin's Collection Blanche remakes the paradigm of the wedding dress for the twenty-first century.

"I don't believe in fittings," Alber Elbaz, creative director of the French couture house told *Vogue* magazine. "Modern life doesn't allow women to take as much time as they used to in the past." For the fast-paced, trend-driven bride, Elbaz created an annual ready-to-wear collection that debuted in Rei Kawakubo's avant-garde concept store, Dover Street Market, in 2008. It was a natural development for the Israeli designer, who was in constant demand for bespoke bridal dresses. Two years earlier, Elbaz had translated key looks from previous years into an all-white collection for the opening of Dover Street Market in London. This gave the designer the idea of applying the concept of seasonal fashion to bridalwear.

Collection Blanche offers a selection of silhouettes drawn from Lanvin's current interseason cruise collection and archival designs—asymmetric wrap dresses, short, fitted sheaths, and classic Grecian draped dresses. These are combined with attention-grabbing decorative details like feather-trimmed veils and oversized bows in a palette of pure white, ivory, cream, and pale gray. Elbaz branches out beyond the main event to include separates—pencil skirts, T-shirts, and cardigans worked in classic bridal fabrics such as lace, silk, and taffeta—to see a bride through the entirety of her celebrations. Offbeat additions—caftans, trenches, tuxedos, bathing suits, and thong underwear—break the rules of traditional bridalwear in recognition of the fact that there is no one-stop solution for modern women. "What happens if you're not a size 2? What if you're fifty? Or if you're marrying for the tenth time?" Elbaz asked *Vogue* magazine. Wearable and a touch nonconformist, Collection Blanche is Elbaz's astute response to the heterogeneous character of contemporary wedding culture: "Weddings are changing their DNA," he said, "and this collection offers alternatives for everyone who hasn't been thought of before."

Monique Lhuillier

"Thoroughly modern Monique" puts a sensual spin on classic bridalwear.

The Philippines-born, Los Angeles-based designer conceived of her bridal business while in the process of designing her own wedding gown, launching her first collection in 1996. She soon won a large following for her delicately embellished gowns characterized by light, lush materials, and a spirit of flirtatious femininity. Sensuality is the thread weaving through all Lhuillier's collections. Season after season, the designer recuts the lingerie-inspired bodices that have become her hallmark, reinventing their style through fresh combinations with classic skirt shapes. The two collections she produced in 2012 artfully demonstrate Lhuillier's range and signature sensuality. In spring 2012, she emphasized a sexy, formfitting silhouette with slinky columns, cut-lace minis, and grand ball-gown confections composed of frothy masses of tulle, raw-edged organza, and layered stiffened-horsehair peplums. Rich in contrasts, the collection highlighted the designer's mastery of the interplay between volume, movement, and texture. The following season she stripped her collection back to a pure, uncluttered aesthetic, creating dresses that stood out in their simplicity: a sporty racerback lace tank dress, tulle crisscrossing the body in a lean and clean mermaid silhouette, and a sleek, unadorned trumpet-shaped dress sculpted in satin matelassé. In every reincarnation, Lhuillier's corseted designs are totally modern, spirited, and unashamedly sexy.

Marchesa

Scene-stealing silhouettes overlaid with ultrafeminine detailing ensure that all eyes are firmly upon the bride.

The British fashion label, famed for show-stopping designs, was founded by Georgina Chapman and Keren Craig in 2004. It was named after the eccentric socialite and fin-de-siècle femme fatale Marchesa Luisa Casati, who famously said, "I want to be a living work of art." The duo launched a high-end bridal capsule collection for Bergdorf Goodman in 2008, applying Marchesa's red-carpet aesthetic to gowns destined for the aisle. Three years later, the label partnered with the grand dame of bridal boutiques, Priscilla of Boston (now closed), to create a lower-priced collection called Eterna by Marchesa, with gowns costing in the range of $1,500–$5,000.

Chapman, who drapes the garments while Craig works on the fabric and

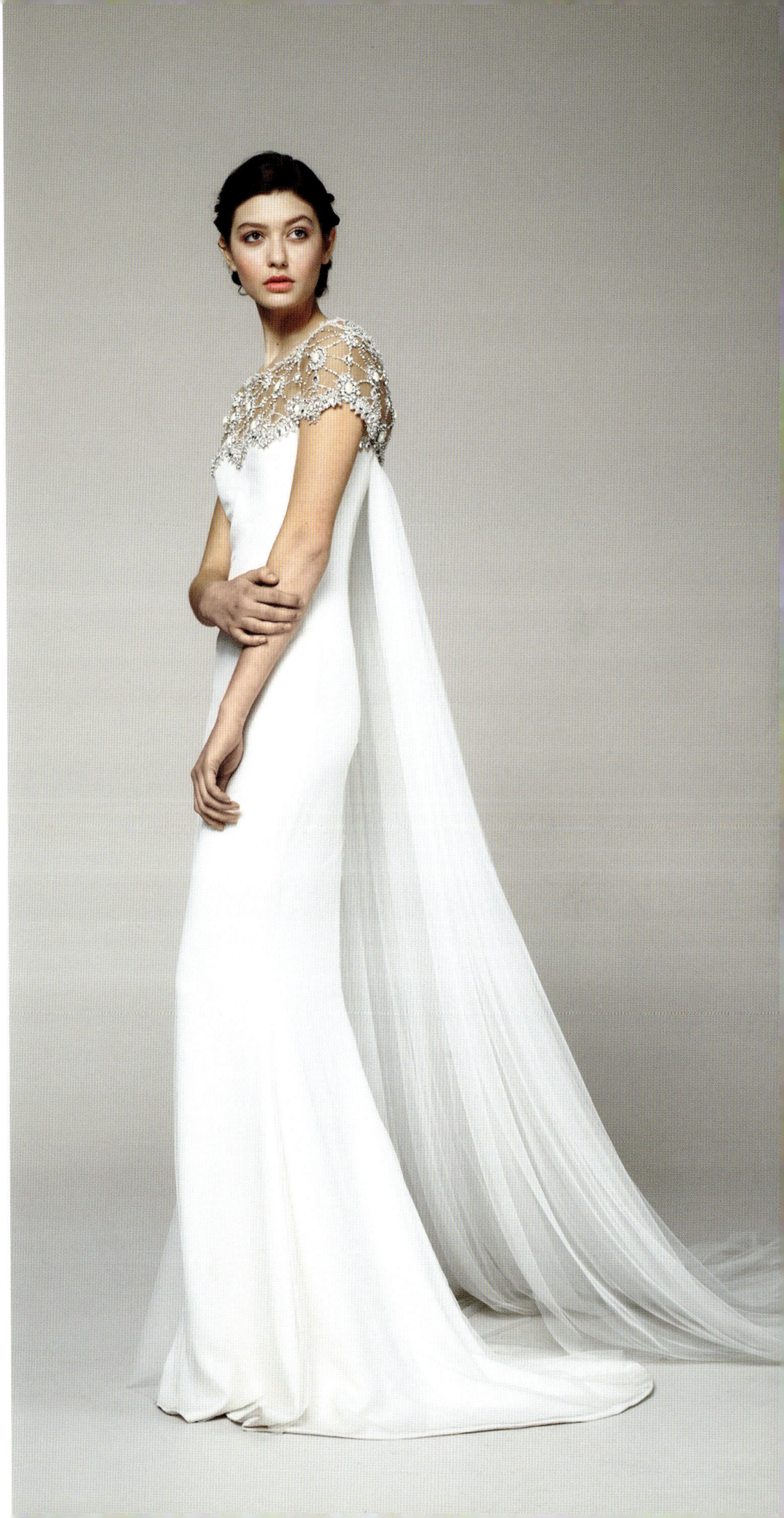

MARCHESA
A dress from the Spring/Summer 2013 bridal collection.

embellishment, defines the Marchesa aesthetic as "feminine touches, dramatic flair, and attention to detail." This translates into wedding dresses marked by striking shapes embellished with sculptural and textural ornamentation. Drama comes from inlaid jewels, Grecian-style drapery, and the cascading ruffles of fabric that are the Marchesa signature. Luxurious silk organdy and chiffon, in Chapman's skillful hands, are manipulated into stiff spirals, waterfalls of petal shapes, and pleated circles with fluted edges exploding across and waving around the body. Chapman has revealed that the design process is the same for bridal styles as it is for her main line—she never designs wedding gowns with trends in mind, preferring instead to focus on inspiration, mood, and the overall silhouette. "I think about everything from structure, style, and fabrics to how the gown will look in photos and the style of wedding," Chapman said. "We do work with themes in our bridal collections, but they are subtle. We have in the past played with ideas of floral lace, romantic fairy tales, and modern adaptations of historical references." For 2014, her ethereal collection of softly layered silk gauze and lace gowns studded with pearls and crystals drew inspiration from the delicate romance of the Bulgarian rose and the assertive sprightliness of the iris.

Marchesa is a firm favorite with celebrity brides. Blake Lively, Nicole Richie, Molly Sims, and Emily Blunt all chose the label because, to quote Lively, "The only designer that really makes you feel like a princess is Marchesa."

Jenny Packham

For brides who dream of golden-age Hollywood glamour, Jenny Packham's floor-sweeping gowns conjure the romance of bygone days.

London-based designer Jenny Packham founded her label in 1988 after studying fashion design at Central St. Martin's College. Over the following three decades, Packham secured an international reputation for her feminine eveningwear, her credentials shown off on the red carpet by a parade of Packham-clad celebrities. Packham's designs even played a starring role in the *Sex and the City* television series. Inspired by the success of her eveningwear business, Packham branched out into bridalwear; her wedding collection gives brides the opportunity to sparkle in the spotlight like a star.

Packham's gowns are created from sensuous fabrics cut into simple silhouettes and embellished with delicate hand beadwork. Plunging necklines, sheer cap sleeves, one-shoulder Grecian drapery, flyaway layers, and oversized flounces are among the most popular of her pretty signature stylings. Slender, languid columns and slips in slippery silk charmeuse and airy silk chiffon are Packham's forte. Decorated with geometric and floral art deco-inspired beading, they subtly evoke vintage glamour. Poured like liquid over the body's curves, these sublimely sensuous gowns are destined to unleash a bride's inner siren.

Elie Saab

Renowned for his flair for drama, Elie Saab can be relied upon for decadent, glamorous wedding gowns.

Legendary Lebanese designer Elie Saab began his couture business in Beruit at age 18. From the start, his atelier specialized in luxurious bridalwear. Saab's collections fuse a Middle Eastern aesthetic with a European sensibility. Cut-to-the-curve dresses are fashioned from yards of richly textured fabrics. Exquisitely embroidered lace and tulle, heavy silks encrusted with sparkling crystals and pearls—often paired with fluid fabrics—are quintessentially romantic and dramatic. Saab is a master of the art of seduction; his signature plunging necklines and subtle interplays of transparencies, overlays, and panels of sheer fabrics are sensuous windows upon bare or lightly veiled skin. Glamorous and sophisticated, Saab's dresses attract princesses and movie stars, but since 2003 he has made his designs available to a wider audience through a capsule collection, Elie by Elie Saab, for Pronovias, Barcelona's biggest bridal brand. The range pays homage to his couture collection, closely resembling its styles and following its attention to detail. Prices start at around $6,000.

Alice Temperley

Alice Temperley's luxe, bohemian gowns exemplify a quintessentially English aesthetic.

British designer Alice Temperley, a favorite of the Duchess of Cambridge and socialites on both sides of the Atlantic, began designing wedding gowns in 2002, two years after establishing her eponymous label. Temperley started her bridal business after her own wedding was featured in *Vogue* magazine: "We got calls from brides wanting something different and at that time there was not much on offer aside from big, puffy bridal gowns. They came to us for something softer and more demure and ethereal." Temperley's girlish dresses, beautifully handcrafted in the finest fabrics, appealed to free-spirited brides. As her success grew, the designer's approach and style matured: "Each dress has to be the perfect blend of functionality and fantasy; a bride must never feel overwhelmed by her dress but [it should] allow them to be the ultimate version of themselves," she stated. In recent years Temperley has sought to capture a timeless elegance by drawing on her archive of vintage fabrics and embroideries, interpreting historical themes and motifs with contemporary sensibility. Her 2013 Titania collection played an old-fashioned tune to a modern beat with an elegant tiered wedding dress, referencing a style popular in the 1950s, and a demure long-sleeved, high-necked blouse and skirt combination, a twenty-first century take on Victorian modesty.

A selection of ready-to-wear designs are available online, and a larger selection of made-to-measure and off-the-rack gowns can be found at the London store and in Los Angeles boutiques, costing from around $650 to $6,500. Gowns made by the designer herself start at $14,500.

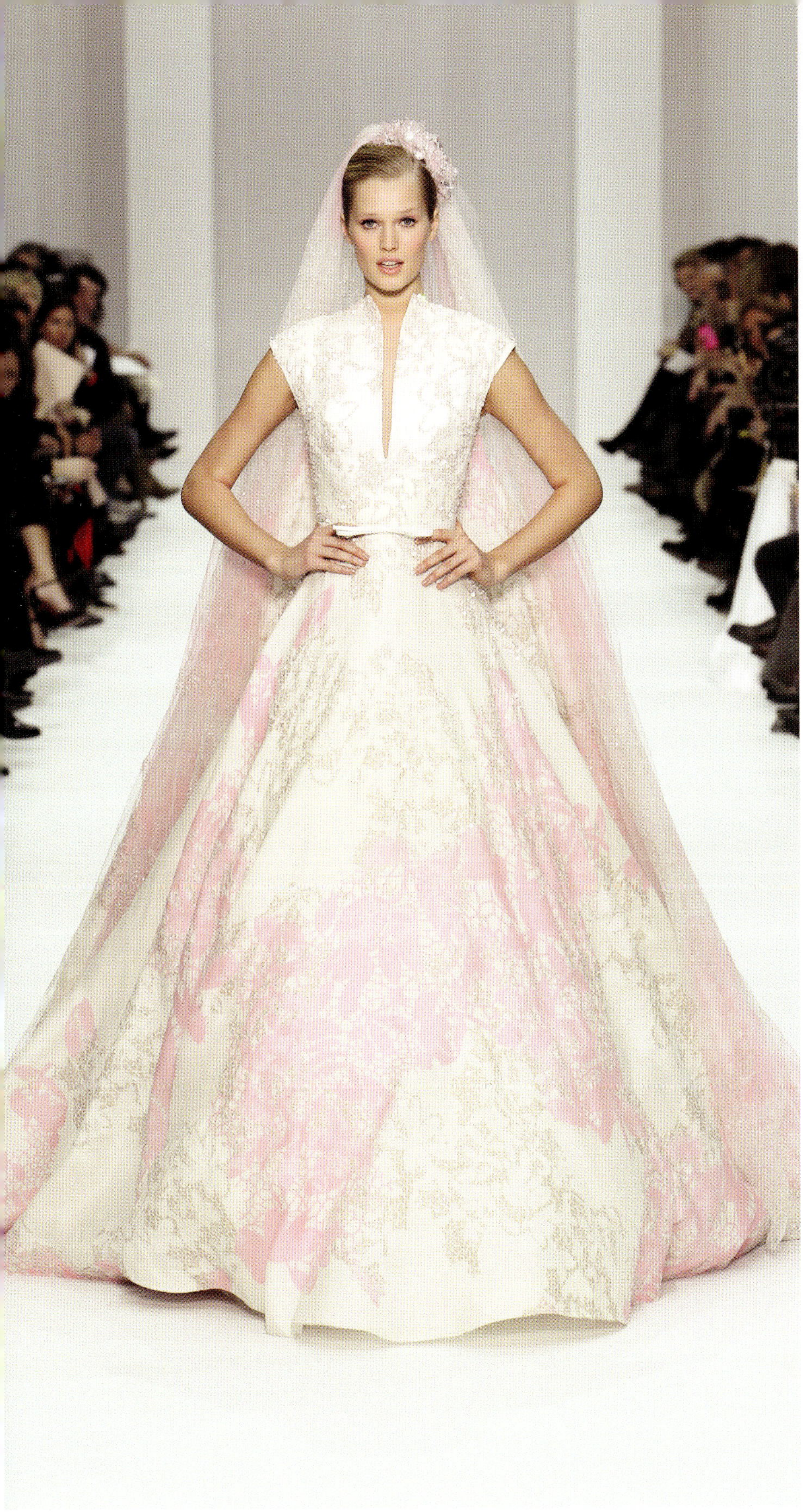

ELIE SAAB
A wedding gown from the Elie Saab Haute Couture Spring/Summer 2012 collection.

Glossary

Alençon lace A needlepoint lace with a floral pattern upon a fine netting ground, outlined with what is known as a cordonnet—a thicker thread raising the edge of the design. Originated in Alençon, France, in 1655.
Appliqué A method of applying decoration to the surface of fabric, typically by stitching cut-out pieces of another fabric onto it.

Bertha A wide, round, flat collar designed to accentuate a woman's shoulders.
Bias cut A technique to make use of the elasticity of fabric by cutting it at an angle of 45 degrees to the selvedge, across the warp and weft threads.
Boat neckline A straight, wide neckline extending across the collarbone, almost to the tip of each shoulder. Also referred to as a bateau neck.
Box pleat A flat double pleat made by folding under the fabric on either side.
Brocade One of a class of shuttle-woven fabrics, usually silk accentuated with metallic threads, with an intricate, often floral pattern. A drawloom is typically used to create brocade. Employing both a standard weft and a supplemental weft during the weaving process develops the detail of the pattern so that it has the appearance of embroidery.
Bustle A structure expanding and supporting fullness at the back of a skirt. The term also refers to draped and gathered fabric at the back of the skirt, lifted up just below the waist.

Cap sleeve A short sleeve extending just over the shoulder.
Cartridge pleat Small, rounded, stand-away folds of cloth used to gather large quantities of fabric into an armhole or the waist without adding bulk to the seam. This type of pleat also allows the fabric to spring out from the seam.
Cathedral train A train measuring approximately 9 feet (2.7 m) from the waist.
Chantilly lace A handmade bobbin lace with an elaborate pattern, outlined with a flat cordonnet (thread or cord-outlined edging), upon a fine ground. Originated in Chantilly, France, in the seventeenth century.
Chapel train A train measuring approximately 3–5 feet (0.9–1.5 m) from the waist.
Chenille A soft, thick-tufted cord of silk, cotton, or worsted velvet used in embroidery or for trimmings. French for "caterpillar."
Chiffon A fine, sheer, plain woven fabric. Woven of alternate S- and Z-twist crepe yarns. Typically made of silk, cotton, or synthetic fabrics.
Cluny lace A strong, heavyweight silk-cotton bobbin lace. Originated in Cluny, France, in the late nineteenth century.
Couching Hand- or machine-sewn stitches that invisibly overcast a thread, yarn, or trim to attach it to fabric.
Crepe A gauzy fabric, either silk, wool, or polyester, with a finely crinkled appearance and a crisp texture.
Crinoline Stiffened petticoat designed to support the skirts of a woman's dress. Originally made of "crin," the French for horsehair, interwoven with hard linen, "lin." After the 1850s the term denoted a rigid petticoat with a cage frame. "Crinoline style" often refers to a dress with a very full, wide skirt supported by a petticoat.
Cummerbund A type of sash or girdle worn around the waist.

Dart Triangular folds sewn into the fabric to fit and shape the garment around the body.
Décolletage Or décolleté, its adjectival form in French. Refers to the area of a woman's neck, shoulders, back, and chest bared by the neckline of her clothing. The term is also applied to a plunging neckline revealing and emphasizing a woman's cleavage.
Dropped waist A low, horizontal waistline that usually falls near the level of the upper hips, visually lengthening the torso.
Duchesse satin A heavyweight glossy satin usually made of silk, tightly woven to create a smooth surface.

Empire A high waistline cut horizontally just below the bust. This waistline creates a long, slender silhouette.

Faille A lightly ribbed, slightly stiff fabric. The ribs are vertical but not prominent. Often made of silk, cotton, or rayon.
Flounce A deep, wide, gathered ruffle used as a trimming.
Funnel neck A high wide neck. In its true form it is made without neckline seams as an extension of the garment.

Gabardine A smooth, durable, and firm, tightly woven twill cloth, usually of worsted or cotton threads.
Gauze An extremely fine, semitransparent silk fabric, similar to chiffon but even lighter in weight.
Gazar A loosely woven fabric with a smooth, crisp finish and a springy, pliable quality. Usually silk or wool, made with high-twist double yarns woven as one.
Gigot sleeve A sleeve that is very full at the shoulder, diminishing in size toward the elbow, and becoming tight at the wrist. Also referred to as a leg-of-mutton sleeve.
Girdle A belt, sash, or decorative item encircling the waist.

Honiton lace A bobbin lace with strong floral motifs upon a typically spotted net ground. Originated in Honiton, England, in the seventeenth century, its characteristic style developed in the nineteenth century.
Horsehair A stiff yet stretchy mesh fabric woven on the bias from synthetic threads. Originally used in crinolines to add volume and shape to gowns; more recently added as a trim on the outside of dresses.

Illusion neckline A transparent panel or yoke attached to or overlaid on the bodice and extending from the bust to the collar.

Jacquard A fabric with an intricate pattern woven on a Jacquard loom. Named after Joseph Marie Jacquard of Lyon, France, who invented an attachment that revolutionized the weaving of figured fabrics.
Juliet cap A close-fitting decorative skull cap, typically crocheted or made of mesh, decorated with pearls, beads, or jewels. Named after the heroine of Shakespeare's play *Romeo and Juliet*.

Knife pleats Pleats turned in a single direction, creating a smooth front.

Lamé A fabric woven with thin ribbons of metallic yarns.

Mandarin collar An unfolded stand-up collar.
Mise en abyme Literally translates as "placed into abyss." The term describes the experience of standing between two mirrors and seeing an infinitely recurring image. In critical theory the term describes self-reflexive meanings embedded in art forms.

New Look The influential hourglass style debuted by Christian Dior in his Spring/Summer 1947 collection, characterized by a slim, nipped-in waist and full, calf-length skirt.

Organdy Very similar in appearance to organza (below), but woven from spun yarn such as cotton rather than a multifilament thread.
Organza A sheer, lightweight stiff fabric that holds its form well. Plain woven from silk with its natural gum intact.

Paillette A small glittering object (such as a spangle or sequin) appliquéed in clusters to ornament a garment.
Palanquin An enclosed chair carried by poles on the shoulders of porters.
Panne velvet A soft, lustrous lightweight velvet with a flattened pile.
Pannier A framework of wire or bone, worn as undergarments in the eighteenth century to extend the width of women's skirts while leaving the front and back flat.
Paper taffeta A lightweight taffeta with a crisp, papery appearance.
Peau de soie A fine, soft, high-quality silk fabric of satin weave with a dull luster. French for "silk skin."
Peplum A decorative gathered or pleated piece of fabric attached to the waist of a dress or a woman's jacket.
Point d'Angleterre lace A combination of bobbin and needlepoint lace. Its origins are uncertain. Some claim that it was originally made in seventeenth-century Belgium and called "English" in order to bypass import restrictions.
Polonaise A gown with a cutaway draped and swagged overskirt, worn over an underskirt or petticoat.
Poplin A strong, plain woven fabric with crosswise ribs that are the result of using finer warp yarns and heavier weft yarns, with a higher thread count in the warp than the weft. Can be made of cotton, silk, wool, rayon, or a blend of fibers.
Portrait neck A wide neckline, softly scooping from the tip of one shoulder to the tip of the other.
Princess line A style of dress that follows the outline of the body. The bodice and skirt are cut in one piece without a waist seam.
Princess seam A vertical seam usually positioned between a side seam and the center front and back, and passing over the bust apex.

Raglan sleeve A sleeve extending in one piece to the collar, sewn to the main body of the garment with a diagonal seam from underarm to collarbone.
Raw silk A stiff, matte fabric made from untreated silk yarn that has not had the sericin (a natural gum that protects the fiber) removed.
Robe de style A dress popular in the 1920s with a tight bodice and full skirts, sometimes supported upon panniers or petticoats.
Rose point lace A complicated, floral needlepoint lace with heavily raised outlines.

Satin A smooth, lustrous fabric, often silk.
Selvedge The tightly woven edge of fabric that runs parallel to the warp, preventing it from unraveling.
Set-in sleeve A sleeve sewn into an armhole.
Shot taffeta Taffeta woven with different colored warp and weft threads to create a changeable, iridescent effect.
Silk A filament produced by the silk worm, known for its luster, strength, and elasticity.
Stomacher A decorated triangular panel that fills in the front opening of a dress or bodice. Stitched or pinned into place or secured by the lacings of the gown's bodice. Worn by men and women in the fifteenth and sixteenth centuries, then by women only during the seventeenth and eighteenth centuries.
Sweetheart neck A fairly wide neckline with straight sides and a concave curved bottom edge, usually doubly scalloped to resemble the top half of a heart.

Taffeta Plain woven, lightweight silk with a fine cross-ribbed appearance; has a crisp quality that holds its shape well.
Toile A preliminary mock-up model of a garment.
Top stitching Usually decorative lines of stitching sewn from the right side (visible surface) of a fabric.
Trompe l'oeil An optical illusion in which a two-dimensional pattern appears to exist in three dimensions. French for "deceive the eye."
True-lovers' knot A decorative knot used as an emblem of love. Composed of two interlocked overhand knots tied from two parallel ropes.
Tulle A delicate, very fine net with a small mesh. Can be made of silk, nylon, or rayon.
Twill One of the three basic weaving methods, twill is a weave with a pattern of diagonal parallel ribs. Achieved by passing the weft thread over one or more warp threads and then under two or more warp threads with a "step" between rows.

Valenciennes lace A bobbin lace with a uniquely open ground and close, even pattern that is not outlined. Originated in Valenciennes, France, in the eighteenth century.

Warp Strong structural threads running the length of a fabric from end to end.
Weft Threads that run from side to side of a fabric, under and over the warp threads.
Worsted A lightweight but strong and durable fabric made from worsted yarn, spun from long, fine combed wool, or wool-blend fibers.

Yoke A shaped panel of fabric across the upper body, from the neck over the shoulders, onto which the main body of the garment is sewn.

Zibeline A thick, soft fabric with a long nap, typically made of wool, but can be made from the hair of other animals. Zibeline can also refer to a heavy silk fabric with a twill weave.

Resources

These sources are recommended for further reading on the dresses and designers featured in this book.

Costume & Fashion: A Concise History, by James Laver, 1969

Fashion: The Whole Story, by Marnie Fogg, 2013

Vintage Weddings: One Hundred Years of Bridal Fashion and Style, by Marnie Fogg, 2011

Vogue Weddings: Brides, Dresses, Designers, by Hamish Bowles and Vera Wang, ed. Chloe Malle, 2012

The Wedding Dress: 300 Years of Bridal Fashion, by Edwina Erhman, 2011

Books by designer

Cristóbal Balenciaga
Cristóbal Balenciaga, by Lesley Ellis Miller, 1993
Cristobal Balenciaga, Philippe Venet, Hubert de Givenchy: Grand Traditions in French Couture, by Christiane de Nicolay-Mazery, 2010

David and Elizabeth Emanuel
A Dress for Diana, by David and Elizabeth Emanuel, 2006

John Galliano
Galliano, by Colin McDowell, 1998

Norman Hartnell
Silver and Gold, by Norman Hartnell, 1956

Charles James
Modern Fashion in Detail, by Claire Wilcox and Valerie Mendes, 1991

Rei Kawakubo
Radical Fashion, ed. Claire Wilcox, 2001

Ann Lowe
The Everything Jacqueline Kennedy Onassis Book: A Portrait of an American Icon, by Kathleen Tracy, 2008
What Jackie Taught Us: Lessons from the Remarkable Life of Jacqueline Kennedy Onassis, by Tina Santi Flaherty, 2005

Mainbocher
Blithe Spirit: The Windsor Set, by Andrew Bolton, 2002

Helen Rose
Grace Kelly: Icon of Style to Royal Bride, by Kristina Haugland, 2006

Yves Saint Laurent
Yves Saint Laurent: Style, by Foundation Pierre Bergé and Yves Saint Laurent, 2008

Elsa Schiaparelli
Shocking Life: The Autobiography of Elsa Schiaparelli, by Elsa Schiaparelli, 2007
Shocking! The Art and Fashion of Elsa Schiaparelli, by Dilys Blum, 2003

Viktor & Rolf
The House of Viktor & Rolf, by Caroline Evans and Susannah Frankel, 2008

Madeleine Vionnet
Cubism and Fashion, by Richard Martin, 1999
Madeleine Vionnet, by Pamela Golbin, 2009
Madeleine Vionnet, by Betty Kirke and Issey Miyake, 1998

Catherine Walker
Catherine Walker: An Autobiography by the Private Couturier to Diana, Princess of Wales, by Catherine Walker, 1998

Vera Wang
Vera Wang on Weddings, by Vera Wang, 2001

Vivienne Westwood
The Englishness of English Dress, ed. Christopher Breward, Becky Conekin, and Caroline Cox, 2002
Vivienne Westwood, by Claire Wilcox, 2004

Yohji Yamamoto
Techno Fashion, Bradley Quinn, 2002

Websites and places to visit

The Valentino Garavani Virtual Museum
valentinogaravanimuseum.com

Australia
National Gallery of Victoria, Melbourne
ngv.vic.gov.au

Powerhouse Museum, Sydney
powerhousemuseum.com

Belgium
ModeMuseum, Antwerp
momu.be

Modemuseum, Hasselt
modemuseumhasselt.be

Canada
Costume Museum of Canada, Winnipeg
costumemuseumcanada.com

McCord Museum of Canadian History, Montreal
mccord-museum.qc.ca

Musée des beaux-arts de Montréal
wbam.qc.ca

Japan

Kyoto Costume Institute
kci.or.jp

Spain

Fundación Balenciaga, Guetaria
Cristobalbalenciagamuseoa.com

Museo del Traje, Madrid
museodeltraje.mcu.es

UK

Aberdeen Art Gallery and Museums
aagm.co.uk

Brighton Museum and Art Gallery
brighton-hove-rpml.org.uk

Fashion Museum, Bath
museumofcostume.co.uk

Gallery of Costume at Platt Hall, Manchester
manchestergalleries.org/our-other-venues/platt-hall-gallery-of-costume/

Museum of London
museumoflondon.org.uk

National Portrait Gallery, London
npg.org.uk

Sudley House, Liverpool
liverpoolmuseums.org.uk/sudley

Victoria and Albert Museum (V&A)
vam.ac.uk

USA

Chicago History Museum
digitalcollection.chicagohistory.org

Cornell Costume and Textile Collection, Ithaca
human.cornell.edu/fsad/cctc.cfm

The Costume Institute, Metropolitan Museum of Art, New York
metmuseum.org

The Fashion Industry of Design and Merchandising, Los Angeles
fidm.edu

Los Angeles County Museum of Art
lacma.org

The Museum at the Fashion Institute of Technology, New York
fitnyc.edu/3452.asp

Museum of Fine Arts, Boston
mfa.org

Museum of the City of New York
mcny.org

National Museum of American History, Smithsonian Institution, Washington, DC
americanhistory.si.edu

Ohio State University Historic Costume and Textiles Collection
costume.osu.edu

Philadelphia Museum of Art
philamuseum.org

Index

Acknowledgments

With thanks to Karen A. Levine, Prestel Publishing; David Breuer, James Ashton-Tyler.
For editorial: Philippa Davis, Donna Gregory, Lucy Kingett, Cathy Meeus, Caroline West. Indexing: Helen Snaith. For design: Simon Goggin; with Lucy Parissi, Yumiko Tahata, Geoff Windram. Picture research: Sarah Bell. Production: Nikki Ingram. Editorial director: Sorrel Wood.

The author wishes to thank Marci Morimoto, Metropolitan Museum of Art, and Su Hepburn, Brighton Museum and Art Gallery.

This book is dedicated to Matt and Ted.

Picture credits

Marshall Editions would like to thank the following agencies for supplying images for inclusion in this book:

Cover: Getty Images
Page 2, 7, 50, 52, 72, 77, 79, 87, 88–89, 126, 130–131, 158, 181 Getty Images; page 8 Sara Jaye Weiss/Rex Features; page 11 Hulton-Deutsch Collection/Corbis; page 12 main The Granger Collection/TopFoto, right From Wikimedia Commons; page 15 main © Illustrated London News Ltd/Mary Evans, left Photo: Nadar, From Wikimedia Commons; page 16, 25, 43, 117, 118 The Metropolitan Museum of Art/Art Resource/Scala, Florence; page 18 © Illustrated London News Ltd/Mary Evans; page 20, 22 Condé Nast Archive/Corbis; page 21 Library of Congress; page 23 From Wikimedia Commons; page 26 main Roger Viollet/Rex Features, right Getty Images; page 29 © Illustrated London News Ltd/Mary Evans; page 30 main © TopFoto, right Chicago History Museum; page 32, 34 Popperfoto/Getty Images; page 37 main © Philadelphia Museum of Art/Corbis, left © Bettmann/Corbis; page 38 Getty Images; page 40 main Getty Images, right Photo: Allan Warren, From Wikimedia Commons; page 44 main © V&A Images/Alamy, left Austin Mutti-Mewse/Hardy Amies Archive; page 46 Time & Life Pictures/Getty Images; page 47, 48 Toni Frissell, Courtesy of the John F. Kennedy Presidential Library and Museum; page 49 © Ebony Magazine; page 53 Library of Congress, Prints & Photographs Division, Carl Van Vechten Collection; page 55, 142 Sipa Press/Rex Features; page 56–57 Gamma-Keystone/Getty Images; page 58 main Sipa Press/Rex Features, right Time & Life Pictures/Getty Images; page 61 AFP/Getty Images; page 62 Fairchild Photo Service/Condé Nast/Cobis; page 63 Arifirfandi, from Wikimedia Commons; page 66 main Courtesy of Victoria and Albert Museum, London, left From Wikimedia Commons; page 66 Library of Congress; page 67 Image Courtesy of Australian Wool Innovation Ltd and the London College of Fashion page 68, 70 Cristóbal Balenciaga Museum, Getaria, Basque Country, Spain; page 71 jaypofromvox, from Wikimedia Commons; page 73 © Bettmann/Corbis; page 75 British Pathé Ltd; page 76 Courtesy of Victoria and Albert Museum, London; page 80 Gamma-Keystone via Getty Images; page 81 s_bukley/Shutterstock; page 83 Zandra Rhodes/V&A Images; page 85 main University for the Creative Arts, left Helga Esteb/Shutterstock; page 90 main Getty Images, right Getty Images; page 93 NY Daily News/Getty Images; page 94 main Time & Life Pictures/Getty Images, right Photo by Christopher Peterson; page 97 main Courtesy of Victoria and Albert Museum, London, right Photo by Ben Weller; page 99, 100 Tim Graham/Getty Images; page 101 © Catherine Walker 2013; page 103, 104 Guy Marineau; page 105 Author: Florian Vincent; page 107 Steve Wood/Rex Features; page 107 Versace; page 108–109 Mark Large/Daily Mail/Rex Features; page 110 main Imogen Eveson, right WireImage/Getty Images; page 114, 180 ©James Wade for Vera Wang; page 115 Nata Sha/Shutterstock; page 121 UK Press/Getty Images; page 122 WireImage/Getty Images; page 123 cinemafestival/Shutterstock; page 124–125 © Reuters Photographer/Reuters/Corbis; page 127 s_bukley/Shutterstock; page 129 Jonathan Becker; page 130 Ed Kavishe/fashionwirepress.com; page 132, 147 Robert Fairer; page 134 main Courtesy of Victoria and Albert Museum, London, right 134 Mattia Passeri; page 137, 139, 140 WireImage/Getty Images; page 145 Rex Features; page 148 WireImage/Getty Images; page 151, 152 © Jacky Naegelen/Reuters/Corbis; page 153 Featureflash/Shutterstock; page 155 main AFP/Getty Images, right FashionStock; page 156 AFP/Getty Images; page 160–161 WireImage/Getty Images; page 162 main Getty Images, right Shutterstock/Featureflash; page 164 JRAA/ZDS WENN Photos/Newscom; page 166 Getty Images; page 169 Fairchild Photo Service/Condé Nast/Corbis; page 170, 174 Fairchild Photo Service/ Condé Nast/Corbis; page 171 main Fairchild Photo Service/ Condé Nast/Corbis, right © Timothy Greenfield-Sanders/Corbis Outline; page 172 Imaginechina/Rex Features; 177 dpa picture alliance/Alamy; page 178–179 AFP/Getty Images; page 179 From Wikimedia Commons; page 183 Marchesa; page 185 Elie Saab.